ALSO BY AARON BOBROW-STRAIN

White Bread: A Social History of the Store-Bought Loaf
Intimate Enemies: Landowners, Power, and Violence in Chiapas

THE DEATH AND LIFE OF
AIDA HERNANDEZ

THE DEATH
AND LIFE OF
AIDA HERNANDEZ

A BORDER STORY

Aaron Bobrow-Strain

FARRAR, STRAUS AND GIROUX ▪ NEW YORK

Farrar, Straus and Giroux
175 Varick Street, New York 10014

Library of Congress Cataloging-in-Publication Data
Names: Bobrow-Strain, Aaron, 1969– author. | Hernandez, Aida.
Title: The death and life of Aida Hernandez : a border story / Aaron
    Bobrow-Strain.
Description: First Edition. | New York : Farrar, Straus and Giroux, [2019] |
    Includes bibliographical references.
Identifiers: LCCN 2018044062 | ISBN 9780374191979 (hardcover)
Subjects: LCSH: Hernandez, Aida. | Mexicans—United States—Biography. |
    Immigrants—United States—Biography. | Immigrants—Mexico—Biography. |
    Mexican-American Border Region.
Classification: LCC E184.M5 B58 2019 | DDC 972/.1—dc23
LC record available at https://lccn.loc.gov/2018044062

Designed by Richard Oriolo

Our books may be purchased in bulk for promotional, educational, or business
use. Please contact your local bookseller or the Macmillan Corporate and
Premium Sales Department at 1-800-221-7945, extension 5442, or by e-mail
at MacmillanSpecialMarkets@macmillan.com.

www.fsgbooks.com
www.twitter.com/fsgbooks • www.facebook.com/fsgbooks

10 9 8 7 6 5 4 3 2 1

This is a work of nonfiction, based primarily on memories shared by Aida Hernandez, her family, and her friends. When possible, these memories have been cross-checked and corroborated with additional interviews, as well as medical, police, school, court, immigration, and other records. News reports, scholarly publications, government documents, and other data sources consulted in the research process are cited in endnotes. In some cases, dialogue was recorded as it occurred; more often, it was reconstructed from the memories of participants. Many names have been changed. A section at the end of the book, titled "About This Book," addresses these and other methodological, political, and ethical questions in depth. Proceeds from the sale of the book will be split equally among the author, Aida Hernandez, and the Chiricahua Community Health Centers to support services for people dealing with domestic violence or sexual assault.

CONTENTS

THE DEATH AND LIFE OF
AIDA HERNANDEZ

PROLOGUE:
THE DEATH OF AIDA HERNANDEZ

Camila looked down at Aida's wrecked body and couldn't see a trace of the cousin she remembered from childhood. Years earlier, when she was a girl living in Douglas, Arizona, Camila would cross the border into Mexico almost every weekend to play with Aida and her sisters. They ruled a gravelly playground near Aida's house in Agua Prieta. They ran free at an uncle's ranch on the outskirts of town. Aida had been the silly, sunlit one. The cousin with the dimpled cheeks and enviable curls.

That girl was almost stubbed out. Her face was swollen, her lips pallid. Matted blood crusted on her bandaged arms. Newer blood soak painted moist shapes on the sheet covering her gashes. A tube stitched into her abdomen leaked sticky pink liquid.

Aida tried to smile up at her cousin.

"It's okay," Camila said. "Just lie still." But Aida twisted on the ambulance gurney, staring up through tubes and leads.

"You're going to be okay," Camila repeated. She didn't know what else to tell her childhood playmate, now twenty and a mother, dying beside her.

The ambulance rattled through Agua Prieta, heading for the border. Camila had not seen much of her cousin in recent years. Camila was determined to stay out of trouble. She wanted to finish school and be a teacher in Douglas, just across the international line from Agua Prieta.

The ambulance jolted over a break in the pavement and Aida shrieked. She had fought to live all day. She'd staggered through the ER doors just before dawn on her own power. She'd survived surgery and conferred with police. "I'm all right," she'd reassured her mother in Arizona by telephone. "Stay there. I'll be fine. Don't try to cross the border."

When a nurse tried to adjust her sheet, Aida had bolted upright to fight against it. She'd been stabbed so many times that she thought the nurse was pulling a shroud over her head.

"I'm not dead," she'd yelled over and over.

Around noon, her father, unable to pay for the private hospital and despairing over the level of care in Mexico, arranged an ambulance to take Aida north. They'd try their luck finding care in Arizona. One last chance to save her life.

Camila had volunteered to accompany her cousin in the ambulance. Crossing the border would be easy for Camila. She was a U.S. citizen, but Aida was not. International agreements allowed residents of Agua Prieta to receive emergency care in the United States. But a lot could go wrong in the crossing, Camila thought.

The ambulance turned north onto Avenida 20. Behind it were the small Mexican border city's high-tech assembly factories, its tin-roofed houses, its broom- and brick-maker districts, and its pirate car lots selling luxury SUVs to the newly narco-wealthy. Ahead lay Agua Prieta's squat downtown, the steel border wall, and then Douglas.

The two towns had been so closely intertwined for so long that some people called them DouglaPrieta. Residents just a few years older than Camila and Aida remembered a time when kids played pickup baseball games spanning both sides of the line. Home plate, marked by a plastic bag, lay in a scrub field on the U.S. side, while Agua Prieta's Calle Internacional formed the outfield. On a day-to-day basis, adults from both countries had scrambled across the ditch or ducked through a ragged chain-link fence to run errands and visit family on the other side. They mingled north to south, and south to north. Longer-term migration followed predictable cycles: the same people crossing the U.S. border at the same point in the same season to tend crops on the same farms. When the season finished, they returned home to Mexico. Year after year.

But in this summer of 2008, the towns weren't as close as they had once been. New policies, new people, new suspicions, and new border crack-downs had pushed a wedge between them.

Avenida 20 was a paved boulevard, so the ambulance picked up speed. It rushed through Agua Prieta's city center past cowboy boot emporiums, dentist offices, and pharmacies catering to American retirees. In the dis-tance sprawled clubs and bars where preppy Mexican teens, Douglas High School students, and drug dealers had partied together behind mirrored glass the night before.

Camila looked from the ambulance window to her cousin.

"We're almost there," she said. The ambulance had gone as far north as it could and turned west onto Calle Internacional. From there it raced along the international line itself. To the right, rusting steel bars blurred by—the latest border wall.

AIDA'S FATHER, RAÚL, followed the ambulance in a battered pickup loaded with family. He pulled as close to the port of entry as the queue of cars wait-ing to cross allowed. Raúl had seen his closest friends die in pitched gun-fights, and he himself had survived torture in Mexico's most infamous political prison. He knew that when it was time to act, you did everything you could do, and then you did a little more. When he'd rushed to the hos-pital just after dawn that morning, he'd grabbed the deed to his house. Even in his panicked state, he knew that he'd need it as collateral for his daughter's hospital bills. When it came to such details, Raúl liked to get it right. And now his girl was dying. His sunlit girl.

He and his daughter had clashed the night before. They'd screamed and yelled, rattling the wood paneling on his cinder-block walls. In the end, she'd stormed out. The twenty dollars she hoped to earn that night was her future, she'd shouted at him—a step toward reuniting with her son. At the hospital afterward, Aida had made sure that her sister recovered the cursed twenty-dollar bill, folded in the pocket of her sliced-off jeans. Now Raúl watched her ambulance pull into an emergency lane on its way to the United States.

FRANCISCO "FRANK" HONE also watched, waiting on the Arizona side as the ambulance exited Mexico and turned in to the crowded border crossing. A Douglas Fire Department veteran, Frank had overseen dozens of emergency transfers across the international line. He knew the drill: the Agua Prieta ambulance driver pulls into an express lane, unloads the patient, and makes a quick stop for Customs and Border Protection clearance. Then Frank wheels the patient toward his waiting rig. This takes place in what looks like a highway toll plaza at rush hour—albeit one bristling with cameras, dogs, X-ray apparatus, and automatic weapons. It was routine, unless something went wrong.

And it seemed to Frank that something had just gone wrong.

At the ID check, inspectors in black-blue uniforms surrounded the gurney, halting its passage with shouts and arm waving. On the Mexico side, a white pickup screeched into the crossing and a family leaped out. Camila unfolded herself from the ambulance's back door. And from the United States, a brass-blond woman carrying a little boy streaked toward the gurney.

Just past Frank, the woman with the toddler collided with a wall of raised palms and shouted commands. It was Aida's mother, Luz, holding Aida's son. She shouldered forward to reach Aida's side, contorting to shield the boy from the sight of his mother's body. The voices of family, border guards, and Mexican paramedics pitched and rolled. Sunday-afternoon shoppers returning to Mexico from the Douglas Walmart stopped to stare.

Pushing through to the gurney, Frank could see the patient didn't have much time. Her face was the color of cigarette ash. Her lower eyelid, when he pulled it down, was white and waxy.

Frank knew border officials weren't heartless. In the hard years when Douglas was one of North America's busiest and most dangerous human-trafficking corridors, he had seen federal agents sobbing over the bodies of dead migrants more than once. But he also knew that even the sickest patient could be refused entry for bureaucratic reasons. Cases like that often came down to a pissing match, he knew. And as a ranch hand turned high school football player turned firefighter, Frank figured that he could piss up there with the best of them.

Frank launched into an argument with the officer in charge, and someone knocked into Aida's gurney. The jolt against her rigid body shook her to life one more time. Aida's eyes startled wide and her voice appeared—first as an exploding howl, then in precise English words.

"Please. I have a son. A U.S. citizen son. Let me pass." Her words brought the fight to a sudden stop.

Frank saw his opening.

"Which one of you wants to be responsible for this woman's death?" he demanded. "If one of you wants the liability, sign this form and I'm out of here."

The group of dark uniforms stared at Frank. And in that moment, barely waiting for a response, he wheeled the patient away—out of one of the most heavily secured sites in the American Southwest.

LATER, FRANK HONE watched Arizona LifeLine II lift off on its way to Tucson's University Medical Center. A crowd had gathered in the border JCPenney parking lot to see the helicopter go. Now they shielded their eyes from the afternoon sun and followed the aircraft rising into the sky. The red shell climbed over surveillance towers and access roads cut in the desert. It skimmed across blue-black slag mountains and skirted one of the world's largest border patrol stations. Then, over the rusty Mule Mountains, it faded from view. Frank looked down at his clipboard and noted the woman's name. Aida Hernandez. Frank knew he had done his best that day, but he also knew that Aida Hernandez would not make it.

NO COUNTRY FOR YOUNG WOMEN

GIRL IN A LABYRINTH

AIDA AWOKE TO THE SMELL of homemade flour tortillas and the sound of her mother singing. Luz always sang the same song while she cooked— "Triste recuerdo" by Antonio Aguilar. Aida thought her mother sang beautifully. She poured out the long notes like honey from her brother's ranch on the outskirts of Agua Prieta. Aida was eight, and her parents were the objects of her deep affection and contemplation.

Aida loved to sit on the couch watching her parents in the morning before school. Raúl and Luz made a funny, mismatched pair. He was in his early fifties, short, and taciturn. She, almost twenty years younger, was tall, loud, and *güera*. Aida didn't understand her father's meetings, or his books, but she knew that he'd once talked with the president of Mexico at a summit in Nogales. Now he worked at a Japanese factory assembling something, Aida didn't know what. To eight-year-old Aida, her mother's work was more exciting. Each morning, after Aida and her sisters left for school, Luz would open the small video and convenience store she ran out of the garage. When school was out, Aida would spend hours sitting beside her mother, surrounded by shelves of snacks and the clatter of dubbed action movies.

Those days had a regular, sunbaked rhythm in Aida's mind. Agua Prieta was balanced on the northern rim of Mexico, tucked away from more important and populous parts of the country. In the 1990s, it had only just outgrown its cattle ranch roots. The city felt both small and large at the same time. Even on cold winter days, the sun was bright and Aida could play outside.

After school, Aida and her two sisters would come home and change out of their uniform skirts. They'd rush through homework under their mother's watchful eye and shoot across the street to the playground. Aida was the middle sister, between Jennifer, age thirteen, and Cynthia, age six. The unexpected new babies, Jazmin and Emiliano, born a year apart, were still too small to count.

Nothing had come between the sisters yet. They ran and swooped and played with abandon. Dizzying themselves on the merry-go-round, their legs sweeping the sky, they squealed together in pure joy. They shot hoops with older boys and climbed anything that could be climbed. They knew every jagged metal splinter, every missing guardrail, and every trip hazard in the playground. They lived for the flawless moment suspended in the air after leaping into space.

The three sisters would only sit still after they had scaled to the top of the monkey bars. Taking in the whole playground, they would perch together at the apex, inventing futures for themselves, their six knees waving in the air.

"I'm going to live in *los Unites* and have a hot husband and daughter named Samantha," Jennifer, the oldest, swore. The others agreed to follow her lead. To prepare for their future lives, Jennifer, Aida, and Cynthia practiced English. Usually this meant mimicking the sounds David Bowie made in *Labyrinth*, their all-time favorite movie. Sometimes they shouted the lyrics of "What's Up?" by 4 Non Blondes, which mostly consisted of the word "Hey" repeated a million times.

"When I'm older," Aida announced one day, "I'm going to live in a Big-Ass City. New York City." With her baby lisp, it came out *"Nuyor-thittee."*

"Of course you are, little monkey," Jennifer answered. "We know you will."

SOME NIGHTS, Luz and Raúl attended a meeting of the Agua Prieta Search and Rescue Club. The girls would slip out to the playground after their parents left. While Luz and Raúl practiced searching for lost hikers with their club mates, Aida and her sisters danced under streetlights. Those forbidden nights on the playground all ended the same way: One of the other neighborhood kids would whistle a warning. Another would yell, "Hey, Hernandezes—your parents are coming!"

Aida and her sisters would rocket off the jungle gym in unison and hit the hard-packed dirt running. Aida knew the routine the way she knew the scars on her knees. She flew over the low fence and spun out of the park. She paused to help Cynthia cross the street, and then all three crashed through the metal gate of their house. Inside, skating across polished concrete, they landed on the couch—just as their parents' car pulled up.

Raúl and Luz let themselves into their modest government housing unit and put down their things. Their daughters peeked up from the video they'd flipped on and were pretending to watch. Their parents wore matching tan Search and Rescue uniforms.

"Labyrinth again?" Luz asked.

Some nights Luz didn't see through the act. On other nights she shouted until the house shook. "I thought I had *girls*. You don't act like girls," she'd yell on those nights. Girls don't scrape knees or play outside after dark, she'd scold. Then they'd eat leftovers from the day's big afternoon meal together, and Luz's consternation would fade.

Days, weeks, and seasons passed in much the same way, there on the northern edge of Mexico. School, playground, *tienda*. Homework, playground, *tienda*. The sisters took care of their new siblings and watched videos. They managed not to break many bones. And they imagined that life would continue this way, like their one brakeless bicycle. And it did, until the night Raúl asked his question and the world fell out of balance.

·   ·   ·

THEY WERE EATING SUPPER. It began like any other bit of conversation.

"Luz, I have a question for you. I want you to be one hundred percent honest with me." To Aida, it sounded ordinary, but Luz set her jaw into a ram.

"Girls, go to your rooms right now," she said, not looking at her husband. It was the first of many bewildering commands Aida would obey that week. Huddled in her room with Jennifer and Cynthia, she didn't get to hear the question or the answer. But she heard the recriminations and the screaming sobs that followed. The chairs clattering to the floor and ricocheting off the walls.

When the babies woke up crying that night, no parent came. Aida and her sisters got up instead and tried to hush them. They climbed together into one bed and pulled covers over their ears to blot out the sounds of fighting. Eventually, they fell into a ragged sleep, curled in one another's arms.

By morning, it all felt like a bad dream. Aida's parents got ready for work as usual. The girls got ready for school. March 8, 1996, passed like many other days.

At school, Aida was ready to learn. The teachers, though, were less than excited to teach. For many of them, teaching was a second or third job. If they showed up late or wandered away from class in mid-lesson to smoke a cigarette, it was only because all the other jobs they worked to make ends meet left them exhausted. Aida knew this because they didn't miss a chance to remind their pupils of how little the Secretaría de Educación Pública paid them.

The morning after the fight, teachers and students alike shivered. The temperature outside rose into the seventies, but the school's cement classrooms gripped the night's cold long after noon. Aida's teeth chattered as she tried to study. After last period, she ran outside to find her father, who always walked her home. Instead, she found Cynthia waiting. The crowded school divided pupils into day shifts and evening shifts. That year, Aida attended school in the day; her little sister went to class at night. Cynthia's appearance on the sidewalk as Aida got out was unusual.

"We gotta go," Cynthia said. She was worried.

To Aida's questions, she only replied, "Just come on. We gotta go."

As the house came into view, a wave of confusion rolled over Aida. Her parents weren't wealthy, but they owned a car. And yet there, idling in front of the house, was a dented white taxi like the kind poor people took when they couldn't use the bus. We never take taxis, she thought.

Luz emerged from the house and stuffed soft garbage bags of clothes into the open trunk, not noticing the girls.

"Mom, are we taking a trip?" Aida asked, thrilled by the possibility.

For the moment, Luz's too-big convenience store sunglasses hid the bruise spreading down the bridge of her nose.

"Mom, answer me."

Raúl appeared next. He called Aida and Cynthia in to join Jennifer, who stood shivering next to an electric heater in the living room.

"Girls, I need to ask you something." Another question from their father. "Girls, do you want to live with me here, or go with your mother?"

The question was incomprehensible. It might as well have been asked in English by David Bowie wearing Goblin King makeup. But Raúl, standing there spent and defeated, clearly expected an answer.

Cynthia looked up at Aida. Aida looked up at Jennifer. Jennifer was four years and seven months older than Aida. She knew everything.

Jennifer stalled, feeling the weight of decision land on her five-foot frame.

"Mom?" she said eventually. "I guess?"

It seemed logical. Girls went with their mothers. No one knew why. Aida and Cynthia nodded in agreement; they followed Jennifer in everything.

RIDING AWAY, the three girls knelt in a row on the backseat of the taxi, watching their father disappear. When he'd walked them to the taxi, telling them he loved them, he had still seemed like the solidest, most reliable thing in the world to Aida. Now he was a bent old man, sinking into the distance. Aida had never seen him cry before.

Aida wheeled on her mom. "What is happening? Where are we going?" she asked. But Luz just stared straight ahead through the cracked windshield. After a few minutes, the border came into view. Little more than a dry ditch and ragged chain-link fence marked the international divide in the spring of 1996.

"Mom?" Aida wanted an answer.

"Shut *up*, Aida," Jennifer snapped. "Just shut up."

No one spoke after the taxi dropped them off at the border crossing. The girls kept quiet at the port of entry, carrying their baby siblings Jazmin and Emiliano and their plastic bags of possessions. Luz displayed a card to the INS officer, and they hustled into a U.S. taxi waiting on the other side. The girls exchanged questioning glances. Anticipation poked in around the anger and confusion.

The taxi pulled out around the border Safeway and JCPenney. In those days, residents of Agua Prieta could easily obtain short-term border-crossing cards that allowed them to visit family and shop in southern Arizona. As a result, a significant portion of Douglas's municipal budget came from sales tax paid by Mexican shoppers. The girls had often accompanied their mother to Douglas on shopping trips or to see their U.S. citizen cousins in Arizona. Sometimes Luz dragged them on long, tedious visits to their family friend Saul's house. But this trip—with all their possessions crammed into a taxi—was clearly different.

The taxi didn't pull into the Safeway parking lot. It passed the street where their cousin Camila lived, and kept going. Soon it left behind the little bit of Douglas that Aida recognized. Against her will, Aida took in the new scenery with rising delight. Her sisters' faces told the same story: the fight, the rushed packing, the taxis—this was not how they imagined going to live in *los Unites* back on the playground, but the ride through Douglas still felt like the beginning of something new. The realization brushed up against sad memories of their father, but Aida and her sisters couldn't help feeling excited.

With a bump, the taxi pulled off the pavement into a dusty neighborhood of strange metal houses on cinder blocks. Aida had never seen houses made of metal before. They *were* going to live in America, she realized.

The taxi delivered them to a dirt-colored brick *casita*. It had a small kitchen, a bedroom, and a miniature bathroom for the six of them. A fridge and stove were the extent of its furniture. Eventually, a man arrived with two mattresses. The girls knew him well. They had played with Saul's children. They'd spent stifling hours waiting in his living room while he and their mother disappeared together.

"This is not right," Jennifer said. She'd put two and two together fast. Aida and Cynthia still didn't know what was happening.

"Fuck, no," Jennifer said.

THAT WAS HOW Aida came to live in the United States. Her new home was in Pirtleville, a dusty neighborhood on the northern edge of Douglas. Mexican American laborers had carved Pirtleville out of scrubland in the early twentieth century. Those original residents had done the dirtiest, most dangerous work at the Phelps Dodge copper smelter, Douglas's main employer at the time. And they did it for half the wage of their Anglo counterparts. The smelter's mustard-gray smoke would settle hard over Pirtleville in those days. It tortured throats and sooted laundry, but residents were proud and independent. For most folks, the sulfurous air smelled like opportunity.

Indeed, Douglas had been a relatively prosperous place during much of the almost a century between its founding in 1901 and the smelter closure in 1987. For a desert outpost whose population never exceeded twenty thousand, the town once had an almost cosmopolitan air.

This story began when the Scottish Canadian adventurer and metallurgist James Douglas journeyed from the East on behalf of the Phelps Dodge mining corporation. In the early 1880s, he worked his way from Albuquerque to Tucson leading a string of pack mules. Then he pushed on to Bisbee and Morenci, where he developed what would become two of the world's most productive copper mines. In the 1890s, he added to Phelps Dodge's growing empire by acquiring mine claims in northern Mexico. At that point, only one thing stood in the way of Phelps Dodge's ascendance as a global corporation: the company needed a smelter in the West and asked Douglas to pick a location.

He chose a spot at the bottom of the broad Sulphur Springs valley in far southeastern Arizona. The Gadsden Purchase establishing the border between the United States and Mexico in that stretch of desert was less than forty years old. The border still felt more imaginary than real in most places. At the time, binational bands of cowboys staged cattle roundups in the spot, drawn by its abundant ground and surface water. American cowboys called the damp oasis Whitewater Draw. Mexican cowboys called it Agua Prieta— "Black Water." The one thing they agreed on was that water aside, the location lay hundreds of miles from anything that mattered and would never amount to much.

James Douglas, on the other hand, saw great promise in the valley's strategic position extending out toward mines on both sides of the border. He gave his name to a burgeoning new town, and twin smelters rose from the desert. After Arizona gained statehood in 1912, a copper star blazed at the center of its state flag. A copper dome topped the state capitol, and Douglas's smelters poured a steady stream of the state's molten sustenance. By the 1920s, the town had nearly ten thousand people, and by the 1930s its smelters could pour almost a million pounds of blister copper a day.

Douglasites called the company PD—as if it were an impressive, benevolent relative known only by his initials. PD's copper built a library, a hospital, and schools. Workers could purchase just about anything they wanted on credit at a modern three-story company store. Copper attracted virtuoso violinists from France and ballet troupes from Russia. The Douglas High School band was big and well equipped. And when sports teams needed to travel to championships on either side of the border, Phelps Dodge covered the costs.

The culture of the company permeated the town built around it. PD's rules were the town's rules—not officially, but in effect. PD's shift whistle governed the rhythm of the town's days. The price of copper governed the rhythm of its years. When the price was high, Douglas boomed. When it fell, the town scrimped. During market gluts and strikes, PD idled its furnaces and the town languished.

In return for benevolent paternalism, the company demanded loyalty and gained a reputation for violent union busting. Not until after 1935, when Congress passed the first national legislation protecting the right to organize and strike, would unions successfully brave PD country. When they did, the International Union of Mine, Mill, and Smelter Workers led the way. Unlike many U.S. unions, "Mine-Mill" championed racial equality.

The union's stance was crucial in Douglas, where the PD smelter followed a two-tier wage system. Anglos received one rate, and Mexican Americans received another, about 50 percent lower for the same work. Race governed what jobs a man could get and how high he could rise in the company. It determined what bathrooms he'd be allowed to use at work and how doctors would treat his family at the PD hospital. Mexican American workers and small business owners in Douglas had long organized themselves in mutual aid societies. Now a national union would help them fight for safer conditions and an end to the two-tier wage system.

PD tried to divide and conquer organized labor, branding Mine-Mill as "the Mexican union" and firing workers who dared to strike. In 1941, however, the U.S. Supreme Court issued a ruling that would serve as a cornerstone of the postwar era of rising wages and declining inequality. The "Phelps Dodge rule," as it came to be called, made it illegal for companies to refuse to hire workers because of union membership. A year later, Mine-Mill won the right to represent workers at the Douglas smelter.

After World War II, union contracts outlawed the two-tier pay rate, and Mexican Americans clawed their way into higher positions in the company. Wages rose steadily from the 1950s to the 1970s. With strong industrial demand for copper in the postwar period, PD could afford it. Workers, company, and town prospered together.

In Pirtleville, kilned-brick ranch houses, some with their own in-law *casitas* like the one Aida and her family now occupied, replaced the community's original adobes. The children of smelter workers could earn college degrees and find professional employment, despite discrimination. Through the postwar period, Douglas embodied the dream of a Mexican American industrial middle class. The town was still, by most measures, a poor place, but it had jobs, schools, a sense of purpose, and a vision of what it could become.

By the time Aida and her family arrived in 1996, though, the town had changed. After PD closed the smelter complex in 1987, the bad air cleared and the good jobs disappeared. By 1996, little remained of the smelter except ghostly slag heaps, residual heavy metals, and a lingering feeling of betrayal. The promise of a Mexican American middle class was snuffed out. In the final years of the twentieth century, Pirtleville, with its population of fifteen hundred, ranked as one of the poorest census-designated places in the United States. When Aida and her family taxied into this dusty outskirt of Douglas, half the children in Pirtleville lived under the poverty line.

2.

ENGLISH WITHOUT BARRIERS

A FEW WEEKS AFTER ARRIVING in Arizona, Aida confronted her mom. The family had gone from a comfortable two-story house in Mexico to a two-room adobe behind Kmart. In the house Saul rented for Luz and her children, a mattress on the floor functioned as communal bed and living room couch. When the children slept, Luz stayed awake brushing cockroaches off the babies' faces.

Aida needed to understand the sudden change in her life.

"What are we doing here?" she asked in the strongest voice she could summon. Since crossing the border, she felt older than her eight and a half years. "Where is my dad, and why is Saul acting like *he's* our dad?"

"You have no idea what you are talking about," Luz said.

"Shut *up*, Aida," Jennifer added for good measure.

Aida knew she had stumbled into the territory of a secret but couldn't figure out how to stretch her small frame high enough to see the whole of it. Instead, she set herself to making her way in the United States. Five months after crossing the border, she entered a brand-new school in her brand-new country, determined to learn.

Like other third-grade girls at Sarah Marley Elementary during the 1996–1997 academic year, Aida dotted her i's with bubbly hearts. She taped pictures of the Spice Girls and Missy Elliott on her binder, wore crop tops, and snapped hair scrunchies like a pro. What people noted most about Aida, though, was her smile. The word people used to describe her was *risueña*—sunny—although the English word "sunny" didn't do justice to the way that *risueña* beamed. Aida lit up a room, even when things were not going well for her, which they usually were not.

Saul had moved the family to a new apartment, the second in a series of whiplash relocations that would define Aida's youth. The new place was an old row house in central Douglas that would once have held smelter workers. The X-shaped former Phelps Dodge hospital marked the end of her block.

Saul, the man pretending to be Aida's dad, had a wife and kids in a nearby town. He moved Luz and her children from one apartment to another like a stone he skipped over water, and disguised the expense by using each place as an office for the transportation company he owned. Saul tried to win Luz's children over at first, particularly the babies Jazmin and Emiliano, whom he showered with gifts. But deep down, he didn't have it in him. Unkindness fell from his mouth, heavy as a car hood with no stick to prop it up.

"*Mira la negra fea*," he let drop as he walked by Aida one day.

She was writing something, a poem or song lyrics. Her left-handed printing smeared on the page.

"You're so stupid. Look at that handwriting." He grabbed the page from her and tore it up. "Do it again and do it right."

Saul tried to make up for insults with gifts but got them all wrong. That spring, he brought over an almost-new bicycle for Jazmin—years before she could possibly ride one. He so clearly favored Emiliano and Jazmin. It ground into Aida, whose prized brakeless bike had stayed in Agua Prieta.

SAUL PUT LUZ to work for his company. Off-duty drivers left their cars in front of the house; Luz and her daughters cleaned them out. Saul set up a radio in their cramped living room, and Luz ran dispatch. Sometimes he would yell at Aida to take over.

"I can't," she said one afternoon, shrinking away.

Saul yelled at Luz to get out of her chair, hauling her up and pushing her out.

"Aida, get in this chair."

"Please, I can't."

He yanked her arm and sat her down. "Just say *cero uno a base*. Zero one to base, come in."

Aida, bouncing in the chair and on the verge of panic, couldn't get the words out. She was terrified of what would follow if she got it wrong.

"What is wrong with you?"

Aida could only make a shuddering hum.

"What? Louder," Saul said, shoving the microphone into her teeth. "*Cero uno a base.*"

Aida tried. She tried to squeeze the words out. She tried with all her little-girl might. But she couldn't.

"Fucking worthless," he growled, and stormed off.

Like this, the household settled into a manic rhythm. With six people in two or three rooms, they lived loud lives. At any given moment, someone had music turned up high. Babies, sibling spats, teenage angst, and television filled in around the music. Most nights, sleep was late and broken by interruption. Privacy was not a concept Aida understood until many years later. She forgot that the intensity of life could have a set point anywhere below maximum.

When Saul stayed with his real family, six people crowded in a tiny apartment almost felt fun. Luz worked endless hours, desperate to keep Saul happy and a roof over her family's head. But at least she worked from home. Radio in one hand and babies in the other, she wrangled the family and, from time to time, cooked meals like the ones she'd prepared in Agua Prieta. Luz had set the family down hard in a new country, but they still had one another and a kind of manic joy.

As soon as Luz received a call from Saul saying that he was on his way, though, the atmosphere froze.

"Turn that music down!" Luz would order, hanging up the phone.

She and the girls would clean frantically—a single unwashed dish or patch of sand kicked in from the patio might cause Saul to explode. On days when she expected a visit from Saul, Luz scrubbed the floor obsessively with Pine-Sol. For years, Aida cringed with the expectation of violence whenever she smelled floor polish.

The house perfect, they would wait. Luz readjusted her hair and makeup. Aida made herself small, fearing what it might mean to be seen or heard by Saul. She never knew what would set him off. Whatever it was, her mother would suffer the most.

Aida learned this lesson shortly after moving to Douglas. One night, a dull thud came from Luz's bedroom, waking the girls. They went to see what made the sound. Saul didn't even pause or look in their direction when Aida and her sisters opened their mom's door. With a craftsman's attention, he rag-dolled Luz into the wall, hauled her back, and did it again. Their mother's body striking the wall was what had woken them.

"Shhhh," Luz managed to say, gesticulating at them to leave.

For the rest of their lives, Aida and Jennifer would remember the animal instinct that followed. They flew at Saul, their fists bouncing uselessly off his broad back. They tried to pull him off. He flicked them away with one arm. Nothing they did made a difference. They yelled for him to stop, swearing and screaming for him to leave. They hoped that a neighbor would hear and help them, and the neighbors could hear everything that happened in that apartment complex. But no one came. And Saul didn't leave.

Instead, he turned on the girls. They could see in his face that he intended to teach them a thing or two about not interrupting, but the lesson never came. Luz cracked across the room. In a concussive flash, they saw Luz shoot out of the background and flatten Saul, who was almost twice her weight.

It was the first time Aida and her sisters had seen their mother being beaten and the first time they saw her fighting back. But nothing surprised them as much as what happened next.

As soon as Luz heard the front door slam and Saul's car start outside, she rounded on her daughters. "Don't you ever do that again! Don't *ever* interfere. Just get away. Just go!"

Luz's rage scared them almost as much as Saul's savagery, but at some level they understood that it was her way of keeping them safe.

From that point on, the girls learned to listen closely to the sounds of violence coming through walls. They could distinguish between a backhand and a closed fist, the scrape of a body hitting a dresser and the thud of a fall. When the noises reached a precise pitch, obvious only to a trained ear, the older sisters would grab the babies and run. They couldn't protect their mother, but they could protect one another.

A SMALL GIRL, jerked from one life to another in a single afternoon, cannot see much beyond her own shock. But even Aida could feel the air of destitution emanating from her new home. From the start, she saw it exuding from Douglas's trailers and crumbling adobes, its wide empty streets, and its countless stores in an indeterminate state of openness. The thrill of living in *los Unites* mingled with sadness and loss. She knew nothing of the town's history, but she could almost feel her body absorbing the past. When Aida played tag with her sisters in a field outside the *casita*, she kicked up traces of that earlier era: dust heavy with arsenic, cadmium, and lead.

The end of copper-based prosperity in Douglas had begun, as many great changes do, with an acute crisis. In 1980, the U.S. economy dipped into economic slowdown, the first leg of what would become a double-dip recession. Auto manufacturers purchased less copper for radiators. Contractors bought less electrical wire, and telecom companies rolled out fewer telephone lines. In April 1982, PD suspended operations across the country to let demand catch up with supply.

At first, the recession felt like others Douglas had weathered before. Residents knew the routine. Families would tighten their budgets. Store owners on G Avenue would struggle to stay open. Kids in college would worry about tuition payments, and women would work harder. They would sell tamales door to door, take extra jobs cleaning executives' houses, and earn grocery money mending clothes. During strikes, women banded together, organizing raffles and collecting donations for families in need. There was a fondness to the way people recalled previous strikes and recessions. They were interludes of solidarity filled with surprisingly happy memories. So residents rallied together and waited for the new crisis to pass and Douglas to return to normal.

But years passed. The belts stayed tight, and people worked harder still. Douglas residents began to understand that this time there would be no return to normal. The early-1980s crisis transformed not just Douglas but the whole world economy.

In the late 1970s, foreign and domestic pressures had fueled double-digit inflation in the United States. Taking over as chair of the Federal Reserve Board in 1979, Paul Volcker vowed to combat price increases by raising interest rates, regardless of the danger. And the danger was clear: high interest rates would stabilize prices and please investors but could also send the economy plunging into recession. Volcker forged ahead, and his decision signaled the rise of a new era of austerity and conservative economics—an era in which the interests of Wall Street would dominate those of Main Street. By 1981, Volcker's leadership pushed interest rates to 20 percent, stamping out inflation and sending the country into a brutal recession.

As hard as it was for U.S. communities, the policy shift rocked Latin America more. Through the 1970s, U.S. banks had fueled a bubble of frenzied lending to what was then called the Third World. These loans bolstered investor earnings and the dubious development schemes of authoritarian regimes. The debt had been manageable, though—as long as U.S. interest rates remained low. When Volcker sent rates skyward, the bubble popped.

In the summer of 1982, Latin American governments, beginning with Mexico, threatened default, and the world economy teetered on the edge of collapse. U.S. commercial banks' exposure to Latin American debt was greater than their combined capitalization. Investment banks were even more heavily leveraged.

Under pressure from northern investors and international financial organizations, Latin American governments responded to the crisis by imposing extreme austerity and breakneck economic liberalization on their populations. These measures extracted money that countries could use to continue making debt payments but also triggered a deep region-wide depression known as the "lost decade." Latin America achieved fiscal solvency and helped U.S. investors earn windfall profits but at the cost of negative growth, unemployment, gutted social programs, and soaring poverty.

Douglas felt the effects of the Third World debt crisis more than many places in the United States, and not just because the crisis fueled increased migration from Mexico. For poorer mineral-producing nations such as Chile, Zambia, and Zaire, the debt crisis generated enormous pressure to extract and sell copper. Exporting as much copper as possible as quickly as possible made short-term sense, even if it caused world copper prices to plummet. For Chile, Zambia, Zaire, and their creditors, the only response to falling prices was to mine more.

In the face of competition from low-cost Third World producers, PD might have diversified into sectors other than copper. It might have invested in technology to make its core business more efficient. The company took a different tack. Following a pattern that would feel all too familiar by the end of the Reagan years, it slashed wages and retreated from its commitments to workers.

When PD workers struck to protest wage cuts in 1983, the company fired and replaced the striking workers. This action would change not just Douglas but the entire country. President Reagan had shocked the nation just two years earlier when he fired and replaced striking air traffic controllers. But they had been public employees engaged in work essential to public safety. Until PD's action in 1983, there were no postwar precedents for a private company firing striking industrial workers on such a large scale.

Thus, despite its small size and remote location, the town of Douglas lay at the center of pivotal events in the rise and decline of U.S. unions. On one end, the 1941 "Phelps Dodge rule" heralded the ascendance of organized labor. It helped set the stage for rising prosperity and falling inequality that would define the postwar period. At the other end, PD's decision to fire striking workers in 1983 was the harbinger of a long assault on worker power.

In the PD company towns of Morenci and Clifton, Arizona, the firings sparked violent clashes between union workers, scabs, the National Guard, and police. In Douglas, long the spiritual heart of PD in the Southwest, 1983 was painful but less violent. There, a wrenching feeling of betrayal was the dominant emotion.

Union supporters shut down Park Avenue in New York. College students across the country rallied for copper workers, and Bruce Springsteen dedicated his song "My Hometown" to strikers during a concert at Arizona State University. None of it mattered to PD. For a company with an atavistic disdain for unions, the crisis of the 1980s was too good to waste.

In previous decades, workers and the company would have finally agreed on a contract. Both sides would have shaken off harsh words uttered in the heat of battle, and everyone would have returned to work. But this time, hundreds of unionized employees found themselves permanently replaced. PD's crew of short-term scabs had become the company's new permanent workforce—and they worked for well below the wage unionized employees had enjoyed. With the company's encouragement, the new employees voted to decertify PD's smelter union.

By 1985, the U.S. economy had rebounded, and PD was again earning healthy profits, despite competition from abroad. Most fired workers were not rehired, though, and the company moved its executive offices out of Douglas.

It was the kind of trauma, both economic and psychological, that few towns survive.

Then it got worse.

In the mid-1980s, environmental science had begun to identify the wide-ranging impacts of airborne industrial pollution. National debate centered on the problem of "acid rain" caused by sulfur dioxide emissions. And in this moment of heightened awareness, Douglas's smelter had just been declared the largest single manufacturing source of sulfur dioxide pollution in the country.

Regulators and a burgeoning local environmental movement demanded that PD upgrade antiquated pollution controls in Douglas. Although the plant remained PD's flagship operation, it was also the oldest active copper smelter in the country. The company refused to spend money on pollution control at what it saw as an increasingly outdated facility.

As pressure from regulators built, local activists held rallies and publicized the myriad health impacts of living near a smelter. Haltingly, Mexican American leaders, particularly those who had fought the company in 1983, began to side with environmentalists. Unbeknownst to both environmentalists and former workers, though, PD had been looking for a reason to close its Douglas operations all along. Relocating the plant in another state would cut labor costs further while avoiding the price of modernizing operations in Douglas. Pressure from environmentalists simply gave PD a convenient scapegoat for its actions.

ON MONDAY, JANUARY 12, 1987, the smelter's twenty-four towering ore roasters began to cool. Its three great reverberatory furnaces followed. On Wednesday, crane operators transferred the last crucible of matte into the smelter's last operating converter, giving the assembled crew its last display of showering sparks and hissing gas. Workers skimmed and dumped slag off the converter top for a few more hours and then, with sullen ceremony, poured a last fluid line of copper into molds. They returned home, as they had always done, at the end of their shift. The town was never the same again.

The firing of union workers and the relocation of white-collar jobs in the early 1980s had inflicted the worst damage already. Still, the blow of the final closure was significant. Douglas's mayor estimated it cost the town another 347 jobs and a quarter of its remaining economic base. New prison construction—the perpetual hope of poor rural towns—would offset the losses, he promised. And it did, in a small way. But Douglas was, simply put, no longer a place of industry. Economic restructuring had gutted the town as thoroughly as rust-belt Scranton or Pittsburgh.

A decade after the smelter closed, about 40 percent of the population lived below the poverty line. And those were the people who remained. By the time Aida began third grade in her new American home, many of the town's residents had already left.

SCHOOL BECAME AIDA'S REFUGE, and Cynthia became her shadow. Aida's younger sister entered second grade as Aida herself entered third. Cynthia had grown quiet since the move, and she followed Aida everywhere. She was not the only shy kid following Aida. The second- and third-grade classes at Sarah Marley had a contingent of new kids who, like Aida and Cynthia, had just come over from Agua Prieta. They fell in together. Outside the vortex of home, Aida had a way of making people feel included and loved. But that wasn't the only thing that endeared her to the other kids from Agua Prieta. All the wrenching changes in her life had re-formed her body into something formidable. Her baby-fat cheeks and dimpled smile disguised a boxer's physique and a direct line to fury. No one bullied the new kids when she was around.

In the classroom, however, some teachers punished Aida and her new friends for speaking Spanish. Others just ignored them. In Aida's language arts class, students took turns reading passages out loud, but the teacher skipped over Aida every time. Maybe he was well-meaning. Perhaps he thought it saved her from embarrassment, but getting passed over day after day felt intolerably cruel to Aida. So she determined that she would learn English as fast as she could.

Aida listened closely to her teachers and peers, echoing under her breath anything they said. She turned strange words over and over in her mouth until her lips and tongue finally made them sound correct. At home, she copied out bits of movie dialogue and song lyrics. Her English got better, but still she struggled.

"Aida Hernandez. You get punished quite a lot for speaking Spanish, don't you?" a teacher challenged her one day.

"Yes, Mrs. Villegas."

Mrs. Villegas figured in the legends of Sarah Marley as an awe-inspiring, poofy-haired tyrant. Her face had been stuck in a permanent scowl for the entire two decades since her giant eyeglasses had been fashionable. Aida's instinct was to run, but the teacher's look intervened.

"Come by my classroom after school today. Don't be late."

That afternoon after the last bell, Aida dragged her feet into the lair of the one teacher even the greenest kid from Mexico knew not to cross. Cynthia followed behind, keeping a cautious distance in case of trouble.

"Do you know what this is, Miss Hernandez?" Mrs. Villegas pointed to a stack of blue plastic binders on her desk. Aida knew. Anyone who watched TV or listened to the radio in Spanish at any point in the 1990s recognized a boxed set of *Ingles sin barreras*, the gold standard of immigrant dreams. It was the blueprint to success, the secret key that unlocked promotions, new cars, suburban homes, and beautiful blond girlfriends.

"I bought this," Mrs. Villegas said, "with my own money. If you'd like to study English after school, I'll be here every day."

AT HOME, everything about the way Raúl had been slashed out of the family confused Aida. Jennifer knew more than she'd say about the reasons for leaving Agua Prieta, but she refused to answer Aida's questions. The oldest sister had struggled with her transition to an American middle school. She began to ditch more classes than she attended. Days spent with her friends extended into late nights out. Sometimes she didn't return home at all. Cynthia, for her part, stayed physically close to Aida but grew quieter and more serious. Aida, Jennifer, and Cynthia were still the Three Musketeers, closer than any three people they knew, but a hairline crack had opened between them.

When Saul went back to his real family, the household breathed again, but the bruises remained. Aida noticed that her mother hadn't sung since they arrived in Arizona. "Triste recuerdo" had become too sad. In simpler times, when she lived in Agua Prieta and her mom had scolded one of the three sisters, the other two would tiptoe up behind Luz. They'd make clown faces and fish lips, doing their best to get the girl in trouble to crack up.

"What are you laughing at, little girl?!" Luz would scream in Spanish, while the other two sisters tried not to laugh out loud. But when they lived in Mexico Luz's fire didn't burn as hot, and her anger would eventually fizzle into good humor. Now they knew better than to even try it.

Aida watched her mother disappear from them as completely as her father had. Luz stopped waking the girls up for school in the morning and no longer checked their homework every afternoon. And as Jennifer quickly realized, Luz stopped keeping track of whether they went to school at all.

Aida helped take over the cooking. She changed Emiliano and Jazmin's diapers and gave them bottles at night. As Jazmin got older, Aida spent hours combing her hair and making pretty pigtails with *bolita* ties. Aida might run off to school with her volcanic black curls in disarray, but her little sister would be beautiful, she vowed.

At school, Aida, Cynthia, and Mrs. Villegas worked together for an hour every day. Soon the whole group of Agua Prieta exiles joined them. English fell into place that year in a way nothing ever had before in Aida's life. Her language arts teacher still skipped her during group reading, but the kids from Agua Prieta didn't get punished as much, and that filled Aida with pride.

One day, when the language arts teacher asked the student on Aida's left to read and then pointed to the student on Aida's right to take the next passage, Aida saw her chance.

She raised her hand and said, "Please, sir, may I read?" The teacher looked dumbstruck, then smiled.

Aida read the short passage and then kept going to the next one and the next one. Finally she stumbled on a word. "Tiny" came out "teeny."

"Tiny," the teacher said, correcting her.

"Tiny," Aida repeated. In her mind, the kids around her cheered.

That spring, as the school year came to a close, Aida's homeroom teacher printed a Certificate of Superior Achievement and Excellence of

Performance for her. She ran home to show her mother and vowed to save the diploma forever.

Delighting in their new command of English, Aida and Cynthia devised a routine to make their mother laugh. They stood next to her, speaking their new language, the one Luz only half understood.

"Cynthia, I have a *big* secret. Whatever you do, *don't tell Mom*," Aida would begin.

"Okay, I promise, I won't tell *Mom*. Tell me your *big secret*."

The two girls said these lines with poorly suppressed giggles and exaggerated winks; Luz didn't take the bait. The joke hit too close to her essential vulnerability. Her daughters could escape to school nine months of the year. But Luz—undocumented with little English, dependent on a violent and controlling man, and struggling to keep a household of five growing kids afloat—was all alone.

Luz spent long hours manning the dispatch radio and cleaning Saul's fleet of vehicles. Working from home let her take care of Emiliano and Jazmin during the day, but it also meant that she rarely went out. Luz needed Saul's permission to leave the house, and he'd know if she disobeyed him. He and his fleet of drivers kept close track of her movements. Just lending a garden hose to a male neighbor could provoke a fight that ended with Saul threatening to cut off financial support.

Luz had a U.S. citizen sister in Douglas whom she could have visited without incurring Saul's wrath, but that would have required explaining her bruises. There were only so many times she could say the hood of a car fell on her while she was checking the oil. So she rarely saw her sister, Camila's mother.

Douglas wasn't yet saturated with U.S. Border Patrol and police, as it would be in the coming years, but Luz was sharply aware of her tenuous status. The border-crossing card she showed at the Douglas port of entry on March 8, 1996, was valid for visits of up to seventy-two hours, within twenty-five miles of the border. It was meant to allow Mexican consumers to sustain Arizona's retail economy—not to live in the state. Saul never let her forget this. Her legal status loomed behind every threat he made.

"Shut up, you stupid woman, or I'll call the Border Patrol," he'd say.

"Sure, go ahead and call the police. They'll bring the Border Patrol, and it won't be me they'll take away."

"Be quiet," he'd scold the girls if they got too loud. "The police will come, and they'll call the Border Patrol to take you away."

On good days, Saul promised to help Luz fix her papers. Part of her wanted to believe this. The other part knew that he already had a legal wife. So she took precautions. When Saul moved them to a new apartment, Luz found a hiding place for each of her children. She tried to turn it into a game.

"One, two, three, go hide! The *migra* is here!" she would call out, and the kids would scatter to their places.

This, like so much else, passed as normal in Aida's new home. Her mother's escape from Raúl had lifted her roughly from one country and set her down hard in another. But most people Aida knew had family on both sides. Crossing the border could be difficult or dangerous for migrants from farther south in Mexico or Central America, but border folk, acculturated to binational living, still moved back and forth with relative ease. They carried themselves differently from other immigrants. Many traced their family's presence in this part of the world to a time before the border existed. They had local knowledge that allowed them to pass—as long as, and only if, they were lucky and stayed out of trouble.

Aida internalized her mother's frequent reminders: "Keep quiet. Don't make trouble." To a certain degree, her mother's habit of looking over her shoulder was contagious. Aida understood that she couldn't participate in certain after-school activities, and even the simplest trip to a store with her mom was a nervous sprint. But eventually, Aida would stop thinking much about her immigration status.

On her own, away from her mother, Aida roamed freely through Douglas. If she had a dollar, she could go to the Circle K across the street to buy ten mini Reese's Peanut Butter Cups. Even very young, she babysat for neighbors. Most women in the apartment complex knew, or intuited, the nature of Aida's home life. They were too afraid of Saul to intervene when he got violent, but they could take Aida into their homes, feed her, and occasionally give her used clothes. An older, housebound neighbor asked her to take out her garbage every evening. Each time she did it, the woman let Aida take a pomegranate from her tree—a thing of pure joy. Aida would sit on her stoop, break the fruit in half, and drench herself in the ruby juice.

It was the summer of 1997, and when Sarah Marley Elementary started again in the fall, Aida knew several different routes to school. She could admire ninety-nine-cent earrings in the stores on G Avenue, and she could shine all of her nine-and-three-quarter-year-old charm on shop clerks. When Aida smiled, even the most suspicious of them stopped puttering over racks of boots and rhinestoned jeans long enough to find a cardboard box that Aida could play with. They'd give her unwanted boxes, and she'd drag stacks of them to the apartment courtyard. There, she and her friends could transform them into labyrinths and forts.

Douglas's big-box stores marked the western edge of Aida's U.S. geography. Memorial Park, with its pool and F-16 Falcon on a pedestal, was her East. Pirtleville and the *casita* where the family first landed after fleeing Mexico, the North. To the south, she could see the old chain-link border fence clearly. Agua Prieta hummed a thousand grown-up steps from her doorstep, but she had begun to forget the other city at the end of her street.

Underneath it all, Aida and her friends discovered a network of municipal storm tunnels. They would wait for Border Patrol shift changes and dash into the gaping mouth of the underworld. The tunnels were big enough in places for the kids to ride their bicycles. And at a spot deep inside the system, Aida staked her shy claim to the new world. "Aida Hernandez was here," she scratched in English on the concrete wall.

On Thursday nights, like everyone else, she watched *Friends*. If she slept well that night, she would dream that she was in *Friends*, and she'd wake up happy. She was a part of America. Despite abundant evidence of Douglas's rough expulsion from the promise of middle-class life, Aida trusted her adopted country's dream. When she and her sisters talked about the future, she proclaimed a vision that was only slightly different from the one she had announced in the playground across the border.

"When I grow up," she said in a voice that had hardened a bit in eighteen months, "I am *not* going to have a husband. I am *not* going to have any kids. I'm going to live in the biggest building in New York, in an all-white apartment, just me and my all-white cat."

3

A SUDDEN STORM

AUGUST 1997

It had been a week of storms in the arid Southwest. The previous night's rain—more than three inches in two hours—washed the sky clean and teased a feathering of green out of the ocher mountains. Rosie Mendoza had lived in Douglas and Agua Prieta for twelve years, but even on a day that clear and beautiful the Sonoran Desert didn't feel like home.

Returning to Douglas after a meeting with Mexican health officials, she observed the effects of the previous night's liquid destruction. Four inches of standing water remained in places around the port of entry. Trash and brush clogged streets. The ditch running ten blocks along the international line and under the port of entry was swollen with muddy runoff.

She had spent the happiest years of her childhood in a tropical estuary on Mexico's Pacific coast, a paradise of palms and mangroves. Prone to biblical analogies, she called her time on the border her "forty years in the desert." Rosie's true home was a green place where water lay thick and slow on the land. Water in the desert, when it came at all, was swift and angry.

Like many newcomers getting their first glimpse of the Sulphur Springs valley, Rosie had cried when her bus from Hermosillo crested the high point outside Agua Prieta back in 1985. On that day, a blue-gray cloud billowed out of the twin smelter stacks across the border in Arizona. Sulfur haze gloamed beneath it, and because the wind blew just right, black fly ash swirled in eddies around her bus. Rosie had not wanted to be on that bus, but foreign factories had begun to open along the border and she needed a job.

Rosie was seventeen when she arrived in Agua Prieta. She had worked full-time since the end of sixth grade. As a girl, she had labored in agricultural fields and helped her grandfather, an indigenous healer. As a teen, she had packed frozen chicken parts at a slaughterhouse. At sixteen, she used her savings to build her mother a house. When the chicken plant closed for a strike, she set out for the border in search of a new job.

Rosie had arrived in Agua Prieta on a Sunday. By Tuesday, she had a job at a Japanese factory. For ten hours a day, she worked with solvents that dissolved her fingerprints and scorched her nasal passages. But the work allowed her to send money to her mom, and Rosie felt as if she were doing something real. She was making a new product that few people on either side of the border had heard of yet. It was an automobile computer system that inflated a fabric cushion to protect drivers in the event of a collision. Air bags, they were called.

On her days off, Rosie crossed into Arizona without papers to harvest chilies, apples, peaches, and pistachios. In those seasons before walls and checkpoints, it was easy for workers to cycle between farm labor in the United States and homes in Mexico. When Ronald Reagan signed the Immigration Reform and Control Act (IRCA) in 1986, Rosie lucked out. The bill allowed farmworkers like her to become legal residents in the United States. She settled in Douglas, married, divorced, and raised five children alone. Somehow she managed to put herself through college. Like her grandfather before her, she became a healer. Her title might have been "social worker," "health promoter," or "victims' advocate," but she was a healer—and a force of nature.

At first, Rosie had worked on any project that seemed urgent. She conducted HIV testing and diabetes education and taught Douglas residents how to protect themselves from heavy metal residues. Eventually, she would focus on sexual assault and domestic violence, topics she knew firsthand. Much later, that work would bring Rosie and Aida together in a crucial moment. But on that August day in 1997, early in her career, she worked in drug abuse prevention. Her meeting with Mexican officials that morning had gone well. They'd discussed ways to coordinate U.S. and Mexican efforts. Like storms, the issues Rosie cared about didn't respect national borders.

WALKING BACK to her office in Douglas, Rosie found a crowd milling around the international line. At the end of July, Border Patrol agents had removed sections of ramshackle chain link between Douglas and Agua Prieta. Everyone agreed that the fence—segments of which dated to the 1950s—was useless, but the Border Patrol's work stirred uneasy feelings. In place of the fence, they planned to erect an eighteen-foot-high barrier of iron bollards along the border. It would stretch a mile to the east and a quarter mile to the west of the port of entry. An ugly barricade cobbled from Gulf War–surplus helicopter landing mats would extend beyond that. Together, they would constitute the most substantial barrier ever installed in this stretch of the Southwest. Rosie and her friends from Douglas's churches and community groups feared the divisive message the wall would send.

For weeks since the old fence came down, Mexican citizens had gathered to chat with Border Patrol agents welding sections of the new barrier. Sweltering in the August heat, agents strayed across the line to buy Popsicles and cold drinks from Mexican vendors. But the crowd on the morning of August 6 was bigger. More than one hundred people lined the Mexican side of the border, pushing right to the crumbly precipice. They spoke in low, angry voices. A woman stood off to the side praying the rosary.

Rosie bumped through the crowd. Short and round with wavy hair and apple cheeks, she found that her warm "sorry"s and "excuse me"s opened a pathway.

She could see yellow police tape on the U.S. side of the ditch. Below, she saw city workers wading in the receding water. Some wore hazmat suits.

Douglas's police chief, Charlie Austin, looked grimmer than Rosie had ever seen him.

Someone in the crowd explained that the Americans had found four bodies in the ditch that morning. One of them, a man, had been pried from the mud just below where Rosie stood. He had come out purple and swollen. Fine gray silt clogged his eyes, nose, and mouth.

Like most professionals who saw extremes of human suffering on a daily basis, Rosie believed that she could not sustain her work without strong defenses. She rarely allowed herself to feel even a fraction of the suffering she saw, and she almost never spoke about the violence she had lived through herself. She helped other people process their emotions and kept her own in check. That morning, though, something gave way.

In the 1980s and early 1990s, migrant deaths on the border near Douglas had been rare. This was clearly changing. The number of bodies recovered in the ditch after the previous night's storm would eventually reach eight—equal to the number of border crossers who died in the entire 260-mile Tucson Border Patrol Sector during all of 1995. No one knew it yet, but the migrants who drowned in this storm were among the first of thousands who would die in the coming years. No one in the crowd could imagine that future. But staring into the muddy ditch, Rosie felt it looming. A jolt of apprehension propelled her out of the crowd.

She ran west along the ditch, looking for a quiet spot away from people. Fifty yards from the port of entry, a bundle of cloth caught her eye, and she stopped short. It looked like a burlap sack floating in an eddy, except, when she focused, she saw that the fabric had arms. And legs.

STANDING ON THE U.S. side, Charlie Austin reckoned that the procession of distended bodies coming out of the ditch was the worst thing he'd seen in twenty-four years as a police officer. Circumspect in speech and angular in bearing, Douglas's police chief appeared cut from the same cloth as Wyatt Earp. In fact, he'd grown up in Bisbee, just up the highway from the O.K. Corral. He squinted at the scene. His sun-blasted face revealed little of the anger he felt. The police chief was a law-and-order conservative, a Christian pastor, and a decent guy. He wanted things to make sense, and nothing about that day made sense.

As far as he was concerned, the border was a homicide crime scene, with the number of victims growing by the hour. He just didn't know whom to charge. In the coming weeks, Charlie concluded that the deaths were easy to reconstruct but hard to explain.

Late on August 5, twelve migrants had met for dinner at a restaurant in Agua Prieta. En route from central and southern Mexico, they were new to the border and full of nervous anticipation. They ate what they could, and the man each of them had paid to guide them to Phoenix reviewed the plan. Then he led them into the night.

The group slipped into the ditch and hurried west along the border, feeling lucky. The fence had been removed, and Border Patrol's night vision cameras didn't work well in the light drizzle that had started to fall. At the end of F Avenue, they located the mouth of a cement storm sewer. They were to follow the tunnel ten blocks north to a manhole opening. If the coast was clear, the smuggler told them, they'd crawl out and make their way to a motel a few blocks from the exit.

They walked, stooped over, and made good progress. Above them, the rain picked up, and they were grateful to be under cover. At Ninth Street and F Avenue, almost directly under the apartment where Aida lived at the time, the twelve migrants and their smuggler paused. A metal ladder bolted to the tunnel wall climbed to a grated opening. Ahead of them, the passage narrowed.

On dry days, Aida and her friends used to sneak into this tunnel to play. She had joyously scratched her name somewhere in the concrete vault. But these people just wanted out. Above them, they could hear the rain intensify. Torrents of water battered into asphalt and cement-hard desert. The sound of a train rumbled somewhere in the distance.

There was no time to react. The water hit them before their brains could register the improbability of hearing a train in a storm sewer. Those who grabbed the metal ladder lived. Those who didn't died. The flash flood swept the unlucky ones away, banging them out of the tunnel, into the ditch, and around the corner. At the end of the run, the current pinned them against a metal grate in a tangle of debris where the culvert dived under the port of entry.

Four adults and a two-year-old girl clung to the ladder for more than two hours. The grate above them was jammed or locked, so they squeezed into the shaft as water pounded below. They were battered and cold but managed to hold on until the flood receded. Bleeding and hypothermic, the survivors staggered to the Loma Douglas Motel, the smuggler among them. At this point, he was probably calculating the scrutiny the deaths would ignite. He dumped the group at the motel with a threat: keep quiet about what happened in the tunnel. Then he disappeared.

Early on the morning of the sixth, the port director, Frank Amarillas, inspected the clogged grate. It had almost flooded his facility the night before. Shining his flashlight at the black water, he saw what he thought was a bale of marijuana floating amid the debris. A smuggler had abandoned his load in the storm, Amarillas thought. It happened often enough. He called for a pole and pulled the bale to shore. From close up, though, even in the dark, he could see that it wasn't a bale. It was a woman.

At 8:30 that morning, Douglas city workers found the bodies of three men. The man that Rosie saw lifted out of the mud was a fifth victim. A sixth man's body appeared a few hours later, and Border Patrol agents detained the survivors huddled in their motel room alone.

On August 17, a second summer monsoon rearranged the ditch bottom again, and two more bodies surfaced. In total, seven men and one woman, ages eighteen to thirty-four, had died. It was not the first time migrants had died crossing the border between Agua Prieta and Douglas. But it was the first time so many had died at once, right in the middle of town. And the dead were from distant central Mexico, strangers even in a place accustomed to the movement of people. Their sudden and public deaths shook both sides of the line.

CHARLIE AUSTIN WANTED to charge the smuggler with manslaughter, but the man had vanished. Besides, Charlie felt that there was something more to the story. It wasn't just a single event. Anyone paying attention could see that migrants were crossing the border in greater numbers every day and were taking bigger and bigger risks to do so. They were coming from distant Mexican states that people in Douglas and Agua Prieta barely knew existed. They were not following the familiar patterns of migration the region had known for years.

Why were so many migrants, with destinations deep in the interior United States, streaming through this place, which had previously mostly seen short-term seasonal migrants? Why were people from faraway central and southern Mexico passing through Douglas?

A young reporter, Xavier Zaragoza, found himself asking the same questions. Part of the last generation of Douglas residents to attend college on smelter wages, Xavier had made it to the Ivy League. He had studied journalism at Brown and had returned to Douglas to take his first real job in his chosen career. On August 6, he had slipped past Charlie's police tape for a closer look at the scene. His work at the *Douglas Dispatch* wasn't scheduled to start for two more weeks, but Xavier was eager.

Over the following months, whenever he asked friends to explain the new face of migration, they gave absurd answers. The most common response ran something like, "You know Mexicans . . . always having babies."

More thoughtful observers blamed the massive influx of migrants on economic crises in Mexico. During the 1980s and early 1990s, foreign investors and the International Monetary Fund had praised the country's pro-market policies. Economic liberalization had generated an expanding financial system, attracted foreign investment, and birthed a growing cadre of Mexican billionaires. At the same time, the Washington-approved policies left many Mexicans far behind. And in 1994 and 1995, a financial collapse triggered by international currency speculators sent poverty and unemployment rates skyrocketing. By August 1997, the meltdown had pushed many Mexicans to seek work in the North. Agricultural provisions of NAFTA, combined with the collapse of international coffee markets, displaced millions more.

As dire as those crises were, though, they did not explain why a wave of migration had come crashing down on *Douglas*—120 miles of empty desert from the nearest major U.S. city.

Xavier eventually found the solution to this puzzle by talking with friends in the Border Patrol. Charlie Austin learned the answer at a briefing with federal officials. After the meeting, Charlie fumed. Why hadn't anyone bothered to inform local law enforcement? Was the Border Patrol that arrogant, or just clueless about the impact of its actions?

Both Xavier and Charlie remembered the words of an Anglo rancher who conveyed everyone's frustration at a town hall meeting with federal officials: "You mean you fucking *planned* this?"

INDEED, WHAT XAVIER, Charlie, Rosie, the Anglo rancher, and even nine-year-old Aida witnessed *was* planned, in a way. The crisis in Douglas was the logical outcome of policies crafted far from the border with little regard for life on the border. And it was just the latest in a long history of policies driven by political interests divorced from the real dynamics of migration and this place.

The border between Douglas and Agua Prieta was established by treaty in 1854. For more than a half century after that, no policies had limited migration from Mexico. In 1917, Congress imposed morality tests and visa fees on entrants from Mexico. Even then, border officials enforced the new rules irregularly. In Douglas, they made little effort to prevent people from avoiding hassles by walking around the official border crossing. Even as xenophobia and the eugenics movement reached frenzied levels in the 1920s and 1930s, lawmakers still imposed no numerical limits on migration from Mexico.

Amid seething nativism during that period, Congress created an explicitly racist immigration quota system. The Immigration Act of 1924 barred people defined as nonwhite from immigrating to the United States and severely restricted immigration by supposedly inferior whites from southern and eastern Europe. On top of that, federal representatives passed legislation designed to make life difficult for "undesirable" immigrants already in the country. But those laws targeted Asian, African, and southern and eastern European immigrants. Lawmakers explicitly excluded Mexicans and other Western Hemisphere residents from the new quotas. Flows of Latin American migrants across the southwest border were simply understood as an integral part of the economy and society of the region.

To be sure, bias still affected the treatment of Mexicans seeking entry to the United States. Border officials harassed and intimidated dark-skinned crossers. When would-be Mexican immigrants "looked poor," agents deployed morality standards and entry-fee rules to prevent them from crossing. And during outbursts of racial and economic animus in the 1930s and 1950s, federal and local officials staged mass expulsions of both Mexican immigrants and U.S. citizens of Mexican descent. These purges—carried out with dubious tactics and disregard for immigration law—affected hundreds of thousands of people and separated countless families.

Nevertheless, U.S. law imposed no numerical limits on legal immigration from Mexico, and the border was essentially open.

When laws did restrict commerce between Douglas and Agua Prieta, smuggling often ensued. Cattle thieves had plied their trade across the border in both directions since the border was drawn, and from 1910 to 1920 U.S. merchants trafficked guns and ammunition to all sides in the Mexican Revolution. During the U.S. Prohibition era, clandestine traffic again flourished. And in the 1980s and early 1990s, the escalating "drug war" again spawned an industry of border evasion. In 1990, authorities in Douglas discovered the first narco-tunnel. Built by El Chapo Guzmán's Sinaloa Cartel, it was more elaborate than the municipal sewers later used by migrant smugglers. It came complete with electric lighting and a trolley for ferrying cocaine 270 feet under the border. At its Agua Prieta end, a hydraulic system raised a pool table in a luxury home's game room to reveal the tunnel's secret entrance.

On a day-to-day basis, though, movement across the border—legal or not—was an open and undramatic affair.

Baby boomers still tell stories of the time when children's games crisscrossed the wire. At the end of a hot day of sandlot baseball in Douglas, legend had it, kids from Agua Prieta would turn themselves in to the Border Patrol. Agents would give each child a Popsicle and a ride back to the port of entry. The story was probably apocryphal and definitely romanticized, but it captured an attitude that was fully real. On any given day, Douglas residents ducked through the fence to buy *pan dulce* and tortillas in Mexico. Business owners from Agua Prieta dashed across to visit their barber. They could have crossed officially through the port of entry, but why bother with the inconvenience?

IRONICALLY, IT WAS a set of liberal reforms that ended the era of relatively free movement across the U.S.-Mexico border. During the mid-1960s civil rights era, images of segregated schools and sadistic southern sheriffs tarnished the United States' image abroad. It had become difficult to convince potential Cold War allies in Africa, Asia, and Latin America that the United States' promise of freedom and equality wasn't hollow to the core. The fact that the country preserved an overtly racist system of immigration quotas didn't help.

So, in 1965, sitting in ceremony at the Statue of Liberty, President Lyndon Johnson signed sweeping immigration reforms into law. No longer would racial restrictions govern immigration policy. Each country in the Eastern Hemisphere would now receive twenty thousand immigration visas a year. African and Asian nations would be eligible for the exact same quota as Germany or Norway. Southern and eastern European countries would also receive the same. Equality had come at last to U.S. immigration policy.

There was just one problem. The new system was fairer for residents of Madagascar and Indonesia—countries whose residents had been barred from immigrating to the United States on racial grounds. But what about Mexico, whose residents had engaged in relatively unimpeded migration to the United States since before the border existed? Countries with little history of migration to the United States received the same quota as countries defined by back-and-forth flows of people.

Most recently, millions of Mexicans had answered the call to pick the United States' food and help run its railroads during World War II. The Bracero Program, which gave wartime migrants from Mexico temporary work permits, was so successful that Congress extended it for two decades after V-J Day. By the time the Bracero Program ended in 1965, the United States and Mexico had become interdependent in ways that few observers on either side of the border wanted to acknowledge. In the years leading up to 1965, as many as half a million Mexican migrants cycled annually through the United States. With a functioning guest worker program and unlimited immigrant visas available to Mexican petitioners, almost all of those migrants had legal status.

The sudden and dramatic change arrived as a one-two punch. First, the 1965 law imposed an unprecedented numerical cap on legal immigration from Western Hemisphere countries. In the years preceding the reform, some 250,000 to 500,000 Mexican migrants cycled legally through the United States. Now no more than 120,000 legal immigrants from *the entire* Western Hemisphere would be permitted. The 1965 law stopped short, however, of extending the 20,000-visas-per-country quota to Latin America and Canada. Mexico could at least claim a big share of the Western Hemisphere's allotment.

That changed in 1976 when Congress amended the original reform bill, extending the 20,000-visas-per-country limit to the Western Hemisphere. After 1976, *all* countries would be eligible for the exact same number of immigrant visas. The new "fairer" system gave Mexico the same quota as

Luxembourg or Bhutan. In subsequent years, Congress closed America's front door further, with reductions in the total number of immigrants admitted legally to the United States.

Thus, between 1968 and 1980, the number of visas available to Mexican immigrants plunged from virtually unlimited to twenty thousand or fewer. Parents, spouses, and minor children of U.S. citizens could be admitted over the cap, but new rules made family sponsorship more difficult.

Did the United States and Mexico respond to this restriction on legal migration by turning their backs on two hundred years of connection and deeply interwoven lives? Did family ties binding the United States and Mexico vanish? Did industries dependent on cross-border movements of people disappear? They did not. Migration continued as it always had. But all of a sudden the same Mexicans who had come and gone from the country legally were now doing so without permission.

When Lyndon Johnson signed the 1965 law, Border Patrol agents arrested around 40,000 migrants a year. By the late 1970s, this figure would skyrocket to between 330,000 and 460,000. Media outlets observed the phenomenon with a growing sense of panic. Many likened it to an unexpected natural disaster. The United States had been hit by a "flood" of Mexicans without papers, a "tidal wave" of "illegals."

In fact, the "explosion" of Mexicans crossing the border without permission was entirely predictable. It was the inevitable consequence of policies that slashed opportunities to migrate legally without addressing the forces pushing and pulling people across the line. People who had lived their lives across two countries legally and peacefully for decades were suddenly redefined as invaders and threats. The "illegal immigrant" was thus invented in Washington, D.C., conjured out of contradiction.

TO MAKE MATTERS WORSE, the dramatic reduction in options for legal immigration from Mexico came just before the 1980s debt crisis hurled the United States' southern neighbor into the worst economic recession in its history and intensified pressures on Mexicans to look for jobs in the North.

By the mid-1980s, the fundamental contradiction in U.S. immigration policy had spawned an even more complicated dilemma: millions of people who lived, raised their children, attended school, paid taxes, opened businesses, sustained local economies, went to church, and joined the military in the United States now lived in the shadow of illegality. Part of the fabric of life in the United States and yet denied formal membership, they were citizens without citizenship.

In 1986, President Ronald Reagan signed the bipartisan Immigration Reform and Control Act. Later condemned by anti-immigration activists as "amnesty for illegals," IRCA attempted to undo problems set in motion by the 1965 reform. Under the bill, undocumented immigrants who met strict criteria could become formal members of their national community. Nearly three million people received green cards thanks to the 1986 law. Seventy percent of them were originally from Mexico.

At the same time, the bill imposed criminal penalties on employers who hired undocumented immigrants. It also provided an at-the-time-unprecedented increase in border security funding.

With these three components in place—legalization, employer sanctions, and border security—Reagan hoped to end the era of citizens without citizenship. Undocumented people already working in the United States would gain legal permanent resident status, while a newly minted focus on enforcement would prevent other people from following in their footsteps.

Rosie Mendoza was one of the 2.7 million undocumented immigrants who benefited from IRCA. Aida Hernandez was one of the many millions more whose presence in the United States after IRCA exemplified the law's failure. The era of citizens without citizenship could not be addressed by simply providing legal status to one cohort of immigrants and then trying to seal the border behind them.

Fueled by debt crisis in Mexico and expanding demand for low-wage workers in the United States, undocumented migration continued through the rest of the 1980s. In the mid-1990s, new financial crises in Mexico sent even more people in search of livelihoods. Rising inequality in the United States drove migration as well. As the U.S. rich got richer, demand for nannies, gardeners, and construction workers soared. Meanwhile, easily exploitable immigrant labor helped keep down the prices of goods and services that middle-class Americans counted on—even as their share of the economic pie shrank.

All of these forces combined to push undocumented migration to unprecedented highs. IRCA's failure was evident to all, and yet the political will to address the problem had vanished. As a result, a girl like Aida growing up American, attending school, speaking English, and staying out of trouble had virtually no possibility of gaining legal residence. Anti-immigrant vigilantes who poured into Douglas in the coming years could scream "Get in line" as much as they liked. There was no line for Aida to get into.

DOUGLAS AND AGUA PRIETA remained largely insulated from the emerging crisis. Aida and her family aside, most of the growing numbers of long-term migrants braving the U.S.-Mexico border in the early to mid-1990s bypassed the remote town. Even as El Paso, San Diego, and other large border cities reported overwhelming influxes, Douglas remained more or less unchanged. Migration through Douglas was still a modest affair. Until 1997, that is, when a sudden storm rolled into town.

At this point, the rancher's question bears repeating: "You mean you fucking *planned* this?"

UNBEKNOWNST TO NEARLY everyone in Douglas, a new enforcement paradigm had come to the border. It debuted in September 1993 when the El Paso Border Patrol Sector chief, Silvestre Reyes, pulled agents off mobile patrols. Breaking with tradition, he concentrated his agents in a static line along a short stretch of the urban Rio Grande. Reyes believed that shutting off unauthorized border crossing in convenient urban areas would force migrants into more difficult terrain. This would raise the human and economic cost of crossing. Reasoning like a microeconomist, Reyes figured that increasing the cost of crossing would lead to fewer people trying. Veteran agents, partial to the thrill of a good chase, hated sedentary days spent "sitting on their Xs," but the strategy worked.

Or half of it did. Thanks to Operation Hold the Line, apprehensions of undocumented border crossers fell by 76 percent in El Paso. The price charged by smugglers soared. Shunted into dangerous wilderness, migrants crossing the border began to die in unprecedented numbers. The program appeared a resounding success.

In 1994, officials in San Diego implemented their own version of the strategy, dubbing it Operation Gatekeeper. There, too, the number of unauthorized crossings plummeted.

And yet "prevention through deterrence," as the strategy came to be called, had little effect on the total number of crossings. Instead, like a pincer moving west from Texas and east from California, it funneled unauthorized border crossings straight into Arizona.

The state had some of the deadliest terrain on the border and only a fraction of Texas's and California's Electoral College votes. Steering a continent's worth of immigrants into the hot Sonoran Desert made cold political sense. The impact on Arizona could be addressed easily, officials argued, by extending prevention through deterrence to Nogales and Douglas. Meanwhile, the political dividends paid out.

In the mid-1990s, Rahm Emanuel, then senior adviser to Bill Clinton, urged the president to take back political ground lost to "tough on crime" Republicans. He suggested a spectacular show of force against undocumented immigration. Clinton scrawled "I agree" and "This is great" in the margin of one of Emanuel's memos. Silvestre Reyes's gambit in El Paso provided a perfect model for this political theater. Unbroken chains of agents watching over deserted urban border crossings made for spectacular photo opportunities. Migrants still crossed the border in growing numbers, of course, but they did so in remote landscapes, much harder for cameras and citizens to see.

The appearance of success attracted money in previously unimaginable quantities. Mushrooming budgets and an energetic new sense of purpose transformed the Border Patrol. Elaborate fences, high-tech surveillance equipment, and thousands of new agents turned the ad hoc strategy into a permanent stance. For decades, the Border Patrol had been a bit player in the pantheon of federal law enforcement. By the turn of the millennium, it was quickly becoming the largest and most heavily funded federal police force in the United States.

In November 1996, Silvestre Reyes rode his success all the way to Washington, D.C., where he would serve as Democratic congressman for Texas's Sixteenth District. And by the summer of 1997, the funnel effect he set in motion hit Douglas like a wall of water.

In 1999, smugglers charged $150 a head for passage from Agua Prieta to Phoenix. A year later, the cost ranged from $800 to $1,300. As predicted, the new Border Patrol strategy made clandestine border crossing more dangerous as well. Deaths from exposure, dehydration, hypothermia, and injury soared in and around Douglas. Whereas migrant death had once been a disturbing anomaly, individual incidents began to lose some of their power to shock residents. But not always.

In July 1999, the young reporter Xavier Zaragoza snapped a photograph for the *Douglas Dispatch* that reminded many readers of August 1997. In the photo, a raging flood pins a man inside a grated tunnel entrance. Three firefighters, heroically roped against the torrent, prepare to cut the bars. They saved the trapped man. Three other migrants were wedged through the grate by the force of the storm that day. They ran aground in the ditch, bloody and pummeled but alive.

And still people crossed. In greater and greater numbers.

4.

MILES OF WALL AND
NO TIME TO SLEEP

LUZ ANNOUNCED A TRIP TO the dollar store across Pan American Avenue, eight blocks from their latest apartment. Aida and Cynthia streaked out the door, itching for freedom. The sidewalk was gritty with gravel under their sneakers. They kicked up stones and flew across heat-warped streets. Luz hustled behind, looking left and right, eyeing the scene, looking for danger.

"Don't run, girls," she yelled after them in Spanish. They ignored her, and she called again. And then once more, angry for real now: "Aida. Cynthia. If you run, the *migra* will think that you're *mojaditas*."

The sisters, ten and eight years old, scuffed to an exaggerated slow-motion stop. Giggling, they switched to speed walking—not dainty swift steps, but giant hungry strides, embellished with feigned toil. Their conspiracy to obey the letter and not the spirit of their mother's law amused them. Except for Pan American up ahead, with its steady flow of traffic to and from the port of entry, the streets were silent. Still young enough not to care, the girls did not take their mother's warning seriously, but they *had* noticed the changes.

IN 1999, BORDER PATROL detained an average of twenty-four thousand migrants a month in and around the girls' new hometown. By early 2000, agents were detaining thirty thousand migrants a month—almost double the population of Douglas itself. Migrants caught and returned to Mexico simply tried again the next night. Even Central Americans flown back to their home countries typically returned.

Frustrated agents employed more brutal tactics, perhaps hoping that increased cruelty would deter repeat border crossing. Agents destroyed water bottles placed in the desert by humanitarian aid workers, stripped detainees of their money and possessions, denied them access to legal counsel, and withheld food and medical care. To disorient and terrorize, Border Patrol sometimes separated women from their groups and deported them late at night and alone into strange cities. To sow fear, agents would separate families: they would deport some members of a family to one border city and the others to cities hundreds or thousands of miles away. In theory, children were never separated from their guardians through this kind of "lateral repatriation," but it happened. A thirteen-year-old girl might find herself abandoned and alone in Nogales, while agents dumped the rest of her family in Tijuana.

Meanwhile, angry politicians made immigration enforcement in the interior of the country more punitive. Backed by President Bill Clinton and approved by a Republican Congress, the 1996 Antiterrorism and Effective Death Penalty Act (AEDPA) and Illegal Immigration Reform and Immigrant Responsibility Act (IIRIRA) brought "tough on crime" tactics to civil, noncriminal immigration proceedings.

The two laws dramatically expanded the range of offenses that disqualified immigrants from legal status. They restricted opportunities to take immigrants' family ties or contributions to the country into account. They closed off routes through which immigrants could win forgiveness or second chances. And stipulations in both laws required that many immigrants await the outcomes of their civil cases behind bars, even when those people were not flight risks or threats to public safety. Propelled by AEDPA and IIRIRA, the size—and lucrative nature—of the country's immigration detention system expanded at an astounding rate. Over the next decades, immigration detention would emerge as one of the country's largest contributors to mass incarceration.

IIRIRA also established "expedited removal," a program of streamlined immigration hearings deployed in the border region. Expedited removal allowed relatively low-level immigration officers to act as judge, jury, and executioner in certain deportation cases. Under it, officers, not judges, could decide complex immigration cases in lightning-quick proceedings with no possibility of appeal. As if that weren't tough enough, officers routinely prevented immigrants in expedited removal from accessing attorneys.

And still people crossed.

Across the border, the influx of hopeful migrants caused Agua Prieta's population to increase by two-thirds in just five years. During the years of Douglas's industrial growth, the Mexican ranch and railroad town had remained small and tranquil. Prior to the late 1990s, contemporary Agua Prieta had roughly two claims to fame in Mexico: the border city's fanatical devotion to baseball and Los Apson, one of the country's most popular 1960s rock bands. The arrival of foreign assembly factories in the 1980s drew job seekers like Rosie Mendoza to the city, but even then Agua Prieta didn't expand as quickly or massively as other Mexican border cities. Prevention through deterrence turned all that on its head.

Hundreds of overcrowded "guesthouses" opened in the Mexican city. Business owners converted their stores, warehouses, service stations, and houses into makeshift shelters. They packed people into cramped rooms and charged twenty-five to forty dollars a night for the privilege. Less fortunate migrants slept on the streets or locked in smugglers' stash houses. The city's taxi drivers grew suddenly rich, shuttling a ceaseless line of migrants to staging areas in the desert.

Later studies would show that the deterrent effects of punitive enforcement played a modest role, if any, in shaping people's decisions to attempt the border crossing. Many migrants had taken out debts of three thousand to ten thousand dollars at 10 percent monthly interest or more to pay smugglers.

With loans coming due regardless of the migrants' success in crossing, people had to keep trying. Reaching a well-paying job in the United States was the only way to make the payments on loans often secured by family farms.

More broadly, sociopolitical forces shaped long-term migration patterns independent of border enforcement strategy. Shifting demand for labor in the United States, economic prospects in Mexico, and violent instability caused by the war on drugs influenced migration trends more than anything the Border Patrol did. Even experiences of cruelty and abuse had a negligible effect on migrants' decision to keep trying. This was particularly true for people fleeing violence or trying to reunite with family members in the United States.

Processing upward of a thousand migrants in a night became routine in Douglas. Arrests far exceeded the capacity of the sector's Border Patrol station. Douglas simply didn't have the infrastructure to deal with the influx. The police chief, Charlie Austin, and his officers could not respond to all the calls about migrants. Groups of young men cut across yards and hid under porches and bushes. Families drank from garden hoses and, when surprised by Border Patrol, left piles of possessions strewn on the ground behind them. Some homeowners left their garages unlocked, knowing that people needing shelter on days above a hundred degrees and nights below thirty would break doors and windows if they had to. Stepping outside to retrieve the morning newspaper, those same homeowners might also find an unknown woman and child slumped in exhausted sleep on their patio furniture.

AT DUSK, Luz would call Aida and Cynthia to come inside during these years. It was better for the girls to stay off the streets when the nightly cat-and-mouse game began. Aida and Cynthia would heed her call, complaining all the way. Then Luz would lock the cramped apartment's doors and windows. Aida noticed that her mother also started locking the car doors. Even with the doors locked, though, the family sometimes woke knowing that someone had crawled inside the car to rest during the active night. The sleepers always left before morning, but Aida would sense impressions they left in the sedan: a slight rearranging of the Kleenex and old soft-drink cups, the sharp smell of fear.

· · ·

IT WAS HARD to say exactly when the situation in Douglas hit its boiling point. But the why was clear.

The crisis had, at first, largely enveloped a small town populated by brown-skinned residents with little political clout. But by early 1999, the massive influx of agents and technology into Douglas had pushed most undocumented border crossers outside the city limits—straight onto land owned by charismatic, well-connected Anglo ranchers. Suddenly political clout was no problem. Politicians and the media tripped over each other in a headlong rush to empathize with the all-American landowners.

Wendy Glenn was one of those ranchers. She and her husband, Warner, had grazed cattle in the vast scrubby basins and rugged ranges east of Douglas since the 1960s. Electric lines hadn't reached their house until 1985. Now they felt as if they lived in the middle of a highway. Night after night, groups of migrants—sometimes a hundred or more at a time—trailed through their property. Harried by Border Patrol, migrants abandoned their possessions in piles, tapped irrigation systems for water, and sometimes robbed supplies. Drug smugglers were worse. They cut cattle fences, careened across the land in ATVs, and threatened residents at gunpoint.

Wendy recognized that undocumented Mexicans had helped build the Glenn Ranch. For decades before prevention through deterrence, a handful of migrants would pass through the ranch every month. The Glenns, like most ranchers in southeast Arizona, would give them food and shelter in return for work. These visitors would chop wood, paint barns, fix fences, and then move on to the next stop in their cyclical journey. Sometimes the same people came year after year. One man, a sharp dresser in a land where clean pressed jeans and a Carhartt vest passed as formal wear, spent part of every year working at a restaurant in Chicago and part of the year at home in Mexico. In between, he'd spend a few nights each at a string of ranches leading from the border to Safford, Arizona. There, he caught a Greyhound bus east. Despite the slicked hair and city threads, he understood ranch work, and the Glenns welcomed his sojourns at their place.

After the buildup of border enforcement, though, that familiar cyclical migration came to a crashing halt. It was too risky to return to Mexico for visits and too expensive to cross the border every year. People like the stylish cowboy settled permanently in the United States. This proved one of the more ironic effects of stepped-up border enforcement: border militarization encouraged undocumented folks to remain in the United States for longer periods. Now, instead of familiar faces, the Glenns saw only strangers.

Wendy bristled at the abandoned belongings, water bottles, diapers, and food wrappers she encountered every day. And she worried about the ominous signs she'd discover. Once she found a whole family's shoes lined up under a tree, the owners vanished without a trace. Another time it was precious family photographs arranged on a rock under a tree in the middle of nowhere. Ranchers found bodies, too: the bloated fly-specked newly dead and the desiccated mummies, leathery after long seasons under the sun.

The new migrants passing through Wendy's land were stressed, terrified, and unaccustomed to ranches. They trampled pastures, left gates open, and dropped animal-strangling grocery sacks. Mostly they kept their distance from locals. Only the most desperate approached the Glenns' house. Once a woman appeared at their door. She had given birth prematurely out in the desert and cut the umbilical cord with a piece of broken glass. She asked if Wendy could help her reunite with her husband in Phoenix.

At first, Wendy would sometimes offer a ride to friendly people she met in the backcountry. Eventually, she stopped that practice. Drug smugglers had pioneered routes east of Douglas and came in increasing, menacing numbers. Fat-wheeled quads, stacked with bales of marijuana, thundered through the night, slicing fences and destroying expensive irrigation equipment. Border Patrol trucks pounded after them, doing just as much damage. Every rancher east of Douglas had stories of near escapes from armed men.

When Wendy spoke out about these horrors, her voice carried authority. Her father had owned a mine that supplied the Douglas smelter with lime. Later he became a state congressman. Her grandfather helped found Douglas. Wendy herself had helped found the Malpai Borderlands Group, a national model for rangeland conservation. In that work, she learned to speak across borders: she could talk to skeptical environmentalists about the importance of ranching and skeptical ranchers about what environmentalism offered their work. When it came to immigration, Wendy had politicians' ears and argued for moderation. The government had to do something to stop people crossing through rangeland, but the answer wasn't open war on immigrants. "A big wall isn't the answer," she would tell Arizona's governor in 2005. The only way to end undocumented immigration and protect ranchers, she argued, was to address the root causes of poverty in Mexico.

Many of Wendy's neighbors were not as evenhanded. Some took a more violent tack in the face of mounting frustration. Larry Vance, a rancher living a mile north of the border, declared that he was done with sleepless nights spent fearing home invasion. He erected a tower on his property and began keeping armed watch. Roger Barnett, one of Douglas's most vociferous critics of undocumented immigration, declared that he would begin hunting migrants on his twenty-two-thousand-acre ranch. "Humans. That's the greatest prey there is on earth," he menaced, and from 1999 to 2006 he followed through on his threat. During this time, the rancher seized and detained thousands of men, women, and children at gunpoint for Border Patrol on his ranch and nearby public lands. Most were undocumented. Some were local Latinos enjoying the outdoors in the wrong place at the wrong time.

Mayor Ray Borane walked a tightrope between sympathy for migrants and sheer frustration. He wrote curt letters to President Clinton and published a blunt opinion piece in *The New York Times*. Instead of blaming people crossing through Douglas, he demanded that Americans take responsibility for the mess. Like Wendy Glenn, he urged a deeper reckoning with the causes of undocumented immigration. Why should one small town have to bear the consequences of politicians' failure to reform immigration policy?

The federal government responded to this outcry, but not by addressing root causes. Instead, it deepened its "enforcement only" approach. Border Patrol rushed reinforcements and resources to Douglas. By 2000, the local station, built to house forty agents, overflowed with almost six hundred. That same year, the agency broke ground on what would be heralded as the "biggest Border Patrol station in the nation." Stadium lighting, seismic sensors, night vision scopes, helicopters, and twenty-foot-tall mobile sky towers looking like two-legged Imperial Walkers from Star Wars followed. Multiple generations of border barrier, each one more imposing than the last, went up and down. An astonishingly ineffective billion-dollar high-tech virtual fence designed by Boeing came and went.

For the young reporter Xavier Zaragoza, it was an exciting time to be a journalist. National and international media descended on Douglas. News outlets declared it "ground zero" for people smuggling, the nation's "new immigration battleground." Prizewinning reporters from New York and D.C. clamored for Xavier's assistance. He took over the *Douglas Dispatch*'s immigration beat and barely slept for eight years. For months at a stretch, when national and international interest was particularly acute, Xavier spent his days escorting teams from news outlets like CNN, *National Geographic*, *USA Today*, and the *Chicago Tribune*. Reporters from Canadian and European newspapers came as well. He took them to see guesthouses and streets filled with stores selling water bottles, backpacks, and cheap boots in Agua Prieta. He'd point out the Douglas used-car lots, tire stores, and gas stations getting rich off smugglers' transportation needs. He'd show camera teams where to set up for a shot of people climbing the fence. At night, he rode along with Border Patrol, taking notes and filming scenes of moonlit chases through desert scrub. In the morning, he filed his stories and started all over again.

What was thrilling for the young reporter was frightening for Rosie Mendoza. She was struggling to raise five children alone amid the growing chaos. As Douglas filled with federal agents in the late 1990s and early 2000s, she taught her youngest son to carry his birth certificate. Border Patrol rarely hassled his lighter-skinned siblings, but the distinctive green-and-white trucks often tailed Rosie's darker-skinned son down the street. Later, when he learned to drive, he couldn't cross the border or pass a highway checkpoint without getting held for secondary inspection and additional screening. He started calling himself "Secondary." It was a joke, but it didn't feel funny.

By 2001, the enforcement buildup managed to divert undocumented crossers from the center of town. More migrants and smugglers poured onto ranch land, but Douglas residents could sleep at night. The number of migrant apprehensions in town fell by 40 percent, and large groups of migrants no longer streamed through alleys and yards with as much abandon. Even Douglasites sympathetic to migrants appreciated the respite.

It didn't take long, though, for people to realize that they had simply exchanged one kind of invasion for another.

"Douglas has become a garrison for a federal force fighting an immigration war," Mayor Ray Borane wrote in a letter to President Clinton. Stadium lights on the border eliminated night, and helicopters beat through the air at all hours. The phrase "border security" slipped off politicians' tongues, smooth and easy. Who could argue against securing the border? Senators, governors, and cabinet secretaries flew over Douglas in Black Hawks, posed for photographs in front of the latest wall, and shook hands with ranchers in town hall meetings. Important men and women from Washington, D.C., and Phoenix drew "lines in the sand" and demanded the border be "sealed." The border was "broken" and the country faced an "existential threat." "Double the Border Patrol" became a frequent refrain. Every politician wanted more "border security," but few agreed on what that meant. The one thing they agreed on was the need for more money. As Christopher Levy, an assistant chief of the Border Patrol, later complained, the lack of a clear definition of border security begot blundering and wasteful spending.

Charlie Austin tried to downplay the need for intensified policing. Douglas hadn't reported a homicide in a couple of years, he would tell readers of the *Los Angeles Times* in 2005. As in other border towns, Douglas's crime rate was relatively low. But, privately, he had to admit that the resources flowing to Douglas law enforcement lifted his spirits. Influxes of federal border security grants allowed him to carry out operations and investigations on a scale he thought few small-town police chiefs could imagine. He was glad to have federal reinforcements and a seemingly bottomless source of funding.

Yet even the conservative police chief reached his limit sometimes. The taciturn Old West cop couldn't stand Border Patrol's daredevil driving. When he saw Border Patrol vehicles tearing through school speed zones at sixty miles an hour with no emergency in sight, he complained loudly. Border Patrol superiors smiled and nodded, but the situation didn't change. In the end, Chief Austin had to provoke a jurisdictional clash to see results: after he ordered his officers to ticket speeding Border Patrol vehicles, things got a little better.

Mexican American residents like Rosie Mendoza and her son grew accustomed to agents following them around town. Encounters with omnipresent Border Patrol fouled even quiet moments of pleasure and reflection. For as long as she'd lived in Douglas, Rosie had loved to hike and picnic in the beautiful country outside town. As border enforcement hardened, though, Rosie's family gave up its outdoor activities. Hiking through the backcountry was no fun when it meant long stops for questioning.

Anglo ranchers, once the Border Patrol's most ardent supporters, learned to suffer roads torn apart by the green-and-white trucks. Agents in hot pursuit crushed irrigation pipes and left gates wide open. With the arrival of drones, seismic sensors, and remote cameras, ruggedly independent ranchers couldn't shake a sense that they were always being watched by someone, even when working alone in the empty desert. One cattleman recounted a call he'd received from a neighbor who flew Border Patrol drones at seventeen thousand feet. The agent was just being neighborly: he'd called to let the rancher know that he'd left his front gate ajar when he left home that morning.

For many residents, the new Border Patrol recruits and federal agents rushed to Douglas on temporary assignment were the worst. Flushed with zeal, these agents were unfamiliar with the ways of the border and truly believed they were at war. They spent hundreds of thousands of dollars in Douglas's hotels and restaurants, but that was often the extent of their connection to the place. A Mexican American law student whose family had lived in Douglas for generations lost his cool after one too many incidents of driving while brown. When the blond-haired recruit pulled him over to ask, "Where are you from?" the young attorney shot back, "Where are *you* from, Iowa?"

DURING THIS FRENZIED PERIOD, Douglas resembled an experiment in the psychology of fear. Residents experiencing similar conditions reacted in wildly different ways. Competing definitions of border security split neighbor from neighbor. Some saw migration as a scourge, a biblical plague. Others read the same signs as a Christian invocation to care for the stranger. Some lived in fear for their physical safety. Theirs were the loudest and angriest voices. Other residents found something of value in quietly embracing the unknown.

In one stretch of heavily trafficked range northwest of town lived two landowners, the story went. One was an elderly woman, living alone. Migrants trailed across her land and sometimes, desperate, approached her house to ask for directions or water. She went about her life, stooping to pick up food tins and diapers discarded by fleeing travelers. She mended her fences when they needed fixing. When people approached her, even at night, she offered water, food, and prayers for a safe journey. It was not that she never felt scared. She was not so brave that drug traffickers swaggering through her land didn't leave her shaken. She simply couldn't see any other way to be in the world.

Her fence-line neighbor suffered the same traffic across his land. Each track, each piece of trash, each sound in the night, inflamed the tightness spreading through his chest and neck. His veins beat like running footsteps almost all the time. He bought extra locks, but they didn't reassure him. He bought floodlights and a surveillance camera. They didn't help. Eventually, the man could not venture anywhere on his beloved land without a small arsenal of guns. Even then, the shadows scared him.

That was Douglas at the end of the millennium.

AIDA ALSO SAW SHADOWS. They moved silently up E Avenue, creeping along the street outside her apartment every night. The newcomers were tired and sunburned. Their travel clothes smelled, even at a distance. To the preteen Aida, migrants rushing through Douglas looked scared and furtive. "Mom, where do they sleep at night after they cross the border?" she asked once.

Luz imagined the worst but tried to reassure her daughter. "They have people who pick them up and take them where they need to go. You shouldn't worry about them." Awareness of her family's vulnerability conditioned even Luz's compassion. "You shouldn't worry about them" was a kindness and also a command. To her daughter it meant, "Keep your head down. Keep your distance." Even if Aida wasn't paying attention to safety, her mother was.

Aida accepted her mother's answer and drifted on to other thoughts. Other Douglasites battled over immigration. Politicians staged photo shoots and newspapers dubbed the town "ground zero," but Aida lost interest.

When she and Cynthia ran into Border Patrol agents getting gas at Circle K, they were confident they knew exactly what to do: they spoke perfect English to each other as loudly and boldly as they could in front of the agents. Aida knew that she and her family were "illegals"—they used that word with each other—but she didn't see herself reflected in the nightly flow of humanity or the desperate plight of migrants. Not yet, at least.

The things that captivated preteens everywhere occupied Aida's attention more than immigration debates: Music. Boys. Math tests. To the extent that Aida perceived migrants passing through Douglas anymore, they were curiosities and objects of sympathy. They dressed funny and spoke strange Spanish. One border crosser, a boy from Mexico's capital city, got stuck in Douglas and began attending classes at Aida's school. Her friends called him *chilango* with a bit of scorn. Aida, on the other hand, marveled at the boy's oversized way of talking. "*¡Chale!*" She stretched her mouth to imitate his slang. "*No mames*," she sang. "*Pinche güey.*"

When Aida's friends interrupted their games to eye southern Mexicans washing at the drinking fountain at the Tenth Street Park, Aida directed them back to playing. We are not the kind of people who call Border Patrol on other people, she told herself with a bit of pride. It's not that she wasn't afraid like so many other residents of Douglas. She was afraid most hours of most days during those years. But the shadows that scared her didn't pass through the borderlands; they stayed.

5

THE NEW MILLENNIUM,
HER OWN QUIET WAR

SINCE THE MOVE TO DOUGLAS, Jennifer had spent less and less time at home. She was distant and irritable. Her anger encompassed Saul, her mother, American schools, and the whole United States. At the nadir, she started lashing out at Aida and Cynthia. And then, in 1998 or 1999, she left for good.

The morning Jennifer ran away, Aida was the only other person home. She watched her sister dump schoolbooks from her backpack and replace them with clothes. She knew what was happening without having to ask and figured it was for the best. On the way out, Jennifer said that a friend would drive her across the border. After that, she'd see what happened.

Aida kept quiet over the next day, even as Luz began to worry about Jennifer's disappearance. She knew that her father would call soon to let them know that Jennifer was safe and would live with him in Mexico. The call came eventually, and then the sisters were two.

This was Aida's fifth-grade year. Things got so bad during that period that Saul bought Luz a house to keep her from leaving. It was a dirty white bungalow with a sharp stone wall around a dirt yard. It had the usual sewer roaches and broken feel, but Aida and Cynthia found a secret paradise in the yard. There, under a thick, strong sycamore, was a cinder-block *casita* with one room, a bathroom, and a metal door that locked. The sisters immediately saw its potential and staked their claim.

A previous occupant had piled the outbuilding with junk and boxes and broken exercise equipment. Aida and Cynthia stacked the junk in a corner, shoved the exercise equipment aside, and scrubbed the place clean. They decorated with dolls and pictures cut from magazines. One of the rumpled storage boxes coughed up a radio that worked.

The two sisters retreated to their hideout whenever they could. They cleaned and decorated and tuned in music. Britney Spears and the Backstreet Boys still fluttered their hearts, but Aida had begun craving Tupac and Snoop Dogg, too. When a good song came on, Aida and Cynthia would lock the metal door, turn up the radio, and dance.

Before they knew it, night would seep into their sanctuary. In the cooler months, it came with mesquite smoke from woodstoves. In warmer months, moths and beetles flicked around lightbulbs. The evening chorus of dogs barking and helicopters buzzing over the border alerted them that it was almost time to leave. Finally, they'd smell grilled meat and roasting chilies drifting across the yard. At this signal, Aida's stomach twisted. She returned to the main house wondering if the food she smelled was meant for her.

That year, Aida felt that Luz spent all of her grocery money on elaborate meals to keep Saul happy. The sisters, on the other hand, often got cups of ramen. Aida was growing, and one Styrofoam Maruchan didn't touch her hunger. "*Tragona*," "*comelona*," her mother would tease, but it wasn't funny.

One night, Aida and Cynthia found a sack of Mexican *birote* rolls abandoned in a cupboard. They were golden and flour dusted and still smelled vaguely of bread. Aida didn't wait to sit down at the table or even get a plate for the crumbs. She stuffed half a roll into her mouth—and yelped. Her teeth ricocheted. She paused for a moment to glare at the basalt-hard roll. Then she adjusted her grip and began to gnaw. Cautious Cynthia followed her lead, sawing and chiseling bread dust with glee.

At the dining room table, Luz had just set steak and rice in front of Saul, but he forked his plate in annoyance.

"Can't they chew quieter?" He directed this at Luz.

The girls went rigid, expecting their mother to lash out at them for upsetting the man. Aida held her roll tight and started to shake.

Instead, Luz reeled on her partner.

"I've already lost one daughter because of you. I'm not going to lose another."

Aida and Cynthia scattered to their *casita* before they could see what happened next. With the door locked and the music on, they didn't notice when Saul left. Nor did they see Luz take her purse and get in the car shortly after that. Only much later, when they smelled burgers frying across the yard, did they venture out of hiding. Luz had gone to the store and returned with the ingredients to make hamburgers and all the fixings for her kids. Later, she showed them an inflatable swimming pool she'd purchased for the yard.

Luz had absorbed the blows of Saul's violence for years. When he lashed out at her children, though, she revolted. Something shifted in her. He had gone too far. That year, Luz made a promise to Aida. "As soon as you finish fifth grade, we will leave him."

SARAH MARLEY ELEMENTARY remained Aida's haven away from home. Any excuse to stay after the final bell was welcome. She played basketball, sang in the choir, and joined the D.A.R.E. program. Luz, exhausted from violence and endless hours of work, did not show up for Aida's games or parent-teacher conferences. But in May 1999, she did show up for graduation.

On the morning of the ceremony, Luz presented her daughter with a new dress. It was long and baby blue with small embroidered butterflies— the exact dress Aida had pleaded with her mother to buy for graduation. Luz brushed out her daughter's bangs and styled her curls to look like Selena. Aida added hair glitter to the look and felt like a sunburst again.

Fifth-grade graduation marked the end of elementary and the beginning of middle school. It was a big deal, and Aida was called up several times to receive recognition. She was so happy she almost forgot her mother's promise.

By the time the event finished, glitter had drifted onto Aida's cheeks and nose, and she clutched a tall stack of awards. She held them up to Luz, one by one, reading the English and explaining what each one meant: "Student of the Month," "Student of the Week," "First Place in the Sarah Marley Mile Run," "Girls' Basketball Team Participation Award," "Honor Roll," and "Certificate of Promotion to Sixth Grade." She wanted her mother to appreciate each one.

"Let's go," Luz replied.

Luz, Aida, Cynthia, Jazmin, and Emiliano walked twelve blocks home instead of waiting for a ride from Saul. Aida, still admiring her certificates, had to run to keep up.

At the white bungalow, Luz ordered the girls to gather whatever they wanted to take with them into bags. As fast as two toddlers, two preteens, and a woman loaded with all their possessions could move, they moved. It was a two-mile walk to the port of entry, but it took even longer through back alleys and side streets. Any of Saul's drivers would have called the boss if they'd seen the family carrying its possessions down the streets.

For the second time in three years, Luz and her children crossed the international line.

PART OF AIDA expected her old life to rematerialize—Mom, Dad, Dad's house, the *tienda*, and the playground. Instead, she got an unfinished cinder-block room near the railroad tracks in one of Agua Prieta's most cutthroat neighborhoods. Mexico was not her place anymore, or her choice.

They spent the last days of May 1999 camped at an aunt's house while Luz acquired a junk car and a place to live. The new house was half built and half in progress, a condition not uncommon in the city's poorer neighborhoods. It lacked door locks, and until Luz installed dead bolts, the five of them squeezed into the car to sleep safely at night. A year earlier, they had locked themselves in their apartment in Douglas and worried about migrants sleeping in their car. Now they were the ones bedding down in a vehicle.

As if to keep the needle of their lives pointing to red in the absence of Saul, Luz began to direct her anger at Aida. Almost twelve, Aida had a new maturity shooting through her blood, and she argued back. One day, Luz and Aida clashed so hard that Luz buckled. She pulled back and begged on her knees for forgiveness. It was too late. While Luz sobbed, Aida stared a thousand miles past her.

Then, partway through Aida's sixth grade, Saul found them. The border was no obstacle for him. He plied Luz with all his feather-haired, ripple-muscled charm, and soon he was visiting regularly again.

Aida endured. She'd lived with violence for so long that she almost couldn't remember another way of life. But she could remember one thing: her father lived nearby. One afternoon toward the end of sixth grade, Aida set off on foot across Agua Prieta to her father's house. And just as Raúl had welcomed Jennifer back a year or two earlier with quiet joy, he also welcomed Aida.

"NOW THAT YOU'RE HERE, there are things you need to know," Jennifer said the first night she and Aida spent together at Raúl's house. Aida understood then that, at last, she would get the truth about her parents' separation. Jennifer didn't sugarcoat it.

"Mom left Dad because Dad hit her all the time, and at the end Dad hit her because she had been with Saul for years. Emiliano and Jazmin are Saul's kids, not our dad's."

All the signs had been there for Aida to put together. Her dad's furious outbursts. The long visits to their "family friend" that Luz had dragged Aida to, Saul's special treatment of Emiliano and Jazmin. But she'd been so little when it happened. Eight-year-olds didn't put clues like that together. She remembered how ecstatic her father had been when Emiliano was born. Finally, a boy after four girls . . . and it wasn't his. That is messed up, Aida thought.

None of it excused Raúl's violence. But it explained a lot about her life.

As Aida grappled with betrayals wrapped around betrayals, an empty space ripped inside her. Luz had raised her with contradictory advice. "Your biggest goal should be to find a man who can support you," she'd say, followed immediately by "Never let what happened to me happen to you." True or not, to Aida's early teen mind her mother's philosophy had wrecked all of their lives. Who is she to tell me what to do? From now on, I live how I want, she resolved.

In this, Jennifer proved an able mentor. For Aida's thirteenth birthday, she organized a party. Before leaving the house, Jennifer took her aside. Long baby-blue dresses with embroidered butterflies were out. Jennifer dressed Aida in a white tube top and baggy pants that slung below her hips. The older sister pulled Aida's hair back tight and wrapped it in a bandanna. No glitter was applied. She brushed on white cake foundation and wings of electric-blue eye shadow. Brown lipstick outlined in even darker brown finished the makeover.

"You should shave your eyebrows, and just pencil them in," Jennifer suggested, but Aida declined. Still, she wore hoop earrings that night and swaggered from the hips. The new look was good.

At the party, Jennifer pressed a warm forty into her hands. Aida drank half of it in one go and liked it.

Aida was only thirteen, but she had seen all that she needed of the world. Enough to know that no one would ever tell her what to do. She remembered herself weak from hunger and punished for not speaking into the dispatch radio. She remembered getting passed over at school and lost in a new country. Not knowing where she'd live next and hustling through the streets with her possessions in plastic bags. And "hide from *la migra*," and "*cero uno a base*." Aida had seen all those scenes through perfectly clear eyes. So if the world blurred and spun a bit when she drank, she was fine with it.

RAÚL WORKED AS a security guard from seven at night to five in the morning. Jennifer showed Aida how to act like a good girl until he left. Then they stripped off their school uniforms and slipped into party clothes. Sometimes they skated back into Raúl's house only minutes before he came home to tumble into bed at six or seven. Jennifer taught Aida how to attend school still high on weed and whiskey. And she helped set Aida up with a guy to teach her the most important lesson of all.

Aida loathed him and the way he pawed her. In all other regards, she was an adept student of Jennifer's life lessons. Soon she surpassed her older sister in the art of smashing into the world. She wanted to be messy and bladelike, and she was.

The playground outside Raúl's house had changed in the few years since they'd played there as girls. All of Agua Prieta had changed since the city found itself thrust into the business of clandestine border crossing. Aida started hanging out with a pack of older kids who convened at the playground every night. They weren't a real gang, but they thought it would be cool to be one. When one of the girls learned to hot-wire cars, Aida and her friends spent their nights fishtailing onto Agua Prieta's paved boulevards and smashing the suspensions of the stolen cars on its rutted dirt roads.

The extended family observed Aida's exploits from a distance. Agua Prieta was still a small enough town that gossip traveled fast, and gossip about Aida provoked knowing head shakes. This one hit *la mera edad de la punzada* hard, they clucked. Aida's family called girls' puberty "the age of the stabbing pain," an apt metaphor. Aida had impaled herself on it fully.

Only when reading books did Aida feel accompanied in life. At some point, she had discovered Sandra Cisneros's *House on Mango Street*. She kept the thin book close and read it over and over again. Esperanza, the main character, was a Mexican American girl Aida's age. Esperanza traversed her Chicago neighborhood in the company of two girls, as close to her as sisters. They found adventures and usually skirted violence, but abusive fathers, sexual assault, and poverty riddled their world. Esperanza survived it all, writing down her story in order to get by. *La mera edad de la punzada* left gashes in Esperanza, and the struggle to make a place in the United States never ceased. Like Aida, though, she vowed to carry on, no matter what. "I have begun my own quiet war," Esperanza wrote, and Aida concurred.

AIDA BURNED THROUGH most of seventh grade this way. She read some, skipped school, and ran wild. Her father didn't know what to do, and relatives, not wanting to bother Luz with bad news, kept her in the dark. Then, one cyanotic dawn, Aida slipped into Raúl's house as usual and found both her parents waiting. Half stoned, the night still vibrating in her head, Aida realized that she hadn't seen her parents together in years. Even though she knew that she was about to get hell, the sight of them sitting at the kitchen table made her smile.

It didn't last long. Luz's stare—which had also become Aida's stare— bored holes in her daughter. Raúl laid out the facts.

"I cannot take care of you while I'm at work, and your behavior of late has been less than correct." He always spoke formally that way. "As much as it brings me sadness, you will need to go live with your mother."

6.

BETTER LIVING THROUGH BORDER SECURITY

POSTERS WENT UP IN THE SPRING OF 2001 advertising a day of Cinco de Mayo horse races. It promised to be a historic event. Reeling from years of record migrant flows and divisive border buildup, the mayors of both Douglas and Agua Prieta wanted to restore a bit of borderlands spirit. They won permission to take down a stretch of border fence west of town. Race organizers would replace the barrier with a plastic railing running straight down the international line. For five hundred meters, a U.S. horse and a Mexican horse would rocket along the geopolitical divide, each one on its own side. Organizers expected ten thousand spectators, half in the United States and half in Mexico. The day's festivities would remind residents what it meant to live in DouglaPrieta, a single community enriched, not endangered, by the border.

Organizers billed the event as Douglas and Agua Prieta's "second annual" International Border Horse Race. The "first annual" race had run forty-three years earlier in 1958, pitting a champion Arizona thoroughbred named Chiltepin against Relampago, one of the most famous horses in Mexico at the time. Relampago, owned by a nightclub impresario from Agua Prieta, won.

In 1958, race organizers staged the match on both sides of the borderline to get around animal quarantine regulations. In 2001, the race would defy another kind of border regime—this one focused on undocumented migrants.

When the day came, Mayor Ray Borane presided over the event with noble words. "They say enemies build walls and friends build fences," he declared. "Well, today we take down the fence to show that we are more than neighbors—we are friends and family."

The races attracted fifteen thousand spectators, far more than expected. Horses with names like El Sapo, El Bobito, and El Rayito thundered down the track in twenty-second flat-out sprints. Between races, Mexican bookies waved rolls of bills and dipped across the line to take bets in Arizona. U.S. spectators hustled across the track to buy Tecate when American vendors ran out of beer. A woman arrayed in a *charro* suit performed an impromptu horse ballet. And the Border Patrol hung back, unwilling to interfere. For some, the binational event seemed as if it might mark the beginning of a new DouglaPrieta. For others, it seemed like a last hurrah.

THE SECOND ANNUAL International Border Horse Race was not the only effort to resist the stiffening border at the turn of the millennium. Around that same time, Rosie Mendoza joined Frontera de Cristo. This was a group of people from Douglas's faith communities horrified by the human cost of prevention through deterrence. Frontera de Cristo worked to mend connections between people and places. It organized development projects in Agua Prieta and education programs for Americans interested in understanding immigration at a deeper level. The group also helped found and staff the Migrant Resource Center in Agua Prieta. Volunteers in the small building on the Mexican side next to the port of entry welcomed recent deportees. They distributed shoes, blankets, hot coffee, and food—some migrants' first meal in days. Volunteers helped the castaways telephone relatives in places like Chicago, Iowa City, and Greenville, South Carolina. They bandaged feet that were bloody and blistered after treks through the desert. Sometimes, they just held people shell-shocked by their violent traverse through Mexico, the desert, and then detention.

When they weren't helping the living, Frontera de Cristo members vowed to remember the dead. Every Tuesday evening, as rush-hour traffic idled through the port of entry, community members carrying white crosses gathered near the wall. Each cross bore the name of a migrant who had died in Cochise County. For as long as it took, the assembled fellowship read each name aloud, followed by a simple cry, *"presente"*—you are still here with us. Rosie Mendoza participated in the vigil often. She called out each name, exactly as written on the cross, as loud as her soft voice permitted. But in her heart, every name she uttered stood for the dead man she'd seen at the bottom of the ditch in August 1997.

ON THE OTHER SIDE of the spectrum, the Old West bluster of angry ranchers drew displays of solidarity from across the country's right wing. Inspired by images of armed residents like Roger Barnett taking a stand against "invasion," anti-immigration activists poured into southeastern Arizona. One of them, Glenn Spencer, had been protesting Mexican immigration to California since the early 1990s. When he heard what was happening in Douglas, he declared California "a lawless, lost state" and decided to make a stand in Cochise County. Southeastern Arizona would be his battleground against what he said was a Mexican assault on white America. Spencer founded the American Border Patrol, an organization with militia trappings, in 2002. After reading about Roger Barnett, the Texan Jack Foote created a similar organization, Ranch Rescue, and began to patrol private land in Texas and Arizona.

Undocumented residents like Aida stayed off the streets when a new contingent of ersatz border defenders rolled into town. Less vulnerable residents openly criticized the vigilante invasion. For some, civilian patrollers were well-meaning imbeciles who got in the way of real law enforcement; for others, they were the shock troops of white supremacy.

If most Douglas residents distanced themselves from militia-style border defenders, the question of what to make of federal forces was more contentious. Was the appearance of heavily armed agents, National Guard troops, stadium lights, fencing, and military-grade hardware a salvation? Or a hostile occupation?

Competing views on border security upended the town. Angry white ranchers drew national attention, but residents' opinions about intensified border enforcement didn't always cleave along racial lines. More than a few Mexican American residents supported immigration restrictions and tougher border security. Years of large-scale migration through the town had exhausted everyone.

Residents also acknowledged that vocal support for border security provided a way for Mexican Americans to position themselves as "real" Americans in the hierarchy of racial nativism. And no other law enforcement agency in the country hired more Latinos than the Border Patrol. "It's kind of like the Irish," one retiree from Pirtleville observed. "When they first got here, they were discriminated against. They didn't get influence or make their way [in America] until they moved into law enforcement."

Prejudice against the new generation of darker-skinned, more indigenous-looking border crossers also inflamed hostility. With their ancestry squarely located in the supposedly whiter reaches of northern Mexico, Douglas's *norteños* sometimes looked down on migrants from southern Mexico and Central America.

Rosie Mendoza was not from southern Mexico, but she came from a northern Mexican family of indigenous descent; this was more common than stereotypes of "white" *norteños* acknowledged. Her grandfather Cipriano had been an indigenous dancer and healer. She herself had first come to the United States without papers. But Rosie's three children, growing up as citizens in post-1997 Douglas, believed that undocumented immigration was something that involved distant strangers—foreign-looking Mayans from Chiapas or Guatemala. They struggled to imagine their mother as "an illegal."

"Is it true that you were a wetback, Mom?" Rosie's youngest son sometimes asked in a teasing tone.

"Mom, guess what?" her teenage daughter might needle. "I'm going to take the Border Patrol exam next week."

"Ay, *mijo*, *mija*, don't you know that Jesus was an illegal too?" Rosie would spar back, and then hug her kids.

Rosie's daughter wasn't going to take the test, but Rosie could have accepted her choice if she did. Rosie even dated a Border Patrol agent for a while. When he brought romantic sushi lunches to the clinic, she made him wait outside so he didn't scare her clients. They kept work talk to a minimum and agreed to differ about the border.

"But, you know, *guapo*," Rosie would tell him to soften their disagreements, "I'm really glad that you have a job."

This was a major factor complicating Douglasites' response to the new paradigm of border enforcement: the town had become partly dependent on border security spending. In fact, increasingly, it seemed to Rosie that border security wasn't much more than a government job creation program. In some respects, she was right: by 2007, one in thirteen employed adults living in Douglas worked for law enforcement. That rate would continue to increase over the next decade. By comparison, only about one in ninety-five New Yorkers worked for law enforcement. In Tucson, the figure was one in a hundred. In Phoenix, only one in two hundred.

For men in Douglas, the rate was even higher: one in seven employed men in Douglas wore a law enforcement badge of some kind. Law enforcement jobs carried wages and benefits that had not been seen in Douglas since the smelter closed. Border Patrol, Customs, Immigration and Customs Enforcement (ICE), the Drug Enforcement Administration (DEA), the Bureau of Alcohol, Tobacco, and Firearms (ATF), police officers, prison guards, and sheriff's deputies constituted a kind of economic elite. Their spending helped keep the town afloat. Children aspired to join their ranks, and even immigrant rights activists made bleak jokes about taking the Border Patrol exam when money was tight. At the community college, a federal grant program helped local students prepare for that test. "Pathways out of Poverty" was its revealing name. Even Aida's family was part of this new economy: Aida, her mother, and her sisters were undocumented, but one of their U.S. citizen relatives worked for the Douglas Police Department. Another one worked security at the port of entry.

Douglas had, in many respects, become a new kind of company town—a Homeland Security company town. But the town's burgeoning new industry did not emulate Phelps Dodge's benevolent paternalism. Nor did it invest in community life as PD once had. As much as Douglas depended on security money to survive, border security never produced the kind of positive ripple effects the smelter had provided. Most of the billions of dollars lavished on border enforcement by Congress flowed to outside contractors. Wall construction, high-tech infrastructure, and even vehicle maintenance enriched firms based elsewhere. When the Department of Homeland Security built a new border wall, it "didn't get the materials from B&D Hardware" on H Avenue, the director of a regional economic development institute joked.

On the personnel front, Border Patrol increasingly hired new recruits from non-border communities, and most new agents refused to live in Douglas. They feared the entanglements that would come with living in a community they patrolled. Most preferred to commute from places like the military town of Sierra Vista an hour away. A top city official described this pattern in stark terms: "It's like the military that goes into a war zone, does its thing, and then goes back. They don't leave any benefit. It's not the same as if they were part of the community."

Two sectors of the economy that even nonresident agents helped keep afloat were Douglas's restaurants and convenience stores. Even that economic benefit came with risks. Owned by a family of Pentecostals, El Chef was one of the town's most popular Mexican restaurants during the boom years of border security. Both Homeland Security employees and the town's immigrant rights activists could agree on its out-of-sight food. The family's vibrant church crossed political divides in much the same way. Services there united undocumented residents and Border Patrol agents in prayer and fellowship. But despite that ability to cross divides, El Chef almost closed when a new-to-town Border Patrol agent believed that he'd been served a drink with spit in it.

After the incident, the agent sent an email to more than six hundred law enforcement officers calling for a boycott. It wasn't the first time Border Patrol agents had targeted a restaurant over an imagined offense. But El Chef was particularly dependent on customers in uniform. The restaurant immediately felt the impact. Ninety percent of its Border Patrol customers refused to return. ICE and Customs joined the boycott. In the end, it took intervention from religious leaders, the mayor, and veteran law enforcement officers to undo the damage.

If PD had been a benevolent paternal figure, the border business was like an abusive stepfather, one young Douglasite who'd moved away to attend law school observed: The purveyors of border security moved in without permission. You were stuck with them. In equal measures, you hated them and you depended on them.

ROSIE THOUGHT THIS analogy made literal sense. Her work exposed her to tragedies of the sort that didn't make headlines on CNN or Fox. She saw the ways expanding security made life *less* secure for many. The glorification of militarized enforcement—and the violent organized crime that followed in its wake—abraded the lives of women in particular. Not all domestic violence and sexual assault could be attributed to militarized masculinity on the border, of course. Many factors complicated the cases that came through Rosie's clinic. But she insisted that common explanations for violence against women—especially ones purveying stereotypes of poor people or macho "Latin culture"—missed crucial factors. The increased vulnerability Rosie saw in her work, she realized, was, in part, the unexamined collateral damage of a border war.

Rosie witnessed the new border regime make women more vulnerable every day. Start with the border crossing itself. Rape was a ubiquitous part of the price women and girls paid to traverse the militarized border. This wasn't an intentional result of U.S. policy, but it wasn't accidental. Since the mid-1990s, the U.S. government's overarching border security strategy was *designed* to make unauthorized border crossing more dangerous.

Once women were in the United States, fear of immigration enforcement also bred vulnerability. Abusers threatened to call the Border Patrol on their undocumented victims. Being pushed deeper into hiding made undocumented immigrants more dependent on perpetrators and less likely to report violence. This was particularly true when U.S. legal residents and citizens committed that violence.

Rosie's Border Patrol boyfriend once defended his job, bragging about the rapists and wife abusers he helped deport.

"That's good," Rosie agreed. "But a lot of the time, when it comes to protecting women, you don't even understand that law you're supposed to enforce. You detain a woman, and you have no idea all the different kinds of visa programs and legal remedies she might qualify for. You just deport her so you don't have to deal with the hassle of getting her a hearing."

Crime rates in Douglas, like those in most California, Texas, and Arizona border communities, were not notably higher than in the rest of the country. But policing had begun to exert an outsize cultural influence on the place. What happened when law enforcement permeated the fabric of a place? Even as she started to fall in love with a Border Patrol agent—a good man—Rosie knew that few professions had higher rates of perpetrating domestic violence than law enforcement. Combined with economic displacement, life in a law enforcement company town bred conditions in which gender violence thrived.

CHARLIE AUSTIN WORRIED about the other side of this equation. Law enforcement buildup had a counterintuitive impact on illegal activity. Instead of saying that Douglas had become a security company town, it made sense to say that it had become a security *and* insecurity company town. As with Prohibition in the 1920s, massive increase in border security made the business of lawbreaking more dangerous but also more lucrative.

During the peak years of the border crisis, it seemed as if nearly everyone made money: grocery stores, hotels, car lots, taxi companies, gas stations all benefited from smuggling. Entrepreneurial locals rented their houses and garages for use as stash houses. And the more vans packed with migrants banged over rutted back roads, the more tire merchants sold.

As prevention through deterrence quintupled the price of unauthorized border crossing in Douglas, ever-more-organized criminal actors sought to enter the market. Drug cartels discovered that they could make more smuggling people than they could trafficking marijuana or meth. They were far more sophisticated and skilled at the work. Watching cartels take over the business of human trafficking was like watching a violent, ruthless Walmart elbow its way into town while the mom-and-pop places went under. Highly profitable human smuggling hardly disappeared in the face of increased enforcement, as policy makers had hoped. It just got more consolidated, concentrated, and sophisticated. And more dangerous for everyone.

For Rosie, this symbiotic relationship sometimes made it hard to distinguish between the harmful effects of law enforcement and lawbreaking. They appeared not as opposing forces but as two different movements of the same machine—a machine that made women more vulnerable to violence. Smugglers preying on migrants and Border Patrol agents enforcing (or abusing) laws both played a role. Each helped strip migrants of money, options, and humanity. When understood as two movements of the same machinery, the fact that organized crime and assault had grown in stride with an expanding border security apparatus was less surprising. Despite abundant lip service paid to protecting migrants from criminal exploitation, in practice U.S. border security policy had outsourced the ugliest work of "deterrence" to violent gangs.

When Charlie retired in 2007, he had accomplished plenty to be proud of in his long career. He had found it thrilling to be at the center of the national drama while free-flowing resources rolled in. And yet he wondered whether it was all worth it. Or worse, if the country's approach to border security had inflamed the very problems he was trying to prevent. So much spending on border enforcement was like a doctor giving medicine to treat a disease unaware that "the disease was feeding off the medicine."

Douglas residents argued about these changes over coffee and sweet bread at La Unica Bakery. They argued over smoky *barbacoa* at family celebrations. When one cousin worked for the Border Patrol and another worked for the cartels, weddings and *quinceañeras* could be tricky. In churches like the one run by the owners of El Chef restaurant, Sunday services could yield strange commensality: a Border Patrol agent deacon might give immigration advice to an undocumented deacon over doughnuts and coffee, each one wondering how an encounter between them outside church would go. By 2001, these kinds of strange relations constituted Douglas's new normal—life in one of the most heavily policed small towns in the country.

7.

DANCE STEPS

AIDA EMPTIED HALF A BOTTLE of Cuervo cut with Bud without anybody noticing. Well, Cynthia saw because she helped. But Luz didn't detect the girls' staggers or inexplicable laughter, and this was lucky. Luz had sworn she would kill them the next time she caught them drunk or stoned. "*Créanme, chiquitas,*" she said. "You are only fourteen, Aida, *por Dios.* And, Cynthia . . . I will kill you." They believed her.

It was the summer of 2002, and Aida had just finished eighth grade in Douglas. Nineteen ninety-nine hadn't gone well. Y2K was a painful memory; even the letters looked forked like gang signs or scissors. And 2001 hadn't improved. It was possible, she discovered, to make the same bad choices about friends in Douglas as she had in Agua Prieta.

"Let's walk," she said to Cynthia. The two sisters sailed out of their mother's house with drunken purpose, no destination in mind. At the Tenth Street Park, the city had stationed temporary basketball nets on a concrete plaza. Two boys were shooting hoops. The ball veered loose, and Aida stopped laughing long enough to pick it up.

"Cynthia, catch." She threw the ball like a bomb going off, wanting to mess something up. Cynthia caught it and passed it back. Aida dared the boys to take the ball away. They stood, mouths open, amazed at their luck. Two hot girls drawing them into a game of keep-away.

Aida singled out the taller of the two. "Who are you?" she said, holding the ball out of reach.

"David."

"David who?" She jumped back to avoid his reach.

"David Rojas."

Aida lowered the ball and stopped juking. "*The* David Rojas?"

He did look exactly like Tupac—all her mooning friends had been right about that. They smacked their lips when they talked about *David Rojas*. Aida could also see that under his baggy *cholo* shirt the boy was cut. She released the ball.

"Let's play."

It was sloppy and the girls didn't care about fouls.

"What grade are you in?" David asked, fending off Aida's hands.

"Just finished eighth, you?"

"Twelfth."

"I heard that you can really dance, Tupac."

"Damn straight."

They played on. Flushed happiness rose to the surface of Aida's drunkenness. David drove at the basket, and Aida grabbed his shirt to prevent the shot. The pocket and part of the front ripped off in her hand.

"That's my new shirt," David shouted, suddenly furious.

"Sorry," Aida howled. She and Cynthia were already sprinting off the court as fast as their feet could take them.

"Can I have your number?" David called out to Aida's disappearing back.

WHEN RAÚL SENT Aida to live with her mother again in that cyanotic dawn midway through seventh grade, Luz realized that she'd have to make changes. And she did. She'd removed Aida from Agua Prieta and removed herself from Saul, this time for good. Six months into the new millennium, shortly after Aida finished seventh grade, she marched her family across the border with a new short-term shopping visa and the intention of staying. Once again, the family fit itself into a bare apartment. Once again, Luz struggled to make ends meet. Without Saul it was harder, but Luz took a job cooking at a restaurant and worked back-to-back shifts, almost without rest. When she wasn't at the restaurant, she took care of her children and earned extra money cleaning houses. A year later, she met Jack.

Jack was an older man with crippling emphysema. He owned a video store in Douglas and worked as a home health-care attendant in Sierra Vista. He had a harsh tongue, but was not a physically violent man. All of Luz's children fell instantly in love with him.

With Jack's jobs, Luz's restaurant work, and the money her girls made cleaning houses when they could, the family still hovered one setback ahead of poverty, but for once they were hovering *ahead* of poverty. When Jack's car got impounded after a traffic ticket and they had to abandon it because they couldn't afford the towing and storage fees, it didn't completely destroy them.

In time, Luz could afford to rent a guesthouse from the owner of the restaurant where she worked. Jennifer, suddenly all grown up at eighteen, newly married and pregnant, followed the family back to Douglas and moved in next door with her husband. This was one good development on the housing front, Aida thought—at least at first.

Aida entered eighth grade dressed like Missy Elliott in an off-brand velour tracksuit, hoop earrings, and a fat-brimmed baseball cap cocked jauntily to the side. Life was better, but her anger had inertia. Extracted from Agua Prieta and returned to the country she considered home, Aida stopped stealing cars and running with tough kids. But her energy still arced bright and destructive. She smoked blunts in the park, drank forties with her sister, and defied Luz as often as she could.

That had worried everyone. Not only for the obvious reasons, but also because Aida's feral entry into eighth grade coincided with the aftermath of September 11, 2001.

When the Twin Towers fell, Douglas, Arizona, went on high alert.

Automatic weapons bristled in the port of entry, and crossing the border took hours. The local economy reeled because Mexican shoppers decided that Walmart's and JCPenney's low prices weren't worth the long waits and intense scrutiny. But the most profound impacts of 9/11 on Douglas would take longer to manifest themselves: In a few years, "Customs" and "Immigration" would become "Homeland Security," highlighting a shift in the way federal forces viewed the border. Border Patrol, originally a minor bureau of the Department of Labor, would emerge as part of Customs and Border Protection, the country's largest police force, armed with influxes of funding and a militarized sense of purpose. After 9/11, the Border Patrol—amped by a belief that the nation's perimeter must be defended at any cost from existential threat—would model itself more and more on the military.

As law enforcement at the border took on the tenor of war fighting, Aida raged through the streets. Mother and daughter scuffled daily, with shouts and stares. Most fights ended with Aida storming out of the house.

"No, you may not go out."

"Try and stop me."

Aida reeled and Luz reeled. They were—in that moment—incapable of peace. Conflict spread and chasms opened between the sisters. It was a season of accusation and counteraccusation, of loud ultimatums and love stripped down to recrimination. The people closest to her pushed her away, and she did the same. She was fourteen. She was adolescent and ancient. She was out of control and largely on her own.

THIS WAS AIDA'S life when she met David Rojas on the basketball court in June 2002. Charming and popular, David was the break-dance king of Douglas High School. He held court on a piece of cardboard laid down at the Tenth Street Park. People spoke of him in awed whispers. They called him "Matrix" because he could run up a wall into a backflip. They called him "Tupac" because he really did look like the rapper, with his shaved head, tight goatee, six-pack abs, and fat lips. He danced, drew brilliant pictures, and got good grades in school. He could lift Aida's spirits as easily as he could windmill on cardboard. He taught her the Wave and a front flip and asked her to sit for a portrait. By the end of the summer, they were dancing together.

David was a party boy—all fun, all the time—but everyone agreed that he calmed Aida. He'd waltzed into Aida's home and won over her mom, drawing pictures for the younger children and flirting with Luz.

"Why don't you speak English, Mrs. Hernandez?" he'd ask.

"How about if you teach me," she'd answer in Spanish, laughing. And David did, listing new vocabulary words and coaching her pronunciation.

When Aida started ninth grade at Douglas High, David helped her with math. He met her after every class and made sure that she reached the next one. Everyone said that he was some kind of genius, and when he promised that the two of them would get ahead together, Aida believed him.

Science and English classes, Aida attended out of pure joy, but math derailed her. She studied hard, but when she sat for tests, the numbers and formulas skittered across her brain, rearranging themselves in kaleidoscopic shapes. Her teacher told her that she clearly understood the math; she just needed to concentrate more. But the harder Aida strained, the more focus eluded her.

While David could skip classes to party and still keep up, Aida found she couldn't. She fell further behind. And with each bad grade, she turned away from school a little more. She exchanged Missy Elliott for Pink Floyd, shedding red tracksuits for black jeans, black T-shirts, black Converse, and black eyeliner. She stopped going to most classes. Her first-semester report card came with three "no credit" grades.

THE LAST THING Aida expected to find at the start of second semester was a place at Douglas High where she felt completely at ease and full of power.

The day she sauntered into Mrs. Olivia Garino's dance room, Aida reeked of weed. The teacher curled her lips and pushed Aida to the front of the room. Even stoned, Aida was astonished by Mrs. Garino's classroom: polished floor and wall of mirrors, each student gently pulling shiny black *zapatillas* out of special cloth bags. Confident boys and girls limbering up to move.

"Okay, Aida Hernandez," Mrs. Garino said, calling her out. "I'd like you to demonstrate this next sequence to the class."

With a single foot, Mrs. Garino executed a pattern of accented taps. It was a simple *remate* from the inventory of Latin American *bailes folklóricos*. Aida watched, her half-staff eyelids widening. The sequence entered her in a way that no math formula ever had. Her nervous energy poured forth, and she produced a precise copy of the teacher's movements. Mrs. Garino frowned.

"Okay, try this one," she said, unleashing a flurry of double-footed stomps, alternating light and heavy, toe and heel.

Aida watched and repeated.

Mrs. Garino frowned deeper. "If you come to class messed up again, even once, you're out."

In dance, the obstacles Aida faced in life became liquid and reassembled into freedom. She lost herself in the footwork and swirling skirts. Intent on the sweet-as-syrup flirtations of a *jarabe tapatío* from Jalisco, Aida's keyed-up brain could finally rest. She committed to Mrs. Garino's class, and by association her other grades stabilized. Between dance and David, Aida felt more alive than she had in years, and she sometimes celebrated this achievement a bit too much.

In February 2003, Aida vanished and Luz spent three days tracking her down. She finally found her daughter squatting in an abandoned building with a group of new friends, strung out on seventy-two hours of strong weed. That was as much as Luz could take. She yanked Aida out of the ruins and sent her to rehab.

For fifteen days, Aida stayed at a drug and alcohol treatment center in Agua Prieta. She did counseling and group sessions and stood still long enough to read books. A psychologist gave her an intelligence test. On the last day of the program, he gave Aida the results.

"You scored higher than anyone else I've seen. You are a highly intelligent girl," he said. "Your behavior is only hurting yourself." Sure, the test's comparison set was entirely made up of addicts, but it was the first time anyone had called her smart. Aida returned to school in Douglas and rode the high for six sober months. She and her mother reconciled as best they could. For an entire half a year, nothing but the pedestrian stresses of looming poverty and precarious legal status assailed her.

AT THIS POINT, at least one of the many disadvantages accumulating around Aida's life might have been removed, if she'd only known it. The family lived in the shadows, but a narrow path to legal residence had opened up for her. In 1994, and again in 2000, the federal Violence Against Women Act (VAWA) had recognized the unique vulnerability of undocumented victims of domestic violence. Undocumented immigrants do not necessarily experience domestic violence at higher rates than the general population, but their precarious legal status empowers abusers. On top of the many barriers all domestic violence survivors face, undocumented immigrants must also worry whether leaving an abusive relationship—or reporting an abuser to authorities—will bring immigration consequences. "Sure, go ahead and call the police," Saul had always told Luz and her family. "They'll bring the Border Patrol, and it won't be me they'll take away."

VAWA sought to atone for this imbalance by opening a path to legal permanent residency for victims of extreme cruelty by U.S. citizens and green card holders. Luz might have been able to pursue legal status for herself and by extension her family. Unfortunately, in the early 2000s, few people understood the law, including law enforcement agents charged with upholding it. Immigration debates roiling in the country drew sharp lines between "legal" and "illegal" immigrants, but Aida, along with countless others, occupied a fuzzy third category. Immigrants in this in-between group probably qualified for legal status but could not obtain it because of fear, limited resources, lack of knowledge, or resistance from law enforcers.

In 2001, the year Aida started eighth grade in Douglas, the Republican senator Orrin Hatch and the Democrat Richard Durbin—both champions of VAWA—introduced another bill that underscored Aida's ambiguous position in the hierarchy of American belonging. The Development, Relief, and Education for Alien Minors (DREAM) Act drew attention to a certain kind of highly deserving undocumented youth. Hatch drew a portrait of this person in his testimony on the bill. "Particularly moving are the stories of undocumented alien children who were illegally brought to the United States through no act of their own," he said. "Many such people have been in the United States for many years, if not the majority of their lives. By and large, these children are assimilated into American culture; they attend school, participate in extracurricular activities, and even go to college. They grow up to be contributors to society, working to better themselves and provide for their families. But the law denies them any chance, no matter what their individual accomplishments, to become lawful permanent residents."

Opposition from Hatch's own party undercut the bill. Similar proposals, introduced multiple times between 2006 and 2012, would suffer the same fate—despite their emphasis on charismatic, innocent, and high-achieving immigrants.

But would the DREAM Act have helped Aida? In many ways, she would have been a perfect candidate. She had been brought across the border at a young age by her mother and was profoundly assimilated to life in the United States. At the same time, Aida's experiences demonstrated the limits of basing immigration reform on idealized portraits of blameless virtue. The DREAM Act left little room for the messy reality of Aida's life. Her family's flight back across the border to escape Saul, for example, broke the bill's requirement of five continuous years of residence. And then there was the question of demonstrating "good moral character." Were Aida's trauma-driven bouts of defiance and self-destruction morally worse than suburban white kids' acts of marauding teenage rebellion? Regardless of the answer, one thing was certain: immigration law and the ever-intensifying policing of Douglas had set Aida up to pay a higher price for her actions than most affluent teens could imagine.

MRS. GARINO'S ADVANCED DANCERS performed all over the state, and Aida vowed to join them. They held car washes to pay for travel, and Aida showed up to help. She felt as if a brightly colored ribbon of happiness connected each member of the troupe. That year, Mrs. Garino laid out a challenge for her beginners: choreograph and costume an original dance to perform at the Tombstone, Arizona, parade. They worked for weeks, choosing their theme—*norteño*—and music, a selection from Los Tucanes de Tijuana. Aida practiced until her feet stung, and on the morning of the performance her heart pounded under a cropped denim cowgirl shirt.

"Please welcome the beginning Baile Folklórico class from Douglas High, performing their own creation," the announcer said when the girls had assembled in front of the reviewing stand.

Our own creation! Aida repeated to herself, a wide smile breaking out across her anxious face. When spectators lining the parade route cheered at the end of the piece, it sounded to Aida like the roar of a full stadium. She decided, at that moment, that she would become a high school dance teacher.

David approved of Aida's plan. He had set his sights on college as well. Thirty years earlier, during the heyday of smelter employment, the percentage of Douglas residents with four or more years of college matched the national average. By the early 2000s, only one in ten Douglas residents over twenty-five had a college degree—half the national average. David wanted to beat the odds. Mrs. Garino approved of Aida's plan as well. She promised to help Aida compete for a scholarship. All Aida had to do was finish high school.

BY THE WINTER of sophomore year, Aida's grades had inched upward. She still skipped classes, though, and got suspended in February. During the enforced leave, she stayed home and helped her mom around the house. One afternoon, the smell of meat frying on the stove sent Aida running to the bathroom.

Jennifer held Aida's hair as she threw up.

"Oh my God," Jennifer said, "you're pregnant!" As usual, Jennifer knew things. With a baby of her own already, she had seen this scene before.

"You're crazy," Aida said. She and David *always* used protection. They had college plans. But the waves of nausea continued, brought on by the strangest triggers. One day, Aida decided she had to face reality. She called Jennifer while her older sister was shopping at Walmart.

"Can you buy me, like, five pregnancy tests?"

When the last pee strip changed color, Aida went completely blank.

"Aida—hello—are you there?" Jennifer asked. Aida burst into overlapping laughter and tears. The two women jumped up and down with excitement. But then Aida froze stiff.

"I can't jump up and down—I'm pregnant! I'll hurt the baby."

At the Chiricahua Community Health Centers, Aida's regular nurse practitioner shook her head and left the room. A counselor took her place.

"You are young and have a lot of life ahead of you. Are you sure that you want to go ahead with this pregnancy?" she asked.

An unaccustomed certainty came over Aida. "I got myself into this, and I need to take responsibility for it."

The woman looked at her, waiting for more.

"What I want," Aida said, "is vitamins and classes. I want to take all the classes and do this right."

The next morning, Aida woke up early to catch David walking to school. She told him the news. His silence lasted too many beats.

"Say something!" Aida commanded.

After a long delay, David replied, "But I wanted to finish school and go to college."

It was not the affirmation Aida had hoped for. "So did I, David." Her stomach lurched and the world spun. "If you don't want to do this—that's fine," she said. "I'll do it on my own."

THE NEWS DEVASTATED LUZ, but later she warmed to its effect on her daughter.

"Thank God, Aida got pregnant," she confessed to Jennifer and Cynthia.

"It finally calmed her down," the sisters agreed.

The thought of living for another person anchored Aida in a way that no one had anticipated. She rediscovered the pleasure of disciplined, organized living—something she had not felt since learning English in third grade. She quit drinking and smoking cold turkey and bought *What to Expect When You're Expecting*. A meticulous, anxious mother-to-be, she came to consider the book her bible. Aida called her nurse practitioner often, worrying about every changing signal sent by the fetus growing inside her. She attended birthing classes and parenting classes, and eventually David joined her. He was not an enthusiastic presence, but he was present.

Aida dropped out of high school and began to work full-time. As a U.S. citizen, born in Arizona, David had more options than Aida. Luz's boyfriend, Jack, got him a well-paying job as a home health-care attendant. He held it for a while and then grew restless. He threw away the good job in health care and escaped to Tucson with friends. He took a job at a fast-food restaurant, earned less, and partied harder. But at least he sent what he made to Aida. Slowly, she accumulated baby clothes, blankets, and a crib.

"Well, we're having a baby. We might as well get married," Aida said during one of David's visits home.

Once again, David's face went blank for too many beats, but he finally said, "Okay."

Luz organized an impromptu wedding, annexing David and Aida's celebration to Cynthia's *quinceañera* ball. Cynthia's gown and flowers were pale blue. Her court of cousins and friends performed a waltz in her honor that they'd rehearsed for months. Aida, on the other hand, chose an ivory dress, full in the waist to accommodate her enormous belly.

Raúl came to the ceremony, and Aida danced with her father for the first time in her life. They curved into each other over Aida's eight-month belly, and Raúl's dismay at the pregnancy melted. Family and friends circled around their warmth. Swaying under the blue lights, cradled by her father, Aida felt social judgment fall away. For the first time in months, she wasn't a pregnant sixteen-year-old disappointment; she was just Aida, surrounded by love.

THE BIRTH TOOK PLACE twenty-six days later in Sierra Vista because Douglas had no birthing center of its own. During labor, nurses complained openly over Aida's anguished body about "babies having babies." Aida would forget the pain of childbirth quickly, but not the nurses' condescending looks. She vowed to disappoint their dire predictions about her parenting skills. David stood by her side and said little.

Hours later, a tiny, perfect boy detonated her heart. She named him Gabriel, the archangel, messenger of God.

DAVID RETURNED TO DOUGLAS, and the two of them saved enough money to make a first payment on a rent-to-own trailer. It was in Sunspots, a horseshoe of battered and burned-out mobile homes that constituted Douglas's worst neighborhood. But someday, if they kept up the payments, the trailer would be theirs. Aida, home with Gabriel, poured her heart into decorating. Scavenging secondhand stores, she collected dark curtains, Pink Floyd album art, and skull knickknacks. Each find delighted her. From the wedding, they had a toaster, a microwave, and a coffeemaker. Aida found a used bed and a television. Once, when gangs battled over Sunspots, Aida had to throw herself onto the floor, shielding Gabriel with her body until the shooting stopped. But sometimes, she could sit with her boy on the plywood stoop, rocking him to sleep in the shade of her very own walnut tree.

Soon after they moved into the trailer, David told Aida that he wanted to show her something. He took her into the bedroom and pulled a wrapped package from its hiding place. He showed her the ripped black-and-white buffalo-plaid shirt, a memento of their meeting two years earlier, neatly folded and saved forever. Aida felt as if she had achieved the American Dream.

8

AMERICAN DREAMING

FROM THE 1960S THROUGH THE 1980S, on autumn Friday nights you could feel it in the air. Teens, their parents, and their grandparents put on extra clothes against the high desert chill and found places in the Douglas High bleachers. While boys in black and gold played football under stadium lights, fans faced the PD complex, which glowed bright as a Christmas tree.

Inside the complex, the players' fathers and uncles and brothers roasted ore, stoked furnaces, skimmed slag, and poured orange ribbons of spattering copper into molds. Inside, the hundred-degree air filled with brilliant clouds of dust and gas and showering sparks. Outside, chill mountain air settled deeper into the valley floor, driving out summer. The crowd snuggled closer for warmth.

If fans were lucky, and work in the smelter had advanced to a particular point that night, electric train cars would appear at the lip of a distant slag mountain and decant molten scoria off the edge. For a minute, fans would forget about the game as liquid light cascaded down the mountainside, shooting fireworks and flashing brighter than the stadium lights. Nighttime slag pours viewed from the stadium were a common enough marvel, so no one cheered out loud. But in that moment of comforting light, the year's troubles might seem a little less acute. The things that divided Douglas might recede a little. At some level, the assembled fans remembered that for all its woes their town was a good place to live. Later, they would recall having felt reassured by the display of tumbling light. Their town had a place in the world.

The smelter closed nine months before Aida's birth. By the time she and David sat as students in the Douglas High bleachers, most of its visible traces were gone. Only the memory remained, sweet and bruised. For Aida and David, finding an American Dream would be more complicated than it had once been, if it had ever been that simple. But Aida, at least, still believed that it was possible—even when her surroundings told her that it wasn't.

DAVID CRASHED IN at 4:00 a.m. Aida had spent a restless night waiting for him. In the long hours, alone with Gabriel, she'd lain there listening to the muffled sounds of her husband partying with his new friends next door. While he partied, she tried to sort out her feelings. She felt ashamed of the puffy eyes, doughy body, and raw nerves of new motherhood. David was disappointed and furious too, she could tell, and that made her angry.

"I'm so tired of you" was the only greeting he could muster. In bed, he pulled the blanket off his wife, wrapped himself up, and turned his back to rest a few hours before his next shift began. Aida curled on her side, freezing. She wouldn't sleep that night.

Other times David suddenly had mountains of amped-up energy. He stormed into the trailer to change clothes after work, said nothing to Aida, and stormed out to party. Or he'd invite the neighbors over. All night the trailer would shake to its thin bones as Aida comforted Gabriel in the other room. David would sleep two hours a night and bolt awake, bristling with energy to fry hamburgers and serve Cokes. One by one, he'd flung aside the things that had made him the David everyone knew. His dancing became graceless and frantic. He stopped drawing. A wild intensity replaced his carefree charm.

At home he spat abuse: "I should never have gotten mixed up with a fucking *mexicana* illegal." Maybe he saw the long tunnel of his future from there and, always bright, understood exactly how it would end: having taken one small wrong step, he would now always be poor. Maybe he just needed the scour of anger to blast away the layers of fryer grease coating his soul. All of his reasons, and his lack of reasons, refined themselves into lead arsenic loathing. Once Aida broached the subject of applying for her legal residency now that they were married. "It's too expensive," David grumbled. "Fucking illegal."

One day, David punched the couch next to her head, leaving an angry divot in the cheap cushion. Another time he shoved her hard out of his way in the galley kitchen. Aida didn't recognize it as violence at first. Once, he drove a knife into the door frame beside her face and said, "You're next."

It's not like he's hitting me in the face, Aida told herself. She stopped her ears against his insults and picked herself up when he pushed her down. If she grabbed a frying pan and hit back, he'd retreat. Aida had lived through much worse.

David homed in on her weakness. He came in one night, high and wild, and grabbed Gabriel out of his crib. The infant's neck snapped back like a wildflower as David tossed him into the air.

Brandishing Gabriel, he shouted, "This is my son and my house. Get the fuck out!"

Aida clawed at David to recover her son. He shoved her aside and made for the car, the worst thing he could do. In the first two years of Gabriel's life, police stopped David for speeding, driving without insurance, and driving with an "extreme blood alcohol level." Aida threw her body in front of the car and begged him not to drive with Gabriel. David relented.

Then it wasn't one night; it was every night. Gabriel became David's weapon. Aida fought to prevent him from harming the boy. When she threatened to leave, David threatened to call the Border Patrol.

"If you leave me," he told her, "I'll make sure they deport you, and I'll keep custody. They will take you away from your son."

Sometimes David kicked her down the stairs, out under her walnut tree, and locked the trailer door on her. David warned her that if she pounded on the door and woke the neighbors, the police would come. David might get a night in lockup, but Aida would be returned to Mexico without her son, he threatened. A lifetime of living in the shadows had trained her not to test this possibility. So she stayed and tried to minimize the damage.

One night after David locked Aida out, an onlooker called Luz. Luz did not hesitate. She, Cynthia, and her boyfriend ran from their home a few blocks away. They found Aida, their sunshine girl, slumped over on the stairs crying. Luz pounded on the door until David opened it.

"This is how this is going to work," Luz informed him, flashing years of lioness rage. "I am taking Gabriel and Aida. Tomorrow you are packing their things and bringing them to my house."

The former break-dance king of Douglas High School halted in mid-fury. If he had seen himself through Luz's eyes for a moment, he wouldn't have recognized himself standing there in a rage. Whatever he saw, he had nothing to say. He crashed through the house and out the back door, slashing across the yard and into the night. The next morning, chastened, he enlisted friends and moved his wife and son's belongings to Luz's porch.

AIDA WAITED FOR the Border Patrol to arrive. They didn't come. David didn't follow through on his threats, and eventually moved to Phoenix. Through 2005, though, immigration controversies shook the town around her. By then, twelve miles of eighteen-foot steel wall divided Douglas and Agua Prieta. More than five hundred Border Patrol agents filled the new station. Detachments of ATF, DEA, and National Guard cycled in and out of town. For the fourth fiscal year in a row, Border Patrol acknowledged a record number of migrant deaths in Arizona. Independent examiners and the Mexican government concluded that the true number of fatalities far exceeded official estimates. While Aida struggled to get her bearings at her mother's house, Rosie and other members of Frontera de Cristo gathered every Tuesday to call out the names of the dead.

Wendy Glenn and other ranchers outside Douglas saw this suffering firsthand. They also saw the impact of desert migration on their land. In

2005, Wendy complained to Governor Janet Napolitano about dunes of trash accumulating in arroyos and pastures. Eventually, volunteers from Frontera de Cristo and other groups, along with workers funded by state and federal grants, would haul away tons of material jettisoned by migrants: plastic bags, water bottles, toilet paper, food containers, shoes, children's toys, precious family photographs, prayer cards, wallets, purses, and letters from loved ones.

During this time, vigilante groups turned Cochise County into a theater of civilian border defense. In April 2005, a thousand volunteers pledged to show up around Douglas to patrol with the Minuteman Project, founded by Jim Gilchrist and Chris Simcox. Faced with the prospect of heavily armed volunteers setting up camp, Douglas's mayor, Ray Borane, spoke bluntly: "It's racism. . . . We don't want them here."

When the Minutemen arrived anyway, albeit in much smaller numbers than expected, the American Civil Liberties Union (ACLU) and the American Friends Service Committee sent legal observers. While the American Border Patrol and Ranch Rescue had channeled righteous anger, Chris Simcox and his partner, the California accountant Jim Gilchrist, also knew how to channel the media. The Minuteman Project quickly gained international attention. Sometimes more reporters converged on Minuteman actions than actual Minutemen. It was not unheard of to see bizarre assemblies form in the desert outside Douglas: a group of migrants, earnestly heading north, stalked by heavily armed vigilantes, trailed by reporters and camera crews, trailed by legal observers from immigrant rights organizations and the ACLU. Xavier Zaragoza, now a veteran journalist, filmed a documentary about vigilante groups.

During this time, Douglas residents turned out for peace vigils. Across the line, citizens of Agua Prieta organized a boycott of Douglas businesses, and several of the town's stores and restaurants reported a significant impact. Activists called on residents to stand up against groups that took the law into their own hands. But in the end, both Douglas's homegrown and outside anti-immigrant groups tended to fizzle or implode on their own. Almost as quickly as the groups converged, ideological infighting, lawsuits, disputes over money, criminal arrests, and feuding egos tore them apart.

In 2004, FBI agents had arrested a key figure in Ranch Rescue after a shoot-out in the parking lot of a Douglas supermarket. A million-dollar civil rights judgment against Ranch Rescue leaders finished off the group. Indeed, "law and order" anti-immigrant groups seemed to have trouble following the law themselves, and not just on the border: the Minuteman cofounder Chris Simcox would eventually be convicted of three counts in a child molestation trial. Another Minuteman leader, Shawna Forde, would receive the death penalty for murdering a Latino man and his nine-year-old daughter in their home. The American Border Patrol founder, Glenn Spencer, would be convicted of assault after threatening the son of a neighbor he believed to be a drug smuggler. And by the end of the decade, Roger Barnett—the original Cochise County migrant hunter—would lose two major civil rights lawsuits. The rancher avoided criminal charges but owed a group of border crossers and a family of Mexican American hunters more than $170,000 in civil damages.

While they lasted, though, border vigilantes once again drew unwanted attention to far southeastern Arizona. Media poured into town, and like moths to security floodlights, politicians followed. Senators, the governor, and the secretary of Homeland Security all visited Douglas. The latter encouraged some by suggesting that Washington would address the root causes of undocumented immigration with a guest worker program. Others reckoned correctly that Republicans would never allow their president's comprehensive immigration reform to advance.

In the face of this turmoil, residents of Douglas and Agua Prieta who enjoyed more day-to-day security than Aida labored to keep alive a positive image of the border. Violent stereotypes of border communities hawked by outlets from right-wing talk radio to liberal Hollywood captured only the tiniest fraction of border life. Nevertheless, in August 2005, Governor Napolitano declared a state of emergency in the state's four border counties. Citing out-of-control crime and violence, the announcement came with millions in additional funding for border town police.

Mayor Borane bristled at the suggestion that his town was unsafe. Charlie Austin accepted the money but agreed with the mayor. Crime statistics didn't bear out the fearmongers. Arizona border towns had lower crime rates in general than the rest of the state. Douglas, for example, reported less than one-third of a murder a year between 1992 and 2012, far lower than both state and national rates. And in an article on Napolitano's emergency declaration, one *Los Angeles Times* journalist noted, "Women in town say the streets are safe to walk at night."

DID AIDA FEEL SAFE in 2005? If she had reflected on the rhetorical war being waged around her over border safety, she might have politely suggested that all parties got it wrong: The violence in Aida's life hadn't come from migrants or smugglers. If anything, it was the ever-expanding Border Patrol and local police that concerned her. She had too much to worry about to give the Chiapans, Hondurans, and gun-wielding vigilantes streaming through town a second thought—except to know enough to stay away.

Aida got wind of a job in Tucson cleaning and staging houses for real estate agents. In 2005, sand-colored stucco developments were metastasizing across the desert. Aida had lots of work. To earn more, she took a job cashiering at a gas station convenience store. She could even afford to pay a woman to take care of Gabriel. She worked and saved and worked, aware that, other than the love she felt for her son, nothing good in her life lasted.

And she was right. The turnaround came fast and hard. By 2006, fewer houses were selling, which meant there was nothing to clean. Then the gas station owner ran her information through an employment eligibility database and fired her. After that, Aida could not find any job that paid enough to offset the cost of hiring someone to watch Gabriel.

Aida did what people in Douglas had always done in hard times: she tightened her belt and tried to wait it out. She made her money last longer than expected. Limiting herself to one sandwich a day freed enough cash to buy baby food and diapers for months. Surviving on coffee and sugar took her a little further. When she finally conceded defeat, her situation was well past desperate.

"If you want my help," Luz responded, "you need to call David first and get him to provide support."

Aida held out one more day, refusing to ask her husband for help. When Gabriel's hunger cries grew eerily subdued, though, it scared her enough to dial the phone.

"There is no way I'm giving you any money unless you come back and live with me," David said on the other end of the line.

Aida explained her desperation. She appealed to David's duty as a father. She fawned, and then she raged. David sensed his power growing and held firm: she'd get no money unless she returned to his side. So Aida fashioned a diaper for Gabriel out of tape and a plastic grocery bag and trudged to a Circle K across town. They waited there on the gum-thick pavement, watching customers come and go with bags of chips and fountain drinks. Eventually, Aida and Gabriel climbed into a white shuttle van.

The van pulled onto Interstate 10 and headed north for two hours through abandoned cotton fields and ghostly developments. It passed turnoffs for the prison towns of Florence and Eloy and sailed across the bone-dry Salt River into Phoenix and a reunion with David.

THERE WAS NO semblance of a relationship after the reunion. David's apartment overflowed with extended family who treated Aida like a servant brought in to cook and clean. David encouraged this treatment. He seemed to think that Aida owed him for his help, even after she found a job at a convenience store and turned her pay over to him. He took her checks and, in return, meted out twenty dollars a week so Aida could buy groceries for herself and Gabriel.

After four months of this, Aida and Gabriel left without goodbyes or regrets.

9

NO COUNTRY FOR YOUNG WOMEN

JAZMIN PERCHED ON THE CHECKOUT COUNTER laughing hard enough to risk spitting out her drink. Aida lip-synched a *banda* song for her while doing a wobbly-kneed Charleston between racks of DVDs. The video store door clanged open, interrupting the floor show. Aida, aged twenty, pirouetted and pointed at the newcomer with a spokesmodel flourish. Returned from her time with David in Phoenix and now living in Luz and Jack's trailer, her light had come back

"Mr. 06664!" she sang into the flashlight she'd been using as a microphone. "Eddie Alvarez, account number 06664."

Eddie gave a sheepish smile. He was, by constitution and choice, a grumpy man, but Aida made him blush with contentment. He knew that

Aida greeted every regular by name and account number, but it still made him feel special.

Aida was good at that. It was the small things that people seemed to appreciate the most, like her remembering names, fixing late returns so there wouldn't be a fee, or offering a movie recommendation. When Aida beamed in their direction, people felt important.

Luz and Jack's double-wide occupied a large lot, scrubby with mesquite and pigweed, tucked behind Sunspots. At eighteen hundred square feet, it was the biggest home Aida had ever lived in. Four separate bedrooms gave its occupants unprecedented privacy. This was a godsend, because, when Aida and Gabriel moved in, they joined Luz, Jack, Jennifer, Jennifer's toddlers, Cynthia, Emiliano, and Jazmin. Depending on the month, the house's population might swell to include friends, cousins, uncles, and grandparents in need of a temporary place to live. Sometimes there were as many as fourteen people sleeping there. But the yard had swings and a kiddie pool where Gabriel and Jennifer's children became fast friends. Life was a companionable chaos.

Tears and recrimination over past conflicts came and went. Luz, Aida, and Aida's sisters found ways to forgive one another. Jennifer had divorced her husband and returned to the family trailer. The Three Musketeers were back, joined by Jazmin, their little d'Artagnan.

Cynthia was midway through high school and took it seriously. She didn't get straight As, but Aida and Jennifer admired her. She would—they believed—be the first person in their family to finish high school.

Aida and Luz went to counseling together for a while, admitting the pain they'd caused each other. Most mornings, Aida dropped Gabriel and Jennifer's son at preschool, still wearing her pajamas, and then picked up sweets from La Unica Bakery. She and her mother would share *pan dulce* and coffee on the double-wide's ample porch. In the relative quiet, Aida and Luz would listen to the mourning doves and talk about their lives in a way they'd never done before. It felt stable, as if it could last.

Aida had even enrolled in an adult high school, hoping to finish her degree. Before dropping out of school to have Gabriel, she had managed to wrangle her reading and science grades into the B range, but math still eluded her. Returning to school meant taking an Arizona standardized math test, and that almost scared her away. When the envelope arrived with her results, though, it said, "Approaches Standard." It gave her hope. After two years of parenthood, violence, and precariousness, she still remembered enough math to almost achieve the standard for her grade. I can do this, Aida thought.

Once again, the reality of poverty intervened. For the first months of Aida's return to school, Luz watched Gabriel so her daughter could attend classes. Child care was an expression of Luz's love. But in the face of her complicated, changeable work schedule, Gabriel's care suffered. Juggling help from other family members kept Aida in school for a bit longer, but time and flexibility are two of the scarcest commodities in a poor community. Just shy of finishing her first semester, Aida quit school again and took up full-time work at Movies 'n' More.

NETFLIX AND REDBOX hadn't quite killed the video store business yet, particularly on the low end of the industry. Jack's shop clung to a loyal band of customers because it rented movies for one dollar, the best deal in Douglas. It wasn't clear the store could make a profit at that rate, but the enterprise was almost too small and informal to get driven under by competition. Jack's emphysema had advanced to a point where he couldn't manage the store, but Movies 'n' More meant something to the family. Free labor gave the store a slight edge, and Aida's nurturing lifted it up.

She loved the place so much. Crammed with racks, adorned with yellowed movie posters, and smelling of stale popcorn, Movies 'n' More appeared dispirited and ratty to some. To Aida, it felt like an oasis.

With help from her mother and sisters, Aida ran the store. She could manage accounts and stock movies while minding babies and entertaining her younger siblings. When Gabriel and his cousin tired of playing in the racks and under the counter, they could nap on a couch in the back room. Customers came for movies but stayed to banter with Aida and play a game at the ancient foosball table. Her sunshine self was back. And in true Aida fashion, she wanted to share it, to let it grow. Bright and entrepreneurial, she kept reaching to make things better.

One day, putting on a DVD to distract Gabriel and Jazmin, Aida came up with the idea of showing free movies for kids. Kids who would buy popcorn, candy, sodas, and *mangonadas*. The idea caught on, and on days when they showed free movies, the store made a profit. Later, Aida helped clean out the store's back patio to rent it out for parties. Aida was rebuilding her life, as best she could.

SITTING LESS THAN a mile from the port of entry, Movies 'n' More attracted police, drug traffickers, and off-duty Border Patrol alike as clientele, but no one bothered Aida there, except to ask for recommendations. Life, it appeared, seemed possible even as migration and border militarization strained Douglas's social fabric.

At the start of 2006, the year of Aida's return from Phoenix, Arizona's governor, Janet Napolitano, pledged $100 million for further border security. Of that, $13 million was earmarked for the expansion of local law enforcement in border counties. An additional $10 million would help cover local law enforcement overtime costs on the border. Millions more would facilitate the prosecution of border-related crimes and encourage cooperation between local law enforcement and the Border Patrol.

If that was not enough, Arizona's conservative, Phoenix-dominated legislature let loose a salvo of bills aimed to make life impossible for undocumented residents. In the mid-2000s, representatives proposed, passed, or moved forward on laws that would deny bail to people charged with felonies and suspected of being undocumented and make it illegal to rent housing to undocumented immigrants. Bills sought to limit state benefits' availability to noncitizens and empower local law enforcement to stop and question suspected undocumented people. Others tried to bar undocumented Arizonans from suing for punitive damages in civil court and to deny birthright citizenship to the Arizona-born children of noncitizens. Few of these bills were expected to survive the full legislature or Napolitano's veto, but they formed a steady, ominous stream. Old constitutional borders between state law and the federal government's responsibility for immigration enforcement had begun to blur.

MEANWHILE, AN UNEASY quiet fell over Douglas. Vigilantes and TV cameras faded away. Flows of migrants through the area dwindled. At first, the funnel effect of border enforcement pushed migrants elsewhere along the border. The area southwest of Tucson saw large increases during this period. But then, by 2007 and 2008, the looming U.S. recession and relatively strong job market in Mexico sliced into the number of unauthorized border crossings everywhere. In 1997, Border Patrol agents assigned to the southern border arrested an average of 216 migrants a year, per agent. By 2008, that number had fallen to 45. In the eyes of many Douglas residents—and some veteran agents—members of the nation's largest and best-funded federal police force did little besides "sit on their Xs" checking their phones.

Border Patrol officials, of course, claimed that declines in border apprehensions proved the success of their efforts. Politicians who had built careers on perennial calls to "secure the border," on the other hand, struggled with the change. Their popularity depended on a perpetual border crisis, and the search for new reasons to increase spending on border security sometimes reached preposterous levels.

In August 2006, for example, three U.S. congressmen from the House Intelligence Committee held an open hearing in Sierra Vista, fifty miles from Douglas. The representatives assembled a panel of Border Patrol officials, DEA agents, and the Cochise County sheriff and peppered them with questions about security.

A reporter at the hearing described how some of the representatives' questions seemed to baffle the experts. Rick Renzi, an Arizona Republican, chased the panelists with leading questions about the supposed rise of Islamic extremism in Mexico and its implications for border security. Darrell Issa, from California, then chimed in, challenging panelists to acknowledge "widely published reports" of Hezbollah operations in Mexico. The one Democratic committee member at the hearing warned against confusing terrorism and immigration. Other panelists tried to educate Renzi and Issa about the complete lack of evidence of suspected terrorists crossing the border, but it hardly mattered. Unsubstantiated rumors of terrorists on the border would prove both resilient and useful as a political tactic, despite continual debunking.

By 2007, enforcement advocates had a new, more well-founded specter to defend against. The previous year, a horrific spike in violence across Mexico had left thousands dead and filled the media with visions of bloodthirsty narco-traffickers running rampant.

Like the Border Patrol's dramatic funnel strategy before it, the crisis in Mexico was a distinctly political creation. In 2006, Felipe Calderón had assumed the Mexican presidency after a bitter and divisive election. Official vote tallies—questioned by many opponents—gave him a 0.58 percent margin of victory. Accusations of electoral fraud multiplied. So, like many presidents faced with controversy and narrow mandates, Calderón declared war.

For decades, Mexican leaders had pursued a strategy of tempering and containing drug cartels, instead of seeking to extinguish them. As long as U.S. demand for drugs remained strong, the argument went, cartels would always exist. The best that Mexico could do was to limit drug trafficking's social impact and spillover violence. For many critics, this strategy reflected corrupt politicians' stake in drug trafficking, but it also produced a stable system in which a few large cartels divided the country, trade routes, and markets with relatively little collateral violence. Calderón's declaration of all-out war against the cartels shattered that stability.

The new fight targeted *capos*—the heads of cartels. But as the government checked off captured and killed *narcos* on its most wanted list, cartels did not implode, as expected. Instead, they grew four heads for every one cut off, multiplying into more than a dozen competing mini-cartels. The unstable new organizations waged open warfare in public places and across increasingly large swaths of the nation. Most regions of Mexico remained far safer than sensational U.S. news reports suggested—far from a "failed state" or open civil war—but something had shifted. As bodies piled up and carnage spread into previously peaceful areas, government security forces gained influence and extended their reach. Military actions—combating cartels but also suppressing political dissent, dispossessing poor people, and protecting foreign investment—claimed growing numbers of lives across the country.

Before Calderón's policy shift, the Sinaloa Cartel, Mexico's most powerful criminal organization, had cemented control over trafficking across the Arizona-Sonora border. By 2008, multiple groups vied for control of important crossing points, Agua Prieta included. Residents came to understand that if you have to live with organized crime, one dominant cartel exercising undisputed power is preferable to many clashing groups. Little *pueblos* south of Agua Prieta felt the impact most. Gun battles on public streets, beheadings, assassinations of government officials, and violent military occupation hadn't reached Agua Prieta yet, but they crowded the horizon, looming ever closer.

Despite doom-laden warnings from U.S. public officials, violent crime from Mexico did not appear to filter into Douglas. The small town continued to enjoy relatively low crime rates, but the foreboding news from across the border was relentless. It began to inform public perception and policy on the American side.

In the two years since her return from Phoenix, Aida felt the change come on like radio waves, intangible yet real. Border Patrol hovered behind her when she refilled her coffee at the convenience store. Agents idled alongside her at stoplights and tailed her when she drove Gabriel to preschool. With the numbers of undocumented migrants crossing the border at record-low levels and falling, agents at Douglas's heavily staffed station had to find something to do. Now they had more time to listen to Douglas Police Department radio chatter and to show up during local law enforcement stops.

To Aida, nestled in her peaceful video sanctuary, crises on the border felt as if they existed in a parallel universe. Focused on motherhood and making ends meet, she ignored rumors of violence in Agua Prieta. Mexico was not her place. And yet she was not entirely immune.

Early in 2008, a routine police stop resulted in Jennifer's deportation. Worse still, her removal came with a five-year legal bar against entering the United States. If Jennifer returned and was caught, she could face criminal charges and time in jail. With no child care and no way to support herself in Agua Prieta, Jennifer left her U.S. citizen son and daughter in Douglas under her mother and sisters' care. For the second time, Aida felt the border slit her family in two.

IN THE SPRING of 2008, Aida was recommending the unsettling border-lands thriller *No Country for Old Men* to any Movies 'n' More customer who'd listen. The store's clientele preferred *Big Momma's House 2*, but Aida charmed a few into trying the Coen brothers.

In one of the movie's final scenes, Javier Bardem's psychopathic hit man waits for a woman he's decided to kill. He sits in her bedroom as she makes herself a cup of coffee in the kitchen, completely unaware of his presence. When she opens the bedroom door and discovers him with his flat face and disturbing haircut, she goes still and resigned.

For some reason, she tells him about her endless money woes.

"I wouldn't worry about it," the killer soothes.

"You don't have to do this," she says, starting to plead for her life.

"This is the best I can do."

Javier Bardem flips a 1958 quarter. By this point in the movie, viewers know that he is offering the woman a fifty-fifty chance to live. What do you do when you realize that living or dying comes down to an endless chain of coin flips?

"No, I ain't gonna call it," she says, staring back at the assassin. She is the first victim to refuse the chance. "The coin don't have no say, it's just you."

Aida's new boyfriend, Alex, seemed like a coin toss that had come up heads. Everything about him was good, except for one problem. He had an unhinged ex-girlfriend who wanted him back. At first, Aida assumed that her frequent encounters with Irma were coincidences. Douglas was a small town, after all. But the number of coincidences added up, and over time Aida realized Alex's ex was following her. Their encounters became run-ins during which Irma made public scenes. She accused Aida of stealing Alex and threatened to report her to the Border Patrol. Aida tried to ignore her, playing and replaying Luz's constant warning to keep quiet and stay out of trouble.

Except for that, Alex made Aida happy. When Jack decided to sell Movies 'n' More, Alex bought the place for five thousand dollars. He treated Aida better than any man she'd known, and she never asked what he did in the store's back room. One of her uncles—a retired Douglas police officer—warned her that Alex received drug shipments from Mexican cartels, but she defended him.

One June day in 2008, a Border Patrol agent ambled up while Alex, Aida, and Gabriel waited in line at a car wash. Alex was a U.S. citizen, and so was Gabriel, but the agent looked long and skeptically at Aida's expired Douglas High School ID. Then he retreated to his car. Standing on the oil-stained asphalt, Aida pictured what would come next—the handcuffs, the slow ride through Douglas, the deportation to Mexico. She thought about losing Gabriel and living with Jennifer in some run-down Mexican shack. When the agent came back, she was shaking with fear.

"I'm going to let you go this time because of your U.S. citizen son," he informed her, handing back the old ID. "But you should know that we've been getting calls about you."

Aida glared at Alex. She knew who had been making the calls.

Over time, Irma's ambushes had grown more menacing. One morning, Gabriel and Aida had been crossing a street when Irma careened around the corner in her car. Aida grabbed Gabriel and jumped back to the curb just before the woman sped by. Now it seemed that Irma had followed through on her threat to call the Border Patrol.

A few weeks after that, Aida woke up to a beautiful midsummer morning. Small creatures stirred in the scrubby lot outside her window. The animal world was awake and taking advantage of the temperate hiatus before July brought down its hundred-degree hammer. Aida followed the animals' example.

Still wearing thin gray pajamas and blue slippers, she drove to La Unica for pastries. She paid for *pan dulce* with a fistful of coins and crumpled bills. Butter stains seeped through the paper bag as she returned home. Her mind drifted toward thoughts of coffee and the company of her mother. She almost didn't react in time when a car cut in front of her and squealed to a stop. With streets as broad and empty as Douglas's on a summer morning, the near accident could only have been intentional. It was Irma, glaring at Aida in her rearview mirror, fouling a perfect morning with sulfurous rage.

Weeks of repressed fury exploded in Aida.

"Enough!" she yelled. In a single unthinking instant, Aida floored the gas, slamming into Irma's car. The next second, both women were out on the street.

"You fucking hit me!" Irma screamed.

"Why are you following me?" Aida screamed back.

"Bitch!"

"Stay away from my son."

"Fuck you," Irma spat.

It was too much. Aida's fist plowed into Irma's nose. Then her conscious brain caught up.

"Shit," Aida moaned.

Irma beamed. She had gotten exactly what she wanted.

AIDA FLED FIVE blocks to Movies 'n' More and called her mom. She searched the street for signs of Border Patrol. The sun-bleached face of Milla Jovovich as Alice in *Resident Evil* stared out the window with her. She knew agents who came in to rent videos. She could picture their records in the store computer and hoped that whoever responded to the call would be sympathetic.

Luz barreled in with Gabriel and Aida's youngest siblings, Jazmin and Emiliano. "What were you thinking?" she demanded. A pair of Douglas police officers, led by Irma, arrived next. At first, it was almost funny. Aida's slept-on hair bounced wildly as she detailed Irma's behavior. The officers struggled to keep straight faces. They demanded calm, trying to assess the gravity of the two women's feud. There was a condescending edge to their response.

"She's not even legal," Irma said. "Check her papers."

On cue, two green-and-white Border Patrol trucks pulled up outside. Irma hadn't called them. They had probably been listening to the police scanner, bored and looking for something to do. Humor bled from the room, and—at that same moment—Cynthia barged in through the back door.

Like a cartoon character pedaling air after running off a cliff, Cynthia knew instantly that she shouldn't be in that spot.

Three agents checked everyone's IDs and chattered on the radio. The Douglas police officers faded to the background, Aida and Irma's fight forgotten. Gabriel watched from his grandmother's arms as men handcuffed his mother and aunt and told them to stand still off to the side. Jack arrived next. He had sponsored Luz's application for residency and shuffled in, coughing, wheezing, and carrying her paperwork.

An agent glanced at Luz's forms and seemed relieved not to have to detain her. This way, there'd be someone left behind to take care of the crying children. The tense circle broke up, and the agents led Aida and Cynthia to a waiting truck. The last thing Aida saw before the steel door slammed on her was Gabriel cantilevering out of Luz's arms, screaming and craning to reach his mother.

Stainless steel and scorching, the truck interior felt like a microwave and smelled faintly of sweat. It lurched forward, and Movies 'n' More disappeared out the wire-mesh window.

"I'm sorry. I'm so sorry," Aida said to Cynthia. "You shouldn't be here. This is my fault."

Cynthia said nothing, swaying with the rough ride. The two sisters went quiet until the truck pulled into the Border Patrol station outside town.

LUZ RAN ACROSS the street from Movies 'n' More to the Mexican consulate. Her sobbing blending with Gabriel's howling, Luz tried to explain the situation. The mother and child's agony was a sight almost beyond bearing, but the consular official had seen it many times before. There was little he could do, he reported. But Luz's eyes blazed with urgency. The official considered the case again.

"Look," he concluded. "With a U.S. citizen son and so many years living in the U.S. and your residency application under way, it's possible that your daughters have paths to legal status."

Luz swept away her tears and kissed Gabriel's forehead.

"The most important thing, though," the official continued, "is that they should not sign anything until they talk with a lawyer."

Luz was already dialing her phone, but the man said it again. "It's critical that they don't sign away their right to a hearing."

AGENTS INTERVIEWED AIDA and Cynthia in the glare outside the station. They didn't even go inside. A vast parking lot encircled them. The compound was twenty-nine acres and almost entirely filled with rows of 4x4s, squad cars, vans, mobile camera towers, and trucks. Slag mountains, remains of the old smelter, sprawled in the east. One ruin atop another.

Aida pleaded with the agents to let Cynthia go. She was weeks away from finishing her last high school requirements. Aida explained that she would be the first person in their family to graduate from high school.

"It was all my fault," she begged. "Please don't make her pay for my mistake."

Aida and Cynthia's speech and bearing took the agents by surprise. "You guys are so American—why are we even deporting you?" one said, joking.

"Well, don't," Aida answered. She looked at the agent as if he were the only worthy person in the world.

"I'm sorry, we have to."

"But look," another agent added, "we can cut you a break." He handed

Aida and Cynthia a form. "Sign this, and you'll be out of here in a few hours. If you don't sign, you're going to be here a long time."

Cynthia's phone vibrated in her pocket, and she moved to pull it out.

The agent moved faster. "Not allowed," he said. He held out his hand for the phone and shut it off.

Luz called Cynthia's voice mail over and over again. Her message was simple: "Whatever you do, *mija*, don't sign anything until Jack gets there."

Even with the declining number of border crossings, Douglas sector agents processed hundreds of migrants some days. There was only so much cell space, even in what was touted as the country's largest Border Patrol station. Encouraging detainees to waive their right to an immigration hearing was the easiest way to keep the system moving. Sometimes agents gave out forms with the "Voluntary Return" box pre-checked.

"Go ahead and sign," one of the agents said, encouraging the sisters. If they signed, he explained, they'd be dropped off in Agua Prieta right away.

"You can come right back," he said, joking. If not, they could spend days in detention. "It won't affect you at all," he promised.

WHEN AIDA AND CYNTHIA finally heard their mother's message, it was too late.

Aida watched Douglas flicker by outside the steel-mesh window. The truck followed the same route as her first taxi ride in the United States twelve years earlier, only in reverse. They passed the Kmart and their old street on the outskirts of town; the turnoff for their apartment near Sarah Marley Elementary; and the big-box shopping plaza that greeted anyone entering the United States.

Aida realized that she had spent more than half her life in that town and felt a wave of sadness, even though she believed she would be back soon. After the adrenaline of arrest and detention, it was the first contemplative moment she'd had. It didn't last long. She and Cynthia were still in pajamas, and inside the truck's tight confines Aida felt eyes on her chest. Five or six young men had been packed in with the sisters. The men reeked of days in the desert and detention. Their clothes were dirty and torn. Cynthia was already calculating how she'd get back in time to finish school, but Aida tensed. She felt the young, hungry men undressing Cynthia with their eyes and braced to defend her sister.

At the port of entry, a gate opened, and the group stepped into a strip of no-man's-land between two countries. Aida hustled her sister away from the men. Ahead, Mexican officials asked deportees for their nationalities, culling Central Americans and steering Mexicans toward a small building just beyond the customs shed. Volunteers from church groups would provide them with help there, the officials said. They could get burritos, coffee, wound care, and a short phone call.

That's not for us, Aida thought. It's for migrants.

Men from the truck shuffled toward the aid station. They were eager for their first meal in days. Cracker packets handed out in the Border Patrol station cells didn't count. Volunteers would treat their bloody feet and locate pairs of used shoes big enough to fit over the bandages. Most of the men would make calls to relatives in the United States. They would weigh the costs of trying to cross the border once more against returning home to places in Mexico and Central America. Or they'd despair at ever seeing their homes and families in the United States again. The Migrant Resource Center would be a lifeline either way. But Aida and Cynthia didn't stop. They were two young women from Douglas, Arizona. They didn't yet recognize themselves in the word "migrant," or understand how similar the stories of the men and women at the center were to their own. Aida and Jazmin were just temporarily in the wrong country.

AGUA PRIETA'S INDUSTRIAL GROWTH appeared chaotic, but it was nothing compared with the upheaval caused by the Border Patrol's new enforcement strategy. After the latest border wall went up and hundreds of new agents surged into Douglas, fewer migrants made the crossing successfully through Agua Prieta. Stuck without resources to return home or continue on, thwarted migrants accumulated there. When Presidents Bush and Obama began deporting unprecedented numbers of undocumented migrants to Mexican border towns, the situation had gotten worse. Agua Prieta's streets filled with trapped, desperate people. Nobody knew how many people lived in Agua Prieta anymore. Was it 60,000 residents or 200,000?

The main street leading away from the border was familiar to Aida, but different. So many people looked as if they'd come from far away. The few men with the cowboy bearing of native Agua Prietans appeared up to no good. *Coyotes* and drug dealers loitered around the crossing, waiting for prey.

Taxi drivers, street vendors, and Mexican police leered at the pajama-clad sisters. Aida lowered her head and took Cynthia's hand. If she kept her eyes focused on the broken sidewalk, no one would bother her, she decided.

Douglas was only a few yards away, but even the air felt different. Aida had once loved this place. Now it was alien. The smell of steak grilling over mesquite coals and the sight of friendly people didn't register. Instead, she focused on the hot bus exhaust and the whiff of sewer. Aida tried to retreat further into the shell of her clothes, but the thin summer pajamas offered no protection.

The two marched quickly at first, hustling away from the border. They passed pharmacies and dentist offices that catered to U.S. patients and hurried farther south, sticking to busy streets. Cement buildings housed the spatchcock commerce of their childhood: butchers next to body shops, paint stores and hair salons, doctors' offices pressed against beer distributors.

When Aida and Cynthia reached familiar streets near their father's house, they paused. From there, they dragged their feet. Now each shop window attracted their full attention. The stopped to loiter in the coolness emanating from air-conditioned fabric stores. Neither woman had any idea how to explain their return to Raúl. They knew he wouldn't be pleased. They dreaded the bare moment on his doorstep in pajamas and slippers. But part of them knew he'd take their arrival in stride. His unusual past had made him nearly impervious to surprise. Even when he and Aida fought in the weeks to come, she drew courage from knowing that his life history coursed through her veins.

TRAUMA RED

PART TWO

10.

HUNGER IS WORSE

An angel was speaking through a loudspeaker outside Raúl's jail cell. He lifted himself from the floor to get a better look out the window. The twenty-year-old's head thundered with the previous night's drinking, but the angel's voice was sweet. The ideas she expressed were new to Raúl. Yet the man who would one day become Aida's father understood them instantly: the people had a right to land, a right to fight for justice, and a duty to stand up to corrupt politicians. Aida's father was a rawboned *campesino* washed up in the city—a peasant from a family of peasants with no land to farm. He heard a crowd cheer the angel, and he wanted to join them.

Vast pine forests, breathtaking canyons, and extreme inequality marked the Chihuahua of Raúl's childhood. During the nineteenth century, some of North America's most important railroad, mining, livestock, and real estate concerns steadily dispossessed the Sierra's indigenous communities and small-scale *mestizo* ranchers. Many of those communities—including Apaches, Tarahumaras, Pimas, and descendants of the soldiers sent to exterminate them—resisted. Pancho Villa was the most famous offspring of this tradition of agrarian struggle, but he wasn't alone. Small communities across the state waged pitched battles against powerful *hacendados*—large landowners—and their private armies. The Mexican Revolution of 1910 arose, in part, from those battles.

After the revolution, Article 27 of the country's new constitution made the nation the ultimate arbiter of private property. The article authorized agrarian reforms to break up estates. This gave small communities the crucial support they needed to reclaim land they had lost. By the 1930s, agrarian reform had begun to carve small pieces out of the state's large *haciendas*, creating collectively owned but individually farmed communal landholdings called *ejidos*. Nevertheless, agrarian reform was easily corrupted, stalled, and stymied by those with the most power. Peasant claims often took decades to work their way through agrarian reform bureaucracies. Opposition from powerful landowners and their government allies gridlocked reform.

By 1963, when Raúl heard the voice declaring the people's right to land, fierce inequality bisected the state: Three hundred wealthy individuals owned almost twenty million acres of Chihuahua's best agricultural and timber land, while 100,000 peasant *ejidatarios* controlled only eleven million acres. Several hundred thousand landless peasants, like Raúl's family, still waited impatiently for the unsteady progress of petitions commenced long before.

In 1960s Chihuahua, *ejidos* grew up on the edges of vast landholdings, but people like Raúl and his mother scraped out their lives on the edges of the edges. Through Raúl's childhood, the family had moved from *ejido* to *ejido*, begging for a chance to rent enough land for a few pigs and goats. The small plots they secured were never enough to get by on. Eventually, they gave up and moved to the city.

For most of his teenage years, Raúl drifted from odd job to odd job in Nuevo Casas Grandes, population twenty thousand. Through his teens, he had no aspiration beyond writing lost and sorrowful *corridos* and singing them at bars. Young and destitute, native to cantinas and day labor lines, Raúl and his friends made easy prey for the local police commander, Chacón, who bore a long scar running up the length of his face. Chacón's work and life pleasure seemed to consist in circulating through town looking for "delinquents" and "punks" to imprison. With waves of peasants pushed out of the surrounding countryside, Nuevo Casas Grandes held no shortage of young men for Chacón to arrest. Jailing and fining them provided much of his income. But Chacón's victims, some of whom were Raúl's friends, didn't always make it to jail. Sometimes, when a young man mouthed off a bit too much, he ended up splayed on the side of a road, "shot in the act of escaping."

The injustice of Chacón's brand of law, mixed with the angel's words, had a powerful effect on Raúl. For the first time in his life, he felt a glimmer of purpose: he would find the angel, learn how to fight for land, and claim a piece of ground for his family.

By the time Raúl paid his fine for public drunkenness and left jail, demonstrators were trickling away from the protest. He looked around the public square for the origin of the radical speech. She wasn't hard to find: light hair, with a flower tucked behind her ear, she was packing up her loudspeaker. His glimmer of purpose gleamed a bit brighter when he saw her. They exchanged names, and then Bertha Prieto changed the course of Raúl's life forever by inviting him to a clandestine reading group for working-class youth.

The reading group gave Raúl the only formal education he'd received since the few years of primary school he completed while moving from *ejido* to *ejido*. Battling his way through pamphlets and books took hours at first. He worked slowly and deliberately, sounding out words and wrestling with unfamiliar concepts, asking his new comrades for help when he needed it. The group was one of several established across the state by Arturo Gámiz, a charismatic young teacher working to encourage a new kind of education for the youth of Chihuahua. Only a few years older than Raúl, Gámiz had fought his way from a small ranch in Durango state to an elite public high school in Mexico City, then to a job teaching primary school in

Chihuahua. The reading group drew Raúl out of cantinas and away from his dissolute friends.

Some of the group's members came from merchant or ranching families and had completed more formal education. Others were just like Raúl, cracked hands and peasant feet barely concealed by city clothes. Gámiz insisted that they learn from one another's experiences and strengths, an approach that forged close bonds and a fierce collective spirit.

Supported by his new comrades, Raúl battled through *La guerra de guerrillas* by Che, the letters of Fidel Castro, and *El comité regional clandestino actúa* by Fiodorov. Each new text exploded in his consciousness, distilling his hereditary contempt for the powerful into blazing certainty. Of the fiction, Gorky moved him most. In *La madre*, he read about Pavel Vlasov, a young man raised by a destitute mother. At a young age, Pavel begins to imitate his absent father, drunken and lost, until one day he discovers revolutionary books. In their pages, Pavel discerns his life's purpose: unbending struggle for a new, better world. Raúl read the book the way he might study a mirror. In reading about Pavel, he found himself.

Raúl joined Bertha's organization, the General Union of Mexican Peasants and Workers (UGOCM). The UGOCM was distinctly reformist, working within the political system. It pressured the government to fulfill its legal commitment to agrarian reform—hardly a revolutionary demand. But a landowner-backed governor and former army general, Práxedes Giner Durán, ran Chihuahua in the 1960s. In Giner Durán's state, even talk of moderate reform was dangerous.

When rallies, legal petitions, and sit-ins failed to move officials, Raúl's comrades embarked on one of the most hallowed practices of nonviolent agrarian mobilization in Mexico—land occupation. After traveling through the night in buses and trucks, an assembly of men, women, and children, sometimes as many as two hundred, would pull up at a piece of uncultivated land owned by one of the state's *hacendados*. Someone cut the fence, and a work army of country folk crossed the line carrying banners and hoes. By lunchtime, they would have erected crude shelters and begun to sow symbolic crops. No one expected the occupation to last. It was a way to dramatize the failure of Mexico's agrarian reform. By that night, or the next night, the army would arrive to begin the beating and burning.

In January 1964, Raúl participated in three of a wave of occupations organized by the UGOCM. Mexican military violently evicted all of them. Seven UGOCM activists died and hundreds more were imprisoned, including the teacher Arturo Gámiz.

RAÚL PARTICIPATED IN his third and last land occupation during one of the Sierra's *fríos negros*, black colds. Freezing fog cracked the pasture grass, and Raúl struggled to erect canvas tarp shacks to protect against the cold. Mexican soldiers seized the property's single well, cut the UGOCM's access to water, circled the plot of land, and waited.

Days passed. Raging thirst drove even the bitter cold from occupiers' minds. Parents gave their children potatoes to suck for moisture, but the group was determined to hold out until agrarian reform functionaries agreed to review their petition.

On the fourth day, the property's owner induced officials to order immediate eviction.

Men and women, their lips bleeding from dehydration and cold, argued over what to do next. Eventually, the meeting broke and they filed out singing. Raúl's comrades walked to the property gate, where the men formed ranks, arm in arm. Occupiers and soldiers stared at each other across the cut fence. Then, in tight formation, the soldiers moved on them.

No one had expected the soldiers to advance with bared bayonets, but they did. The jabs and slices reduced the organizers' formation to a shamble. Other soldiers started to drag the men away, but the organization's women surrounded them. For a moment, the balance tipped as the women refused to let the soldiers pass. A confused pause hung over the field until the army plowed through.

Soldiers sack-hurled men identified as leaders onto trucks, injured or not. All others, including Raúl, were shoved onto the vehicles they had come in. The army carted them back to Nuevo Casas Grandes, where Raúl helped take lacerated and beaten comrades to the hospital. Then he returned to the plaza to demand information about the detained leaders.

An anxious crowd milled around the public square. Rumors buzzed through the group as everyone waited for someone to tell them what would happen next. A year had passed since Raúl first heard Bertha's voice in that same plaza. Now it was Bertha who turned to Raúl and asked if he would speak. Inflamed by the violent treatment of his friends, inspired by his studies, and fixing his gaze on Bertha, he began.

In his rough peasant voice, inflected by the formal sound of Marxist literature, Raúl didn't stop at denouncing military repression. He explained the whole political economy of authoritarian Mexico from Spanish conquest to postrevolutionary crony capitalism. The effect was electric.

He rose toward a grand finale: "It is not right that thirty-six million Mexicans live like this. We have a right to a modest life of justice, work, and well-being." He'd stolen the last line from Fidel Castro, but the crowd roared. News of Raúl's speech passed from person to person across Chihuahua, a currency that gave them hope. Eventually, it would reach the ears of the teacher Arturo Gámiz as he sat in his prison cell in the late spring of 1964.

TO ALL APPEARANCES, Mexico was a democracy. It had experienced thirty years of presidential transitions uninterrupted by coups or generals. Elections unfolded regularly and efficiently, complete with opposition candidates. If the winners always came from one party—the Insitutional Revolutionary Party (PRI)—it was, to many people's way of thinking, a sign of that party's appeal, not of electoral fraud. As a general rule, the PRI system avoided outright repression in favor of patronage and co-optation. The army, rural police, and political bosses were happy to assassinate and torture opponents when they deemed it necessary, but they preferred to purchase loyalty and peace.

Under PRI rule, Mexico had experienced twenty-four years of unprecedented economic growth and rapid industrialization. Cities swelled with a burgeoning working class, an emerging middle class, and all the material trappings of modern life. Economists called this postwar boom "the Mexican miracle," but the country's modernization had sharpened inequality.

The countryside felt this contradiction most. Not only hadn't the benefits of modernization reached rural Mexico, but the country's economic development and trade policies taxed farmers to pay for urban progress. Unable to make a living in agriculture, millions of rural Mexicans poured into shantytowns exploding on the edges of prosperous cities. Those who remained in the countryside toiled even harder to survive.

Agrarian struggles intensified as contrasts between the promises of progress and conditions in the countryside sharpened. Agrarian struggle had never been without risks, but the number of peasant land reform petitioners killed by military forces and landowners' hired gunmen soared in the early 1960s. These forces frequently ambushed agrarian leaders, assassinating them when they traveled on rural roads. Sometimes government forces detained and tortured the leaders of peasant land reform before turning them over to landowners' hired guns.

It wasn't just leaders who felt the impact of repression. During March and April 1963, for example, the army retaliated against land reform petitioners by deploying troops and armored cars to level the towns of San Luis Acatlán, La Gusanera, La Barra, Papanaca, and Contepec de los Costales in the state of Guerrero. In the early 1960s, the facade of Mexico's apparent democracy began to crumble. Mexicans were waking up to the fact that they lived under a dictatorship. It was a rude awakening.

Gámiz, jailed for participating in legal protests, concluded that if the government treated its people like this, the people must take up arms. After supporters secured his release, he swore that he'd never return to prison. Nor would he ever file another futile land reform petition. Instead, he set out for the mountains, where he planned to meet his longtime friend and fellow collaborator, Salomón Gaytán, to plan a revolution.

MEMBERS OF the Gaytán family grew up resisting powerful men. José Ibarra, ruler of vast extensions of rich timber and grazing land, was one such man, and he was the Gaytán clan's nemesis. Ibarra treated large swaths of the region and its people as his personal fiefdom, even exerting the medieval practice of *derecho de pernada*—the right to claim any woman in his domain for sex. When Ibarra pursued a woman from the Gaytán family, retaliation came swiftly: In May 1964, Salomón Gaytán and Antonio Scobell Gaytán ambushed José Ibarra's brother, Florentino. In addition to helping engineer the Ibarras' despotic control over land and people, Florentino had ordered a popular land reform organizer assassinated several years earlier. The Gaytáns filled him with bullets.

Army and rural police stormed through *ejidos* and the mountain backcountry, harassing and torturing peasant families in a scorched-earth search for the killer. By the time Gámiz reunited with the Gaytáns, they all understood that they would probably die fighting. And so they prepared to die fighting for change. High in the mountains of Chihuahua, they began to assemble Mexico's first modern revolutionary force, the Grupo Popular Guerrillero, the Popular Guerrilla Group (GPG). When Raúl received the invitation to join, he returned home, said goodbye to his mother, and then found Bertha to tell her the news.

"Are you sure about this?" she asked.

"It's my obligation," Raúl answered in his most formal voice. "I need to fight for more than just land for myself. I need to fight to change the whole system for everyone."

HIKING TO the GPG's first camp took two days. Twelve recruits ascended the mountains, staying off main roads and eating deer they shot on the way. Sympathetic *ejidatarios* gave them shelter, hopeful that the abuses of Ibarra's men would be brought to an end. One village under Ibarra's tyrannical rule had lost its main well when Ibarra's men claimed it exclusively to water his cattle. The one-room schoolhouse in another village had been turned into a stable for Ibarra's livestock.

Over the next year, the GPG's ranks fluctuated between fifteen and seven. Many city recruits could not stand the endless marches across rugged terrain, nights spent in caves, or the frost on their eyebrows when they woke up. They moved constantly, never camping in the same place more than two nights. Rural police, torturing their way through the municipality's ranches and farms, were never far behind. But half lost in the pine forests and ravines of Chihuahua, chased by police and hunger both, Raúl experienced an intensity of friendship he would never know again. The wretched conditions bonded the men.

One night, so hungry he couldn't see straight, Raúl watched a comrade take a spoonful of broth. Blinking, he asked the cook, "Did you add rice?"

"We are out of rice," the cook replied.

"So what's this?"

The men stared at the spoon.

"I guess they're maggots," the cook declared. "But who cares—hunger is worse." The men laughed, picked maggots out of the pot, and continued their meal. Things could have been worse. The forest was still around them. They slept deep in its shadows.

MEANWHILE, THE REGION'S rural police intensified their search for the GPG. They tore through remote villages and ranches, exacting reprisals and demanding information about Gámiz and the Gaytáns. Finally, they captured, tortured, and strung up one of the Gaytáns' nephews, a boy of ten. The note they pinned to his dangling body was a message for the GPG: "We're coming for you."

Raúl's small band decided it was time to act. They planned to surround the Rural Police headquarters at the Ibarra estate and use a Molotov cocktail to force its occupants out into the open. They hoped for the element of surprise, and they would need it: their complete arsenal consisted of a World War II–era infantry carbine, two hunting rifles, and three .30-30s that might have seen action during the 1910 revolution.

Of course, nothing went according to plan—least of all the element of surprise. Barking dogs woke the detachment before the GPG was in place. Police troops streamed out, confused but armed and shooting. Miraculously, the Molotov cocktail found its way into the wooden building, though, and all six rebels managed to find cover and return fire. The standoff lasted thirty minutes as a blaze spread behind the police.

Raúl yelled into the glowing night, "You're brave when you're up against defenseless peasants, women, and children. Let's see your bravery now!"

Just before the roof caved in, the post's five *rurales* and the region's infamous commandant surrendered. Arturo Gámiz, once opposed to violent revolution, ordered the men to form a firing squad.

"It doesn't make sense to kill them," Raúl argued.

"That's the whole plan—it's why we're here."

Raúl saw a bigger picture. "The newspapers are already calling us assassins, cattle thieves, and criminals."

"Fine," Gámiz said, shooting the commandant in the leg and stalking away.

When Raúl learned how Chihuahua's newspapers reported the attack, he was pleased to hear that the usual talk of assassins, cattle thieves, and criminals was notably absent. Instead, they commended Arturo Gámiz for his act of mercy.

AFTER THE SKIRMISH, Gámiz laid out a challenge for the GPG. In the summer of 1965, the group would make its way to the outskirts of Mexico City, where sympathetic ex-soldiers would teach them to behave like a real fighting force. Then they'd strike. Years of inequality and authoritarian rule had primed Mexico for a new revolution, Gámiz argued. With a little luck, all it would take to unleash that energy was one spectacular public action.

The training went well, and that fall, the men agreed they were ready. The young guerrillas left Mexico City and returned to the North. Their objective was an army barrack protecting the town of Madera, Chihuahua. It was a strategic spot guarding a railroad yard and stockpiled with weapons. But more than that, Madera served as a commercial and transportation hub for the state's vast timber estates. A powerful forestry company owned the building itself. This epitomized the oppressive partnership between the PRI and wealthy landowners. It was more than a barracks; it was an emblem of the David-and-Goliath struggle for land in Mexico. Gámiz's men chose a symbolic date for the attack as well. They would launch their revolution on September 16, Mexican Independence Day.

11

MADERA

THAT FALL, THE MOUNTAIN RAINS were relentless. As the day approached, Arturo Gámiz divided his force of about twenty men into three groups. Salvador Gaytán and another brother set off on foot to retrieve the group's new automatic weapons from a cache in the mountains. Four university student recruits made their way into Madera, charged with scouting the battlefield and returning with intelligence. The rest of the group, including Raúl, camped in the mountains outside town.

Raúl kept his mind focused on thoughts of revolution to distract himself from the physical discomfort. September 16 came and went as the rains continued. Neither the scouts nor the two men bringing better weapons arrived. Gámiz postponed the attack, and Raúl settled in for more waiting.

A train left Madera every Tuesday and Thursday, and one of the GPG had heard rumors that most of the soldiers in the barracks would leave for Ciudad Juárez on that Tuesday's run. Only a skeleton force of two platoons, twenty-two soldiers, would remain at the base. Come what may, Gámiz decided, the GPG would attack on Wednesday.

Tuesday brought no news of Salvador, his nephew, the automatic weapons, or the university students sent to scout Madera. The garrison's soldiers did not appear to have boarded the train for Ciudad Juárez. The plan had fallen apart, but Gámiz was out of patience.

"Tomorrow is the day," he told the twelve assembled men. Really they were boys—young schoolteachers, students, and peasants like Raúl. Pablo Gómez, a medical doctor, was the only person in the squad over twenty-five. At thirty-nine, Gómez had worked within the Mexican political system for years before taking up arms. He had run unsuccessfully for congress and battled bureaucrats and landowners for legal land reform. Under the slick wet pine trees that afternoon, he counseled delay.

"Are you afraid?" Gámiz snapped. "If anyone is afraid, he can stay behind." Gámiz was poised to act, to press the trigger that he believed would unleash mass popular uprising against the government.

"It's not that, Arturo."

"Well, good. Tomorrow is the day. If we win, great; if we lose, *ni modo*."

Gámiz's "*ni modo*" hung over Raúl. No English translation could do justice to the phrase, but its meaning was intuitive to Raúl. *Ni modo* summed up his feelings precisely: this is bad, but we are already as good as dead, so all we can do is accept that fate and soldier on.

The doctor stopped arguing, took out a pencil and a page from a school notebook, and sat down to plan the attack.

WITH SEVEN THOUSAND inhabitants, Madera was surrounded by the remains of two of the largest private estates in Mexico. The U.S. copper-mining baron William C. Greene had established one of them in 1906. The newspaper titan William Randolph Hearst had developed the second. Between them, the two estates encompassed more than two million acres of timber and some of the best agricultural land in Chihuahua. For decades, they had supplied lumber and provisions for, among other ventures, the mines that fed Phelps Dodge's Douglas smelter.

Peasants had begun soliciting the redistribution of Greene's and Hearst's properties in 1917. In the 1930s, President Lázaro Cárdenas, Mexico's foremost champion of agrarian reform, tried to satisfy their legal demands. Gunmen paid by estate managers killed the federal agents sent to enact his decree. In the 1940s and 1950s, politically connected Mexican investors took over the two properties, and peasants' legal appeals stalled.

The town of Madera had been founded to serve as a company town for Greene's Sierra Madre Land and Lumber Company. In 1965, Greene was long gone, but the town was still a commercial hub for the region, defended by the GPG's objective: a two-story army barracks alongside the railroad yard. The barracks made a tempting target. If most of the Madera garrison had, in fact, shipped out, a large cache of weapons would be there for the taking. All of Raúl's comrades knew that the Cuban revolution had begun with a bold and lopsided attack on a military barracks just twelve years earlier. They also knew that the attack on the Moncada Barracks in Cuba ended with most of the rebels dead and Fidel Castro in prison, but someone had to start the revolution.

Raúl contemplated the GPG's current arsenal. Their thirteen weapons included a small collection of military carbines—.30-06s and M1s—a single-barrel shotgun, and several hunting rifles. Beyond that, they had Molotov cocktails, assorted pistols, a few sticks of dynamite, and homemade grenades of dubious manufacture. The modern carbines aside, they were armed with relics and antiques. If, as it seemed, the Madera garrison hadn't left for Ciudad Juárez as planned, the GPG would need more than history on its side to succeed against ten platoons of well-equipped soldiers.

Ni modo, Raúl thought. Hadn't Father Miguel Hidalgo launched the war for Mexican independence with nothing more than a mob of Indians armed with rocks and sticks on September 16, 1810?

"Someone has to start this revolution," he said out loud.

AT 5:45 IN THE MORNING of Thursday, September 23, 1965, precisely following the plan sketched out on paper the day before, a GPG rebel fired one shot at the barracks' main door. "Surrender! There's no hope for you!" he yelled exactly according to script.

From there, everything went as badly as possible.

Just after the first shot, the headlight of a locomotive parked on the tracks switched on, blinding Arturo Gámiz, Salomón Gaytán, and two others. A bullet hit Salomón as his arm reared back to throw a grenade. Salomón died before he hit the ground. The grenade exploded in his still-warm hand, killing Arturo Gámiz standing next to him.

They were mere seconds into the attack.

Soldiers poured out of the barracks. Black clouds of smoke billowed out behind them. Raúl thought that was a good sign, but when he heard the sound of men dying around him, he guessed they weren't from the other side. Taking cover behind the roundhouse and then behind a telegraph pole, Raúl fired his .30-06 for an hour and a half before he knew, definitely, that the battle was lost. Soldiers with a heavy machine gun had circled behind the GPG. Pinned down in both directions, Raúl waited to hear someone shout the code word, *Águila*, to signal retreat. He wondered if there was any-one left to give the order.

From his vantage, Raúl saw the outcome of the battle. Most of the men he'd endured cold and snow with, studied Marx with, breathed vaporous shapes into the mountain winters with—men he'd laughed with as they picked maggots from their soup—lay twisted in unnatural positions around him.

A wailing cry pierced the smoke and confusion.

"*Águila*. I heard it—let's get out of here," Raúl yelled. He could see only one other rebel from his position.

"No—that's just a dying soldier screaming. We stay and fight!" the man replied.

Raúl felt an exploding needlework of shrapnel in his thigh. A bullet shattered a spare rifle magazine he had stuffed into his pocket. The maga-zine stopped the bullet from hitting his femoral artery, but dozens of shell fragments drilled deep into his thigh.

"I think it's just us two left," Raúl called, feeling pain shear up and down his leg. As he spoke those words, a third rebel careened by and disap-peared into the smoke. Soldiers inched forward toward Raúl.

"Cover me," Raúl's comrade yelled, sprinting across the railroad yard. Raúl fired his .30-06 until the man reached the trees. Then Raúl forced him-self to his feet and ran after, oblivious to the pain.

He hit a cornfield, flailing through the stalks. Burnt-yellow plants closed behind him as he ran on. The cornfield spat him out into an open lot, and he could see the logging road into the mountains. Army vehicles clogged it, pouring upward, chasing survivors and deploying roadblocks. Raúl rolled into a muddy ditch and waited for them to pass.

His leg began to go numb, and Raúl willed himself onto his feet again. He made it at last to the group's rendezvous site at an apple orchard outside of town. No one was there to greet him, and no one arrived as he waited.

Raúl staggered blindly into the mountains, moving through forests and fields, avoiding roads. He lost track of the days. Leg throbbing, he had no food and drank ravenously from streams. On what might have been the fifth day of his flight, Raúl followed the sound of barking dogs to a cluster of houses. Its occupants might turn him in, but *ni modo*. He knew that he would die soon if he didn't find food and shelter. It took almost everything he had left to crawl through the brush, looking for a place to hide his rifle.

A boy stood over him. Raúl was an apparition caked in mud and blood, his clothes shredded, shoes barely on his feet, frantically shoveling pine duff over a rifle. Terrified, the boy bolted.

A group of gnarled *ejidatarios* rode out of the village to find him in the forest. Raúl tried to explain who he was and where he was coming from. The men already knew. Reports of the attack—and the massive army retaliation against civilians—had spread through the Sierra. They contemplated Raúl in silence. By some imperceptible agreement, they decided he wasn't a threat, and the group relaxed. Someone took cheese and a bottle of milk from a saddlebag and handed them to Raúl. He drank the bottle in one draw, warm milk pouring down the pine needles and stubble on his chin.

The cowboys took Raúl to a house, gave him clothes, and treated his wound. Someone told him that he was at an *ejido* near Presón del Toro, forty kilometers from Madera by road. Raúl had no idea how many off-road kilometers he'd crossed to get there.

Raúl recovered for two days. By the second day, he had enough strength to talk to his saviors in his stiff, formal way about the revolution of the proletariat and the emancipation of the peasantry. The cowboys listened impassively and nodded politely while he finished. When an army patrol passed outside, though, they hid Raúl on a board in the ceiling rafters. Raúl's leg still oozed blood. He could do little more than hobble clumsily around the farmhouse, but he knew that for his rescuers' safety he couldn't stay another night.

Raúl moved through the mountains, looping north toward Nuevo Casas Grandes, sheltered by sympathetic peasants and a network of radical students. An uncle harbored Raúl for a time and filled him in on news about the attack. Eight of his thirteen comrades died at the barracks. Governor Práxedes Giner Durán had ordered their bodies loaded onto a flatbed truck, paraded through Madera in the rain, and dumped in a pile outside the city hall. He refused family members' requests to retrieve their dead, decreeing that soldiers throw the bodies into an unmarked mass grave.

"They were fighting for soil," Giner Durán told his men. "Well, give them what they wanted."

The widow, daughter, and niece of Dr. Pablo Gómez defied the governor's orders, walking stone-faced through a phalanx of soldiers to leave flowers on the grave site. Two days later, five hundred people from across Chihuahua marched to the grave, led by women relatives of the dead.

Raúl took in the news. The GPG had stirred something in Mexico. Even the governor had made a mistake: he had accidentally broken from the official practice of labeling the GPG bandits and cattle thieves. He'd spoken the truth; they were fighting for soil.

IN THE END, the attack did not spark a mass uprising. But in the short run, it swung the pendulum from repression toward co-optation. Hearing news of the attack, President Gustavo Díaz Ordaz immediately decreed that twelve thousand acres be granted to an *ejido* outside Madera. Governor Giner Durán, true to his repressive past, unleashed a wave of violence on the countryside, but even he had to make concessions. Within weeks of the attack, he had approved the redistribution of ninety-six thousand additional acres to create a new *ejido* in the area.

Decades later, historians would credit the GPG's assault on the Madera barracks with much more than catalyzing land redistribution. It was the first example of Cuban-influenced guerrilla action in Mexico. While it didn't spark a mass uprising, it did inspire groups across the country. In the 1970s, a group of urban guerrillas took the name *Liga Comunista 23 de Septiembre*, the September 23 Communist League, commemorating the date of the action in Madera.

Later still, there would be a novel about Madera by the well-known

Mexican author Carlos Montemayor. There would be anniversary conferences, memorials, retrospectives, and a melodramatic movie. Prominent national magazines would dedicate issues to Madera's legacy. The GPG's
quixotic action helped stir a much larger movement for democracy. After
almost four decades and through many twists and turns, that movement
would eventually end the PRI's single-party rule. But all this lay in the far
distant future for Raúl. First, he would have to survive the year.

12.

EXILE AND BELONGING

MAKING THEIR WAY THROUGH AGUA PRIETA toward Raúl's house, Aida and Cynthia stopped at a chain supermarket to cool off. The refrigerated air in Casa Ley smelled of Mexico: scented laundry soap and a whiff of ripe fruit. They browsed in the makeup section and wandered through aisles of familiar brands. Each interesting consumer item delayed the moment when they washed up, grimy, half naked, and homeless, at their father's door. Aida clacked through racks of clothes. Polyester blouses, cool to the touch. The kinds of anonymous shirts a person might wear to blend in anywhere.

"You know," she said, "some of these shirts don't have security tags."

They shed their pajamas in a changing room, feeling safer at last in real clothes. For the next several blocks, they talked and laughed, confident their exile in Mexico would be short-lived. They debated different ways to cross the border.

At the playground near their father's house, they paused. The steel equipment had aged. Paint flecked off the jungle gym. Years of feet had dug shallow grooves under each swing seat. So much time had passed since they'd stood in that park as girls. Unwelcome teenage memories of the playground came up like ice picks. Aida thought of her year drinking, stealing cars, and fighting on that ground.

Since leaving Mexico, Aida had made a stable place for herself in Douglas, seen it battered apart, fought to make a new place for herself, and then, just when she felt secure again, one stupid argument had wrecked everything. She felt sick. The only unruined part of her life was Gabriel, her beautiful boy. He was so at ease with himself and smart. At four, he could almost read.

Thoughts of Gabriel quickened Aida's heart. Luz would take care of him as well as she could, Aida knew. That was lucky. But Aida didn't know—couldn't guarantee—that Gabriel would be safe without her, alone in the constant chaos of Luz and Jack's double-wide. Nor was she sure that *she* would be all right alone. Without Gabriel, her life was just one bone-cracking punch after another. His presence anchored her to the world. Maybe it was wrong for a mother to depend so entirely on a small child, but those were the facts. Even a short separation made her feel like a satellite spinning out of orbit into the blackness of space.

Luz would not be able to bring him to Agua Prieta. Leaving the country would invalidate her residency application. Besides, as much as it hurt to admit it, Aida didn't want Gabriel in Mexico. Like many people living in the United States, Aida had acquired a deep fear of the country from television news in the past few years. Nightly coverage of Mexico on Arizona channels was a horror show of shootings, decapitated bodies, narco-kingpins, and the unmarked graves of tortured women.

Nothing is going to keep me in this country for long, Aida swore to herself as she and Cynthia approached their father's house.

They knocked on the door. Despite the lack of forewarning, Raúl accepted his daughters' return with characteristic composure. If Aida's past behavior still disappointed him, it didn't show. His partner of several years, on the other hand, made no secret of her displeasure at having to take in someone else's eighteen- and twenty-year-old children. Jennifer already lived with them, unable to find a job in Agua Prieta since her deportation. Now they'd have to feed and house two more people? Raúl busied himself with practical concerns: Where would the girls sleep? Could a job be found for them at a maquiladora, one of the foreign-owned factories that had sprung up in Mexico? Raúl's partner fumed.

"It doesn't matter," Aida said to Cynthia. "I've got a plan. We'll be gone as soon as the weekend comes."

Her plan worked. Maybe too well.

THAT SATURDAY, Cynthia called her boyfriend in Douglas.

"We're going to party in Agua Prieta tonight," she said. "Bring a friend for Aida."

They met at Pachanga's, a nightclub near the border crossing. Jennifer remained at Raúl's house. She had been formally deported, not voluntarily returned. The sisters' understanding of immigration law was weak, pieced together out of rumors and anecdotes, supplemented by half-remembered encounters with Border Patrol, a surprisingly unreliable source. They did know one thing for certain, though: you didn't want to get caught in the United States with a five-year bar in your record. It would be a long time before Jennifer tried to make her way home.

When the collection of bars and clubs just south of the border shut down at 3:00 a.m., Cynthia's boyfriend directed his car into the long line of young Americans weaving through the port of entry after partying in Mexico.

If challenged when their turn came, the sisters would say that they lost their IDs at the club. The United States would soon require passports for people crossing from Mexico, but for the moment immigration officers had enormous discretion. Crowds of drunken revelers staggering north would make the agents impatient and exasperated. Encountering two English-speaking women in the company of U.S. citizens, they would probably just pepper them with detailed questions about Douglas. Where had they attended elementary school? Who were their favorite teachers at Douglas High? What street was Food City on? Aida knew that she and her sister would make convincing U.S. citizens. Cynthia's boyfriend didn't even know that they were undocumented; his reaction wouldn't give anything away.

Dancing at Pachanga's, Aida drank enough to calm her nerves, but not so much that she'd make a mistake under questioning. Cynthia, far more anxious about the plan, availed herself of a few too many one-dollar tequila shots. But Aida could still handle her.

The boyfriend pulled to a stop at the inspection booth and shut off his car. The officer pulled himself away from a computer screen and glanced lazily down at them.

"U.S. citizens?" So bored.

"Yes, sir," they said as he pointed to each one of them. Cynthia perked up enough to chime in with the others.

"IDs?"

The two boys passed their driver's licenses out the window. "I'm sorry, sir," Aida added in perfect English. "We had kind of a rough night and lost our IDs at Pachanga's." He studied her face for a moment, and she rolled her eyes and shook her head—as if scolding herself ironically. The guard barked with laughter.

"All right, go ahead," he said, waving them on.

Cynthia's boyfriend turned the key. The car coughed several times, sputtered, and gave up, stalled dead. They were stuck in a no-man's-land crawling with cameras, hidden microphones, immigration officers, and X-ray units.

"Shit!" Aida said. Her mind went to images of secondary inspection rooms with fluorescent lights and latex-gloved officers. Then she had a more immediate problem.

"Um, sir," she said to the officer glowering down at the stalled car, "I think my sister's going to be sick. Can I . . . ?" She pointed at a garbage can well inside the United States.

"Go on."

Cynthia finished heaving into the barrel, and Aida looked up. They were home. The bright lights of Walmart and the UETA Duty Free store felt like spotlights over a movie opening. She wanted to dance. The immigration officer left his booth and walked toward them. He stopped at the side of the car and spoke.

"Pop the hood, man. I'll give you a hand."

THE DREADED CROSSING was so easy it was almost laughable. For the whole next week, Aida couldn't stop shaking her head. All her adult life the border had weighed on her. Even during her most carefree moments, its walls, fences, agents, and lights bristled on the edge of her peripheral vision. It was a constant physical reminder that no matter how at home she felt in the United States or how much she contributed—working, raising Gabriel, paying taxes—she was still excluded from full belonging. Like a tree gnarling around a fence post, she'd grown up twisted by the border into an irreconcilable position—fully a part of the Douglas community and yet alien to it.

Now, for the first time, Aida felt what it was like to be an unencumbered citizen, moving effortlessly from one country to another. Until that week, she hadn't realized how much she wanted that inkling of normalcy, or how good it would feel. The immigration officer, waving her on, had recognized her as a whole person. For that instant, she wasn't the jittery little girl neighbor ladies took pity on and fed because they knew she needed to get away from Saul. She wasn't the receptacle for anyone's "worthless bitch" remarks. No "go ahead, call the police, and see who gets in trouble." She wasn't the pregnant sixteen-year-old nurses shook their heads at, not even making the effort to do it behind her back. She was someone who didn't have to efface herself. She was Aida, coolheaded and capable of slipping between nations as if the world were her borderless plaything.

CYNTHIA RETURNED TO finish high school, and Aida settled back into the rhythm of shelving videos and entertaining children while living in Jack's trailer. In less than a week, life inside the double-wide returned to normal.

The first Saturday after returning home, a cousin invited them to celebrate his birthday at Pachanga's. Another cousin promised to walk through the port of entry with them. Aida didn't think twice about not going.

They walked across the border. This was going to be a wild night—better not to drive. A few hundred yards south of the crossing, Agua Prieta's Saturday-night pageant of cruising automobiles inched around the blocks of nightclubs. Bumping music, laughter, and the clink of bottles beckoned. Pachanga's, their destination, sat two blocks past the border, surrounded by bars, a strip club, a shady hotel, and the Mexican customs impound yard.

Pachanga's facade, with its slapped-on onion dome, offered a cut-rate imitation of the arabesque style prized by *narcos* in the 1990s. "*One Thousand*

and One Nights style" had come to symbolize the gaudy aesthetic of narco-culture: life is to be enjoyed immediately and wildly in the face of inevitable violent death.

Luis Pericles Drabos, a popular Greek Mexican former mayor of Agua Prieta, was said to own Pachanga's along with other bars, strip clubs, a liquor store, and a seedy hotel in town. Parents on both sides of the border told their children to stay away from the place. This just made it more attractive. Douglas High School students lined up outside to be frisked before entering. Affluent Mexican teens queued beside them. Soldiers from Fort Huachuca in Arizona flocked here, too, dancing and drinking next to cartel *sicarios*.

Any anxiety Aida felt about the border lifted when she stepped inside. Reggaeton pounded into her chest and a wing of cousins enveloped her. Her feet didn't touch the floor; she was carried away.

The club was a black-lit frenzy, all elbows and glistening necks, all loud celebrations of dancing and sex. An old feeling of freedom surged into Aida. She became liquid, inseparable from the pulse and throng.

At some point, the music lurched to a stop, and the DJ announced a singing competition. The birthday boy chose a sentimental drunken *ranchera* and belted out the verses. Aida and her cousins came in at the chorus. They won.

Their prize was a bottle of tequila and a bucket of beer chasers. By the time the club spat them out onto the street, the bottle was empty, and the bucket had been refilled and emptied several times. Aida was not prepared for the decompression. The stillness outside Pachanga's plowed into her. Inside, where she was braced by music and lights and friends, the world's riotous spinning felt rapturous. Outside, she was a vomitous, staggering drunk.

Somehow Cynthia and her cousin got Aida to the border-crossing entrance. They could see that she couldn't make the rest of the way on foot, much less stand in front of an officer and answer questions. They considered their options and decided to leave Aida propped against a wall. They would cross and then return with a car. Concentrating as hard as she could, Aida watched her sister and cousin disappear into the border crossing. When they were gone, she slumped to the ground and clung to the gyrating sidewalk.

· · ·

AIDA'S SURROUNDINGS CAME into view, sunlight punching through cheap curtains.

"I am not supposed to be *here*," she said when she realized where she was. Confusion turned into anger. Jennifer stood over her, laughing and offering a glass of water. Aida saw the familiar cinder block and wood paneling of her father's house.

"I was out last night with friends," Jennifer said, her voice grating in Aida's head. Driving home, she had seen a shape lying in the street that looked like her sister. The resemblance had been strong enough that she made her friends stop. They managed to drag Aida into the car and bring her back to Raúl's.

"But I'm not *supposed* to be here; they were coming back for me."

"You were lying in the street."

Aida's situation sank in. She would have to wait until the next weekend to cross the border again. She would miss work in Douglas, and Gabriel would be alone with Luz.

She felt agitated getting out of bed. In the kitchen, Raúl's partner glared at her when she took an apple from a bowl on the counter. Aida hated herself with a shocking clarity. What a fucking *idiot*.

When Aida called home, Luz, grumpy, put Gabriel on the line.

"Mom, can you please come home?" The boy sounded small and abandoned.

Aida hung up. The room had begun to revolve again, only now she was sober. She felt as if she were standing on the edge of an unbelievably high tower, the air thin and dizzy. Her heart pounded, and burning crackled from her sternum to her fingertips. A terrible awareness hit her with a smack: I'm having a heart attack. Blackness clouded the edge of her vision.

Frightened, she clattered down the metal stairs of Raúl's house into the tight gangway. The pressure buzzed in her temples and strangled her breath. She needed to escape this place—to return home immediately, take Gabriel in her arms, and swear to him that she would never ever leave again. She insisted that a friend of Jennifer's drive her to the border.

"No way. It's Sunday afternoon. You can't cross now," he said. The friend's mother worked at the port of entry. He understood its rhythms and weak points, but Aida was gasping for air now. Her words came out in choking gulps.

"I can't wait a week. I need to be home now."

Jennifer and her friend followed as Aida ran to the port of entry. Outside the crossing, the friend made a final attempt to dissuade her, but she cannoned through the sliding doors, not hearing words.

THE OFFICER WAVED her forward. He made the same gesture a thousand times a day, slouched in his uncomfortable steel chair. His body armor was sweaty, and the utility belt poked awkwardly into his waist when seated.

"U.S. citizen?"

All the adrenaline that had carried her across town vanished. Lacking any plausible explanation for her presence, she stood there blank and ashamed. She wanted to run and knew it was too late. The lead-faced officer registered her wavering state as something he'd seen before: the reaction of a drug mule who knew the jig was up.

"U.S. citizen," she said, too late and without conviction.

In a side room that everyone in Douglas and Agua Prieta knew existed and hoped to never see, they told her to spread her legs. The female officer's latex-gloved groping revealed nothing, of course, so Aida sat. From time to time, an officer came in and threw out a few questions.

"If you made a mistake, it's better to just come clean now," they said to encourage her. "Just tell us what's going on; maybe we can help."

One officer just stared at her as if he were trying to read an invisible bar code printed on her forehead. Mostly they just joked with her, promising to clear all this up as soon as possible. The room had no windows or clock, and she lost track of time.

Suddenly officers with purpose and serious expressions appeared, carrying handcuffs and no jokes. The intimate entanglements of life in a border security company town had snagged her again. One of Luz's older cousins, a teetering obese man whom Aida called "uncle," worked for port of entry security. He'd seen Aida led off for questioning and, wrestling with his conscience, finally decided that he had to tell someone she wasn't a citizen.

After the uncle's report, deportation bureaucracy snapped into place. New officers swept her away and others pressed her fingers onto a digital pad.

"Let me ask you again—are you a U.S. citizen?"

"No, sir, I'm not."

Aida explained that she'd lived in the United States almost her whole life. She had long ties to Douglas, and a son. Questions poured out of her mouth at every stage. Would they let her call her mother? Could she call the consulate? Could she have a lawyer? She repeated her request several times. Each question fell into a canyon of silence and routine. Officers who, an hour earlier, had made a show of befriending Aida now didn't look up from their screens.

"Sign here." The officer pushed a form at her, and she signed. Protesting would have done no good. The hurried judgment misspelled Aida's name; part of its cut-and-pasted text used the pronoun "his" instead of "hers."

IT WAS ALREADY late when officers motioned her to follow them. They handed her copies of the paperwork and then marched her to a gate in the steel wall. With no way to tell time, she was shocked how many hours had passed. Agua Prieta's polluted sunset had come on like a sick headache and settled into darkness. The small clangor of Monday night's party scene had begun to stir: little bursts of laughter, cars honking, and music in the street hit her like a second hangover from the night before.

Still dressed in the party clothes and high heels she'd put on thirty hours earlier, raw from adrenaline and lack of sleep, Aida started the long walk to her father's house. Again.

13.

LA ROCA

WALKING THROUGH AGUA PRIETA in the dark, Aida kept to the main streets, taking no shortcuts. Passing cars, scattered streetlights, and a few open restaurants made her feel a little safer. Dogs on rooftops barked, following her progress through the city. During the days that Aida had spent at Raúl's before crossing the border the first time, she'd heard newspaper trucks blaring lurid headlines through static-fuzzed loudspeakers. Decapitated women had been found somewhere, maybe Ciudad Juárez, or was it Agua Prieta? Aida couldn't remember exactly, but the dead women crowded her mind. They were dark company as she walked alone, still in party clothes.

After fourteen blocks, her route edged around the city cemetery for a quarter mile. She crossed the street and quickened her pace. A woman could get dragged into the dark necropolis so easily. She could be pulled down behind the concrete crypts, and no one on the street would hear her struggling.

Passing the Velcro factory, Aida knew she was almost to Raúl's. Night shift was in full swing. At last the playground came into view, and then her father's house.

Raúl greeted Aida with resignation. In her hands, she held crumpled paperwork that would make border crossing too risky and maybe end her chance at ever gaining legal residency in the United States. From a legal standpoint, lying about her citizenship at the port of entry was the worst thing she had ever done. An I-860 form, smeared by her sweaty hands, notified her that she'd been subject to expedited removal.

Most immigrants facing deportation, particularly those who had lived in the United States for long periods, had a right to a hearing before a judge. A hearing date gave immigrants time to learn about their rights and hire legal representation, if they could afford it. At ports of entry, though, or when individuals were detained within a hundred miles of the border and during their first fourteen days in the United States, ordinary officers could serve as judge and jury rolled into one in expedited removal proceedings. They could summarily deport people, with no right to a hearing. It was unclear whether immigrants in expedited removal had a right to an attorney at all. Either way, denying access to attorneys was common practice and sped the process even more.

The flash judgment carried a five-year bar from entering the United States for any reason. There could be severe criminal penalties if Aida were caught crossing again.

Immigration attorneys often say that their area of law is, after tax law, the most complex body of American jurisprudence. Nevertheless, it took two officers at the port of entry relatively little time to decide Aida's case. In a limited sense, the officers' call had been correct. Aida had, as charged, attempted to talk her way into the United States—an act of fraud, even though it had been quickly recanted. On the other hand, the cut-and-pasted text and spelling errors in her paperwork spoke of a hasty proceeding. If Aida had been allowed access to a lawyer or been granted a hearing before a judge as she requested, the U.S. system of rights and due process could have functioned. As it was, the officers overlooked, or ignored, the fine points of her case—and her possible pathways to legal residency.

COOPED UP IN Raúl's house, Aida tried her best to hate the United States. Her country had rejected her; she would reject it. With no other option open to her, Aida vowed to make a life in Mexico. Once she had money and a place to live, she'd send for Gabriel. Like other U.S. citizen kids with Mexican parents stuck in Agua Prieta, he could commute to school across the border.

The morning after her deportation, Aida set out walking. As an outgoing English speaker, she left the house thinking that it would be easy to find decent work at a foreign factory or a dentist office catering to American patients. By afternoon, her confidence had dwindled. Ejected from the United States as an "illegal alien," Aida wasn't quite legal in her birth country either.

Seven months after Luz took her family to live in Douglas, Mexico had adopted a national ID known as the Clave Única de Registro de Población (CURP). Aida had grown up in the United States, spent almost two-thirds of her life there. She considered herself American. Getting a CURP would require spending money for documents, copies, and notary stamps. It would take hours on line at Mexican offices. The whole idea of the process annoyed her. Getting a CURP would mean giving up a central piece of her American identity. But without the eighteen letters and numbers, Aida couldn't work legally in Mexico. Without a CURP, she was a kind of alien in two countries. And as she discovered that day, her hair made it worse.

Aida had always loved her wild ringlets; they stood out in northern Mexico, where most people had straight hair. But as more and more of the migrants stranded in Agua Prieta came from Central America, her hair took on a different meaning. When friends used to tell Aida that her curls made her look Honduran, she took it as a compliment. Now it was a curse. Her day of office visits revealed that no one would even consider hiring a Honduran-looking woman without a CURP.

That week, Aida argued nonstop with her father. After the last fight with Luz in 1996, Raúl had stopped drinking, but he was still a hard man, haunted by traumas he kept at bay by establishing a formal distance from other people. Not surprisingly, tensions flared between the bullheaded twenty-year-old, reeling from dislocation, and her stern father.

Later, they would disagree about whether the stubborn daughter had refused to ask for help in paying for a CURP or whether the stubborn father had refused to offer help. Under other circumstances, this kind of misunderstanding might have been a natural and necessary stage of acclimatization between a young woman, just out of adolescence, and her rarely seen father. But deportation, exile, and separation from Gabriel raised every emotion to an extreme pitch. In the end, Aida and Jennifer left Raúl's house in search of other lodging.

As the sisters left, a slow realization scratched at the inside of Aida's skull: without money to process a CURP, she could not earn money, and without money she was well on her way to becoming one of the city's stranded denizens. The options for stranded women in Agua Prieta were not good.

In one sense, Aida and Jennifer were lucky. Unlike many other recent deportees, who could be found squatting in abandoned buildings or sleeping on Agua Prieta streets, the sisters knew the city. And compared with Tijuana or Ciudad Juárez, Agua Prieta was a quiet, relatively safe place. But as was often the case in their family, theirs was an uncomfortable kind of luck. Jennifer's ex-mother-in-law owned a house in Raúl's neighborhood. Jennifer had remained close to the woman, even after her marriage ended in ugly fights. The woman was happy to help her former daughter-in-law, with one caveat: they would have to share the house with Jennifer's ex, who'd also been deported. The sisters considered the ex-mother-in-law's offer and decided it was the best they could do.

A cinder-block wall split the small house into two apartments. Aida, Jennifer, and Jennifer's two toddlers took one side; Jennifer's ex occupied the other. The man seemed to have ties to gangs and drug dealers and made no pretense of rekindling a friendship.

Aida's instincts told her to give the man a wide berth. The sisters watched him closely and slept together in one bed at night, prepared to fight. In the mornings, they searched for work, pacing Agua Prieta from end to end.

Several days passed like that. Occasionally, shop owners and secretaries showed Aida kindness, apologizing and wishing her luck. Other times, employers informed her that they had no openings before she could even speak. What food the sisters acquired went mostly to Jennifer's children.

One evening, Aida and Jennifer's U.S. citizen aunt arrived with bags of groceries. Never had plastic Walmart bags looked so beautiful. Aida and Jennifer ate tortillas and eggs and cheese and saved the rest for later. Just looking at it and knowing they had food for several days filled the sisters with new courage. The next morning, the endless walking and rejections felt easier.

When they returned to the divided house that afternoon, their feet and lower backs protesting from hours pounding concrete, the groceries were gone. Aida and Jennifer hadn't eaten all day, and hunger tumbled over them. Aida stood at the empty refrigerator willing the food to reappear. They'd picked up Jennifer's children from Raúl's house, and everyone expected a meal.

"He stole his own fucking children's only food," Jennifer howled in disbelief.

The next morning, they took jobs they'd been hoping to avoid: waitressing at La Roca, an uninviting bar near the border wall. They'd had the offer for several days but hadn't considered it seriously until Jennifer's kids cried with hunger.

La Roca sat on a main street around the corner from Pachanga's. Pericles supposedly owned it too, but La Roca fell several slippery social rungs below Pachanga's aspiring narco-chic. The sisters' first night was almost amusing. Aida and Jennifer felt like extras in an awful *telenovela*. La Roca was threadbare and sour, lacking even the most basic bar decorations. A dark passage connected it to El Greco Hotel—which was less a hotel than a structure renting concrete rooms by the minute. El Greco, in turn, connected to Wau Wau, a popular strip club. If people wanted a fun atmosphere and cleanish seats, they went to Wau Wau, not La Roca. La Roca, it seemed to Aida, mostly served as a place for business meetings—the kinds of business meetings attended by men in gray suits who talked with men in crocodile boots, their bodyguards attentive at the next table over.

Aida found that she had a talent for keeping her distance without appearing aloof. She dropped bottles of beer at tables and skipped off, her warm smile covering a hasty escape. Away from customers, the bartender offered Aida and Jennifer a free sample of coke. They declined. One of the other waitresses offered them something else.

"You see that," she told Aida, sliding back to her post at the bar after having disappeared into the hotel for a while. "I just made a hundred dollars in fifteen minutes. You could too."

"No, I'm not like that," Aida answered.

"You're crazy," she said with a frown. "It's easy."

LATE THE SECOND NIGHT, Aida was lugging a cooler of old ice to the back patio when she saw an apparition in the adjoining hotel. A woman in a tight blue dress was being yanked up the stairs by one of the ugliest men Aida had ever seen. The woman kept tripping as she tried to keep up. For a fleeting second, she turned to look back at the lobby and her eyes met Aida's. Aida went as cold as the slurry in her cooler. She recognized the woman; they'd gone to elementary school together years earlier and played in the park outside Raúl's house when they were kids. Berenice was her name. Aida used to call her "Bery Nice."

Now the woman's eyes discharged an electric, raw hatred. For a second, Aida thought that Berenice intended that hateful look for her, and didn't understand what she'd done wrong. Then she knew: the woman's disgust was not for her. It was a deep self-loathing.

That will never be me, Aida vowed. Never.

Back at the bar, a customer with a blue baseball cap pulled low over his eyes wouldn't leave Jennifer alone. He'd sent other waitresses away all night, insisting that only Jennifer serve him. Sometimes when that happened, Aida knew, it ended with a nice tip. But it didn't end this time. Around closing, the man followed Jennifer to the bar. He stood too near to her, saying nothing, while she cashed out. Jennifer moved away. He slid closer. Jennifer said something to the man, and he responded by grabbing Jennifer's arm hard.

"Let's go," he said, loud enough for Aida to hear across the room.

Jennifer pulled away, saying, "No, I'm not like—"

Aida was already flashing across the room, slamming her drink tray into the man. He staggered back against the bar. Before he could recover, Aida landed two shattering punches, one on his hard, high cheekbones.

She grabbed Jennifer, and the two of them clattered out onto the street.

"Ow, my fucking hand," Aida howled as she shook it out.

The sisters were laughing, hightailing it down Panamerican Street, a hysterical solidarity arcing between them.

"We didn't get paid!" they realized. And they couldn't go back.

They kept running, elbow to flying elbow until they were breathless and far from La Roca.

"Shit, we didn't get paid."

IN THE DAYS that followed, Aida worried more and more about Gabriel. She ached to hold her son close, but something stubborn and proud prevented her from sending for him. Not until I have a job, a safe home, and food, she told herself. She didn't want Gabriel squatting in an ex-relative's house, going hungry, or attending school in a strange country. She wouldn't compromise.

The small amounts of money she managed to borrow from relatives disappeared for groceries. Why was Agua Prieta so much more expensive than Douglas? No wonder anyone who could crossed to shop at Walmart. A CURP number would solve most of her problems, Aida believed, and the copies and notary stamps wouldn't cost much. At most, she figured, it would take sixty pesos, six dollars. She could save that, little by little. But Aida was impatient and growing more restless by the minute.

Eighteen days after the expedited removal, La Roca's manager telephoned Raúl's house and left a message. She apologized for the way things had gone at the bar. There was no possibility of paying them, not after they left with such scandal, but she had another proposal. She wanted Aida and Jennifer to bartend at Pachanga's. She would pay them twenty dollars a night.

Aida considered asking Jennifer to go with her but decided not to subject her sister to another night in the Pericles empire. She'd do it herself. Twenty dollars would transform their situation. One shift at Pachanga's would pay for a CURP, and then she'd find a better job. Pachanga's was clean, familiar even. The bartenders wore white T-shirts. There might be drugs, but no pressure to go off with anyone. She'd probably see people she knew from Douglas. She could handle one night, one shift.

That afternoon, the manager led her into a conference room filled with businessmen. Aida turned on a beaming smile and held it while the men ogled her. None of them said a word, but they must have communicated something to the manager. She said, "Let's go," and swept Aida out of the room.

She would start the next night. Saturdays were the busiest, and the manager needed another English speaker. Aida hesitated.

"I need time to arrange for someone to pick me up after closing."

"Not a problem. It's your first night; I'll give you a ride home."

Aida dressed deliberately before her shift. She pulled her hair into an austere ponytail and wore no makeup. She thought about borrowing a miniskirt and high heels but opted, instead, for her everyday black jeans and favorite black Converse All Stars. She'd be working, not dancing.

When Raúl heard the plan, he got angry.

"If you don't want to get in trouble in this life, don't mess with that kind of thing—Pachanga's is not an advisable place, Aida," he warned.

Jennifer joined him and begged her sister to reconsider. They'd start a new round of job inquiries at the factories Monday morning. This time they'd find something, she promised.

"Monday, we'll go get my CURP," Aida said, correcting her, "with my twenty dollars."

Watching Aida get ready later that evening, Jennifer thought about how beautiful her sister looked. With her long hair pulled back, her face was open and bright. How could the same mouth that roared with so much savage fury at that man at La Roca also produce that galaxy-wide smile?

She half swallowed a final plea: "Aida, please don't go?"

But Aida was tired of arguing. She was tired of being six dollars short of a CURP card and a grocery bag away from dinner. Her next words came out like pistol shots: "I. Want. My. Son." The argument was over.

Right before leaving, Aida pulled on her favorite white T-shirt. Silk-screened on its back were two angel wings, reminders that she carried Gabriel, her archangel, with her always.

14.

THE RAILROAD YARD

AIDA WANTED TO DO THE JOB RIGHT. All the doom-laden portents she'd brought to work—her father's and sister's warnings—gave way to more immediate matters. Could she make drinks correctly, keep track of swirling orders, and count out change? Usually dance music lifted her into another plane, but Aida stiffened. Where did the empty bottles go? What had the lead bartender told her about the price of Modelo Especial?

She was the only woman tending bar. She was afraid to make a mistake and conscious of the attention focused on her. But the lead bartender had been kind. He introduced her to the other staff and gave her a cursory tour of her duties. Slowly, she eased into the work.

Acquaintances from Douglas pushed their way to the bar, shocked to see her on the other side.

"What are you doing here?" they asked. She must have heard the question a hundred times.

"I always wanted to try bartending," she told them, forcing as much cheer into the words as she could. "There definitely aren't jobs like this in Douglas!"

She laughed loud and poured friends' drinks with an extra flourish. But inside, Aida winced. Most of her friends and acquaintances didn't know that she was undocumented. Even though deportation was as much a part of daily life in Douglas as *quinceañera* parties, Aida felt ashamed—different. She refused to admit what had happened to her.

Her friends seemed to accept her excuse and move on, not knowing how entirely alone their surprised expressions made Aida feel. She would snap back to life, though, when the lead bartender signaled his crew to set up rows of shots. Aida splashed a high unpracticed arc of tequila into rows of glasses. Her laughter was real in that moment, shoulder to shoulder with the other bartenders yelling in chorus at the expectant throng, "Tequila shots *por un pinche dólar.* Come and get it."

Near closing time, a white spotlight aimed at a low stage replaced the spinning dance-floor show. Movement slowed and the crowd quieted. The DJ announced a dance competition—cash prize for the sexiest performance. Three women climbed onto the stage, introduced themselves, and began to writhe.

At first, the women laughed awkwardly in the spotlight. Then, glassy-eyed and drunk, with their hair sweat-slicked to their faces, they gave themselves over to the act. It was not a kind of dancing that Aida liked. One of the women sailed her T-shirt across the crowd, followed by a bra, which provoked wild cheering. Aida reddened and started clearing empty bottles. The dancing women were gorgeous, but she couldn't stand the looks on their faces. They worked too hard for the small prize. It didn't seem right.

Someone called for the "girl bartender" to get on the stage, and the crowd turned his words into a chant. Aida backed away. Hands shoved her forward. She ducked under outstretched arms and slipped into the women's room. Aida locked herself into the safety of a stall with shaking hands and waited.

She had no idea how much time passed before she left the bathroom. Mostly she concentrated on not thinking about what was happening outside, and not breathing the bathroom air. The stall smelled of perfume, urine, and vomit mixed in an unventilated blender. When she finally emerged, the lights had changed again. It was brighter, and bouncers were urging people to leave.

The other bartenders banged racks of glasses and counted bottles. Cleaners started to sluice buckets of soapy water across the dance floor. The manager appeared, handed Aida twenty dollars, and then disappeared again. Empty bottles rattled into a metal garbage can somewhere.

"Aida, the ice."

Aida dumped bins of beery ice into a sink and then found a rag to wipe down the counters. More lights came on. In the sick white glare, Pachanga's looked decrepit. Sticky stains covered every surface. Aida knew that she'd leave reeking of alcohol.

No one talked more than strictly necessary, but Aida felt a kind of camaraderie with the closing crew. They were quiet, but in it together, late-night service workers, hurrying to go home. Aida reached into her pocket to touch the twenty-dollar bill, ATM-crisp. More practiced bartenders started to drift away, alone and in small groups. She finished sweeping a section of floor and took out a bag of garbage. Only a few other people remained at the club, and a guard was getting ready to lock the doors. No one had given Aida a list of jobs, so she took a final look around and walked outside to wait for her ride.

JENNIFER STIRRED AWAKE, expecting to feel her sister's warm body beside her. Then she remembered. Her phone glowed 3:00. Closing time. Aida would be home soon. Jennifer closed her eyes and nestled into the sheets, but sleep didn't come. She sat up and then lay down again. Her phone glowed 3:20. She imagined Aida skipping into the room, trying to be quiet, but unable to contain her excitement. "Twen-tee dollars, baby," she'd say, doing a dance. Jennifer closed her eyes. Outside, it began to rain so lightly that she could smell it more than she could see or hear it. Sleep didn't come.

A ROLLING PARTY of tricked-out cars had packed the streets of Agua Prieta's club district just a few hours earlier. All Saturday night they'd cruised in a slow rectangle, lit by neon and happy voices, trunks buzzing with scudding bass. Couples kissed in the shadows, pressed up against adobe walls. Their friends hooted encouragement. Now, two hours before sunrise, the street was completely empty except for trash and the faint impression of a summer rain. Exhaustion crept in at the edges of Aida's consciousness. The fine rain picked up, and she began to look around.

For all its rapid growth, Agua Prieta was scabbed with empty space. Near the border, the city's downtown disintegrated quickly into dirt roads and empty buildings. Across from Pachanga's, an abandoned railroad yard looked dark and feral, uttering strange noises in the night.

Aida pressed herself against the club's locked door. At 3:30, she told herself that the manager was probably busy tallying receipts or out depositing the night's cash. Around the corner from Pachanga's, a long row of unfinished or abandoned buildings gaped in the night, missing doors and walls. During the boom years, smugglers took them over and used them as stash houses. Their ceilings were black with campfire smoke. Their walls were sticky with the residue of other people's worst nights.

At 3:45, Aida's promised ride had still not appeared. Aida cursed; the manager had forgotten or never intended to carry through on her promise in the first place. Aida's mind spun out scenarios. She had watched far too many slasher movies during all those years at Movies 'n' More. She could picture every possible fate awaiting a woman alone on the edge of Agua Prieta's railroad yard. At 4:00, tears and rain mixing on her cheeks, she decided to hide in the doorway until first light and then run home.

By the time the white sedan pulled to a reassuring stop beside the club, Aida's angel T-shirt was soaked through. The driver wasn't Aida's manager. Aida had long since given up hope that her boss would show up, but she thought she might at least send someone in her place. The man in the white sedan identified himself as a waiter from another one of Pericles's clubs and leaned over to open the passenger door.

Aida gave the driver her address. He smiled. He looked like a dark falcon, strong and not unkind. They were, Aida thought, comrades in the society of late-night bar workers, this new world she'd joined for just one night. The car shifted into drive, and the man asked if she knew any place to buy beer at that hour.

AIDA SHOULD HAVE wondered why someone who worked for Pericles didn't know about the all-night liquor store a block away. Pericles owned that, too. She should have wondered how a waiter could afford such a nice car. She might have run when he left her alone to buy beer. But she didn't. She wanted to be home, in a bed. She wanted to show Jennifer the twenty dollars and celebrate this doorway that opened to their future. She wanted to sleep before the light of day.

THE REALIZATION CAME first as a drowsy question: Why is he turning here? Suddenly the question had Aida's full attention.

"Where are you going?" she yelled.

When the car bumped into the railway yard, her question became a certainty.

"This is not the way to my house."

The driver stopped the car and leaned over to kiss her. She flinched and the kiss missed. His mouth collided with her shoulder. She jabbed at him with her left arm. He recoiled in surprise. With her right hand, she struggled to open the door.

The latch became a plastic riddle, cryptic under her fingers. How many millions of times had she opened a car door without thinking a second thought? The man yelled words Aida couldn't make out and bent over to pull something from the space between seats.

She kept rattling the door handle. He made a noise, and there was a strange squelching pressure in her side. It felt more odd than painful. She twisted to work the door better, and agony shot through her side. Another thrust hit her torso. This one tore and flamed.

It occurred to Aida that the man was stabbing her.

Bemused surprise came first, icing over into fear. Just like in a horror movie, time got slow and viscous. The space between stabs stretched wide, and she considered her collapsing life. Unbearable regret flashed across her mind, images of Luz and Raúl. Saul. David. Then Gabriel—the angel—glowed overhead, and she was all fury.

She landed blow after blow with her left arm. This slowed the man down, but the knife still found its way through. Bones in her hand splintered. Her wrist frayed from parrying the blade. Everything went black. An eternity passed. And then she was out on the ground, running.

AIDA STAGGERED OUT of the railroad yard, heading toward Panamerican Street. Behind her, the sedan's headlights burst on, and she cringed. Aida listened hard for the car's approach. Instead, it roared off in the opposite direction. Aida stumbled ahead, gripping her abdomen as if she were holding her insides in, which she was.

Under streetlights she saw her white angel T-shirt turn sopping black. Squishing excess blood. Her arms were gloved in slick liquid up to the elbows.

A trickle of drivers dragging themselves home from bars mingled with early risers on their way to work. Aida tried to wave, bent over and still holding her stomach. Drivers steered around her, one after another, unwilling to stop for a thousand selfish reasons.

"Hey, girl, you wanna party?" Samuel Escobar rolled down his window. He was hoping for one last chance at fun before calling it a night. But the sight of blood seeping between Aida's arms sobered him instantly. He jumped out of the car. It was a risky move in a country where police treat Good Samaritans as convenient scapegoats. Aida fell into the car and Escobar drove.

By the time Aida opened her eyes, she had slid in her own blood to the car floor. They were stopped in front of a private hospital. Aida levered herself out of the car and swayed through a door marked *Urgencias* on her own two feet. Escobar sped away.

Later that morning, Agua Prieta municipal police accused Samuel Escobar of the brutal attack on Aida Hernandez.

15

THE BLACK PALACE

THE LAST TIME POLICE HAD COME at dawn for Raúl was 1971. They'd smashed down the door and dragged him into the basement of a government building. Police lights flashing in front of his house in the summer of 2008 brought him back to that place again. Before he unlatched the metal door—before the officers in their tamarind uniforms could deliver the news about Aida, the worst news he had ever received in his perilous life—Raúl paused. He took a slow yogic breath and stifled his fear of police.

AFTER FLEEING MADERA in 1965, Raúl spent years on the run. Much of this time, he managed to live an ordinary life. From time to time, he connected with other revolutionary groups, joining their efforts for a while and then moving on. During one of those engagements, he was shot in his good leg by police.

In 1971, Raúl found his way to an armed cell operating out of Mexico City. Facing continual repression, the unit was closed and distrustful. They vacillated over accepting a new recruit but finally agreed to send him on a mission. From the start, Raúl knew the plan was ludicrous. The group wanted to "expropriate" a strongbox of cash rumored to exist at the municipal headquarters of the ruling PRI in Mexico City. The robbery couldn't possibly succeed, Raúl understood. He also knew that if he wanted to join the cell, he'd have to demonstrate discipline and courage.

Raúl escaped from the harebrained operation with his life. Some of the cell's other militants weren't as lucky. Raúl made his way back to his apartment after the failed robbery and collapsed into bed. A few hours later, at 6:00 a.m., police smashed down his door and dragged him away. In the concrete basement of a government office lit by a single bulb, Raúl met, for the first time, people he had always known existed. People who could beat him senseless for fifteen or twenty minutes without leaving a visible mark. Two of them held his head under freezing water until he passed out. They called this a *pozoleada*, a serving of pozole stew.

"Would you like another serving of pozole? No? Well, tell us about your comrades."

"I'm Raúl Florencio Lugo," he repeated. "I was one of Arturo Gámiz's men. I participated in the attack on the Madera barracks, September 23, 1965." Raúl had decided to give the interrogators as much information as possible about people who were already dead. He was blindfolded so he couldn't anticipate the gut punch when it came.

"Tell me about Genaro Vázquez instead."

"I was in Guerrero, but never met Genaro."

It went on like this for a long time before the interrogators gave up. Eventually, they dragged him out of the basement and propped him in front of a battery of press photographers. After the photographs, they drove him to the Lecumberri prison, the Black Palace, as it was known.

LECUMBERRI WAS AN Italianate castle built by the dictator Porfirio Díaz between 1885 and 1900. It loomed large over the east side of Mexico City, and even larger in the Mexican imagination. From Pancho Villa to student protesters who disappeared after the 1968 Tlatelolco massacre, much of Mexico's Left had passed through Lecumberri. As a result, Raúl had a rough idea of what awaited him when he entered the dark edifice.

He sat in a windowless iron isolation cell for the first seventy-two hours. Walls and doors were relentlessly blue. Carceral scientists deemed the color calming, but seventy years of scratching and scouring by inmates gave it an angry look. The din emanating from the general population areas outside his cell was deafening. Lecumberri roared like one of the city's most dangerous neighborhoods.

Porfirio Díaz had desired a modern prison for the modern country he hoped to build. In it, prisoners would interact and self-govern, creating a new society for themselves. Like Díaz's capitalist modernity—which dispossessed millions, enriched U.S. and Mexican elites, and sparked the Revolution of 1910—Lecumberri's modern society reeked of dystopia. Boss prisoners controlled every aspect of life, running drugs, prostitution, stores, and cafeterias. New prisoners' possessions were confiscated and sold back to them. Ability to pay determined everything. Did you spend your days in a private, protected cell? Could you only afford to rent space under a bunk in a crowded room for one short shift a day? Did you sleep on the stone toilet-room floor, ordered to work for your keep? Bosses' henchmen enforced order armed with knives, handguns, and buckets of ice water that could kill a person during Lecumberri's freezing nights.

Alone in Lecumberri's intake unit, Raúl prayed that officials would assign him to O-West, the political prisoner wing. There, in a newly constructed building, separate from the general population, self-government worked. Or so he'd heard.

THE GUARDS TAKING him from H to O-West seventy-two hours later halted at the unit's gate. Guards rarely intruded on the world beyond that entrance. Raúl still felt raw and unhinged by torture and fear, but as soon as he passed into O-West, he knew that he had found a new family. Prisoners representing the entire alphabet soup of armed revolutionary groups lined the central hallway to greet him. He recognized members of the CAP, the MAR, the ACNR, and other organizations—even a few comrades from his years in Chihuahua. The assembled crowd cheered O-West's new arrival. Everyone had known in advance that he was coming, thanks to the newspapers, radios, and televisions in abundant supply throughout the wing. Political murals covered the fawn-colored walls. Doors remained open, and Raúl saw cheerful gatherings inside cells. Groups of prisoners laughed, held political debates, and played guitar. Chalkboards hanging in different rooms displayed evidence of prisoner-taught classes.

That night, guards left dinner outside O-West's entrance. Raúl watched, impressed, as a group of three prisoners, assigned through a rotating schedule of jobs, improved the meal with collectively purchased ingredients in a common kitchen. Mostly, though, Raúl noticed that O-West overflowed with books. They bulged out of improvised shelves and covered desks and tables. Inside many cells, young bearded men with spectacles clattered at typewriters. O-West seemed more like a college dorm than a prison.

But it was a prison. Like most of the other men, Raúl had not gone to trial yet and had no idea how many years would pass before he even learned the length of his sentence. As much as he structured his days with political discussions, confinement still wore at him. He taught guitar classes, practiced martial arts, studied English, and composed revolutionary *corridos*, but isolation swallowed him. Inmates in O-West could receive visits at any time, but he had no one to visit him.

Days dragged into months and then years. O-West could feel like a family, a utopian collective even, but Raúl struggled to find his place in it. Most of the prisoners were university-educated intellectuals. He was a peasant from the mountains of Chihuahua with six years of primary school. Fissures between revolutionary factions became canyons in the geological time of incarceration. Raúl redoubled the walls of his clinical, rational, revolutionary affect, pushing emotion down and out. The prisoners had a saying: A golden cage doesn't cease to be a cage. Slowly, *el carcelazo*—the dreaded prison depression that erased whole lives—closed in on him.

Felipe Villanueva recognized the symptoms: Raúl alternated between deadened stupor and lashing anger, a clear sign of *el carcelazo*. Villanueva was an older leftist who had taken it upon himself to visit political prisoners without friends or family in Mexico City. He asked Raúl what would help him. At first, Raúl resisted. He needed nothing. He was fine. But slowly, Villanueva drew him out and began to find small ways to support him. When Raúl's depression deepened, Villanueva recommended yoga.

In the early 1970s, few Mexicans had heard of yoga, but Villanueva shared mimeographed pamphlets and a book. On the next visit, Raúl asked if Villanueva might be able to search out other sources.

Like a prisoner in Plato's cave imagining a world from shadows— thanks to incarceration with university radicals, Raúl could converse about Plato now—he pieced together a practice of yoga from the mimeographed sheets and blurry illustrations. Villanueva brought more material, and Raúl's practice expanded. Yoga, to Raúl's way of thinking, reconciled his insistence on emotional control with his agitated body. Almost any obstacle in life, he came to believe, could be overcome through mental and physical discipline centered on conscious breath. Through rigorous training, he could learn to control fear and stabilize his emotions.

Four years after Raúl entered Lecumberri, a judge declared him guilty of criminal association and possession of a firearm. His sentence was five and a half years. The final eighteen months would be served in the Santa Martha Acatitla Penitentiary on the outskirts of Mexico City, only a few kilometers from the compound where, ten years earlier, the GPG had learned the rudiments of war.

By the time he transferred from Lecumberri to Santa Martha Acatitla, Raúl had written and illustrated his first memoir, *The Assault on the Madera Garrison: Testimony of a Survivor.* Pedro Marín Zárate, another jailed guerrilla, volunteered to edit and type the manuscript.

Raúl had internalized the formal language of his movement. He punctuated his everyday speech with phrases like "the objective conditions for armed struggle" and "the scientific study of reality." But the memoir's language was simple and blunt. It traced the coming into political consciousness of a landless peasant with little formal education. "In jail, I heard a voice over a loudspeaker inviting people to a political meeting of peasants demanding land," it began. "It should be clarified, though, that my reasons for being in prison had nothing to do with revolutionary action."

One hundred brief pages later, it ended with Raúl, alone, remembering his fallen comrades and walking through the mountains. "Fully convinced that I had to keep struggling . . ."

After finishing his memoir, Raúl received a visit from a MAR militant who had just won release from another political prisoner unit. She had grown up in Chihuahua, and the two connected. She appreciated his political writing but also encouraged him to write about his method for keeping sane in prison. Raúl set himself to the task, scratching out the first lines of a new book. "In this study," he began, "we will not address the so-called science of yoga, nor any spiritual version that claims to take man to unachievable supernatural places like states of enlightenment and astral projection. Those do not reveal, nor clarify, the true finality of yoga." Instead, Raúl charted the "real achievements" of "one of the greatest disciplines exercised by man."

Not only had yoga saved him from despair, but the breathing patterns and flowing movements he practiced on Lecumberri's bare concrete floor filled him with a feeling of rigorous self-control. Yoga, he promised readers, "regularizes sleep, stabilizes emotions, and controls fear, anxiety, worry, anger, and all the negative effects those have."

This time, Alejandro López Murillo, one of the charismatic founders of MAR, helped Raúl edit and type the manuscript. Raúl taught himself to draw and supplied rough pen illustrations. His friend from Chihuahua found a publisher. When Raúl walked out of Santa Martha prison in 1976, he had an advance on the publication of his yoga manual, now with the distinctly bourgeois title *Health and Beauty Through Yoga*.

THE MONEY EARNED by his yoga book didn't last long, and soon Raúl made his way north to live with his sister in Agua Prieta. He hadn't returned to the North since fleeing Madera in 1965. At first, he made a small living teaching yoga at a city gymnasium, but the former cattle town wasn't quite ready for yoga. Maquiladora jobs could be had easily on the border, though, even if they paid a pittance. If he took a factory job, he could transition into a position organizing workers as part of a PRI-affiliated union.

Raúl gave up yoga instruction and began to manufacture seat belts—but not before meeting a young woman. Luz had defied her conservative father by enrolling in a yoga class. Raúl had watched as the fiery seventeen-year-old argued in the street outside his gymnasium. Her father was a blunt ranch hand and a professional boxer, but he was no match for his daughter. Luz was exasperating, Raúl thought. But for the first time in a long time, something like attraction stirred in the ex-guerrilla.

Raúl and Luz married after a short courtship. He rose to an important position in the local maquiladora union and dabbled in state politics for a while. Neither endeavor lasted long. Raúl's vision of social justice was too uncompromising to mesh with the PRI's ideologically flexible politics of accommodation. Life settled into a quiet routine of factory work punctuated by occasional moments in the national spotlight during anniversaries and remembrances of "Madera 1965." With Jennifer's birth in 1983, followed by Aida's in 1987 and Cynthia's in 1989, Raúl's life centered on the difficult task of raising three girls who blazed as bright and unpredictably as their mother.

16

TRAUMA RED

VOICES. LIGHT.

A sheet pulled over her head.

Aida struggled to sit up—to refuse the sheet—but her lower body didn't respond.

Reassurance. She'd misunderstood the nurse's intention. The sheet was not a shroud.

She was not dead yet.

CURTAINS CIRCLED HER. Camila, her cousin, poked through, turned white, and backed away. Jazmin sat beside the hospital bed. Where had Jazmin come from? She was supposed to be safe at home in Douglas, not in Agua Prieta.

Darkness.

AIDA WOKE REMEMBERING the blood-slick sliding out of Samuel Escobar's car. She remembered stumbling through glass doors into the Hospital Latino. Jennifer had taken Jazmin's place next to the bed. She tried to say something to her older sister. A plastic tube tugged inside her nostril.

"Do you have my pants?" Aida formed each word painstakingly. "You need to take the money."

"It's okay, Aida. Just rest," Jennifer said, hushing her.

"No, you need to take the money." Aida shifted uncomfortably, agitation rising. "Take it. Use it."

They'd sliced Aida's jeans off in the emergency room, the waist sopping with blood. The pants dried stiff, in a heap. Jennifer found them and brought Aida the twenty-dollar bill. Folded several times over during Aida's nervous wait at Pachanga's, it looked tiny and insignificant. But when Jennifer slipped it into her pocket, Aida relaxed and lay still again.

SOMEONE PRESSED A PHONE to her ear. She reached to steady it. Her left arm crackled—dried blood and hospital tape. It startled her. Her inflated hand looked ready to pop, a ghastly shade of mulberry.

"Mom," she said into the phone. "Mom, I'm okay."

"I'm coming. I'm bringing Gabriel." Luz's Spanish was high-pitched, delirious. Aida could picture her on the other end of the call, tearing out the door of the Douglas trailer.

"No, Mom. Stay there. I'm fine." Aida was half aware that crossing the border would void her mother's green card application. She was even more certain that she didn't want Luz to bring Gabriel across the border to the Hospital Latino. She didn't want her son to see her die.

OUTSIDE THE CURTAIN, Aida heard her father arguing. He'd handed over the title to his house as collateral for the cost of Aida's surgery. Now hospital staff wanted him to purchase plasma and medicine with money he didn't have. If you can't pay for these, they told him, she will have to go somewhere else.

Luz's brothers and sisters, nephews, nieces, and their boyfriends and girlfriends converged outside Aida's hospital bay. They poured out sympathy and advice. Some promised financial help. Raúl sealed himself off from the clamor. Nothing but the logistics of survival existed for him. The hospital was prepared to give up, but he wasn't. There had to be a way to save Aida.

POLICEMEN PUSHED INTO the curtained enclosure around her. A photograph of Samuel Escobar appeared in front of her face.

"No," she croaked, "he was the one who saved me." The police looked nonplussed as Aida signed a statement that would exonerate Escobar. The man who'd dropped Aida off at the hospital had been the easiest person for the Agua Prieta police to accuse. Now they'd file her case away and forget it. They had other, more pressing concerns.

Earlier that summer, cartel hit men had executed a police officer three blocks from the Hospital Latino. Multiple bullets skewered his partner, who lived somehow. Before that, Agua Prieta's police chief took forty gunshots and died at the same hospital where Aida lay. Other officers just disappeared, kidnapped or fled. The army reinforced Agua Prieta, but the message from cartels to police was as clear as the painted sheets that hung from overpasses in the nearby mining town of Cananea: Join us or die. Rumor had it that 10 percent of the Agua Prieta police force had quit in the weeks before Aida's attack.

Even if Agua Prieta's police hadn't been under siege that summer, they probably wouldn't have taken Aida's case seriously. Attitudes toward violence against women in Mexico were changing in the late 2000s, but public officials and residents of Agua Prieta still found ways to blame the victims. "Public women"—the kinds of women who worked outside the home at foreign factories or, even worse, went to nightclubs—brought violence on themselves, the argument went. Mexico's federal legislature had passed a sweeping law for the prevention of violence against women in 2007, but implementation lagged. A later study would show that only 7 percent of victims of violence against women in Mexico received protection orders under the new law.

Aida's identification of Samuel Escobar saved an innocent person from jail, but there would be no further investigation of the attack.

SINCE AIDA'S DEPORTATION, thirteen-year-old Jazmin had taken on much of Gabriel's care. She dressed and fed her nephew and made sure he got to preschool every morning. Taking care of Gabriel consumed time that she could have spent at church, but she didn't mind. The Pentecostal community she'd found, almost by accident, had become her haven away from the chaos of daily life. But she owed Aida more than she could ever repay. In the years of Saul, Aida had never hesitated to insert herself between the old man's anger and his daughter from another family. When stress, injuries, and overwork incapacitated Luz, Aida stepped in as one of Jazmin's mothers. When Jazmin thought back on her childhood, her memories of care all included Aida: Aida sitting on the couch in one of their temporary abodes brushing out Jazmin's fine black hair; Aida packing her school lunch, adding special touches like sandwiches cut into crescent smiles. Taking care of Gabriel was the least Jazmin could do.

Soon after the attack, Jennifer had telephoned Jazmin from Agua Prieta. The younger sibling left Gabriel with Luz and flew across the border to the hospital. Of all the immediate family members, Jazmin was the only one with a valid border-crossing card in 2008. She pulled a plastic chair up to Aida's bed and refused to leave her side.

Meanwhile, Raúl learned from a relative that Arizona's Medicaid program might cover emergency care for Aida. Hope sparked in him. While Raúl arranged a Red Cross ambulance to take Aida to the border, Jazmin held her hand.

AROUND MIDDAY, about eight hours after the attack, the movement of doctors, nurses, and police wound down. Jazmin was alone with Aida, gently holding her undamaged hand. Relatives milled outside the curtained enclosure. Words of worried conversation and whispered logistics ebbed, and Jazmin barely noticed. At first Aida tried to talk. Later, only faint periodic squeezes reassured her that Aida was still alive. Watching her sister disappear beside her, Jazmin clung to girlish memories of Aida caressing her hair. She wept quietly, remembering Aida cooking pancake breakfasts for Jazmin and Gabriel at the trailer. She had made smiley faces out of chocolate chips on each one.

Then there was only weeping and urgent "I love you"s, and an ambulance pulling away from the Hospital Latino in the afternoon glare. The border. The battle over Aida. And the helicopter flight.

. . .

THE CALL CAME to the University Medical Center in Tucson in clipped noun phrases. "Trauma red." "Ongoing catastrophic blood loss." "Unknown surgery in Mexico."

Surgeons in green and ER doctors in blue hovered outside the helipad elevator. News of a mystery operation conducted at a Mexican hospital gave an extra dose of adrenaline to the wait. Border traumas usually followed a certain script: they were either spines shattered falling off the wall, extreme dehydration, or exposure from freezing nights in the desert. This call felt different.

When the elevator doors opened, the quiet choreography of a well-practiced dance began. Aida arrived with a tube in her nose and a tube in her side, both siphoning blood from her stomach. A nine-inch zipper cut ran up her abdomen. Fast labs put rough numbers on the scale of her bleeding: she'd lost at least 40 percent of her body's blood over the past ten hours. But she clung to life.

Rolling toward the trauma bay, Aida remained semiconscious, half answering questions. Five times in the past ten hours, she had summoned all her remaining force for a cause. At the railway yard, she had fought to escape her attacker. At the hospital, she had battered her way through terror and confusion to make sure that Jennifer took the twenty-dollar bill. Even lacquered in blood, the money was the key to her future. It had been earned at too high a cost to waste. She had reassured her mother over the phone, saving Luz from a headlong rush into a canceled green card application. She had roused herself to clear Samuel Escobar's name after police suspected him of the attack. And finally, she had pleaded with U.S. officials at the border to let her cross.

Now she was nearly dead. Her tissues were suffocating. Her arteries no longer held enough red blood cells to carry oxygen through her body. Her heart raced to keep the blood she had left flowing. A weaker person would have already died.

THE ER TEAM faded to the background. This was not their area. Everything depended on the trauma surgeons. They reached into Aida, manually feeling for cuts and leaks, pushing aside deep tissues and viscera, searching methodically through the warren of her abdomen, stapling and draining as they went. Two and a half years later, members of the same team would save the Arizona congresswoman Gabrielle Giffords's life after an assailant shot her outside a Tucson shopping center. There was a kind of democracy in the trauma bay, all ruptured bodies looking very much alike.

LUZ, JACK, LUZ'S SISTER, and Jazmin packed into Jack's car for the two-and-a-half-hour drive to Tucson. Raúl negotiated an extension on his border-crossing card and was able to join them. Aunts and cousins followed behind. Only Cynthia stayed in Douglas, nervous about Border Patrol checkpoints. Luz didn't want Gabriel to see his mother in pain. So in a frantic split-second decision she later regretted, she left the boy with David's mother.

For the first few miles, climbing out of the Sulphur Springs valley, the occupants of Jack's car conferred loudly. Expressions of angry disbelief clashed with conjectures about what would happen in Tucson. Then one by one the passengers dropped into silence. For the final hundred miles, no one said a word.

A priest met them in the waiting room. Luz was Catholic. Raúl believed in the struggle for earthly justice. Jazmin attended a Pentecostal church. But that day, each of Aida's family members followed the Catholic priest in a daze as he arranged them in a circle and began to pray.

The waiting room clock marked out hours. Luz paced jagged circles or drummed her nails on the chair rest. Jazmin rocked softly in her seat. Raúl folded in on himself, concentrating on breathing. Every time the interior door opened, they all startled, met the staff member's informationless eyes, and sank back into waiting.

AIDA BUCKED AWAKE, punching and kicking her assailant. She clawed at his face and thrust his knife arm away. The movement jerked out an IV and brought nurses running. For the first day, they tied Aida's IV arm and one leg to the bed to restrain her battle reflex.

Slowly the present and immediate past came into focus. Begging for her life at the border crossing was seared in her mind, along with a glimpse of Gabriel looking stricken. She half remembered rising over the strip mall parking lot in a red helicopter, the Dollar General store sign glowing yellow as Douglas disappeared below. At the hospital, people in blue and green scrubs had swum around her, asking urgent questions. She had wanted to help them, but their words ricocheted off her consciousness. She remembered those details. But she could not, as much as she tensed her drugged brain, pinpoint what had happened to her before walking into the hospital in Agua Prieta.

When she woke fully, a nurse untied her hand. Finally free, Aida lifted her gown to look at the place that hurt. She saw stapled and taped slices in angry yellow, red, and purple running up and down and across her stomach and side. She had no idea how they got there.

She keened for her mother. "Mama, what's happening to me?" she asked.

THE SURGEON IN Mexico had performed competent initial repairs. Even so, Aida had arrived with only minutes left to live. In recovery, the provenances of her pain were hard to count: The attacker's knife severed nerves in her liver and deep tissues. Blood-swollen hematomas groaned against the sacs containing her kidney and liver. When the second surgery opened her insides to air, her intestines spasmed into paralysis. A third excruciating surgery reassembled her shattered left hand and wrist.

In the haze of recovery, a bright new memory formed in Aida's mind: She imagined that somewhere over southeastern Arizona her heart had faltered, exhausted from pumping empty arteries. Then it stopped. And then, an eternity later, it had begun to beat again. In that lacuna between death and life, Aida remembered seeing a vision of Gabriel. Her son bound her to return to the earth, to return to him. Gabriel gave her the strength to continue.

Medical science did not support Aida's new memory. With such low blood volume, Aida's heart would never have recovered if it had stopped beating for even a moment. But the vision of her death and resuscitation felt so visceral and real that it became truth, accepted by her family and friends. Even without scientific backing, the story of Aida's death and revival crystallized onlookers' admiration for the young woman's spirit. Aida had died, and Aida was alive.

IN THE HOSPITAL BED a few days later, Aida's gown rode up, exposing her pubic hair. Luz leaped to fix it.

"Cover yourself up, *hija*. People can see your—"

"Mom, I died and came back to life. I don't care who sees me."

Raúl appreciated his daughter's courage and reminded her of the Mexican saying "*Todo tiene remedio, menos la muerte*"—everything can be fixed, except death. When her courage faltered in the face of pain, he told her, "You survived death. You can do anything."

After a few days, Aida took her first slow steps. Supported by a walker, pulling her IV stand, she balanced around the ward. Physical activity unleashed breathtaking pain, but she fixed her mind on returning home to the son whose image had saved her.

Luz had kept Gabriel away from Aida at the border and in the parking lot after the attack. When he cried for his mother, Luz had done what adults did when the truth was simply too much to ask a child to hold: she lied. Luz told Gabriel that his mother just wanted to see what it was like to fly. That had perked up Gabriel. The four-year-old was fascinated by the helicopters that buzzed daily over the border. For a moment, he was envious and a little proud of his mother. But then, with the adults distracted by planning and lamentation, a girl, five or six years old, walked up to the boy.

"Your mom's dead, you know," she said with a shy smile, satisfied to possess secret grown-up information. The boy looked back at her, stunned. A moment ago, he'd been thrilled to see a real helicopter up close. He'd been told to imagine how fun it would be for his mother to fly. Now his heart cracked wide open, and there was no coming back from that. Luz and other adults shooed the girl away, but the damage was done.

After that, nothing would convince Gabriel that his mother was still alive. Not even the rasping voice calling from Tucson, which sounded only a little like her. His mother was dead, Gabriel repeated to David's family in a flat voice. The distress this caused others when he said it caught like a flame, threatening to burn him out. Aida needed to return.

She pestered the doctors so often to release her that they gave her a task to focus on: when she passed gas, they informed her, it would indicate that her mangled intestines had begun to work again and she could go.

It hurt to laugh, but jokes were inevitable. So much depended on a fart. But how could she fart, Aida worried, if the doctors wouldn't allow her to eat? On her sixth day in the hospital, Aida pulled Jazmin close and whispered, "*Hermana*, can you sneak me some food from the cafeteria?"

Cellophane-wrapped key lime pie had never tasted so divine or done such important work.

AIDA LEFT TUCSON with a thirty-day immigration parole to receive follow-up care in the United States. Humanitarian parole was a strange contrivance of logjammed immigration law. It allowed Aida to be present in the United States without legally admitting her to the country. The border wall wrapped around her body as she left the hospital. Physically, she existed inside the United States; legally, she floated outside.

Her mental state matched the unusual legal status. Her physical wounds had begun to heal, but the attack had cut her in places she couldn't yet fathom. She was barred by law from the United States, but she could return home to Douglas.

When Aida struggled out of the car outside her mother's trailer, Gabriel stood dumbstruck on the porch. His mother had come back from the dead. Aida stumbled to him, hugging him as hard as her mangled belly would permit.

It seemed as if an hour passed. Luz, Jazmin, and Cynthia crowded around Aida and Gabriel on the porch, but neither mother nor son pulled away. A summer monsoon, shoveling hot, wet air over the Gulf of California and rolling hard across northwest Mexico, broke over Douglas that afternoon. The roof rattled. Mesquite thorns scraped against the trailer's metal walls, and Gabriel held on to his mother, back from the dead.

Finally, he pulled away. "Mom, please don't ever go away again," he said in a tiny voice.

"Gabriel, I promise—I will never leave you again."

She held his head, one hand still encased in gauze, and stared into his eyes. She repeated her promise. She looked into his eyes. She squeezed his chubby hands.

And then the darkest part of her story began.

SLIPKNOT

PART THREE

17.

LUCKY EMA

A quarter of a world away, forty minutes' drive south of the equator, Ema Ponce had finally settled on a college major: systems engineering. She had earned a promotion at work as well. Now, instead of selling tickets in a metro bus booth, she supervised accounting at the beginning and end of shifts. Mostly, though, she directed her energy into the place where she stood at that exact moment: the left wing of a dirt pitch, listening to a cheering crowd.

Every time Ema pulled on her battered cleats and stepped onto the field, she marveled at what soccer did to her. Off the field, she was a small, somewhat shy twenty-three-year-old raised by a single mother on the razor edge of Ecuador's middle class. On the field, she felt as massive and sharp as the Guagua Pichincha volcano towering six thousand feet over Quito. She was a force, hurling herself through the thin air of Ecuador's skyscraping capital.

Ema's teammates arrayed themselves around her, wearing the orange and gray of the Guipuzcoa soccer club. Some of them were stretching calves and quads. Others bounced in place, ready to begin. They were notorious. They were fierce. In five years together, they'd fought for more than just goals. Ema looked up, found her mother's face in the concrete stands, and double-checked her place in the defensive line. She tensed for the official's whistle.

It was a life. A real, solid life with hope and a future, *compañeras* and a consistent paycheck, a place to live and enough food to not have to wonder if it would last. It would last. How could it not? With her team arrayed around her and her mother making the trip to see her play, so much had changed in just five years.

EMA'S EARLY LIFE was marked by violence and flight. Her first memory was not the swift, cold river rushing down from the high Andes through her village in Cañar Province. It wasn't her grandmother's prosperous market stall on the edge of that river. Or even the hours she spent playing underfoot in the market, asking to weigh out fistfuls of corn and yucca or bundle sweet greens into bunches.

Ema's first memory was of her father crashing home, drunk and belligerent, knocking aside the dinner plate her mother held out to him. Ema was three and a half. At five or six years old, she asked him why he beat her mom.

His answer confused her for decades: "She asks for it."

By the time Ema was eight or nine, her mother had had enough. Ema's father had gone to work in New York and never sent money home to support his family. When he returned, ready to resume his old ways, Ema's mother fled with her children to Ecuador's capital city.

In Quito, Ema's mother rented a room in a *hotel de mala muerte* near the cathedral. Ema saw things for which she had no words yet: syringes, drunk-rolling muggers, prostitutes. To her immense luck, the family did not get stuck in that place. Ema's mom eventually secured a job at a bakery owned by a cousin in a pleasant hamlet north of the capital.

The town of Mitad del Mundo, as the name suggested, owed its existence to a stone monument commemorating an eighteenth-century expedition by French geographers to measure the exact middle of the world. Modern GPS would reveal that their calculations, and subsequent monument, missed the equator by 240 meters, but for Ema everything about her new home felt right.

During those first years, Ema's mother, Luisa, struggled to make ends meet. Sometimes the family subsisted on nothing but weak tea and fried onions. At other times they managed a middle-class existence by Ecuadorian standards.

Two important discoveries coincided with this period of middle school and early high school. They changed Ema's life even more than the flight from Cañar.

The first was the riotous nightly soccer match that broke out in the street in front of her house. Kids made goals out of rocks and played with a tattered indoor soccer ball. When cars needed to pass, the game paused and then resumed in full fury. The conditions were crude, but the play was fast and skilled. Ema watched out her window for weeks, unsure whether a girl would be allowed to take part at that level. When she finally ventured onto the concrete pitch, she found that she could, and more.

Ema began to join organized clubs and school sides. Soon she anchored competitive teams in tough leagues. One year, one of her teams reached the championship round in a tournament. Ema was at home with a fever and flu, but her coach went to her bedside to persuade her to play anyway. Ema dragged herself onto the field and staggered around for the full ninety minutes. Somehow she scored a goal, and the team won. She was that kind of player.

Ema's success led to the second great discovery of her young life. When Ema was thirteen, her mother found money to enroll Ema at an experimental private high school focused on math and science. She thrived in the school's hands-on technical curriculum while continuing to excel on the soccer field. This brought her to the attention of Daniela, a seventeen-year-old running for student council president. Daniela asked Ema to join her campaign team and invited them all to attend a meeting at her apartment.

Ema had never seen anything like Daniela's home. It was modern, all dazzling glass and light—like Daniela. The candidate swept Ema into the open living room. She was extroverted, quick-witted, and beautiful. Ema realized that the apartment belonged to Daniela. The girl's parents had an immense house of their own outside town, and even that they rarely occupied. Business travel took them out of the country often. Daniela offered refreshments and then draped herself onto the couch as they waited for the rest of the campaign team. But the others wouldn't show; Daniela had made sure of that.

"I have no idea where everyone is. Let's watch a movie while we wait," she suggested.

They bantered over the video. Daniela's running commentary made Ema laugh, and, miraculously, each of Ema's attempts at wit had the same effect on Daniela. She felt smarter, more sophisticated in this bright space. When the credits rolled with no sign of the rest of the campaign team in sight, Ema knew that she should head home. But she couldn't pry herself away.

"You're into me, aren't you?" Daniela said as Ema stood up.

The words didn't sound accusatory or arrogant. They were a line cast into unknown waters. Daniela's sudden vulnerability disconcerted Ema even more than the question.

"Don't be nervous. It's okay. I'm into you, too," Daniela continued.

Ema recoiled: "I don't know what you're talking about. You're crazy."

A WEEK LATER, Ema saw Daniela in the stands at one of her games. Ema made uncharacteristic mistakes that day. She sliced easy shots and tripped over the ball. After the match, Daniela found her embarrassed on the sidelines. They sat together near the field, plucking grass stems and talking. The older girl apologized for her forwardness.

"Come to my house on Saturday. I'll make you dinner to make up for it," she said. "And I'll tell you something that will change your life."

The dinner came in courses, on fancy dishes. Ema refused to eat. She put down her soup spoon.

"Would you just tell me what you're going to tell me?"

"No, it's okay. Just eat."

A minute passed. Ema stared into her potato puree.

"Okay," Daniela said, relenting. "I know why you look at me the way you look at me. The same thing happened to me. I've been exactly where you are right now."

"But that kind of thing isn't right."

"What kind of thing?"

"Girls and girls." Ema didn't look up from the soup.

"Well, that's all I wanted to say."

Daniela and Ema finished the rest of the meal in awkward silence. At the door as Ema went to leave, Daniela spun her around and kissed her mouth. And Ema kissed back.

EMA'S MOTHER, a conservative Catholic, didn't learn of the relationship. The girls kept their growing love tucked away in private places and secret glances. They sat together in patches of grass outside their school, tracing the tiny scars on each other's knees. Or they let themselves settle into each other, ever so slightly, sitting side by side at a movie. Ema's mother complained about moral corruption infecting Ecuador, but Ema and Daniela's bond was chaste and timeless. Mostly they talked, filling the years of their adolescence with endless, earnest dialogue about politics, soccer, science, and the nature of love. When Daniela enrolled in a premed program at the elite Universidad Central del Ecuador in Quito, Ema found a high school in the city and commuted. Together they explored the capital's small world of lesbian bars. Ema began to play in Quito's city leagues. Sometimes they found quiet places where they could hold hands publicly in a country that had decriminalized same-sex relationships only a few years earlier.

As time passed, their age difference grew more significant, not less. Busy schedules and, in Ema's case, endless bus rides eroded their bond. When Daniela received a scholarship to study medicine in Cuba, they said a tearful goodbye in the airport. Ema promised to join Daniela on the island as soon as she finished high school. But they both knew how it would go: they'd send sporadic emails for a few months, get busy with other concerns, and never see each other again.

Ema spent her last year of school at a public *colegio* in Mitad del Mundo. By the end of the final semester, she had convalesced from the end of her relationship with Daniela enough to begin dating again. Anytime she went out with a girl, though, Ema worried that her fiercely Catholic mother would catch her. Mitad del Mundo was still a small town.

During the last week of exams, Ema invited her occasional girlfriend Ana to stay with her. Ana's parents had thrown her out of the house in the middle of finals. This didn't surprise Ema, who had her doubts about Ana. Ana was a difficult person to bring home, nothing like the kind and clever Daniela. Ana seemed to lack both scruples and discretion and spent the day at Ema's house making loud, lewd suggestions that they go up to her bedroom. Ema squirmed away from her friend and took refuge in studying. She had passed her two hardest finals already. Only one easy test in drafting stood between her and a degree.

At dinner that night, Ana played footsie and groped Ema under the table. Ema pulled away. But when Luisa bent down to recover a spoon elbowed off the table at a particularly poorly timed moment, she saw enough to understand everything—instantly. Seeing Ana's hand snaking up Ema's thigh, Luisa assembled years of misread clues into a new picture of her daughter.

Ema tensed for an outburst, but her mother said nothing. That scared Ema more than yelling would have. After dinner, Luisa blandly suggested that the three of them watch a movie. Only Ana, oblivious, registered the film as it flicked by. Ema's mind raced with frightful scenarios of expulsion and forced conversion therapy. Luisa's mind clicked and whirred, fighting for traction—until she abruptly snapped the TV off.

"Ema—outside, now." Her eyes shot into Ana, telling her to stay put. On the patio, Luisa impaled her daughter with questions.

"And Daniela? Was she a girlfriend too?"

Ema planted her feet, an internal goalie telling her to form a wall.

"I'm a lesbian, Mom. I like women."

Luisa hit Ema hard across the face. It was the first time she'd ever struck her daughter, and the blow left the hot red shape of a hand on Ema's cheek.

Early the next morning, instead of passing her last high school exam, Ema left home. The next months went by in a blur of bus stations, odd jobs, and relatives fooled by lies about leaving home after a fight with her mother over a boy. She slept in an uncle's auto body shop in Cañar and at a hotel in Quito worse than the one she'd known as a girl. She entombed herself in the worst parts of Quito's underground lesbian scene, a world of sad bars, coke, and bulbous alcoholics. Sour romances came and went, brief, flinching encounters that left her feeling even worse. One night, a stranger stopped her on the street to talk. The unexpected conversation finally nudged Ema out of her stupor.

"Family is the most important thing, *mija*," the stranger said. As they parted ways, she reached into her purse to give Ema bus fare home.

LUISA RECEIVED HER daughter back with tears and a condition: Ema could return home if the two of them went to therapy together. At the first session, the psychologist asked them to state their goals.

"I want my mother to accept me for who I am," Ema said.

Luisa countered, "I want my daughter to realize that she's not a lesbian."

They visited the psychologist weekly for months, and Ema reenrolled in school. In the Ecuadorian system, she was required to retake her entire last grade. As the year progressed, the therapist's true intentions revealed themselves.

"To heal," she said one day, "you must renounce lesbianism, have sex with a man, and accept God."

Ema continued to keep her appointments because she'd promised her mother that she would. But each visit sliced another chunk off Ema's soul.

"You must have sex. With a man," the psychologist said during one session when Luisa was present. "If you need help, I can arrange it."

"I think we're done," Luisa said.

Ema's mother stopped the therapy sessions and took her daughter's eternal soul into her own hands. She disconnected the internet and monitored Ema's phone. Ema continued to frequent lesbian bars but persuaded an acquaintance to pose as her "boyfriend" around Luisa. In this way, mother and daughter instituted a loose détente. Dissimulation allowed space for their old closeness to return. They learned to ignore big differences on key questions—like Ema's sexuality and Luisa's religion. Their relationship improved.

Months passed like this. The two women applied themselves to rebuilding their connection, hoping that the places where it had broken would grow back stronger. And they did, until Luisa discovered an overlooked message from a lover in Ema's voice mail.

"You are still at it?" Luisa waved Ema's phone at her daughter.

Ema saw their armistice disintegrating in her mother's angry glare, but then something shifted. Luisa tossed the phone onto the couch.

"Just learn to erase your messages, okay?"

Ema sat transfixed on the couch, looking at the phone and wondering what had just happened. Five minutes later, her mother reappeared.

"Tell me the truth—you really don't like boys, do you?"

"No, *Mami*."

Suddenly there was a softness between them that had been absent for almost a year. In the conversation that followed long into the night, Luisa finally disclosed her deepest fear. The therapist had convinced her that gay relationships led to drug use and crime.

"Mom, I want you to know what I do when I'm not here," Ema said with a bolt of inspiration. "You should see for yourself."

LUISA ROCKED IN the folding chair, arms crossed over her chest. Ema, perched next to her, tapped the polished floor nervously, waiting for the film to start. Leticia Rojas, one of the founders of the Causana Foundation, a lesbian feminist organization, had taken Ema under her wing. The older woman shared advice about relationships and family and taught Ema to think politically about her identity. After Luisa bared her soul, Ema asked Leticia if she could bring her mother to the organization's film and discussion series.

That week's offering was a saccharine, made-for-television movie with Brooke Shields and Whoopi Goldberg. Ema barely glanced at the screen. Instead, she watched her mother's reactions in the blue glow. In the film, a lesbian couple in Florida had a child, but the mother died of lupus. In a time before civil unions or same-sex marriages, this left the second mother with no parental rights. Whoopi Goldberg, a curmudgeonly civil rights lawyer, fought to keep the grieving family together. Luisa's sister had died of lupus, and this unexpected correspondence unlatched something. Ema saw it flash onto her mother's face.

The lights went on, and Leticia opened the floor for questions and comments. Luisa sat, impassive and inscrutable, taking in the conversation.

"We have time for one more question," Leticia said.

Luisa's hand drifted up. Ema blanched, but Leticia gave her a reassuring look. Luisa laid out her reasons for opposing same-sex relationships. She had clearly spent the evening assembling this speech. The foundation encouraged frank, open discussion, and the audience listened carefully. What ensued was nonconfrontational. Testimonies and answers, questions and admissions, poured out on all sides. When the conversation finally wound down, long after the appointed hour, Ema realized that she had forgotten to breathe for most of the night.

Mother and daughter departed through a gauntlet of hugs. In the diaphanous mountain air outside, Luisa was quiet, lost in thought. But when, a while later, the Causana Foundation inaugurated an informal soccer program in La Carolina Park, Ema and her mother could be seen playing pickup games together. In 2003, the informal soccer program crystallized into the Saltamontes de Venus, Ecuador's first all-lesbian soccer club. The team lost every match by lopsided scores, but Luisa cheered from the stands.

SALTAMONTES DE VENUS coalesced over several years, its political profile and soccer skills developing in tandem. Nearly half the lineup quit after a decision to come out as an openly lesbian project in 2006, but Ema remained. League officials harassed them. More than once, men barged into the team's locker rooms with video cameras, hoping to catch "obscene acts" on film. Often officials found pretexts to disqualify the team from important tournaments. And whenever the women played, the stands filled with hecklers. But insults and adversity stiffened the team. To Ema's surprise, they began to win.

Almost a decade had passed since the Ecuadorian Constitutional Tribunal decriminalized same-sex relationships. But the landmark ruling reflected a country deeply ambivalent about LGBTQ people: even as it overturned laws against same-sex relations, the tribunal concluded that homosexuality might be a "dysfunction or hyperfunction of the endocrine system" to be treated medically, rather than criminally.

For Ema, though, there was nothing unhealthy about the team, and she flexed her political muscle on the field. By August 2008, with a new start at college, a promotion to supervisor in her job, the embrace of an awakening lesbian community, and her mother's love, Ema felt the elements of her life arranging themselves into a beautiful future.

18

ALL THE MONSTERS AT ONCE

AIDA'S CLOSET DOOR CRACKED OPEN, revealing a slash of darker black inside. She watched from bed, holding her breath, willing herself to get up and run. Fingers curled around the door, sneaking it open wider. Aida flinched, bumping into Gabriel, asleep beside her in Jack and Luz's trailer. Her son didn't stir. The closet door opened fully. She watched Jennifer's ex-husband step out naked. He tiptoed to the foot of Aida's bed, all of his body showing. Next to the bed he stopped and leered.

Aida screamed and snapped on the light. The room was empty, except for Gabriel. Everything looked as it should: Aida's Pink Floyd wall hanging, Gabriel's Legos strewn on the floor. The knob on the door to her bedroom rattled. Someone pounded on the other side. Luz called to her daughter through the hollow-core door. Aida stammered a response and inched across the floor to unlock the room.

Luz consoled her daughter and settled her back into bed. Aida still couldn't sleep. She stared at the ceiling, listening to her mother's footsteps retreating down the hall. Luz hadn't locked the door behind her, Aida realized with a jolt. She launched herself out of bed, pressed the lock button, and then froze. Had anyone locked the front door of the trailer?

Aida listened to the satisfying thunk of the dead bolt. She tested the door, peered through the front window to make sure the porch light was on, and shuffled back to her room. She pressed the lock button on her door and contemplated Gabriel. He splayed on the bed, innocent, oblivious, exposed.

Aida returned to the front door. She hadn't forgotten to lock it, but she unlocked and reshot the bolt, just in case. The porch looked darker than she remembered. Had the porch bulb blown? Aida flicked the switch on and off. It worked fine.

The push-button lock on Aida's bedroom door felt cheap and flimsy. She could have snapped the knob easily if she hadn't just been stabbed. But it was too late at night to change the lock. Aida persuaded herself to let it be until morning and sagged to her bed.

Exhaustion pulled at her. The doctors told her to rest as much as possible, but she kept waking up through a haze of painkillers. A force stronger than exhaustion propelled her out of bed. Maybe she'd check the closet again. The small nook held only her clothes and shoes, but as she stood in front of the closet, it occurred to her that she might have left the front door unlocked.

"Aida—go to sleep," Cynthia moaned from her room.

"Just a second." She'd go back to bed as soon as she checked the lock again.

IN THE DAYS since returning from Tucson, Aida had shown off her wounds to a stream of visitors. Relatives and friends from Douglas filed into the trailer to marvel at her perseverance. Some visitors showed real sympathy; others came only to indulge their morbid curiosity. Many felt guilty for having turned their backs on Aida, the wild teen-mother high school dropout. She greeted each the same, lifting her baggy T-shirt in a defiant display of angry flesh.

"Look at this," she told them all. "I died, and I lived."

Visitors left Aida's bedside awed by her strength. They commented on the way she still beamed optimism into the room, even though she was clearly in pain. By surviving death, Aida had, in some small way, rewritten the rules of life for everyone. Each of the pilgrims left her bedside resolved to be a better person. They stepped off the trailer porch committed to making more of their lives.

But when the goodbyes faded and the door swung shut, Aida coiled into herself. She felt safest locked in her room, playing Legos with her son. The boy had wavy brown hair, dimpled cheeks, and a tendency to watch his mother like a hawk for signs of distress. She saw everything she had once loved about David contained in him. He was poised and smart. He had the focus of an engineer when he dedicated himself to his meager pile of mismatched Legos. Aida marveled at the beauty of each spaceship and superhero car.

Several times a day, Aida assured her son that nothing he did had caused her long absence. She fumbled to explain the deportation and attack in words he could understand. In some ways, this wasn't hard: She barely remembered it herself. The attack had sheared off whole sections of her memory, leaving only disorienting blanks and her family's version of events. Speaking to Gabriel, Aida could only explain her situation in the vaguest of terms. But even speaking about it like that would make her heart race and the room spin. Instead, she said that Mexico was full of "bad men," and left it at that. Part of her knew that it was wrong to talk about her parents' home country—full of good people—in such a brute way. But she couldn't muster another explanation for Gabriel. As a result, he grew up, like so many Arizonans, fearing the country on the other side of the wall.

When Aida sobbed for no reason, Gabriel would tell her she was okay in his child's voice. Already, Gabriel was learning to take care of his mother.

She would look up from sobbing and choke out her own reassurances. "I know, honey. It's going to be okay."

He'd accept this with a bucktoothed smile, trusting his mother.

· · ·

OUTSIDE THE BEDROOM, away from Gabriel, the world had become too unreliable for Aida to bear. Common household objects pierced her with splinters of memory. Certain smells hurled her into the path of panic. It terrified her that such ordinary things could undo her this way. The steady movement of time became unreliable, fragmenting and rearranging itself. Aida could not remember whether she spent eight days in the hospital or two months. She did not know if she had snuck across the border one time or many times. She did not know how long she'd lived under Saul's roof, or how long she had waited outside Pachanga's. She felt twelve years of danger blazing in the present moment. Her survival instinct shoved all other ideas out of her mind. She had no past and no future, only the unceasing signal to run or fight—*now*. And she saw no way out. No path forward.

Her mother and sisters would try to talk her down from bouts of howling anger, but their consolations morphed into recriminations in her mind. Aida would fling off her family's sympathy and storm back into her room. The only solution to the continual assault of fear was to avoid as much of the world as possible.

When needed, Aida could build herself up to joke with visitors, but she couldn't focus on people in the way she had before. Conversation passed through and around her without registering. Words darted out of reach. She grinned and repeated platitudes about survival, but inside she was counting the minutes before she could rush back to the safety of her locked room. The thought of venturing onto the porch, or beyond, left her quivering, her hair slicked to her face with a sudden cold sweat.

The worst part was the temporary nature of her permission to remain in the United States. As the end of her monthlong humanitarian parole approached, Aida could barely step off her front porch, much less contemplate going back to Mexico. Images of the attacker returning to finish his work flicked at the edge of her consciousness every waking moment.

A white sedan had followed women who looked like Aida down the street in Agua Prieta, she heard—or thought she heard—from one of her visitors. Was the attacker stalking the streets in search of her? The husband of one of Luz's friends said he had overheard a man at a barbecue in Agua Prieta bragging about "finishing off" the Pachanga's bartender.

Thinking about the imminent expiration of her humanitarian parole gutted Aida all over again. Someone had broken into her father's house, she heard. The man searched the place but took nothing except Raúl's address book. Aida berated herself. Had she given the man in the white sedan her father's address? If she went back to Mexico, would he know where she lived?

Raúl visited Aida in Douglas. Since Luz had left Saul and found Jack, Raúl and Luz had reconciled. This allowed him to visit his recovering daughter at least once a week. He treasured these moments with Aida, but her stories about the persistent stalker didn't make sense. Her certainty confounded him.

"Aida, no one broke into my house," he said. He had no idea how she'd come to believe otherwise. Her sisters debunked rumors of women being followed by a white sedan in Agua Prieta as well. Even if the man was still searching for her, Cynthia and Jennifer told Aida, she'd be safe as long as she kept out of sight of Border Patrol in Douglas. For once, the border wall would protect her. But Aida persisted. Her whole being told her that these things had occurred. The man was still out there, in Agua Prieta, looking for her. Mexico hadn't felt like her real home in years. Now the country at the end of her street wasn't just alien. It was an active threat to her existence.

In calm moments, Aida suspected her sanity. Why would her brain try to deceive her so cruelly? In aroused moments, Aida couldn't fathom why her family would deny these stories, which were so obviously true. Sometimes the two suspicions overlapped and entangled: her brain was betraying her; her family was lying to her; her brain lied to her; her family betrayed her. One certainty tightened around another: if her own mind and family couldn't be trusted, she would have to be even more vigilant. The circle of people she could count on cinched down to a single four-year-old boy.

RAÚL BEGAN TO TEACH Aida the meditation techniques that had helped him endure Lecumberri. Focusing on her breath, Aida could drive panic into the background but not escape entirely from its grip. On the afternoon of September 15, 2008, it took an hour of shaky meditation just for Aida to gather the courage to leave home for her final postsurgical checkup. Thirty-six days had passed since the attack. Her permission to stay in the United States would expire at midnight. Luz drove her to the clinic.

They rounded Douglas High, "Home of the Bulldogs" and Aida's abandoned dreams. The route passed within a few blocks of the house Saul now shared with his "real" family. Next, a corner of the Tenth Street Park, where she'd met David, flicked into view, and then they entered the sparse downtown. Douglas's business district looked familiar, but there was nothing there for Aida. Movies 'n' More had closed in the months since her deportation. Her former boyfriend Alex, who'd bought the store for five thousand dollars, was, by that time, in prison, just as Aida's uncle predicted. In the short time Aida had spent in Agua Prieta, Alex had been arrested for drug possession with the intent to sell. That afternoon, he was two weeks into a three-and-a-half-year sentence.

Aida and Luz pulled up to the Chiricahua Community Health Centers clinic well after Aida's scheduled appointment, but the nurse practitioner saw her anyway. Elizabeth Fabry had been Aida's health-care provider for years. She had coached Aida through pregnancy and motherhood. That day, she fought to hold back tears while releasing the staples running up Aida's belly.

During the appointment, Aida searched for a way to explain what had happened in Agua Prieta, but her story came out in fragments. The shards were enough for the nurse practitioner to grasp one thing, though: Aida could not return to Mexico that night, no matter what her documents said.

Fabry stepped outside the exam room and made a telephone call. She returned a little while later and promised to write a letter to immigration officials on her behalf. As Aida prepared to leave, there was a soft knock, and the door pushed open.

For some reason, Aida didn't startle. She was so folded into herself, cowering on the vinyl exam table, that she had to crane her neck to see the newcomer, but she didn't feel fear. The woman had dark curls like Aida's, but none of her sharp angles or hairspring tension.

"Rosie, she can't go back to Mexico," Fabry said to the woman. "You've got to find a way to help her."

ROSIE MENDOZA'S ENGLISH was rougher than Aida's, but it conveyed gentle confidence, even in its errors and hesitations. Aida felt completely understood without having to speak. The woman, standing there with a sad, kind face, looked past Aida's baggy T-shirt and through the defensive inward curve of her chest.

At Rosie's request, Aida stumbled through her story again. Rosie's face darkened as Aida concluded. The social worker's expression was kind, but she appeared deflated.

"I don't think that there's anything I can do for you," she said at last.

Rosie's tone indicated both that not being able to help devastated her more than anything and that she found herself in that powerless position far too often. At the time, U.S. immigration courts almost never approved asylum petitions related to violence against women in Mexico. There was little Rosie could do with Aida's story, but she vowed to try. She contemplated the young woman in front of her. Aida had one hand buried between her legs and the other unconsciously twitching up to conceal her face. She sat bowed over, a posture, Rosie thought, of suffering that went far beyond the body. There was more to this woman's story than the recent attack, Rosie realized. She could read it on Aida's face.

"I want you to come back to the clinic and talk to me another day, and we'll see if there's a way to help you." Rosie worked up a reassuring smile. "For now, go home. Try to stay out of sight, and don't despair."

In gratitude, Aida summoned every remaining bit of her old radiance. Smiling hurt in so many ways that she could not finish the expression, but Rosie completed it for her.

THAT OCTOBER, Aida turned twenty-one. The day was overcast, and she stayed home. She found it nearly impossible to control herself when she hid in her room; she certainly couldn't go out. The slightest perception of provocation could result in Aida's exploding with anger: a friendly suggestion from Cynthia, a dish returned to the wrong cabinet or left in the sink unwashed, an offer to drive her to the store. Almost anything could hurl Aida into a wild rage. She smashed dishes on the kitchen floor. She upended chairs and tables. The thin paneling around her home splintered under her fist.

Afterward, the fury drained, and Aida would collapse into a heap. She couldn't understand why her family didn't see how exposed she was. Her family didn't seem to care that her attacker might find her. They didn't see the leering way all men looked at her. Her family's refusal to see the dangers looming at every turn confounded Aida.

Anger provided her with a brief respite from fear, but no matter how much she raged, anxiety still rolled back through her.

Luz, Jack, Cynthia, and Jazmin began to alter their behavior to avoid triggering Aida's attacks. They spoke less, never knowing what words might unhinge her. They began to go about their days as tense and alert as a bomb disposal team.

In their own ways, all the women in the house had been in the same place before. At forty-eight, nineteen, and thirteen years old, Luz, Cynthia, and Jazmin each understood violence and trauma. But the 180-degree alteration of Aida's personality caught them unprepared. The worst came when Aida, in mid-rage, went stony. Her eyes glassy, her voice suddenly quiet, she would hiss terrible, unfounded accusations at her family. No one had loved Luz, Cynthia, and Jazmin more than Aida, so no one could deliver such precisely targeted pain.

An hour or two later, her face looking like a rotten peach, Aida would reemerge from her room. Her palms were bloody from digging in her nails, trying to squeeze herself back to sanity. Calm now, Aida would prostrate herself in front of the person she'd eviscerated, weeping apologies and begging forgiveness.

"I don't know why I said that. I didn't mean it," she'd groan. Sometimes she just rocked back and forth repeating, "I don't know what's happening to me."

Occasionally, she came out of her room with no memory of what she'd done or said. If one of the women—perhaps too wounded to let the matter drop—enlightened her about the blank space in her memory, Aida unhinged again.

"Why are you making up lies about me? What is wrong with you people?"

A YEAR PASSED with no sign of improvement, and Luz lost her ability to nurse her daughter through her "moods." The two women were match and gasoline. In the wake of arguments, Aida's remorseful supplications grew even more desperate. She was terrified that her mother would throw her out of the trailer. Catastrophic sequences buzzed in her head while she tried to sleep at night. She saw herself wandering homeless with Gabriel in the back alleys of Douglas. She was preyed upon by clones of her attacker hiding in the high grass of vacant lots. She was living in abandoned houses with drug addicts who tortured Gabriel. Sometimes she envisioned institutional shelters staffed by people who abused her son when she turned her back. And no matter how sickeningly distinct each nightmare appeared, they all tumbled toward the same end: deportation, Mexico, and Gabriel looking on as his mother was murdered.

On her best days, Aida could half relax on the porch while Gabriel played with his cousins in the yard. It took effort, though, to suppress the constant alarms shooting through her body: There were snakes in the yard. And cacti. The swing set was too rickety. The older kids played too rough. Gabriel could snap his neck on the threadbare trampoline. If he ventured into the ankle-deep kiddie pool, Aida's heart pounded. Eventually, the sparking fears would overload her system, and she would sweep her son back into the safety of their curtained bedroom.

The bright boy began to struggle with school. Mirroring his mother, he forgot things. His birthday. The order of numbers. The name of his school. When someone asked Gabriel his teacher's name, he grinned awkwardly and started to squirm. Gabriel had displayed early signs of reading in preschool, but confined to his mother's narrow world, he regressed. Once precocious, he forgot the alphabet.

"Your son is not okay," Luz said one day. "He needs help. It's not good for him to be closed up here." To emphasize this point, she picked up Gabriel and started to walk away. Aida lunged at her mom.

"You don't know anything about what's good for him." Aida tried to detach Gabriel from his grandmother's arms. "He's my son."

Luz kept walking, and Aida, not wanting to hurt Gabriel, stopped pulling. Luz was just taking Gabriel to play with his cousins, she knew. But something Aida couldn't control pushed her after her mother and son. Moving through the trailer, she knocked over furniture and pulled knickknacks off shelves. In the kitchen, she collapsed onto the floor holding on to her mother's feet.

"I know you're right, *Mami*. I know he needs to play. Just not right now. Please."

.   .   .

MAYBE IT WAS just Aida's old habit of keeping appointments. Perhaps she felt an obligation to the woman who had listened to her so closely at the clinic. Or maybe it was an inspired glimmer of self-preservation. Whatever the reason, Aida forced herself out of the house for her follow-up appointment with Rosie Mendoza.

It was evening on a Tuesday. Rosie had just returned to the Chiricahua Community Health Centers after attending the weekly border vigil. The Border Patrol's fiscal year had ended the month before, and with it came the death count for 2007. Two hundred and two migrants had died in the Tucson Sector, which included Douglas. Eighteen times more than had died in 1998. More than had died in 1998, 1999, 2000, and 2001 combined. The tack of new white-painted crosses clung to her hands. So did the sting of each name. Attending the vigil had left her unsettled and yet, somehow, closer to God and her faith.

Aida straightened on the plastic chair in the cool clinic and started to lift her shirt.

"It's okay," Rosie said, stopping her. "I don't need to see. I will believe you no matter what."

For three months, Aida's puckered and angry red scars had been her most important proof. To people who saw her as small and broken, they said, "I fought. I survived." And now this woman sitting opposite was offering to take her on faith. That trust loosened Aida. For an hour, she clawed out the story of what had happened to her. The chain of small mistakes. The deportation. La Roca and Pachanga's. The railroad yard and the flight to Tucson. Her memories of the attack itself had not fully reassembled yet. So she gave Rosie chips and splinters. The white sedan. The wrong turn and the attempted kiss. She described the first stab, the fight, and her arm shearing away blows. The squishy feel of blood in her angel-wing T-shirt. Rosie didn't flinch.

Rosie said little during the hour. Two thoughts vied in her mind: This girl is powerful. She fought for herself, fought not to be raped. She lived. And then: I have no solution for her troubles.

When Aida finished, Rosie explained that the attack in Mexico would make no difference to immigration officials. If it had happened in the United

States, that would be another story. Or, if Aida had experienced violence or abuse at the hands of a U.S. citizen. Aida replied that the attack in Agua Prieta was the only "real" violence she could recall. But that evening, Aida stopped Rosie often to ask her to explain terms that she didn't understand. She inquired about the intricacies of the immigration system. Rosie did her best to answer.

A girl who tells her story and asks questions—that is a good sign, Rosie thought.

"We'll talk again in a couple weeks," she offered. It was the best she could do. A new possibility might open up. If not, talking clearly helped. It was not much, Rosie acknowledged, but it was something.

Aida left ignited with hope. Rosie returned home full of despair. Aida's feeling didn't last. By the time her mother's car pulled up to the trailer, all the monsters were back. Rosie's despair only grew deeper.

"You look tired, Mom," Rosie's daughter said in Spanish when she walked into the house.

"I am, *mija*." She went straight to her bedroom, and her daughter followed.

"Can I do anything, Mom?"

"I need to shower and sleep."

That night, Rosie's son made dinner. Her daughter brought her tea in bed. This revived her, and in the morning she rose, knowing that she would try again. She would help someone, even if it wasn't Aida.

19.

THE HEALER

WHEN ROSIE MENDOZA FINISHED SIXTH GRADE, her father informed her that school cost too much. Money flowed swiftly when he bought alcohol for himself and friends. But there would be no more money for school uniforms or textbooks. Rosie had taken to school like shrimp to a netter's lamp in the mangroves tangling the edge of her town. Her father—a mean drunk and professional failure—resented learning. So, at eleven years old, Rosie quit school and went to work. In the evenings, she consoled herself with cheap government editions of world classics. Under the light of a single mothy bulb, she read the *Iliad*, *One Thousand and One Nights*, and the poetry of Sor Juana Inés de la Cruz. Cicadas, chattering palm fronds, and the sound of the Río Fuerte oozing into the sea accompanied her fictional escapes. In the ferocious heat of day, as she detasseled corn or stooped over onion fields, her head buzzed with Scheherazade and Helen of Troy. Stories of women in tight spots kept Rosie Mendoza going.

At thirteen, Rosie found temporary refuge away from her father's house with the help of her maternal grandfather, Cipriano. Cipriano practiced the indigenous art of a *huesero*, a combination of chiropractics, massage, and herbalism. Together the two of them would walk from town to town in the fertile valleys of Sinaloa. They made an amusing pair: Cipriano had the lanky build of a Tarahumara marathon runner. Rosie was short and round and skipped to keep up. When they arrived in a new town, Rosie helped raise a tent in the market. Then she sat in the shade and watched her grandfather treat peasants bent by stoop labor and malnutrition. Sometimes she prepared tinctures and rubs, infusing *hierba del manso*, basil, rosemary, and cannabis in oil. Mostly she kept quiet, watched, and listened.

Rosie's grandfather could read a patient's life history from the articulation of her bones or the torsion of his spine. He treated anyone who appeared at his tent seeking help—even if the person could offer nothing more than a single orange as payment. In the evenings, Rosie and Cipriano would take down the tent together. On festival days, Cipriano would put on shell anklets and a deer-head mask and dance through the night.

Rosie spent two of her happiest years wandering the countryside with Cipriano. Then her father moved the family north to Hermosillo, the state capital of Sonora, a blazing scab of concrete in the desert. After the move, Rosie's earnings supported the family. She got a job cleaning chicken guts and packing frozen chicken tenders for export to the United States. This allowed her to save enough money to make a down payment on a house for her mother. It was a single cinder-block room in an illegal land occupation, but it didn't belong to Rosie's father.

When she was able to save more, Rosie purchased bags of cement or zinc roof panels to expand the house. Providing a stable place for her mother and siblings to live filled her with so much pride that it was easy to eschew spending money on herself. But when the slaughterhouse began to cut wages and the union announced a strike, Rosie fell behind on her monthly house payments. So she set off to the border to look for work.

AFTER LIVING IN Agua Prieta for a time, Rosie married a man nineteen years her senior. It was a mistake, she knew almost right away, but she wanted a family. The two of them worked in Agua Prieta during the week. On weekends, they joined the steady stream of farmworkers crossing back and forth between Sonora and Arizona in those days before the border hardened. In 1986, they learned of IRCA, an immigration reform signed into law by Ronald Reagan. IRCA offered a route for some farmworkers to become legal permanent residents of the United States. Rosie and her husband qualified. They settled in Douglas, where Rosie found work at a T-shirt factory. She had two children and another baby on the way when reading an unexpected job ad changed her life.

Wanting to earn extra money, Rosie answered a call for a night DJ at a Spanish-language radio station in Douglas. She had no experience but persuaded the station manager to hire her. Five nights a week, she would finish her shift at the T-shirt factory, cook dinner, and then head to the studio. Her program began with a message to her children, who slept with the radio next to their pillows.

"Let me say good night to my babies. Good night, my babies," she'd whisper over the air. Then she'd hum a Spanish lullaby. "Don't worry, dear listeners," she'd say, breaking off her song, "I am not going to torture you with my singing anymore."

Rosie addressed her radio persona to women of the double shift—women who worked long days in factories and fields followed by long nights at home.

"This song is for all the ladies mopping right now," she'd say. "*Eso sí, que limpiecito se está quedando.* You're getting it so nice and clean—but, *oye*, you missed a spot over there," she'd say with a laugh. "*¡A bailar con el trapeador, mis comadres!* Let's get dancing with that mop, my ladies!"

It was as if Rosie were speaking directly to every single one of her listeners. Women would call the station, amazed. How did Rosie know that they had been mopping at that very moment? they asked.

"All you *señoras* making dinner right now. You know what? Take a break today," she'd say some nights. "Just make your husbands a sandwich—they'll be fine."

Spanish radio on the border meant *norteño* music—*rancheras, corridos,* and Mexican *cumbia*. Rosie hated *norteño* music. Instead, she'd play Cuban salsa, *jarocho* from Veracruz, real *cumbia* from Colombia, and the music of all the great rock bands of Mexico. Listeners complained at first and then embraced the change. When Rosie came back on air after a song, they could tell by her hard breathing that she'd been dancing in the studio.

During the early 1990s, border radio stations from San Diego to Brownsville had Chalino Sánchez in heavy rotation. He sang *narcocorridos*—folksy ballads about drug traffickers. And of all *norteño* music, Rosie hated *narcocorridos* the most. Her fans would call in waves begging her to play Chalino Sánchez. Eventually, they called just to provoke her into entertaining rants against the singer's glorification of violence and his wailing oompah-oompah sound.

On air, Rosie laughed and teased, but off air during song sets she began to have long conversations with callers. She listened to them the same way her grandfather had watched his patients. She could tell from the pitch of a woman's voice when something was wrong—sometimes before the caller knew it herself.

Most women in Douglas did not have the phrase "domestic violence" or "sexual assault" to describe their experiences in those days. But some of what the callers confided in Rosie in those off-air conversations seemed too big to gloss with the indifferent labels they used. Rosie didn't understand much, but she had experienced enough violence in her life to know that what her listeners told her about wasn't "boyfriend troubles" or "just how men are." She began to compare notes, asking other callers for advice, piecing together bits of instinct and insight. She found that callers valued her counsel.

She learned from the callers as well. One in particular, an older woman named Mary, seemed to have all the information Rosie lacked.

"Mary, isn't leaving your husband without a court order a crime here, like it is in Mexico?" Rosie asked one night.

"No, *mija*, that's not a crime in the United States."

"So, if she leaves, she won't lose her children?"

"No, *mija*."

LISTENING, ASKING QUESTIONS, and connecting woman to woman, Rosie realized that she could do a lot of good for others. And that she needed to do better for herself.

"Rosie," Mary asked one day after putting in a request for music from her native Veracruz. "What's wrong, *mija*? There's something in your voice today."

"Just problems with my husband. Nothing."

"Are you kidding me?"

Sitting in the studio with upbeat *merengue* as a backdrop, Rosie talked for the first time about things that had happened to her as a girl. She didn't go into the details, even with Mary. As much as she loved listening to and helping others, she abhorred talking about her own pain. But over time, she came to trust Mary. She explained about her drunken father and the abuses of her early life. How, later, the long shadow of violence destroyed her chance at love with her childhood sweetheart, the one man who had made her feel whole and good.

Before moving to tropical Sinaloa, Rosie's family had lived in the state of Durango. She survived her first ten years of life in a house with her father's extended family. It was a wretched and unhappy time. Her uncles and older cousins selected Rosie as their chief victim. When the male members of the family weren't molesting her, the women harassed and disparaged her. For the first years of elementary school, Rosie didn't speak a word. She made no friends. Shame over the things men and women did to her in the private corners of her home left her mute. Kids threw stones at her, the solitary girl.

Then her father moved the family to Las Grullas, Sinaloa, a village of shrimp fishers where the great brown Río Fuerte met the Pacific Ocean. The move saved her life. On the first day of school in Las Grullas, Rosie made her first friend. She had walked into the overcrowded classroom, expecting the worst. Expecting insults and stones. Instead, a boy offered her his chair. That year, the two of them would walk to the beach or along the riverbank together, talking about books. She brought him burritos for lunch when he had no food of his own. He introduced her to other kids. For the first time, she ran and played like a child.

As they got older, Jorge and Rosie grew into a couple. They swam together in the river and exchanged dreams for the future on its banks. When Rosie's father uprooted the family again, this time to move to Hermosillo, Jorge proposed.

Rosie wanted to say yes. But six years of heaven in Las Grullas couldn't erase the scars of Durango. Sixteen-year-old Rosie still carried so much shame. She couldn't find the courage to say yes. She couldn't detangle love from fear, sexual attraction from abuse. Though Jorge had stuck by her side and refused to give up on her no matter how crazy she got, Rosie pushed him away, certain that she was unworthy of his love.

YEARS LATER, in Agua Prieta, Rosie learned that Jorge had married someone else. Out of regret and self-hate, she responded to the news by agreeing to marry the first man to express an interest. That was the story of Rosie and her husband. Through their entire marriage, she addressed him with the Spanish honorific *Don* out of respect and submission both. Rosie hadn't worked fewer than two jobs in decades, but she mustered energy to become the perfect wife. She cleaned and ironed his clothes and got up early to dust and mop before work. She cooked for him, and he threw the plates at the walls. He deposited her paychecks in a private bank account and made Rosie beg for grocery money. He abused her verbally but rarely hit her. Mostly he laid into the children with his belt.

"Rosie, that's not normal," Mary said.

"I know."

"Rosie, you need to take your children and leave."

"Can I do that?" It had not occurred to her that she would be allowed to leave.

"You can, and I'll help you."

Mary found an abandoned trailer for Rosie to rent. After her husband discovered where she lived, he would park in front, yelling insults and threats. Together, Rosie and Mary figured out how to get a protection order. When he broke the order, they figured out how to get the judge to enforce it.

One day, Rosie's supervisor at the radio station called her into his office.

"If you are going to raise three kids alone, you are going to need help," he said. He explained that she could apply for state-subsidized health care and gave her the number for legal aid.

"You need to quit one of your jobs, because you don't make enough to live, but you make too much to qualify for assistance," he informed her.

Rosie quit the T-shirt factory and found time to learn English and attend school. She hadn't been to school since sixth grade, but the GED came easily. She finished an associate's degree at the community college in Douglas and then a B.S. at a Baptist university in Sierra Vista. She was one of the only nonmilitary students at the school and learned to defend herself arguing with classmates about immigration.

Rosie thought a lot about her grandfather during this period. She realized that Cipriano had seen straight through to her fear and shame. That
was why he had offered her the chance to work as his assistant. The days spent
walking with her grandfather, helping set up the tent, sitting quietly reading while he mixed his tinctures, watching how he worked with people—all
that had been a chance for her to heal. Feeling a debt to her grandfather,
she studied harder, setting her sights on a career as a social worker. Just as
her grandfather had helped her, she would help others.

In vast, underserved Cochise County, this meant wearing many hats. She
volunteered in efforts to prevent lead poisoning in mining communities,
ran HIV outreach programs, worked on drug prevention, and administered
a grant from the EPA to improve air quality in Arizona by paving dusty
streets in Mexico. More than anything, though, she watched women for signs
of domestic abuse and sexual assault. She became a professional healer, a
version of her grandfather. He had helped others, sometimes in exchange
for nothing more than a piece of fruit. Simple and beautiful and, when it
came from the heart, it was enough.

20.

LEAVING THE WORLD AND FIGHTING TO REJOIN IT

AIDA FOUND THAT SHE COULD TALK for hours about anything in Rosie's office at the clinic. The more she trusted Rosie, the deeper she went. As the social worker had suspected, there was a lot more to Aida's pain than the attack in Agua Prieta. During their third visit, Rosie asked about Gabriel's father. Technically, Aida and David were still married. David had disappeared, and Aida had no time, energy, or money for a divorce.

"Did he ever punch, kick, or hit you?" Rosie eased her question into the conversation.

"Not really."

Rosie waited.

"Not like *hitting* hitting. Just like punching the wall next to me." She remembered the trailer shaking on its cinder blocks. She remembered the knife scraping against the doorjamb beside her head.

"Not *violence* violence. Just normal stuff."

Rosie continued to maneuver questions into their discussions. Did anyone ever try to force you to have sex with them against your will? Did you feel safe with your mother's boyfriends? Did Saul or David ever threaten to turn you over to the Border Patrol?

Aida answered truthfully and then steered the conversation back to the attack in Agua Prieta and her immediate fears. She'd do anything for Rosie but didn't see why that ancient history was relevant.

Only after listening to many such back-and-forths did Rosie make her move.

"Aida, that was domestic violence. That was child abuse. You were the victim of violence all those times. Domestic violence. Child abuse. None of that was acceptable."

Aida stared back. It was not a brilliant lightbulb moment, but recognition passed across Aida's mind.

"Yes, I know it was domestic violence." Aida half believed these words and half said them because she knew Rosie wanted to hear them.

That's a start, Rosie thought. Still in her early twenties, Aida had accumulated enough trauma in her dancer's frame to buckle almost anyone.

IN 1980, the American Psychiatric Association added post-traumatic stress disorder (PTSD) to its *Diagnostic and Statistical Manual*. Drawing largely from the experiences of war veterans, the association defined PTSD as a constellation of symptoms emerging after a traumatic event outside the range of normal human experience. Controversial at first, the diagnosis eventually took root in psychiatric practice and American popular culture. Its medically validated description of nightmares, flashbacks, avoidance behavior, estrangement from loved ones, hypervigilance, and explosive anger resonated with survivors of trauma and the people who cared for them.

What soon became apparent, however, was something more ominous and disturbing than the diagnosis itself: for large swaths of the world's population, ongoing extreme trauma was not outside the realm of normal human experience. For many people—whether civilians living in war zones or women enduring domestic violence—extreme trauma was all too normal.

The American Psychiatric Association later removed references to the unusual nature of trauma-inducing events, but Judith Herman, professor of psychiatry at Harvard and pioneer in the study of PTSD, argued that the association could have gone further. Working at the Cambridge Health Alliance's Victims of Violence program in the late 1980s, she observed a marked difference between the accepted definition of PTSD and the experiences of a subset of her patients. These were people for whom trauma hadn't struck in the form of a single, acute incident like a bomb blast or flood. Instead, as political prisoners, women in situations of extended domestic violence, and children exposed to prolonged abuse, they had assimilated violence and powerlessness into the core of their being, over long periods of time.

For these patients, distinctions between real and unreal, past and present, dissolved in terrifying ways, and a barrage of accompanying conditions piled onto the more common symptoms of PTSD. Adults like Aida who experienced repeated traumas at a young age seemed particularly vulnerable to this more complex version of the disorder.

With Rosie's help, Aida started treatment for PTSD. She saw a psychiatrist who worked with Iraq War veterans, and, in the process, Judith Herman's language of complex PTSD (CPTSD) became a way to understand her experiences. Naming her condition gave her a sense of control. But the language of psychology told her that healing from CPTSD blossomed in safe, stable spaces. In her case, poverty, undocumented status, and the constant specter of deportation infused every bit of daily life with instability and peril.

When Aida left the trailer to take Gabriel to school or to pick up Jack's medicine at Walmart, she avoided catching glimpses of Mexico peeking through at the dead ends of north-south streets. The slightest mention of Mexico in ordinary conversation could undo a week's progress. As could the prickly feeling of a man eyeing her on the street. Or the olive-green uniform of one of Douglas's five hundred Border Patrol agents. It wasn't clear how Aida could carve even a small redoubt in her precarious world, but she tried.

With the help of hypnosis and talk therapy, Aida's amnesia receded. Details of the attack returned. Pieces of her childhood fell into place. She learned to wrestle violent flashbacks into the coffers of memory, where they belonged. Sometimes it worked, and the past felt less electrically present.

Sometimes it didn't. And eventually, the terror and rage always came crashing back.

Worse still, even as Aida struggled to get better, Gabriel continued to decline. At first, Aida's family and friends thought he was joking, but the boy had, in fact, lost the ability to speak Spanish. Luz, who spoke little English, talked to her grandson as usual, but Gabriel just stared back, his head bobbing and a nervous grin taped to his face. Aida prompted him to respond.

"Come on, Gabriel, talk to your grandmother."

"Yes, Grandma," he said in English.

"No, in Spanish," Aida insisted.

"I don't speak Spanish, Mom. That's for Mexico, where the bad men are."

Gabriel's cousins and friends at school often played in Spanish. When this happened, he refused to join them. Frustrated and shy, he would implore them to return to English. Aida watched him closely during those interactions, trying to determine whether the boy understood Spanish and just refused to speak it or whether he had truly blocked the language out of his mind. Sometimes it seemed like the latter.

In Douglas, less than a third of the population spoke only English at home. Gabriel, already isolated by his mother's illness, had suddenly become even more of a minority. Kids who had mocked him for his strange, shy manner now teased him in Spanish. His closest friends cast quizzical looks at him when he went silent; sometimes they laughed. And Aida, chemically wired to perceive threats in even the most innocent behavior, responded to this treatment by swooping in to save Gabriel. They spent even more time alone together at home.

Visits from Raúl punctuated their isolation. He still spoke to his daughters in clipped, formal phrases, but now raw emotion pulsed behind each word. For years, Aida's indomitable will had grated against his own rectitude. Her ferocious decisions and reckless certainty had regularly left him clenching his fists and stewing in silent recriminations against the way she thrashed through life. Refusing to have an abortion at age sixteen, running headlong into motherhood, crashing across the border, defying all warnings about Pachanga's. Now Raúl understood how much they were alike—a survivor and a struggler. There was dignity, he knew, in the simple act of continuing to live in a world where you were not meant to survive.

Raúl sat with Aida and Gabriel, teaching them yogic breath. He guided them into simple yoga poses and spoke of letting stray thoughts float by without leaving a mark. This seemed implausible to Aida at first. Her intrusive thoughts screamed with such brute physical force. Not paying attention to their warning bells felt crazy. But Aida let Raúl work. Some indestructible fragment of her old personality told her to trust him. When Raúl visited, her mood careened toward optimism. Like anyone learning meditation, she tried to force negative thoughts out of her mind. Tension radiated out of her yoga poses. But she persisted.

"You've gotten through the worst," Raúl told her. "Now you just need to get through the fear, and you are strong enough to do it."

She believed him. Standing in chair position, *utkatasana*, her knees bent, arms outstretched, sometimes for ten minutes or more, she grasped the mental control Raúl so admired. With her body in the shape of a human lightning bolt, her mind stilled. Raúl told her that she was "reconnecting with the universe."

"*Papi*, guess what," Aida would say, greeting him when he came to visit. "I've been practicing. I'm reconnecting with the universe."

And she was. But between 2008 and 2011 in Douglas, Arizona, the universe itself was somewhat bruised.

IN THE 1970S, the noted sociologist Kai Erikson began visiting communities hit by catastrophe. Over the next twenty years, he researched places erased by floods and poisoned by seeping toxics. He spent time in communities blindsided by plant closures, ground down by disinvestment, and torn apart by war. In the end, this research led him to conclude that places, like people, could experience trauma.

It didn't matter much whether the collective blow came instantaneously, as it had in Hiroshima. Or if it evolved over centuries, as it had on some Native American reservations. Erikson wrote that communities could experience "a blow to the basic tissues of social life" so fundamental and deep that it "damages the bonds attaching people together and impairs the prevailing sense of communality." By 2008, Douglas, Arizona, had experienced not one but two traumatic blows to its collective fabric. When the furnaces went cold, Douglas lost its purpose and place in the world. In some ways, this was worse than the resulting loss of jobs and tax revenue. The militarization of border security had a similar effect. For more than a century, Douglas and

Agua Prieta had effectively been one community. Families, businesses, churches, schools—everything—ignored the geopolitical line. But as the border hardened, attitudes changed in tandem.

These traumas did not break Douglas entirely. Organizations like Frontera de Cristo and the Chiricahua Community Health Centers and people like Rosie worked to undo damages inflicted on the country's "new immigration battleground." In doing this, they reassembled DouglaPrieta, little by little. In the years immediately following Aida's attack, residents also came together around new community festivals and the redevelopment of downtown. Mayors searched for new industries and investment to replace the smelter. With the help of private funds and grants, they restored the three-story Phelps Dodge company store to create an elegant government service center. The remote customer service company ACT opened a call center on Tenth Street, and rumors of a new port of entry reserved for trailer trucks raised expectations of increased cross-border commerce.

New subdivisions were green-lighted in the hopes of attracting retirees or enticing Border Patrol agents to live in the community they policed. And someone painted a to-do list on the terra-cotta theater where John Philip Sousa played in Douglas's heyday. The sign read, "Install steel trusses, new roof, stage renovation, restore facade, replace seating . . ."

IF AIDA SAW traces of these efforts, though, they didn't register. The world Aida fought to reconnect with looked splintered and unpromising. Across the United States, the middle class and working poor fought to maintain the income levels they'd enjoyed in the past. In postindustrial Douglas, the trajectory was clear and indisputable. Good jobs could be found in law enforcement, corrections, and other government agencies, but unemployment rates hovered over 10 percent in 2009 and 2010. Real household median income had shrunk by almost 20 percent between 1980 and 2010.

Women felt the brunt of Douglas's decline. They were less likely to find employment in either law enforcement or lawbreaking and more likely to experience the violence of militarized life. A third of Douglas households earned less than the federal poverty line, but more than half of female-headed households were poor. This was almost double the national poverty rate for female-headed households.

Even if Aida could achieve enough mental stability to hold down a job, few options were open to her. With legal status and a high school degree, she might have found work at the prison or Border Patrol. With just legal status, she could have qualified for work at the call center or one of the many stores catering to Mexican shoppers. Those jobs, however, paid a median wage of around fourteen thousand dollars—below the federal poverty line for a mother and son.

Without legal status, even those jobs were out of reach—along with nearly all federal public benefits. Gabriel, as a U.S. citizen, qualified for food stamp assistance, though, and Aida steeled her courage enough to walk into the office and file an application. She shook with terror through the whole interview, her mind spinning out the dangers of interacting with government officials. But she willed herself to get through it, because there was nowhere else to turn.

Gabriel's father had all but disappeared. Once he had appeared unannounced at the trailer with fifty dollars for his son, but that money was long gone. Rumors of his whereabouts suggested that his absence was for the best. There might have been a warrant for his arrest in Phoenix; he'd been charged with aggravated assault with a deadly weapon against an underage girl in New Mexico.

ON AGGREGATE, the children of poor parents who scrape, sacrifice, and do everything right will end up worse off than the children of inattentive wealthy parents. The monthly shortfalls of food, the inadequate medical care, the stress of unstable housing, the parents whose precarious work won't allow them to shuttle kids to practices or music lessons all add up, each tiny deficit compounding into great disadvantage. Trauma and violence arise from and amplify this pattern. Even children exposed to trauma secondhand do worse in school, get sick more often, and die younger than other kids.

Before Gabriel, Aida had barely noticed the poverty around her. Now it felt bottomless. And Gabriel was now also old enough to understand how poor he was and how far he'd fallen behind other kids in his class. This awareness sharpened his suffering, and he fell further behind. In lucid moments between flashbacks and night terrors, Aida saw how trauma can pass from mother to daughter to son like an awful family heirloom. Her whole being strained to give Gabriel a different life.

More than anything, she wanted to get better psychologically so she could provide for her son. She started seeking out Rosie *before* worries snowballed into crises. She'd arrive at the Chiricahua Community Health Centers just after dawn and wait on F Avenue for the clinic to open. Then she'd hover in the lobby, waiting for Rosie to review paperwork and finish her coffee. For fun, she held the door for the day's early patients, greeting each newcomer with a smile. Her excitement was contagious. At first the front desk staff wondered who she was. Later, they just shook their heads. "That's Aida—waiting for Rosie."

Over time, Rosie shared her own story with Aida, something she rarely did with clients. She spoke of Durango and Las Grullas, her husband's abuse, and how she pushed herself to earn a college degree. Aida recognized this shared intimacy for the rare gift it was and marveled at Rosie's ability to thrive in the face of adversity. With each conversation, Aida lost a small part of her pain. Rosie would see Aida around town, often at the grocery store. The younger woman would beam when she saw her friend and counselor. In an instant, she was the sunlit girl again.

"Rosie, it makes me feel so good to talk to you."

"I'm always here for you," Rosie would reply, equally chipper. But she could see from the frown lines and near-empty cart that Aida was sliding deeper into poverty.

When she noticed this, Rosie would help. She had connections with affluent churchgoers and could assemble packages of donated goods for clients in need. One time when Aida's situation had gotten particularly perilous, Rosie arrived at the trailer carrying a bag of used clothing. Gabriel pulled each item out and admired it like a kid at Christmas. He held up a marvelous pair of red Converse shoes in his new larger size. A barely used reversible Tommy Hilfiger jacket looked as if it would make him invincible at school. A T-shirt with a T. rex driving a monster truck elicited an uncontainable "Whoa!" He would wear that shirt as many times a week as his mother allowed, until his body bulged through the seams and it fell apart.

Jack had dwindling savings and a monthly disability check that covered his medicines and oxygen. Luz worked long shifts in the restaurant kitchen and filled any remaining time with housecleaning and elder-care work. When she could leave the trailer without breaking down, Aida helped her mother clean houses. If there was one job Aida could do in those days, it was housecleaning.

Even in quiet moments, Jazmin noted the change in her sister. Aida had always been a little hyper—quick with compliments, smiles, head bobs, and prone to spontaneous bouts of dancing. As a small girl, Jazmin had loved walking around town with her older sister. Aida was the kind of person who skipped down the street clacking a stick along front fences like a girl in a black-and-white sitcom from the 1960s. Hand in hand, they had made a joyous scene like Norman Rockwell *en el barrio*. Now Aida's frenzy scared Jazmin.

When Aida couldn't help Luz clean for money, she hurled herself into taking care of the trailer. She scoured at hurricane speeds, often repeating the same section several times. She scrubbed dishes so hard that her rubber gloves shredded and her face glistened with sweat. At the end of the day, she'd collapse, drained and exhausted, but sleep wouldn't come. Sometimes, after staring at her bedroom ceiling for hours, she'd bolt upright. Still smelling of cleaning product, her palms wet with nervous sweat, she'd stalk around the house until she found more things to organize or scrub. This kind of frenetic energy could last until nearly dawn, inevitably followed by a long period of inky depression. Aida could glaze over for days, stunned and unable to leave her room.

Even fifteen-year-old Jazmin could see that Aida catapulted herself into nerve-jangling cleaning in an attempt to keep one step ahead of fear. Jazmin wanted to grab her sister and anchor her to the ground even for just a moment. If Aida would have permitted it, she would have sat with her, brushing out her hair, whispering that she was safe, just as Aida had done so many times for her.

As bird boned and frail looking as Jazmin appeared, she had somehow survived the chaos and abuse of her early life relatively unscathed. She was unafraid of the world and doing relatively well in high school. She owed that, she knew, in part to Aida's protection. If Aida hadn't brushed her hair, made her breakfasts, and shielded her from blows all those years, who knows how she would have turned out. Now Jazmin wanted to instill her sister with the same iridescent sense of safety that she had felt in her care.

Watching her older sister feverishly cleaning the house, Jazmin wished that something could wash away Aida's pain. Aida brushed past her concern, making a show of her autonomy. Aida still saw herself as the person who did the caring in that trailer.

By 2010, Jack had company sitting around the oxygen tank: Fulgencio, Luz's aging father, also crippled by emphysema, had moved into the trailer. Aida took charge of the two men's care. She kept track of their medications and monitored the levels in their tanks. On good days, she accompanied them on short walks, waiting patiently, a hand on each man's elbow, as they struggled to catch their breath. Mostly, she sat with them, listening to Jack's cranky complaining and her grandfather's wandering stories.

Aida had not spent much time with her grandfather as a girl. The frail man who spent his days sitting under a tree, gasping for air, had once been a rugged cowboy, amateur boxer, and barroom brawler. For weddings and *quinceañeras*, Fulgencio would put on his one tailored *charro* suit and his best gray Stetson hat. In those moments, he looked as if he'd stepped out of a movie from Mexico's golden age of cinema: dashing, handsome, prone to leaping onto horses and flying off with *señoritas* in a cloud of dust.

Luz tensed around him and rarely spoke of her childhood. Aida suspected that as a father Fulgencio had alternated between neglect and abuse. But all the brutality had long since drained out of the disabled man. Around Aida, his big-boned frame bent in gentle submission. To her, his hard hands, wrecked in a pile on his blanketed lap, looked capable, not ominous. She had enough distance from his past to delight in his accounts of epic fights and breakneck rides. He conjured a time when bars in Agua Prieta had swinging doors—just like in Western movies—and Aida was besotted. She doted on him, preparing coffee in the old-fashioned manner he preferred and passing as much time as she could at his side.

The two of them made an odd-matched pair sitting side by side in the yard, one leaving the world, the other fighting to rejoin it.

21

THE "SHOW ME YOUR PAPERS" STATE

ON MARCH 27, 2010, WENDY GLENN heard her friend Robert Krentz make a crackling call to his brother Phil over a radio channel used by ranchers outside Douglas. Phil couldn't understand the call due to poor reception, but he got the impression that his brother had stopped to help an injured migrant. Phil tried to call Robert back. His calls went unanswered, and communication ceased. This didn't strike Wendy as unusual at first. In the rugged country east of Douglas and north of the border, a person got used to long stretches without human voices.

In this land, cattle grazed in broad, scrubby basins slung between broken peaks. The colors were rust red, blood red, cochineal, sand, and tan. Dry washes, fringed by the only green around, had served as north-south highways in this region since before the Anglos or Spanish. Wendy had surrounded herself with the history of this crossroads: stone tools, Clovis points, Neolithic pots carefully glued together. Bits of Spanish ceramic, U.S. Cavalry rifles, the skulls of mountain lions, deer, bear, and jaguar, fossils, mineral specimens, and remnants of the copper industry.

Wendy Glenn was of this place. Her father had owned a mine that supplied the Douglas smelter with lime. Later he became a state congressman. Her grandfather helped found Douglas. Her husband, Warner, tall, sunburned, and not prone to talking, was a renowned tracker and mountain lion hunter. He was, in fact, one of the only people alive to see a jaguar in the wild inside the territorial borders of the United States—and he'd seen a jaguar twice. As a teen and young adult, their daughter, Kelly, was, literally, the poster girl for Ruger rifles.

Around six that evening, Phil Krentz came to find Warner. The sheriff's Search and Rescue team had begun to look for his brother Robert, and a Department of Public Safety helicopter was on the way. Phil hoped that Warner would join them. Warner was the best tracker in southeast Arizona.

Together Warner and his granddaughter scoured the Krentzes' thirty-five-thousand-acre ranch. Just before midnight, they received word that the Department of Public Safety helicopter had spotted a quad in a ditch. Robert Krentz lay sprawled next to his vehicle, killed by multiple 9 mm gunshots. Skid marks indicated the spot where he'd tried to leave the scene in a hurry, and a set of footprints led away. All night, Border Patrol followed the tracks, straight through to a dead end. In the morning, Warner found a different trail. This one led to a point almost twenty miles south, where it too ended. At the border.

Police never caught Krentz's killer. Theories about the murder quickly cleaved around familiar political lines. Longtime critics of ranchers' stance on immigration speculated that Krentz, or his son, had gotten involved with a cartel, taking payments for access to the ranch. Others imagined Krentz as a hero, dying while defending America against alien incursion. More likely, the popular fifty-eight-year-old had just stumbled into the wrong place at the wrong time. Thanks to Border Patrol's success funneling clandestine border crossings into the terrain outside Douglas, there were many wrong places and wrong times to be found.

One thing folks from across the political spectrum agreed on, though, was that the killer himself was probably dead. Cartel *capos* dealt with him, the theory went, because he'd drawn too much attention to an important smuggling route. Indeed, in the heated political context of Arizona in the spring of 2010, Robert Krentz's killing drew a *lot* of attention.

THE YEAR 2010 had begun tense and only gotten worse. Just after the New Year, a Border Patrol agent shot and killed a man near a popular jogging and picnicking spot outside Douglas. That same month, Arizona's Republican governor, Jan Brewer, called for draconian cuts to social services in the state. The 2008 recession had hit Arizona particularly hard, and Brewer looked to balance the budget by slashing funds for health care and education. Her proposal would have kicked 310,000 low-income residents off the state's Medicaid program, cut funding for mental health services, eliminated full-day kindergarten, and ended coverage for most organ transplants. At the local level, Douglas's city council began the year contemplating layoffs and austerity.

That winter and spring, legislators in Phoenix clashed over a controversial bill called S.B. 1070. The legislation proposed some of the harshest state-level statutes targeting undocumented immigrants—and documented people who interacted with them—in generations. Maricopa County, home to Phoenix and its suburbs, had experienced a dramatic influx of Latino residents during the past decade and boiled with white rage. The FBI reported that hate crimes had increased 28 percent in Arizona between 2008 and 2010.

State legislators could not directly regulate immigration; only the federal government held that power. Instead, the bill, authored by Kris Kobach, a Kansas politician and anti-immigration activist, sought to discourage and punish undocumented immigrants by criminalizing everyday life. S.B. 1070 promised to make it a state crime for undocumented people to be present in Arizona, to apply for or hold a job, and to solicit work on the street. It created a misdemeanor crime of transporting an undocumented person, even if that person was a member of the family. And it authorized police to execute warrantless arrests of anyone they suspected had committed an offense that made them deportable. Most controversially, though, the law required law enforcement officers to check the immigration status of anyone they thought might be undocumented.

Critics dubbed S.B. 1070 the "Show Me Your Papers Law." Arizona police chiefs, some of whom vocally opposed the bill, worried that it would force officers to engage in illegal racial profiling. Tucson's police chief, Roberto Villaseñor, warned that the law "drives a wedge between us and the community." Mass protests spread across the state.

ROB KRENTZ'S MURDER on March 27 exploded this already polarized situation. Krentz hadn't been just any rancher. He descended from one of the first Anglo families to raise cattle in the area. He had played for the Douglas High School Bulldogs football team when it sought the state championship in 1968. He had served as president of the Whitewater Draw Natural Resource Conservation District and as a board member of the Malpai Borderlands Group and the Arizona Cattle Growers' Association. He was well known and well loved.

Politicians streamed into southeastern Arizona to pay respects to the family. National media converged upon Douglas once again. Governor Brewer used the occasion to lambast President Obama's handling of border policy, reiterating her demand for the deployment of National Guard troops. The "migrant hunter" Roger Barnett rushed into the spotlight, issuing strong statements about the need for tougher border enforcement.

On March 31, Congresswoman Gabrielle Giffords met with 350 people in a field outside Apache School, a desolate spot near the Krentz ranch. Ranchers from across the county had turned out to express their outrage at the murder and what they perceived as the federal government's failure to protect them from border violence. Flanked by Border Patrol and law enforcement representatives, Giffords sat at a plastic table, her back against a brick wall. Rows of bowed sunburned, white-haired, and cowboy-hatted heads faced her. Beyond that, newspaper reporters and TV crews milled in the pink twilight.

The mood of the meeting tacked between respectful mourning and frank anger. By any statistical measure, the region was safe. Douglas had averaged less than one-quarter of a murder a year during the previous ten years. Krentz's killing was one of seven reported that year in the entire 6,219 square miles of Cochise County. Crime rates in Arizona border towns were not rising. In fact, violent crime rates in Arizona border towns were lower than those in the rest of the state. And nationally, study after study showed that undocumented immigrants committed fewer crimes than their citizen counterparts. If anyone was unsafe, it was undocumented immigrants themselves, subject to rape, robbery, and murder during their transit of the desert. Rosie and Aida understood the fundamental vulnerability of undocumented crime victims intimately. But to ranchers, seeing their world turned upside down, the numbers were irrelevant.

Giffords called for the deployment of additional National Guard troops on the border. The Republican senatorial candidate J. D. Hayworth took that further. He demanded the mobilization of both the army and the National Guard. Another audience member called on Border Patrol to shoot first and ask questions later.

The Krentz family issued a more diplomatic statement: "We hold no malice towards the Mexican people for this senseless act but do hold the political forces in this country and Mexico accountable for what has happened."

In Phoenix, the Arizona Cattle Growers' Association gathered at the capitol, promoting a security plan titled "Restore Our Border." The state senator Russell Pearce, S.B. 1070's sponsor, convened a special hearing to create another venue for ranchers' testimonies. Pearce had tried and failed four times to pass legislation as extreme as S.B. 1070. In the Krentz tragedy he must have sensed the perfect political moment to advance his campaign against undocumented immigrants.

Janet Napolitano, Arizona's former governor and now U.S. secretary of Homeland Security, sent airplanes, drones, and helicopters to patrol the desolate land east of Douglas. By later that summer, a new deployment of National Guard soldiers reached the border. Increased Border Patrol presence brought some relief but also tore up roads and trampled land. Ranchers like John Ladd who had called for increased law enforcement grew to resent smug federal agents swarming around their ranches as much as they hated undocumented immigrants.

To Wendy, the federal response seemed too little, too late, and of the wrong sort. She appreciated Border Patrol agents for their grueling, thankless work, but she reflected that the only way to address undocumented immigration was to create "a border where people could come in legally at Douglas and get the right passport or visa or whatever and either get a work permit if they wanted to work or, if they wanted to study for a few years, get citizenship."

Perhaps the only unequivocal winners in the aftermath of Robert Krentz's killing were the politicians championing S.B. 1070. Public outcry over the rancher's murder proved enough to tip the balance in favor of the controversial bill. Governor Brewer signed it on April 23 and received a bump in popularity that galvanized her flagging reelection campaign. Russell Pearce, the Arizona state senator who sponsored the bill, was elected president of the senate. And Kris Kobach rode its passage to election as Kansas's secretary of state. Brewer and Kobach would go on to play roles in Donald Trump's election and administration.

IN JULY, a federal judge issued a preliminary injunction blocking the most controversial components of S.B. 1070, pending the resolution of multiple lawsuits, including one filed by the Department of Justice in Washington. But, even frozen in legal limbo, the law continued to divide Arizona. S.B. 1070 would require police officers, with minimal training in federal immigration law, to question anyone they stopped about his or her citizen status if they had a "reasonable suspicion" that the person was in the country without authorization. The bill's framers struggled to explain how this didn't lead to racial profiling. Only 15 percent of Latinos in Arizona were undocumented, but this law felt like a declaration of open season for racial harassment on all Latinos.

AT A MAY 12 Douglas City Council meeting, amid discussion of road repair and a Department of Homeland Security grant application for police intelligence software, community leaders asked local politicians to pass a resolution against S.B. 1070. The Presbyterian minister Mark Adams, a longtime organizer of the weekly border vigil, urged council members to take a stance against the law. He argued that this would help repair damaged relations with Agua Prieta. Other speakers warned that the law would have a negative economic impact and that it would virtually require racial profiling. Groups across the country were preparing to boycott Arizona, but the law had already hurt Douglas: Mexican shoppers—the city's most important source of sales tax revenue—were refusing to patronize Douglas stores.

Days later, the resolution's backers organized another display of strength: two hundred people marched down Pan American Avenue to the port of entry, demanding action against S.B. 1070. As in other protests across the state, Douglas participants called attention to the bill's apparent endorsement of racial profiling based on visual appearance: A young girl wearing green antennae carried a sign that asked, "Do I Look Like an Illegal Alien?" Another sign read, "[I'm] Not Illegal, I Tan Easy."

Ever since the punishing strikes and environmental struggles of the 1980s, Douglas had been politically subdued. The town was not known for organized protests or social movements. But 200 people marching down Douglas's streets was the proportional equivalent of 100,000 people marching in New York City. The outcry against S.B. 1070 felt urgent and important.

As these events unfolded, Douglas's city attorney released a memorandum on S.B. 1070. The bill would have little real impact on local procedures, he argued: Douglas police already cooperated with Border Patrol and had done so for more than a decade. Douglas police officers sometimes held suspected undocumented immigrants until the Border Patrol could come to take them away, the memo reported.

Resolution backers fought back: Unlike the town's current policy of limited voluntary law enforcement cooperation, S.B. 1070 *forced* local jurisdictions to participate fully in the business of deporting community members. Worse still, it contained numerous minor provisions aimed at criminalizing relationships that were inescapably part of the social fabric in a town like Douglas. Under the new law, Jack could be charged with migrant smuggling if he was stopped while driving Luz and Aida to the store. As political theater, conceived in white suburban Phoenix and anti-immigrant think tanks in other states, the bill was already driving a wedge between the two halves of DouglaPrieta.

As was often the case with border controversies in Douglas, an 80 percent Latino town, sides did not split neatly along racial lines. Instead, debate fractured along lines defined by decades-old political cliques and ideologies. These divides reflected differing degrees of openness to change and uncertainty. And they mirrored people's positions in the border security industrial complex.

Del Cabarga, a leader of anti–S.B. 1070 efforts in Douglas, embraced his Mexican roots wholeheartedly. He was a third-generation American but visited Agua Prieta without fear nearly every week. He led foodie tours of Mexico and owned a cabin in the mountains of Sonora. It was Del's retreat, a whisper of cool air and pine trees. Del's cousin in the Border Patrol, on the other hand, lived with an ever-present awareness of violence in Mexico. He couldn't fathom why his cousin would willingly expose himself to such extreme danger. His mission was to protect Douglas from the horrors across the line.

Mayor Michael Gomez, by his account one of the first Mexican American dentists licensed in Arizona, helped rally support for border security in 2010. His resentment of the influx of new migrants passing through Douglas was bolstered by the stories he heard from his Border Patrol agent son-in-law. The mayor spoke with evident pride about the safety of Douglas under his administration. The town proper hadn't seen a single Class 1 felony during his time in office, he bragged. But Gomez's wife found herself feeling increasingly afraid and on the defense. Even as crime rates remained low, they began to lock the door to their house. Like many other Douglasites, Gomez also stopped crossing into Agua Prieta. While he opposed S.B. 1070 because its many mandates would tax city resources, he instinctively supported tougher border policies.

In the end, the council voted 5–1 to adopt the resolution against S.B. 1070.

At the next scheduled city council meeting, Gomez launched a discussion on a new resolution. This one demanded increased border enforcement. It called for stepped-up deployment of "physical and human resources as required to secure Arizona's borders and protect its public safety personnel and citizens from criminal activities."

Responding to the changing geography of migrant flows, Border Patrol had reassigned almost two hundred Douglas station agents to more active sectors in recent years. Now Gomez wanted them back, and more. If passed, he informed the council, the resolution would go to the League of Arizona Cities and Towns and rise from there all the way to Washington, D.C.

Nothing stayed secret long in a town the size of Douglas. Supporters of the anti-1070 resolution had learned of Gomez's plan and filled the council chambers in anticipation. The group waited through twenty agenda items and then blasted the mayor. One after another, residents testified that they already felt safe in Douglas. The town didn't need more Border Patrol or National Guard troops. Del Cabarga reminded the gathering of Agua Prieta and Douglas's long history of close, amicable ties. Ginny Jordan, a community organizer and daughter of one of the town's early Mexican American city council members, praised Douglas's low crime rate. She warned of the impact the resolution could have on tourism and cross-border business. A Catholic nun spoke for organizers of the anti-1070 march. And the city council members argued among themselves.

Gomez began to fume. He railed against undocumented immigrants flooding the community and committing crimes. The mayor's daughter lambasted the audience. His wife, known for her laser stare, glared. But late that night, the council voted 5–2 against the resolution. Gomez seemed to take it personally, and opponents heard him promise that he'd have a surprise in store for the council at the July 6 meeting.

Over the Fourth of July weekend, people opposed to S.B. 1070 and intensified border enforcement fanned out into community events. In three days, they collected a symbolic 1,776 signatures on a petition supporting their cause. The equivalent of more than one in ten residents of a town reluctant to engage in political protest was willing to speak out against recent events. Armed with this backing, advocates for more welcoming pro-immigrant policies felt confident entering the meeting on July 6.

They arrived early and sat at the front. Then ranchers began to file into the chambers. By the time Gomez reintroduced his resolution for a second attempt at its passage, the crowd had overflowed the chamber and clogged the lobby. More than two dozen constituents spoke that night. Del, Ginny, and others spoke against the resolution as tension boiled into outright conflict. When Ginny spoke, Mayor Gomez interrupted to disagree with her point. Three-quarters of the speakers clearly supported Gomez's resolution. Of that group, more than half—most of them ranchers—lived outside town. Wendy Glenn joined the ranchers decrying the lack of security, and Susan Krentz, Robert Krentz's widow, walked to the lectern as one of the final speakers. She held a photograph of her husband in front of her as she praised the resolution.

In the end, the council rejected Gomez's resolution again. By fall, members of the group formed to oppose S.B. 1070 mobilized a campaign to recall the mayor. After an acrimonious year, the effort fell short of reaching the ballot, dismissed by a judge. But the embattled mayor did not seek re-election. Danny Ortega, the city's next mayor, would work with the city council to repair relations with Agua Prieta and champion Douglas as a "welcoming city."

A new chief of the Douglas Police Department, hired after Charlie Austin's retirement in 2007, understood the dangers of involving local law enforcement in the federal business of deporting community members. Alberto Melis had already begun working with local groups to disentangle public safety officers from immigration enforcement. Rosie Mendoza had collaborated with him to ensure that city police did not question residents reporting domestic violence about their immigration status. The chief and the social worker both knew that involving local police in immigration enforcement helped criminals: evidence from around the country showed that immigrant community members, both undocumented and documented, were less likely to report crimes, come forward as witnesses, press charges against perpetrators, or share valuable information with police investigators when they feared that talking to police might have immigration consequences.

But some level of cooperation between Douglas police officers and Border Patrol was still standard practice. For now, arguing loudly with a boyfriend, failing to signal a turn while driving, or committing a minor misdemeanor could still land Douglas residents in the hands of the Border Patrol. Small slipups carried steep prices for people like Aida. With or without Gomez's resolution, Ortega's counterefforts, and the new police chief's goodwill, hate-filled rhetoric flooded the state of Arizona. Douglas police officers continued to hold suspected undocumented people for Border Patrol. And the walls severing Aida from her community rose higher.

22

WHAT CARE CAN DO

AIDA WOKE TO A GLISTENING VEIL of snow outside her window. It was such a rare, delicate substance to behold in Douglas. Hoarfrost on mesquites took her breath away. She began to hop around her bedroom, pulling on warm clothes and shouting to wake her sisters and Gabriel. The snow and bright winter light gushed through her veins better than any antidepressant medication. The whole trailer should be leaping out of their covers and joining her, she decided. She rushed to slide her thickest socks over sleepy Gabriel's hands, urging him to hurry. This joy wouldn't survive the noonday sun.

Cynthia and Jazmin moaned when Aida woke them.

"Come on—for the kids, get up for the kids."

Jazmin let herself be pulled out of bed. Jennifer stumbled around her room, dressing her son and daughter in as many layers as she could fit over them. Cynthia grumbled harder and refused to surrender her warm blankets.

Outside, snowballs flew, wet and delicious. Laughing, Aida, Jazmin, and the children ducked and slipped, their cheeks red and sock-gloves soggy. Aida instructed the children in the art of rolling a snowman base. There wasn't enough snow to build anything, but they loved watching a ball grow bigger and bigger, plucking up twigs and leaves, leaving the ground exposed. Jazmin, shimmering with happiness, watched Aida. Her sister had come a long way in recent months.

It was true. Between 2010 and 2012, the kind of care and support most people take for granted began to form around her. She couldn't afford the medicines a psychiatrist had prescribed for her, but friends and family proved just as effective.

Journalists, academics, and political groups in Mexico had rediscovered the history of the GPG. Raúl received invitations to speak at conferences, newspapers and magazines ran features about his life, and he opened up to Aida about all that he'd survived. It exhilarated her to feel a blood connection to someone so principled and brave. His gentle coaching in the discipline of breath and relaxation took on new potency once she understood what Raúl had overcome. Knowing Raúl's blood ran through her veins steeled Aida against fear.

Rosie provided a different kind of inspiration, nudging Aida to imagine a life beyond bare survival. Rosie had survived violence like Aida and remade her life by helping others. On days when it felt as if the worst were behind her and she allowed herself to imagine a future, Aida wanted to follow Rosie's footsteps. If Cipriano, the indigenous healer, was Rosie's guide, Rosie was Aida's. She vowed to get better, finish high school, and go to college to become a social worker.

"Rosie, I want to *be* you," she confided to the older woman.

Aida's efforts to rejoin society also got a nudge from another, more unconventional friend. She'd initially met Alvaro Andrade in high school. He had grown up in one of the mansions across from the Tenth Street Park. In more prosperous times, the places were homes to bankers and PD managers. During the bleak early 1990s, Johnny Depp, Jerry Lewis, and Faye Dunaway had supposedly rented Alvaro's house for a time. That was a roommate situation as surreal as the inexplicable movie they filmed together in scrubland outside Douglas.

By the time Alvaro was in middle school, federal agents were Douglas's upper crust, and his father was a customs agent at the port of entry. Alvaro grew up with U.S. citizenship, a cavernous bedroom all to himself, and more material comfort than almost every kid he knew. It was enough to riddle him with eternal unease and a creeping sense of dread.

When Alvaro and Aida had met in high school, Alvaro's life revolved around ear-shattering metal. He and his band named themselves Atrest, after a single word engraved on a tombstone deep in the Douglas cemetery. Alvaro and his friends decided that the inscription wasn't a family name. It was a botched "At Rest," carved by an illiterate mason. Rest was a mistake, they figured. Just one chisel slip away from death. And so: Atrest.

Soon Atrest was playing to large crowds in Agua Prieta and then touring the Southwest. They played any venue they could find, enjoying their unexpected ticket to small-time fame. They played community festivals, charity events, and small clubs all over southern Arizona and northern Mexico. And so for a time, Alvaro escaped the grip of Douglas, and he and Aida fell out of touch.

Alvaro's rise, like most musical endeavors, didn't last long. Atrest came crashing down in an implosion of pills and booze, and Alvaro stumbled back to Douglas. Instead of moving back to the big house, he squatted in a windowless concrete room with no heat and went long stretches without eating.

Alvaro turned twenty in August 2008, a few days after the attack on Aida. He hadn't thought about his old acquaintance for years, but for some reason she came to mind that day. Celebrating with friends but feeling completely alone, he had stumbled into a vacant lot filled with pigweed and mesquite thorn. For the first time in years, he noticed the stars, an enormous vault of light so sharp and clear that he could read the label on his forty of beer. As he looked up into the night, his mind drifted from the wreck of his own life to wondering what had happened to Aida.

Unbeknownst to Alvaro, that night Aida lay in the University Medical Center. While Alvaro stared into the stars and listened to the universe, his old friend fought for her life. Alvaro threw away his beer and breathed. He sensed a connection to Aida, wherever she was, and vowed to track her down.

In the morning, mostly sober, he felt a trace of Aida still clinging to him. He asked around about her and learned nothing. Finally, a month later, he found her, returned from the hospital, recovering in Jack and Luz's trailer. At their reunion, Alvaro discovered that his connection to Aida back in early August had been stronger than he could have imagined: Piecing together the family's account of Aida's attack and salvation, he realized that his father had been on duty at the port of entry that day. When the paramedic Frank Hone tried to wheel Aida across the border, Alvaro's father had been part of the group that tried to stop him.

"Damn, this place is strange" was about the sum total of Aida and Alvaro's reaction. She forgave his father without hesitation. Luz hesitated but then agreed. Alvaro's father had just been doing his job.

"Check out my scars again," Aida said, changing the topic.

Who does that? he thought. Who bounces back from death like that? Alvaro marveled at her strength and the speed of her physical recovery.

It would take many more visits, and their growing friendship, for Alvaro to fully understand how far from recovery Aida was. What Alvaro could see, though, was that only a few months after the attack she looked healthier than he did. Strung out and rail thin with red-rimmed eyes, Alvaro looked as if he needed more help than Aida. Something about her calmed the buzzing in his head.

But it wasn't Aida he was attracted to. In the coming years, Alvaro and Jennifer became a couple. It was a mismatched, turbulent affair that in retrospect Alvaro mostly enjoyed because it brought him closer to his friend Aida. Alvaro moved into the trailer during that period—what was one more person, amid the chaos of relatives, friends, and Aida's attacks? Aida hardly even noticed the extra mouth to feed and man to clean up after. The whirling tornado of her housework took on everything in its path.

The trailer had a hole in the roof above the stove and a hole in the floor next to the toilet that Alvaro and Aida tried to repair. But even in that condition, the trailer was more of a home to Alvaro than the windowless dump he had fallen into after his band's collapse. With a scraggly goatee and his hair pulled back, he looked Jesus-like. And even with the pills, he had a gentle manner to match. He spoke quietly and deliberately. Atrest's end had made him philosophical. When Aida was able, she sat on the porch for hours talking with him, watching the kids play, and reflecting on their lives. Like a more spiritual version of Raúl, Alvaro asked questions about the universe and their place in it, and Aida listened, rapt. But Aida's attacks took Alvaro off guard.

Sometimes, when panic overwhelmed all of her resistance, the Aida he knew dissolved. In those moments, often on her knees and elbows, beyond words or actions, all she could do was emit a ragged, stuttering moan. When Alvaro heard this, he couldn't not laugh; it just came out.

"Uhhh. Uhhh. Uhhhhhhh." Alvaro imitated Aida's lowing in a teasing voice.

The object of his imitation looked up at him. Her distorted face looked like smashed fruit. Her hair, slick with sweat and tears, stuck in her mouth. This made Alvaro laugh harder.

"Uhhhh. Uhhhh," he repeated.

Aida stopped making the noise. A black sucking silence engulfed Alvaro's fake moans. And then, bit by bit, her face recomposed. It was like watching the film of a car accident in reverse. Each piece of her face started unbreaking and regluing, returning to whole. And then she laughed along with Alvaro.

Only Alvaro could do that, Aida's sisters thought to themselves.

Alvaro's ability to calm Aida wasn't limited to the shock of imitation. For some reason, seeing Aida transform into a completely unrecognizable, alien entity, driven by fear and rage, didn't scare Alvaro as much as it scared others. Over time, with Aida's help, he learned the right combination of words that, when repeated mantra-like, could bring her back:

There are people who love you.

You are not a bad person; you are just sick.

You are safe, even though your brain is trying to tell you you're not.

It's just your PTSD talking.

You are safe.

You are loved.

You are safe.

AIDA STILL STRUGGLED to calm herself, but for once, between Raúl, Rosie, and Alvaro, she had people around her who could. Little by little, the attacks receded. She emerged from her house more frequently, volunteered in Gabriel's classroom, and cared for a bedridden elderly friend of her mother's. Rosie persuaded her to volunteer at a Relay for Life race, and Aida received praise for her work with youth participants in the charity run. Aida had begun to learn how to live without fighting or fleeing. She felt part of the fabric of Douglas again and imagined someday earning the kind of acceptance other residents were born with.

WHEN ALVARO FORMED a new band, Aida followed him to practices. While the group played, she sat on a broken sofa, feeling the sound razor through her. Most people wouldn't equate death metal with relaxation, but somehow the jarring music quieted her mind. Inspired by the rockers, and helped by a tattoo artist and body piercer in the band who offered his services for free, she pierced her lip, nose, and brow. With each spike, her fear of stabbing ebbed. For a time in high school, she'd dressed exclusively in black T-shirts and jeans. With her Pink Floyd wall hanging, skull rings, and fondness for Guns N' Roses, she considered herself a fist-pumping rocker in a town of foot-shuffling *norteños*. During the intermittent periods when she'd happily taken care of Gabriel behind the counter at Movies 'n' More, Aida had worn bright colors. She thought of her look from those years as "Latina soccer mom"—not quite pink sweater sets, but almost. Now, with hardware accenting her face, she gravitated back to black and began to acquire tattoos.

For Aida, inking and piercing, done by the new friend, were a kind of therapy. They exposed her to needles and blood in a way that reframed memories of stabbing and hospitals. Each mark was a beachhead—a place where she had reasserted control over her physical being. She felt pride in her body for the first time in years.

To Rosie, the new look threatened Aida's ability to stay in the United States. Rosie continued to insist that despite the deportation, false claim of citizenship, and humanitarian parole overstay, Aida might still have a chance at legal residency. Because she was the mother of a U.S. citizen, a victim of domestic violence at the hands of her U.S. citizen husband, and a caregiver for Jack, the immigration system might just move for her. The odds were not great, though. Aida's false claim at the border, deportation, and visa overstay weighed heavily against her. But she had no criminal record, and that helped. At a minimum, she might have a case for legal residency under the Violence Against Women Act, which protected some undocumented victims of domestic violence perpetuated by U.S. citizens and legal permanent residents.

Aida adored Rosie. During her worst days, she held on to Rosie's words like a smooth, magical stone. Rosie's kindness sustained her. But Aida drew the line at following Rosie's advice to apply for residency. Approaching the authorities petrified her. Every time Rosie mentioned legal residency, Aida would politely agree, knowing deep down that she'd never follow through. The authorities might condemn the violence she had suffered, and this might offer a chance at legal status, but Aida also knew that those same authorities had helped make the world that had almost killed her. They were not to be trusted. She refused to apply. When Rosie arranged for her to meet an attorney, Aida found some crisis exploding in the trailer that required her immediate attention at the exact time of the appointment.

Rosie understood why Aida would want to keep her distance from immigration officialdom. Still, she hoped the young woman would take the chance. She kept Aida's file open long after the clinic's policies told her to close it. But what Rosie couldn't understand was Aida's new look. If Aida applied for legal residency, or encountered the law in some other way, officials would not see beyond her new piercings and *chola* swagger. They wouldn't see the person who battled through PTSD to care for Jack, her grandfather, and friends. They'd overlook the devoted single mother and miss the woman who cultivated a sense of dignity out of surviving in a world she was not intended to survive.

All that would be invisible. Officials would see nothing but a metal-pierced delinquent.

23.

SLIPKNOT

THURSDAY, JANUARY 5, 2012, was the kind of day that had inspired Douglas civic boosters to write rapturous tourism pamphlets for more than a century. While the rest of the United States stumbled through cold gray winter, Douglas prepared to enjoy its eighth day in a row of sunny seventy-degree weather. The previous day's *Douglas Dispatch* reported on a quiet New Year's Eve, marked by a few stray gunshots and a single DUI.

New census numbers, cited in the same issue, confirmed that Douglas, like so many small towns across the country, had lost residents the year before. This day's *New York Times* offered even starker news. "Harder for Americans to Rise from Lower Rungs," the front-page headline read. The story described a growing consensus among researchers that upward economic mobility for low-income people in the United States had stagnated, particularly compared with other developed countries. During the past decades, the land of opportunity had tilted steeply against poor people.

The grim news about economic mobility might have surprised Aida. She still believed in the promise of the country that she'd embraced as a young girl at Sarah Marley Elementary. She knew she would find a way to finish school someday. She would earn diplomas and become a counselor like Rosie. She would escape Douglas and live in a big apartment in New York City with Gabriel. It just might take a while.

Christmas had come and gone in a particularly bleak manner that year. Luz and Jack managed to wrap a few presents, of the most practical kind, for Gabriel. Aida, still unable to work, had little to give beyond kisses. Gabriel waited all morning for the Lego set that he'd had his heart set on. He pretended not to be disappointed. The forced cheer he dashed over his sadness pierced Aida even more than her inability to give him the one thing he desired. He was too good at accepting disappointment for such a small boy. After Christmas, Aida teetered on the edge of a familiar pit. She was so aware of having messed up so many parts of her life. She knew that she'd gone down so many ill-advised alleys and made so many poor choices. But the one thing she could not mess up was being a good mother to Gabriel. Not if it killed her, she thought.

January 5, 2012, dawned so clear that mountains deep in Mexico and far north in Arizona seemed to rise out of the edge of Douglas. The bright morning lifted Aida's spirits. Even if failing Gabriel on Christmas still ached, she had kept one promise to him: she had not left his side since returning from the hospital. More and more, she managed to volunteer in his classroom, attend parent-teacher conferences, and cheer for him at school performances. She had also broken a chain of child abuse that stretched as far back as anyone could remember. She had never hurt Gabriel, and that, in her family, was not nothing.

When Jack announced that he'd run out of one of his medicines, Aida volunteered to go to Walmart for him. Luz drove. Aida put on a light cotton sweater just right for the perfect winter day.

Mother and daughter walked into the superstore's welcoming blue light, enjoying each other's company. Luz wandered off across the shiny floors and overstuffed aisles to pick up a few items the trailer needed—toothpaste, Kotex. Aida waited in line at the pharmacy.

At first she ignored the post-Christmas end cap display of miniature Lego kits. Their six-dollar price was six dollars more than she had in her empty wallet that afternoon. But the prescription took ages to fill. She dawdled alongside the Lego display, anxious, her fingers brushing the tiny boxes. Sixty-odd pieces and a figure. The pharmacist called Jack's last name, and she turned away, relieved.

As an afterthought, she tipped a box into her purse.

LUZ AND AIDA paid for the prescription and sundry items. Aida chatted with the checkout woman. Luz was silent, her mind back at the trailer with her father, Fulgencio, who was clearly dying. At the door, Aida tensed. Remembering the Lego kit, she hesitated. And then she stepped out into the afternoon. During the years since returning from the hospital, she'd often had the metal song "Dead Memories" by Slipknot stuck in her head. "When I got away, I only kept my scars," she hummed. "The other me is dead." "I can't go back again. I can't go back again." Her life was a slipknot. Tug one way and it came free and undone; tug the other and it strangled tight.

The alarm was more of a tone than the piercing bell she'd expected. She considered running, but security was already there.

Aida's shoplifting was a minor misdemeanor. Young adults in a hundred white suburbs across the country got featherlight slaps on the wrist every day for the same offense. But this was Arizona in 2012. Aida and her family understood the severe consequences of turbocharged immigration enforcement all too well.

THE U.S. LEGAL SYSTEM does not consider deportation a punishment. Removing an undocumented immigrant is simply a civil, administrative correction of that person's status. As a result, deportation proceedings lack many of the due process protections found in criminal courts. But for Aida, sitting in a cell at the Douglas Police Station waiting for Border Patrol, the hairsplitting arguments of distant judges couldn't have felt more absurd. At best, Aida thought, she faced heart-wrenching exile from her family and home; at worst, she faced death at the hands of an unsated killer.

Aida threw up until there was nothing left in her body but dry heaves punctuated by panicked sobs. The cell reeked, and the other prisoners edged away. Aida was too afraid to feel embarrassed.

"WHAT'S *WRONG* WITH YOU?" The policeman's words sounded sympathetic, not angry. He led Aida out of the cell and sat her on a bench. Douglas's police station occupied a building that had been the town's elegant train depot, once the bustling hub of an international copper industry. The room was polished and ornate. The officer gave Aida a bottle of water. She composed herself in fits and starts—enough to blurt out a rough outline of her story.

"I'm going to help you," he said. The officer placed a call to the Border Patrol, and when the standard pair of agents arrived a while later to collect Aida, a supervisor accompanied them. They interviewed Aida outside. The three agents stood with their feet spread, hands on hips, in a triangle around her. Railroad tracks beside the station glinted in the sunset, disappearing south. Just beyond Aida's view, she knew, they led straight to the abandoned railroad yard in Agua Prieta where the attack occurred. Where she'd be by nightfall.

"Calm down." For a while that was all the agents said. "You need to calm down." As if this were something Aida could control. Fulgencio used to tell Aida stories about fighting to pull a roped and rearing stallion back to earth. Reining in a full-blown PTSD attack was like that. But somehow Aida found the strength to do it.

"I can't go back." At first she begged, then the words took on the sound of a declaration. "I'm afraid to go back."

For years, Rosie had told her that she had rights. Now she found her voice and would not stop. She explained and appealed as the supervisor looked on. Her life story poured out in torrents until the man gestured at her to stop. Another agent told Aida to take out her piercings. The Border Patrol agent held out a plastic baggy for the jewelry, but Aida was too nervous. She fumbled and threw the studs and bars onto the ground.

"I don't care—I don't want them. You have to listen to me." She pressed on with her story.

The agent handcuffed her, and the supervisor spoke.

"You're going to have an opportunity to tell this to a judge who will decide whether you can stay." U.S. law required the supervisor to say words like that whenever immigrants expressed a credible fear of returning to their home country. Federal statutes and international treaty obligations guaranteed that immigrants expressing credible fears of returning to their home countries were entitled to a hearing in front of a judge. In practice, agents often failed to follow the law, preferring the streamlined convenience of expedited removal. This time, though, the system worked.

"But I'll tell you," the supervisor warned, "you're going to be detained for a *while*. We don't know how long. It could be months. It could be more."

Aida would be separated from Gabriel for months. She would not be with Fulgencio when he died. As with deportation, the legal system did not classify immigration detention as punishment, but conditions could be worse than those in many criminal prisons. And in the end, a Border Patrol agent at the station told her later, she would still have virtually no chance of winning her case.

"Okay," Aida answered. "But it's what I have to do."

GOING AWAY TO COME BACK

PART FOUR

24.

EMA'S JOURNEY

BETWEEN 2006 AND 2009, the Causana Foundation's soccer team had gotten better and stronger. Ema and her teammates had a lot to prove to the hecklers and league officials. More than once, league governing bodies had come close to expelling the team. Officials forced them to change their name from the vaguely suggestive "Saltamontes de Venus" to "Guipuzcoa," the name of a Quito neighborhood. But the team played on.

In July 2009, conflict with the league came to a head during a day of matches at La Floresta stadium on the northeast side of the city. Guipuzcoa's game ended without incident, and the team filtered into the stands to watch the next contest. Spectators noticed and began to jeer. It was the usual provocation, but one spectator began to film the women's reactions. In a flash of defiance, two Guipuzcoa players kissed on camera. The mob that formed in response to this open show of affection drove Guipuzcoa from the stadium.

League officials finally had the pretense they needed. Later that week, they unanimously voted to expel the team for "obscene acts." And this, in turn, gave the team what it needed—an act of overt discrimination that could be challenged in court.

Led by the team captain, a young law student, Guipuzcoa sued and won a partial victory in court. But the league refused to reinstate the team. The Causana Foundation, supported by allies from across Ecuadorian civil society, fought back, taking the case to a higher court. Ema marched with her teammates and helped stage sit-ins. They wore their uniforms and chanted, "*¡Chucha con chucha, es nuestra lucha!*" Ema's little sister joined one of the protests, and the two of them laughed together at the vehemence with which the straight girl shouted, "Cunt with cunt, that is our fight!"

As the next ruling approached, the team staged a roving soccer match through the center of the city. It culminated in an elaborate public kiss. Once again, the team prevailed in court and the league refused to comply.

The legal process dragged on for years, and the team disintegrated, members drifting off to play for other clubs. They'd won the preliminary legal battles and influenced public opinion in ways that would reverberate through Ecuador for years. The victories exacted a toll, though. Months of struggle, constant intimidation by Guipuzcoa's critics, and, worst of all, the steady dissolution of the team itself wore at Ema and her comrades.

Around this time, Ema's economic situation began to disintegrate as well. The company she worked for ran into financial trouble and fell behind on paying its employees. Ema and her colleagues kept showing up for shifts, hoping the problems would be resolved and back pay would arrive. After a few weeks, employees with families to support left in search of other jobs. Ema made it a couple months. Her savings from the job had lifted her into Ecuador's middle class and paid for college. Now they were gone.

For the next few years, Ema subsisted by cobbling together whatever employment she could find. She worked as a bank teller. She sold cell phone plans. For a time she traveled around the country administering the country's census. None of these paid enough, or left sufficient time, for Ema to continue her studies. The comfortable future she'd imagined for herself just a few years earlier disappeared from view. In its place loomed loneliness, desperation, and the dark side of Quito she remembered from earlier forays. Through it all, discrimination shadowed her. Bosses made thinly veiled comments about her sexuality. Coworkers grumbled about working with a *marimacha*. Sometimes she'd be let go for no reason. The country's new constitution barred discrimination based on sexual orientation, extended some rights to same-sex couples, and condemned hate crimes. But on a daily basis—in the workplace, on the sidewalk outside gay bars, and on the bus home from work—Ema experienced threats and harassment. Outside the protective circle of her team, the specter of antigay violence and discrimination compounded Ema's economic woes.

In 2013, Ecuador's Constitutional Tribunal refused to hear the team's appeal, leaving its fate in limbo. But by then, Ema had left the country she loved.

IN THOSE DAYS, it was not hard to find Ecuadorians departing for New York. Around 550,000 Ecuadorians lived in the United States, about a third of them undocumented. A large proportion of that population lived in or around New York City, including Ema's sister, whom she hoped to join. Asking around, Ema learned that her cousin's former nanny, Juana, was in the final stages of planning the trip. Juana had already researched routes and *coyotes*, and Ema trusted her. Juana's former charge—Ema's cousin—had already made the journey north.

Gathering money took a while, but eventually Ema and Juana boarded an airline flight bound for Honduras, with a transfer in El Salvador. Thirty-eight other hopeful clients of the same smuggling operation accompanied them. Once it landed in San Pedro Sula, Honduras, the group would face a four-thousand-mile overland journey, three perilous national border crossings, and a minimum of three nights of bushwhacking through the Sonoran Desert—all entrusted to the tender mercies of transnational criminal organizations.

Anyone who watched the news in Ecuador had heard of the massacre of seventy-two South and Central American migrants by the Zetas Cartel at a ranch in northern Mexico two years earlier. Accounts of more mundane extortion, rape, and kidnapping jumbled in Ema's mind.

Ema and Juana had paid their smugglers extra for "special treatment"—the "deluxe package." But in practice, that meant little. Before leaving home, Ema and her mother had worked out a set of code words in case she fell into the hands of another band of smugglers or her own guides turned on her. It was not uncommon, she knew, for smugglers to hold their charges captive until family back home paid extra "fees."

If anyone in the group was detained by authorities before reaching the U.S.-Mexico border, they'd also face extortion and abuse. And then a long flight back to Ecuador. For Ema, repatriation would mean having to start—and pay—all over again.

AS THE PLANE climbed over Ecuador's snowcapped mountains and green coastal plains, Ema felt a pang of loss. Homesickness pushed aside fear of the unknown. Even as they leveled off over the Pacific Ocean, she was unprepared for how much Ecuador pulled at her to stay. She thought about her summer working for the census. She had traveled for months with a group of young survey takers. They'd covered the country in canoes, buses, and pickup trucks, from the high Andes to the Amazon basin and hissing humid coast. It opened her eyes to the majesty of her country. On a syrupy Amazonian tributary, two hours' journey in a dugout canoe from the nearest road, she interviewed women in huts raised on stilts. In a gray coastal village outside Esmeraldas, Afro-Ecuadorians spoke Spanish so fast that she couldn't understand them. One afternoon, she stooped to enter a shack on the outskirts of a town in Imbabura Province. Bottle caps, used as clever improvised washers, prevented nails from pulling through the house's cardboard siding. Inside, an old woman prepared soup for the unexpected visitor. Ema set down her clipboard to take the bowl from the woman's wrinkled hands. The soup was salty hot water with two noodles—all the woman could offer and more than enough.

Before taking the job with the census, Ema had not appreciated her country. Now, leaving, she wanted to hold on to its verdant plantations and misty Pacific coast, the boiling Amazon, and the snowcapped volcanoes. More than anything, she wanted to return to her mother.

Ema and Luisa had had a long goodbye in Mitad del Mundo. Talk of money transfers, code words, and contacts in New York camouflaged their grief. Paying thousands of dollars in smuggler fees consumed their attention.

Ema had emptied her own savings and taken out small loans to cover the costs. Luisa wanted to help more. She'd begun saving for college, where she wanted to study to be a counselor. She'd be a much better therapist, Ema said, breaking down, than the horrible woman they'd seen together during the year of their schism. Just five years ago, they'd battled over whether Ema could be "cured" of her sexuality. Now her mother was saving to study so she could do better for other families. As the two women held each other for the last time, Luisa's college plans crystallized their reconciliation. They were a kind of amends. Of course, Luisa still insisted that Ema use those college savings to help pay for the trip.

Not long ago, Ema reflected in her window seat, she'd been on the way to friendship, family, education, and a moderate degree of comfort. That future still felt like her real life even as it disappeared beneath the clouds. Her new life felt like a movie happening to someone else.

EVEN IN HER most pessimistic calculations, Ema had not imagined that the journey could end so quickly. But there she was, three hours after leaving Ecuador, standing in line for customs and immigration at the San Salvador international airport watching officials arrest members of her group. One by one, the Ecuadorians presented themselves for inspection. The immigration officers looked cranky and uncomfortable, sitting in their booths, reviewing passports, and snarling questions. From her place at the end of the line, Ema noted that the woman in booth seven was the worst. Other officers occasionally waved one of Ema's group through to the next stage. The woman in seven signaled for police to whisk the aspiring immigrants away every single time. Ema counted the bodies ahead of her, trying to estimate her chances of getting line seven. The math didn't look good, and she racked her brain for a plan. When the woman in booth seven gesticulated for Ema to step forward, she took Juana by the hand and pulled her along.

"Say you're my girlfriend," she said to Juana.

"What is the purpose of your travel?" the officer asked, contemplating Ema and Juana's high heels and professional dress.

Ema let fly with her hasty plan. "We are going to an international congress of lesbians in Honduras," she said, giving her best impression of eager anticipation.

The officer stiffened and stamped their passports, in a sudden rush to be done with the two women.

OUTSIDE THE SAN PEDRO SULA AIRPORT, crowds of South Americans found drivers using code words given to them by contacts in their home countries. "*Tigre*," Ema and Juana repeated to a succession of taxi drivers until, at last, a man nodded and gestured impatiently for them to climb into his packed car. It *was* like a movie, Ema thought, streaking through the sultry Honduran night. The successful escape in El Salvador and the secret-agent car ride made her feel like a heroine, not a victim.

More exchanges of code words followed. Ema handed over another thousand dollars in cash at a nondescript house crammed with Colombians, Peruvians, and Ecuadorians. She received tortillas and coffee in return. The men operating the stash house all called one another Marroquín—Marroquín Uno, Marroquín Dos, Marroquín Tres—and organized their charges into platoons: Alpha, Beta, Delta. Ema couldn't help but admire the military precision of the operation.

That night, she and Juana squeezed aboard a van. There were thirty men and women and their suitcases in seating designed for fifteen.

AS THEY APPROACHED the first of many police checkpoints that night, Ema rehearsed a Honduran accent in her mind and tried to remember facts that would help her pass as a native. It was hopeless, she realized. No one would confuse this dangerously overloaded van for a local tour group.

The police waved the van through the stop without comment. Dark uniforms and the dull glint of guns passed in the night.

Hours later, they stopped in a spot away from lights and houses. The hiss of tropical insects and the murmur of a river filled the darkness. Humidity breathed off thick vegetation. Men appeared, startling the group with shouts.

"That's Guatemala across the bridge," a man hollered as his team herded the group like animals. Yelling and sudden movement after hours of hushed immobility panicked the group. Commands, getting louder and more urgent, propelled them forward. Ema ran along with the stampede, her suitcase banging against her leg. She lost sight of Juana in the darkness.

"You fall behind, you get left behind," someone said.

Pushed by her companions, Ema lurched forward. The bridge was temporary but well constructed out of rough timbers. There had been no time to change in San Pedro Sula, so her high heels clutched for traction on the slippery wood. Halfway across the river, one heel stuck in a crack and she broke it off, still running breakneck.

On the other side, she leaped into a waiting truck, terrified of getting left behind. The skin of her fellow passengers pressed against hers. They were all slippery with sweat. Older women breathed hard, recovering from the sprint.

"Everyone, off! Hurry, get into the woods." Shouting from new men twisted the group of South Americans around. Unbribable police had appeared nearby. "Scatter!"

Ema crouched under a bush until dawn. Insects gnawed at her thighs, and sticky liquid dripped on her arms. She strained to hear a signal from the smugglers. Her fear of getting arrested by Guatemalan police paled in comparison to her terror of getting left there. Sometime in the blue-green morning, the truck reappeared and Ema emerged from hiding. Her legs ached and itched. She was a new person, she realized. The cocky, border-guard-defying heroine of the day before had decomposed in the night. All that remained was an unadorned certainty that she would survive this journey, no matter how ugly it got.

JUANA ALSO SURVIVED the night in hiding and rejoined Ema and the group. Over the next days, men in snakeskin boots shuttled them from station to station. They paused at a three-story apartment building in the capital and a bleak hotel on the edge of some unknown village. In the city of Huehue-tenango, eighty-five miles from Mexico, their guides locked them in a compound for two weeks because the border was "hot."

Ema introduced herself to her warden the same way she had approached everyone who intrigued her through the journey.

"What's your deal?" she asked, striking a confident footballer pose. "Single? Married? Divorced? Gay? Student? What?"

"Married," the young man said. "Christian. Evangelist for God."

This puzzled Ema. "If you're an Evangelical Christian, what are you doing smuggling people?"

"We are here to help," he said with a smile. "God is with migrants."

A family of smiling Evangelical Christian smugglers operated the clandestine way station. Once a luxurious mansion complete with pool and gardens, the property was enormous. Sylvester, the lanky young man, showed Ema and Juana to their assigned quarters, a former chicken shed. Inside, piles of blankets awaited. They reeked of the sweat of hundreds of previous guests, but the shed was luxurious compared with where Ema and Juana had stayed the night before.

The Evangelical smugglers mixed missionary messages with logistical updates. Other smuggler way stations operated as prisons. Here, the administrators allowed their charges to venture into town in small groups to purchase cigarettes and food. Ema and Juana spent most of their time sitting by the pool; they couldn't believe that they were sitting by a pool. The water was dirty and the weather too cold for swimming, but the two women imagined themselves on a kind of vacation.

For hours on end, they spoke of home. Juana told Ema about the children she'd left with family members. Together they tried to level the impossible scale of immigrant sorrow: the future, on one side, family and roots on the other. One night, the Evangelicals cooked *mote* for the Ecuadorians. The warm stew of boiled corn was the typical dish of the region where Ema had spent her early childhood. For the first time since leaving home, her stomach unclenched and the anxious grumbling that had plagued her since Honduras stilled.

IN 2012, an average of three hundred migrants a day set out from Guatemala en route to the United States. On average, two hundred Guatemalan migrants a day returned to the country, deported by Mexican or U.S. officials. Those numbers didn't include migrants from other countries sent back to their home countries, even farther from their destinations in the United States.

Debt burdens crushed both groups. The more Border Patrol's strategy of prevention through deterrence inflated smuggler fees, the more migrants turned to moneylenders. This debt, secured by homes and farmland, created cycles of return migration: the only way migrants deported by U.S. or Mexican authorities could hope to repay their original loans was to take out new loans and try again to reach the United States. With interest rates on migrant debt reaching as high as 10 to 12 percent per *month*, no job that returned migrants could find in their home country could possibly pay enough to avoid default. Ema hoped to reach New York on her first attempt. She couldn't imagine what she'd do if she were caught and returned home.

For many years, tales of the U.S. Border Patrol tormented the sleep of Ecuadorian migrants en route. Failure took the definite and tangible form of shackled prisoners wordless on a charter flight to Quito. But in recent years, Mexican officials had begun to terrify Ecuadorians even more. Backed by hundreds of millions of dollars in U.S. aid, Mexico had militarized *its* southern border.

Ema learned that stepping across the line between Guatemala and Mexico wouldn't be difficult. They'd cross amid the steep canyons and coffee plantations of the Sierra Madre de Chiapas, where the border was almost invisible. After that, the trip would get difficult. Mexican authorities had, effectively, transformed the routes between Guatemala and the United States into a "vertical border." Checkpoints, raided hotels, searched vans, and boarded buses hardened this flying barrier. As on the U.S.-Mexico border, increased enforcement pushed migrants further into the shadows and the grasp of organized crime. At best, Mexican authorities ignored the kidnapping, extortion, rape, and killing of migrants tangled in the vertical border. At worst, they participated. Human rights groups estimated that some twenty thousand migrants went missing every year in the passage from Guatemala to the United States.

WHEN WORD THAT the route into Mexico was clear spread to the former chicken shed, Ema felt brave and ready. She also found that she could no longer hold down food. Her stomach twisting, Ema said goodbye to the kind Evangelicals and climbed into the back of a pickup truck. By now, the press of elbows and unwashed bodies against her face in the back of a vehicle was second nature. The neck-snapping progress across countless speed bumps between Huehuetenango and the border hardly registered. The group rode jammed together, and then they got out and walked. The international divide came and went unremarked. Pine-oak forests and steep cornfields extended, unbroken and identical, on both sides.

Ema only truly realized that she'd entered Mexico when a new, rougher crew of smugglers took over. The new men packed Ema, Juana, and the rest of their group into a caged pickup truck covered with a tarp. Exhaust gassed into the enclosure through holes in the floor, and passengers fought for a few square inches of breathing air. Ema hadn't eaten in thirty-six hours when the truck groaned into motion. This was a blessing and a curse. Even for people grown inured to close conditions and rough travel, this leg was hard. The truck pitched and rolled over ruts. When the journey ventured onto paved roads, the route kinked and curved. The drivers took corners so tight and fast that Ema swore she could touch the front hood of the vehicle from her spot in the back as the truck bent around hairpins. To her left and right, passengers who had eaten before the trip turned green. Unable to move in the tight space, they vomited on themselves and their companions.

In Tapachula, Chiapas, a sweltering border city reached after hours on this circuitous route, men herded the group into an underground bunker. They looked like men accustomed to killing, so Ema obeyed. At first she moved into the dim light cautiously; then a smell quickened her pace. The crude concrete lockup made Ema nostalgic for her Guatemalan chicken shed, but it was filled with the smell of exquisite soup. The nearness of chicken, *chayotes*, potatoes, and carrots pushed away Ema's exhaustion and fear.

Famished, her stomach still contorting from the trip, she sat at a long table. She wolfed the broth placed in front of her, spilling almost as much as she got into her mouth. Then she gagged. The food was heavily spiced; the greasy *caldo* contained enough chili to make even the Mexican smugglers stream tears. The dish was a jagged world away from the bland white foods Ecuadorians preferred—potatoes, rice, boiled corn, and smashed plantains. Her lips blistered. The innocent-looking chicken wasn't salvation; it was a kitchen knife stuck in her sternum.

From that day forward, constant stomach cramps and diarrhea marked Ema's journey through Mexico. Migrant lore overflowed with hushed accounts of robbery, assault, and extortion. Premonitions of carnage to come could be seen on the cruel faces of the men who controlled their lives. Deep in the Sonoran Desert of Arizona, everyone knew, stood trees that groaned under the weight of multicolored foliage—the underwear of raped women, displayed as trophies. But for Ema, the gut pain of hunger and acid spice was more immediate.

"YOU LOOK LIKE a smart one. Would you like to help me?" This man didn't scare Ema the way the others did. Somewhere in Oaxaca, he approached her with an unexpected bargain.

"You'll travel up front with me, stay in a better room, and eat better food."

Ema waited for the catch, knowing that she'd do just about anything short of sex for different food.

The man explained that police rarely searched women at checkpoints. If police caught him with large amounts of cash, things would get complicated for the group. At best, he'd have to spend their food money on extra bribes. At worst . . . Ema seemed steady, he told her. Would she be willing to let him tape packets of bills under her shirt and jeans? Ema agreed, and removed her clothes so the man could strap bundles of five-hundred-peso bills the color of dried blood to her waist and crotch.

Just shy of the next checkpoint, Ema realized that the smuggler hadn't been right about the police. The group had pulled into a roadside restaurant with a good view of the checkpoint. Ema watched as the police separated out the women and patted them down. She stared at her curves in the restaurant bathroom mirror. The damp, scratchy packets were invisible to the eye, but not to probing hands. If she ran, with or without the money, smugglers would almost certainly kill her. If police found the money, she might be flown back to Ecuador. Thousands of dollars and weeks of suffering would have been for nothing. And that was if she was lucky. She didn't want to think of Mexican prison or what else the police might do.

The only idea that occurred to her was preposterous, but preposterous had worked in El Salvador. Ema tousled her hair and slipped into the front of the truck. By the time the police peered into the cab, Ema had keeled over in the seat with copious drool running down her chin, breathing heavily like a passed-out drunk. No one disturbed her.

For the rest of the journey through Mexico, Ema sat in the front seat, slept alone, and ate yogurt, plain rice, and unspiced chicken. When the man needed money for expenses, he peeled bills off her body. A little bit of the heroine had returned.

TWENTY YEARS EARLIER, Altar, Sonora, 60 miles south of the Arizona border and 120 miles west of Agua Prieta, had been a tiny cattle town, drifted over with tumbleweed and desolation. By 2012, thanks to the Border Patrol strategy of funneling hundreds of thousands of border crossers into the Arizona deserts, it had become a metropolis of migration.

As crossings between Agua Prieta and Douglas dwindled in the mid-2000s, Altar exploded into North America's most important migrant staging ground. The dying cattle town became a city. A dozen hotels and an unknown number of guesthouses opened to welcome the influx of migrants. Tarp market stalls lined Altar's crowded streets, selling everything migrants needed for the next stage in their journey. Matte black plastic water jugs, camouflage backpacks, bedrolls, and replacement shoes hung in copious displays on every corner. Shoe covers made of carpet remnants had appeared on the market in recent years. The innovative design promised to blur one's tracks through sandy washes and open country. Moneyed travelers from *tierra caliente* could purchase winter coats, warm hats, and extra socks for the freezing desert. And for luck, *milagros* and prayer cards abounded.

Every morning, a priest at the Nuestra Señora de Guadalupe church off Altar's main plaza blessed crowds of pilgrims about to venture into the desert. Outside, even more people milled around the square, waiting for meetings with smugglers. The streets ringing the plaza were a carousel of battered vehicles. A fleet of two hundred vans shuttled groups to border-crossing points along what was probably Mexico's most heavily trafficked remote dirt road.

When Ema entered her group's next stash house, the sight reminded her of concentration camp photographs: rows of plank bunk beds stretched into the darkness; the shocked white eyes of the beds' occupants stared back at her. It was easy to tell which people had already attempted the crossing and which ones were, like her, just starting off. Newcomers' nerves jittered with anticipation; veterans just looked stunned. Feet, poking off the end of bunks, pussed with blisters. Thorn and spine scrapes carved up arms and faces. And underneath all those visible scars, traces of deeper hurts roiled.

If the desert traverse through rugged country patrolled by the United States' largest federal police force and crisscrossed by millions of dollars' worth of military surveillance technology weren't difficult enough, violent transnational criminal organizations now controlled most routes. As in Agua Prieta and Douglas, the growing difficulty of making it through Border Patrol's gauntlet raised smuggling tariffs. Higher price tags, in turn, attracted cartels that wiped out mom-and-pop smuggling operations and smeared the desert with blood.

Sexual assault was endemic, and few migrants escaped without facing some form of robbery or extortion. Billions of U.S. taxpayer dollars spent on enforcement-only immigration policies had, by 2012, created vast territories of violent disorder on the border. The road ahead of Ema and Juana was profitable for criminals and police agencies but painful for people with no choice but to proceed.

In most ways, Ema was one of the privileged in Altar; she had taken few loans to pay for her journey. Indigenous Mayans from southern Mexico she met had taken out three-thousand-dollar loans at 12 percent interest a month, secured by their small plots of corn and beans. Failure to reach jobs waiting in Georgia, Florida, or Nevada would result in their family's eviction. No matter what deterrence Border Patrol erected, those migrants would try again.

Other migrants had been caught and deported, their entire savings spent or stolen. They lingered at the guesthouses, unable to pay smugglers for another attempt, lacking money for bus fare home. Ema's arrangement for the trip from Altar to Phoenix covered as many attempts as it took. Once she reached Phoenix, it wouldn't be hard to make her way to New York. Reaching Phoenix was the key. She hoped that it would take only one try.

OVER THE NEXT WEEK, Ema and Juana made two forays into the United States. Each time, their group squeezed through the wire west of Sasabe, Arizona, in the dead of night. Whatever belongings they'd managed to hold on to that far into the journey were transferred into backpacks. Each person carried two gallons of water, along with packets of crackers and tins of tuna stuffed into pockets. They were prepared for a two- to five-day trek, but each time, the group advanced no more than a few hundred yards before their guides gave the signal to retreat. Attuned to clues Ema couldn't discern, the smugglers decided the route was "too hot."

Sometime late in February 2012, Ema and Juana joined a new group for a third foray into the desert. They left at 3:00 a.m. Their guide warned them to dress like men—"just in case." If Border Patrol caught them, he advised, try to speak *como mexicanas.* Assuming that they weren't selected for criminal prosecution for misdemeanor "unlawful entry," Mexicans were dropped back at the line after a few days in detention. U.S. officials returned

South Americans home on airplanes, long flights on which to contemplate the money and time they'd lost.

RAINDROPS FELL LIKE stones on Ema's frozen arms. A few minutes earlier, their guide had stopped them on a bluff to watch how quickly a desiccated creek bed could fill with fast-moving water after a sudden downpour. It was a warning for anyone who thought sandy basins offered easier walking than rocky highlands.

The *coyotes* kept the small group together and paused, briefly, for stragglers. This was the extent of the "special treatment" Ema and Juana had purchased. The smugglers kept the group moving with few rests through the night, the next day, and into the second evening. But they didn't threaten or steal.

At night, the group sensed Border Patrol all around them. Lights flashed, tires crunched over rock, and helicopters plied the distant dark. This was the busiest desolate wilderness in the world.

Ema startled out of a brief, dense sleep during the second night. She couldn't see the smugglers. Juana was gone. The crackle of an approaching truck had scattered the group. Ema scraped under a low thornbush to hide and collided with another woman. Together they held their breath until the truck disappeared.

At daybreak, a group of six Ecuadorians and three Guatemalans, not all from Ema's original party, gathered in a clearing, arguing about what to do next.

"What about you?" the woman who'd shared Ema's tree asked.

Ema had a little water, a few oranges, and a cigarette lighter. Her backpack was gone. So was Juana.

"I'm not going back, and I'm not going to die here," Ema replied. She figured that she could make her way north keeping aligned with peaks in the distance. A few people accompanied her. Others preferred to wait for Border Patrol.

Ema led the group to a high point where they could see a road. It was Highway 86 connecting Tucson and the Tohono O'odham nation, in whose territory they'd spent the past two days. The group followed the road, hoping for a ride from a sympathetic driver. Eventually, they came to the edge of a town. Barking dogs surprised the group on the outskirts of the settlement. It was just a recording piped through a loudspeaker to scare migrants away. They should have heeded the warning.

Instead, desperate for their ordeal to end, Ema and her new companions dropped their supplies and cantered into the clearing. Maybe they could pay someone to drive them the final sixty miles to Tucson.

THE POLICE OFFICER forced them to their knees in the gravel outside a house. Border Patrol came later and took the five men and two women in Ema's group to a small forward operating base. A man in green pushed a dented steel clipboard at her.

"Sign here."

"What is it? What am I signing?"

"Receipt for your money. Sign. Please."

Ema squinted at the paperwork. Even with her meager grasp of English, she could tell that it wasn't a receipt. She had handled money and paperwork every day in her job. Next to a checked box, she puzzled out words to the effect of "I give up my right to a hearing before the Immigration Court. I wish to return to my home country."

"I want to talk with a lawyer," she said.

The man shrugged.

Ema would get to talk with a lawyer. But not for weeks. First she would be stripped and scrubbed and dressed in forest green at a for-profit detention center.

25.

THE UNDERWORLD

AIDA SPENT HER FIRST DETAINED NIGHT sleepless on the floor of a concrete cell in the Douglas Border Patrol station. She felt sick and bruised. The last sixteen hours spun in her head. The beautiful morning, Walmart's comforting sheen, tipping the Lego set into her purse, and the cell in the old railway station. The Aida who'd defiantly thrown her piercings on the sidewalk and insisted on her right to stay in the United States felt like another woman. Only a numb certainty remained: "I can't go back. I can't go back." She pictured Gabriel alone in their bed, a ten-minute drive away. "I will never leave you again," she had promised him just three years earlier.

The next morning, agents escorted her to a van idling outside the station. It would take her to Tucson, they said. The man who drove the van told her to expect worse conditions there. Architects had designed the Tucson

Border Patrol holding facility to keep detainees for a few hours or maybe a day. But in 2012, people often spent a week there before embarking on the next stage in their journeys through immigration detention.

Aida tried to peek into the cell awaiting her while an agent processed her paperwork in a kind of foyer. Through the single thick-glass orifice, she glimpsed a narrow concrete room and a bench. Behind that a low wall partly hid a steel toilet. Any undocumented immigrant in Arizona had heard of these holding cells. Universally, they were known as *las hieleras*, the iceboxes.

An agent told her to take off her light cotton sweater and gestured her inside. The room was colder than her cell in Douglas, which had been bone breaking. She wouldn't have believed it possible to make a room colder. In Douglas, she had shared her cell with several women. Now she was all alone, shivering in a loose V-neck T-shirt. Of the blankets strewn around the room, she picked the one that showed fewest signs of use and no inexplicable stains. She wrapped herself in it and lay down on the bench. Bright fluorescent lights never dimmed. People came and went outside the cell twenty-four hours a day. A loudspeaker somewhere in the facility looped an audio recording listing the many dangers migrants faced if they tried to cross the border again. It played over and over. But light and noise couldn't hold back a wave of exhaustion.

Ten more detainees arrived while Aida slept. The new women emitted the unwashed smell of weeks in transit and days lost in the desert. Some stepped gingerly over the dirty floor. Open sores and blisters the size of eggs made it impossible for them to wear shoes. Aida bolted up from sleep to this sight—and a sinking feeling. Her period had come.

Over the course of that day, ten more detainees appeared. Aida gave her blanket and bench to a pregnant woman. A box of food appeared. The women rummaged through what appeared to be sacks of discarded McDonald's hamburgers. Aida heard a woman complain that she'd bitten into a maggot. Aida forced herself to nibble at a burger anyway. She knew that her mental state deteriorated if she didn't eat. By the second day, though, when nothing but more old burgers appeared, Aida's body rejected the meal. After violently gagging on the green meat, she joined the rest of the women in eating only the snack-sized saltine packets accompanying the burgers.

The detainees organized themselves according to unspoken rules. The pregnant women received blankets, enough floor space to lie down, and any edible food that appeared. The rest did their best to sleep sitting up. Early in the second day, the toilet paper ran out. Taking a linguistic cue from her cellmates, the guards, and prison signage, Aida asked for more in Spanish. Border Patrol agents ignored her, shaking their heads and waving clipboards to suggest that they were too busy to respond.

Suddenly it hit her—why was she speaking Spanish? The next time the cell door opened, she switched to English.

"Look, I've been in here for days. I have my period. Can I please get a box of Kotex?"

The difference was striking. A box of Kotex and a roll of toilet paper appeared a while later. Aida took a couple tampons and passed the container around the room. Several of the women's faces glowed with palpable relief.

Once a day, agents ushered the cell's occupants into the processing foyer while a janitor mopped. This was their one chance to stretch without worrying about bumping into someone.

One agent, hunched over his laptop screen like an olive-drab bear, played Guns N' Roses on his phone. Aida gravitated toward him. "Sweet Child o' Mine" was her favorite song. Life before her arrest had already receded to a distant, dreamlike plane, but she still remembered the way Alvaro's band would sometimes halt their anarchic wailing to play the song just for her. It calmed her.

"You know what I'm doing?" the agent said when he saw Aida looking at him. He grinned up at her, and Aida flooded with hope that he might help her out.

"No?" he asked, then tilted the screen so the whole room could view it. It was a glamour shot of the most beautiful king cab pickup truck Aida had ever seen.

"Thanks to you all"—he waved at the room full of exhausted women— "I can buy this truck."

ON THE FOURTH DAY, Aida worked up the courage to ask for soap. She couldn't take the accumulated grime of the place or the dried blood between her legs. She felt more unclean than she'd ever felt in her life. To her surprise, a sympathetic agent found time to bring soap and a towel. After receiving these goods, the detainees organized themselves again. The women confined alongside Aida clung to the norms of civilization, even in that place. They took turns holding up a blanket so each woman could wash out of view of the male guards and security camera.

The fourth night, enough women had been taken away that the group decided to try sleeping lying down. Aida encouraged the pregnant and older women to claim spots first, then took the last piece of real estate: wedged behind the half wall, her face pressed against the toilet. The concrete floor oozed damp and cold, but stretching out fully felt glorious.

Aida woke well before dawn. Her eye itched furiously, crusted over with dry pus. It was the hour when women were shipped out to the immigration prison at Eloy, Arizona. For days, agents had told her that Eloy would be her final destination. It was a vicious cathouse, they'd murmur with mock dread. Some of the agents clearly enjoyed unnerving detainees. Eloy was full of the worst criminals in the immigration system, guards told Aida—murderers, drug-dealing matrons, Salvadorian gangbangers. All of them were lesbians, one agent teased. Get ready to be a sex slave: "You're meat."

The word bounced around Aida's head that morning as she waited her turn to board the bus. An agent called to her, and she braced for one last insult. Instead, the man sat her down on a bench and spoke kindly.

"Hernandez, I want you to think of this as a blessing in disguise."

Aida winced. What did he know about blessings? But the man pressed on past Aida's blank stare.

"I'm sure you're going to get your papers. Just go to Eloy and do what you have to."

Somehow that helped. Not everyone was an asshole.

THE BUS WHISPERED through Tucson in darkness. Aida formed an instant bond with two women her own age, also born in Sonora. One of them had grown up in Tucson, so they spent the first minutes of the ride with their faces pressed to the window. Each time they passed a familiar corner, the woman gasped a little. Streets where Aida's new friend had walked her dog, intersections remembered from her daily commute, and restaurants where she'd eaten fish tacos all looked alien when lit by streetlights and seen through smoked glass. After only five days in the *hieleras*, the known world had changed into something distant and strange. When they felt Interstate 10 buzzing under the bus, the three women tried to sleep, huddled together for warmth.

Aida stirred awake and saw that the bus was parked in a gravel lot. Blue light suffused the desert. Outside she could make out the Corrections Corporation of America (CCA) Eloy Detention Center. Raúl's stories of the severe Black Palace, where he'd spent his years as a political prisoner, filled her head with images of stone penitentiaries. This, on the other hand, looked like a suburban warehouse. Aida peered through the double layer of chain link and razor wire—the one thing marking the building as a prison—searching for any clue of what her life would be like inside.

Just as U.S. law does not consider deportation a punishment, immigration detention centers are not categorized as prisons. But anyone paying attention knew that private companies and the government modeled most of these detention centers on medium-security criminal prisons. They looked like prisons, sounded like prisons, and felt like prisons. A rank of women in blue scrubs filed out of a door, sauntering across the gravel yard and disappearing into another door. These were the sadistic gang members Border Patrol agents in Tucson had warned her about, Aida thought. Her new friends must have been thinking the same thing, because they exchanged worried looks and spoke almost in one voice.

"We need to stick together in there. No matter what happens, we watch out for each other."

Aida felt as ready as she could be, but the bus showed no sign of leaving the parking lot. Her friends eventually stopped pledging mutual defense and fell into silence. Receiving no explanation for the delay, each passenger retreated into her own solitary thoughts of what lay beyond the double fence. Aida's stomach turned with hunger. Since breakfast in the trailer almost a week earlier, she'd eaten nothing but rotten hamburgers and saltine crackers. Someone in Tucson had informed her that prisoners in Eloy would steal her food if she didn't fight to save it.

An hour passed before the bus hissed, lurched forward, and rolled softly through a gate, crossing over to the other side.

A STEEL DOOR closed behind her. Latex fingers probed Aida's mouth and body, a camera flashed, her street clothes disappeared. For the first time in her life, Aida showered in front of other people, with no curtains or stalls. The icy water whipped her breath away, but after five days in Tucson it felt good to get clean.

Scrubs appeared, a sick shade of forest green. The rest of the world was primary blue and white. The steel doors were blue, the bolted chairs were blue, the metal trim around each ballistic glass interior window—blue. The prison surrounded Aida with enough relentless, calming blue to drive a person mad.

The three young Sonorans reunited in a crowded waiting room—relieved smiles all around—and sat together in their identical clothes. From time to time, a guard appeared and called out prisoners' names. Bit by bit, the room emptied. Aida's new friends went first, casting worried glances back at her as they disappeared. Aida was fully alone.

"Hernandez. Charlie 204." The guard looked up from her clipboard at the room. Aida stood up, her heart pounding, and followed her into the sunlight. The guard led her along a concrete path to Pod 200.

Aida expected a room packed with murderous *cholas*. As the blue door opened, she imagined gangbangers sporting aggressive braids and toothbrush shivs. Stressed, sweating guards would strain to contain the violence or, worse, give up altogether.

Instead, entering Pod 200 for the first time, Aida saw a gaggle of Latin American housewives watching soap operas. Some of them appeared to be making lipstick out of Red Vines. Aida looked at her escort for confirmation that this was her destination. Pod 200 seemed more like a gossipy hair salon than the nightmare described by Border Patrol agents in Tucson.

"Take my advice, Hernandez," the guard said in a matronly voice as they stepped into the common area. "You need some water. You're dehydrated. And try to get some sleep."

Aida reeled. She had steeled herself to resist bedlam. Over five days, she'd armored her soul, preparing to do hard time while wrenched from family and home. The gaiety of Pod 200 felt like an insult.

"How can people enjoy themselves in a place like this?" she muttered under her breath. "What do those ladies think this is? Vacation?"

The guard, still spouting tidbits of health advice, chaperoned Aida to a door on the ground floor of the motel-style pod. C204 was uniform blue and white, of course; one of about thirty double-occupancy cells, equipped with a toilet, a metal bunk bed, a dented mirror, and a plastic lawn chair. Aida sank onto the bed and refused to leave.

"WHERE YOU FROM?" The two women didn't knock or wait for answer. They were in their early twenties like Aida and spoke in clipped tones, neither agreeable nor unkind.

"Don't even think of crying, new girl," the first one said, observing Aida's face. "If you cry, they're gonna take you to psychiatric, and you do not want to be there. They take all your clothes off, and you're alone in a cold, empty room."

Aida stared at the two women, dumbfounded. She couldn't tell if this visit was intended to welcome or intimidate her.

"Plus," the second woman added, "we're all going through the same thing. So . . ."

Aida shook off the hospitality committee, moved to the bed, and curled into a ball. Later, more strangers tried to wake her for dinner. She held on to the thin mattress, unwilling to move. Night passed. Someone tried to persuade her to eat breakfast, but she slept on. By first count, a guard arrived to force her out of bed. Aida stood up, famished, knowing that she'd survive her time at Eloy through strict regimen and defiant silence.

After lunch, Aida asked a guard for paper and a pencil and scratched out a schedule for herself: 7:00 a.m., wake up; breakfast; clean cell; watch the news; return to cell for the day's first lockdown; reading time.

The pod had its own book rack, and the whole prison—built for fifteen hundred segregated men and women—counted on a single shared library. Just as Raúl had found comfort in yoga during his prison term, Aida now found her refuge in reading. Threadbare hardbacks and rumpled bestsellers, each one stamped with the name of some other public library to which it had once belonged, kept her alive through the first weeks. She read a book about the Buddha, the Bible, and a compendium of faerie stories from different cultures around the world.

After lockdown, a shower, lunch, one hour of yard time, and then back to the cell for more reading. Dinner, nap, TV in the common area until lights-out.

Aida stuck to her monastic vow, speaking only when necessary and only to guards. A ten-minute telephone call ate a shocking percentage of the twenty-dollar commissary money Luz sent each week in lieu of visits. Aida rationed her phone minutes to talk with Gabriel. If time remained on her card, she dialed Rosie. Talking with her friend and counselor lessened the overwhelming solitude. Disembodied phone conversations with her family, on the other hand, only accentuated her isolation. She called anyway, because the telephone was all she had. Luz couldn't take time off from work on the days Eloy permitted family visits, nor could she afford gas for the 350-mile round-trip. Gabriel, halfway through first grade, could not comprehend his mother's disappearance when Aida tried to explain it over the phone.

"I am in a huge house with a lot of women waiting to see a man, a judge," she said. "He's the one who will decide if I go to Mexico or get to stay home."

"Okay." He sounded puzzled.

"You understand?"

"Yes, but, Mommy, can you please ask him if you can come home just for today and then go back at night?"

"It doesn't work that way, honey."

"Okay, but can you tell him to let you out so you can take me to Walmart?"

She didn't cry on the phone, but afterward she returned to her cell, closed the door, and wept.

During those first months, she buried herself in creating drawings for Gabriel, desperate to cheer him up from a distance. First, she made a small green Hulk accompanied by the words "Be Strong!" Every week after that, she mailed a different cartoon figure, imagining them taped up on every surface in the trailer, reminding him that she loved him.

AIDA DISCOVERED a shelf of immigration law books and pamphlets in the central library. She'd received a "Notice to Appear," listing the government's allegations against her, along with notification of an initial hearing in February. She was the one person in her pod fluent in English, but the papers might as well have been written in Urdu. When she showed the Notice to Appear to a sympathetic guard, the woman just shook her head and said, "That's a lot of charges."

In early February, Aida attended a presentation in the visitation room by a volunteer attorney, Charles Vernon. A recent law school graduate, Charles was not much older than Aida. He had just joined the staff of the Florence Immigrant and Refugee Rights Project (FIRRP), an organization whose small team of pro bono attorneys did everything they could to help the approximately twelve hundred people in Eloy who couldn't afford to hire a private attorney on any given day.

It was Charles's first presentation, and already he looked harried and overwhelmed. His Spanish was not very strong yet, and coworkers had warned him about the difficulty of presenting to women. Women detained at Eloy, they said, tended to have more traumatic pasts and more complicated cases than their male counterparts.

Aida watched Charles struggle through the presentation and joined the crush of women around him when he finished. She realized that some people in the room hadn't understood a word he said, between his rough Spanish and the complexity of immigration law. But something had clicked for Aida.

Though FIRRP could directly represent only a hundred people at Eloy that year, its presentations helped almost nine thousand detainees understand their basic rights and remedies amid the intricacies of immigration law. Even more crucially, the group's attorneys coached more than six thousand people through the process of fighting deportation on their own and helped hundreds more win release on bond. The work was first aid and emergency surgery, not holistic medicine, but Charles knew that it could make a difference in individuals' lives. In this case, it did.

Aida and Charles sat down together in a cubicle away from the general visitation throng. In time, Charles would become a seasoned and successful senior attorney and coordinate FIRRP's entire pro bono program. For the moment, though, all he could do was promise to look up the answers to Aida's questions. That was enough. She looked as shell-shocked as Charles felt after his first presentation, but inside her head gears began to turn.

Tagged at the end of every dense form she received from the government was a waiflike notice: "For information on Immigration Court procedures, please consult the Immigration Court Practice Manual." Most women in the pod couldn't even read the advice. Aida could, but up to that moment it had seemed, at best, unhelpful and, at worst, a cruel joke. Now she wondered how she could get hold of the *Immigration Court Practice Manual.*

THE ANSWER, as it turned out, was a half-hidden corner shelf in the prison library. Law materials did not circulate, so Aida began to spend as much time as possible in the corner with the thick textbooks and thin how-to pamphlets. First things first, she figured out how to petition for release on bond.

It was difficult to gauge what logic, if any, governed judges' willingness to set a bond in any particular case. From time to time, a guard would appear in the pod, paperwork in hand, call someone's name, and trumpet the words everyone wanted to hear: "Roll it up. Your bond came through." No coherent thread united the cases of women who received bonds, Aida gathered. Even the amounts were unpredictable, ranging from zero to thirty-five thousand dollars.

Aida reported what she'd learned about bonds during her weekly call home. Luz insisted that they hire an attorney, but Aida wasn't convinced. Luz's income barely stretched to cover Gabriel's expenses as it was; any extra money should go toward him. She'd figure out the case herself, Aida maintained, not quite sure that she would. But Luz pressed on: her daughter needed help. Eventually, they agreed that Luz would somehow find a thousand dollars to pay an attorney from Phoenix to help Aida petition for release on bond.

AIDA ATTENDED HER first hearing alone. Early in the morning of February 15, she and eight other detainees squeezed into Judge Richard Phelps's closet-sized courtroom. This was each prisoner's first encounter with Eloy's immigration court. The atmosphere was subdued and anxious. Women sat in back, the men in front, and everyone had been instructed not to look at the other prisoners.

"Good day," a cheery disembodied voice declared. "This is the beginning of your removal proceeding."

An audio recording of Judge Phelps's opening remarks played for just over twenty minutes. He spoke slowly and clearly, with just a hint of western drawl. He sounded like the white-hatted sheriff in a movie. He could have been a professional announcer. Itemizing detainees' rights to appeal his decision, the judge sounded like someone explaining the rules of a fun contest.

Aida concentrated, but the details blurred together, a jumble of options and consequences, ifs and thens, requirements and ramifications. The words were crystal clear and impossible to fathom.

You can request additional time to prepare your defense, the voice said. You can request pre-conclusion voluntary departure. You can have your whole hearing taken care of today. Your time in Eloy—in the United States—can all end this very hour.

When the recording finished, the real Richard Phelps spoke. His voice was still kind but more harried. He intoned the rote formalities convening an initial master hearing. A court official recited the names of nine respondents:

Cuenca Salazar, Roberto.

Serrano Salazar, Ramiro.

Delgado Hermosillo, Salvador.

Leyva Morales, Dennis.

Ruiz Gonzalez, Rogelio Quique.

Hernandez, Aida.

Aida's heart bounded when she heard her name, but the litany continued without pause.

Saenz Gervacio, Benigno.

Ruiz, Graciela.

Afrassa, Abaeze Tadesse.

The translator stumbled over the final name, pronouncing it as if in Spanish.

Not a single respondent came to the hearing with an attorney.

Judge Phelps asked if anyone needed more time to prepare a defense. Remembering Charles Vernon's advice, Aida raised her hand. She was the first person to raise a hand, and it was the right decision. She'd cleared her first hurdle. Of the eight remaining detainees in the room, three would lose their case that same morning, be ordered removed, or, in one case, accept voluntary departure. Three would be ordered removed soon afterward. Two would eventually win release from Eloy on bond and argue their cases from home. Five years later, only one of those other respondents would have secured legal status in the United States.

A DETAILED LETTER from Charles Vernon arrived through prison post around the time of Aida's first hearing.

"After talking with you last week, I researched your unusual case," it began. In easy-to-understand language, he recommended that she apply for a remedy similar to asylum called "withholding of removal." To start this, she should fill out an I-589 form. "I must let you know, however," the letter continued, "that these types of cases can be very difficult to win for people from Mexico."

Immigration courts were notoriously skeptical of asylum claims from Mexico. That year, more than 9,000 Mexicans would apply for asylum in the United States. Only 126 would receive it. A judge might, on the other hand, be willing to issue a withholding of removal, a lesser form of protection than asylum. Withholding of removal would give Aida permission to remain in the United States but also place her in permanent immigration limbo: she could return to Douglas and, for a fee, work legally in the United States. But this lesser form of protection offered no pathway to a green card or citizenship. In some cases, the government could choose to deport people granted withholding of removal to a country other than the one they fled. More commonly, the government might indefinitely limit recipients' freedom to move within the United States.

Unfortunately for Aida, asylum claims must be filed within a year of entering the country. Aida had been in Arizona for four years since the attack in Agua Prieta. Asylum was out. Aida might win legal residency if she reconciled with David and he petitioned for her. But withholding, Vernon concluded based on the small part of Aida's story that she had shared with him, was her primary option.

Nevertheless, a growing number of immigration attorneys believed that women's experience of gender violence in Mexico and Central America fit the criteria for both asylum and withholding of removal. Women facing extreme and rising levels of violence in Mexico should be able to prove that they were members of a social group likely to face cruel and inhumane treatment if returned to their home country.

Elizabeth Juarez, the attorney Luz found money to retain, was less sanguine, as were most immigration courts at the time. She flipped through Aida's carefully collected paperwork skeptically and offered to resubmit Aida's bond petition. For a thousand dollars, she would wrangle Aida's request for bond into a more convincing package and accompany her to the bond hearing. There was nothing else she could do. Aida's case had no effective defense, Juarez believed. But with luck, she could win Aida's release on bond.

Aida hoped it would work. She imagined what Juarez's fee could have bought Gabriel. Clothes that fit, better food. A thousand dollars was a lot of Legos, and Aida really didn't want to think about what Luz had forgone to scrape together the payment.

A little less than a month later, the bond hearing ended almost as soon as it started. Aida's humanitarian parole—the strange bureaucratic contrivance granted after her surgery—made it almost impossible to qualify for release on bond. Parole had permitted her physical body to remain inside the United States while never allowing her legal persona into the country. Any ordinary undocumented border crosser or visa overstayer at Eloy was at least understood to have entered the country, but not Aida. She couldn't be released on bond if she wasn't in the country.

There was barely time to feel the stinging regret from having wasted a thousand dollars. Without pause, the summary bond hearing morphed into Aida's second immigration court appearance. The hearing began with dispiriting news and got worse. The government opened by lodging two additional allegations and an additional charge against Aida. Really, these were nothing new. The government had simply forgotten to include her expedited removal and five-year bar in its first charge sheet. But the sound of allegations accruing against her hit like slugs.

It didn't surprise Aida when Elizabeth Juarez petitioned to withdraw as her representative. They'd agreed that Juarez would represent her only at the bond hearing. But the speed of the process, the flash of papers, and the ritual exchange of legalese undid Aida. The attorney stood while the judge punctiliously ran through the approval process, and then she rushed to gather up her files, ready to leave.

Phelps looked to Aida. No one wanted to be in that room. Watching immigrants defend themselves alone in deportation proceedings had to be one of the most painful exercises in the American judicial system. "Ms. Juarez has filed a request to withdraw and no longer represent you. Is that all right with you?" he asked. Aida mustered a "Yes, Your Honor," but as Phelps launched into the final pronouncement, she clutched at the attorney.

"Can I ask for more time?" she asked in a deflated voice. Maybe she could still figure out a way to fight her case on her own.

"If you want to," Juarez replied, a bit too quickly, and then added more reassuringly, "He'll ask you if you want more time."

JUDGE PHELPS GRANTED Aida three more weeks—enough time to coil deeper into solitude and despair. She spoke to guards when she needed something and spent her time reading. The few connections she made with other women in forest green were fleeting. Every weekday evening, the residents of Pod 200 gathered around the Spanish-language TV watching *telenovelas*. Even the Chinese and Indian women, who spoke no Spanish, preferred the camaraderie of watching gaudy Mexican soap operas in a group to the solitary English TV. Most nights, Aida sat alone at one of the steel tables, secluded in a community of fifty women. Those women, each enmeshed in her own story, trials, heartache, and hopes, at least had one another. Aida sat with them, but apart from them, watching English movies alone through earbuds.

26.

AIDA'S VOICE

THE FIRST PORTENT OF CHANGE came in paperback form. There it was in the library: the familiar cover, the three long-necked, black-haired women. Their skin glowed golden against misty jewel tones. Lettering looking crooked and handwritten announced, *The House on Mango Street*.

Aida hadn't thought again about the one friendly Border Patrol agent's suggestion that Eloy would be a blessing in disguise. Nothing redeemed the place, with its impossible jurisprudence and soul-destroying separation from home. But then she stumbled upon the book. Maybe I *am* supposed to be here, she thought. Maybe there is a point to all this.

Aida flipped the thin book open to her favorite part—the protagonist Esperanza's prose poem about four skinny trees growing outside her apartment: "Four skinny trees with skinny necks and pointy elbows like mine.

Four who do not belong here but are here. . . . Their strength is secret. They send ferocious roots beneath the ground. They grow up and they grow down and grab the earth between their hairy toes and bite the sky with violent teeth and never quit their anger. This is how they keep."

Aida's heart pounded. This is me, she repeated to herself as she read: "Keep, keep, keep, trees say when I sleep. They teach. When I am too sad and too skinny to keep keeping, when I am a tiny thing against so many bricks, then it is I look at trees. When there is nothing left to look at on this street. Four who grew despite concrete. Four who reach and do not forget to reach. Four whose only reason is to be and be."

From that day forward, Aida slept with *The House on Mango Street* under her pillow and returned again and again to its brief, uplifting branches. Esperanza's words still intoxicated Aida with the hope that comes from having been understood by another person, just as they had when she was a teenager. But, with Aida locked inside the steel and concrete of Eloy, they took on a new meaning, all the way to the book's final page: "I have gone away to come back."

ONE DAY IN the cafeteria, packed with women, Aida took her usual seat alone. To her surprise, a tablemate leaned forward and spoke to her, as if to a child. The other eaters looked on, curious. The woman's words came out in halting, carefully formed English: "Would . . . you . . . like my bread?" It sounded as if she had practiced the question in preparation for approaching Aida.

"*Sí, por favor. Muchísimas gracias,*" Aida answered.

"*¿Hablas español?*" the shocked diners exclaimed.

"*Por supuesto.*"

Later, alone in her cell, Aida rolled the encounter back and forth in her mind. The women of Pod 200 hadn't known that she spoke Spanish. It stunned her. My God, she thought, there are women here from all over the world—Mexico, Ecuador, Guatemala, El Salvador, China, India. Women with incredible stories. Women who have seen places and lived lives I can't even imagine. And we are all stuck here for months, maybe years. What am I doing? I could make friends and learn things. "Four who reach and do not forget to reach," the book under her pillow said. I will reach, Aida vowed. I will get something out of my time in this horrible place, not just fester.

The next day, Aida was still pondering this thought, half watching the news, when a new detainee tapped her shoulder. Aida pulled out her earbuds, surprised. No one had ever interrupted her morning routine.

"Excuse me, young lady, I'd like you to help me." The woman had arrived the day before. She was decades older than anyone else in the pod. When Aida had seen her poking around her new home, she looked severe, even mean. Her touch was gentle, though, and her words affectionate.

"I'm Tomasita," she said. "I heard that you knew how to fill out bond forms. Would you help me with mine? I don't speak English."

The angry wrinkles of her face had rearranged themselves into happy crinkles. Tomasita was asking Aida for a favor, to work on her behalf. But to Aida, the request felt like a hand extended across a chasm. She almost jumped out of the plastic chair.

"Of course I can help," she blurted. Women sitting at the next table exchanged surprised looks.

That night, Aida stayed up late deciphering Tomasita's forms and returned the completed documents to her in the morning. Detainees who barely spoke English charged twenty dollars in commissary credit for translations. Aida just asked Tomasita to pray for her. She could tell that the older woman was religious, and her request produced an enormous smile.

Almost as quickly as she had donned it, Aida discarded the hard shell she'd worn since arrival. It was like rediscovering home after a long exile. An earlier version of Aida still existed under the rage, and she allowed it to peek out. She tried to befriend everyone, even the indigenous Guatemalan girl who couldn't possibly have been eighteen. During rec periods, the Guatemalan girl knelt in the gravel yard and keened, her arms thrust up to the sky. Most other detainees kept their distance from her. In a lucid moment, the girl mumbled in broken Spanish to Aida that a man in the desert southwest of Tucson wearing a green uniform with a gun on his belt had "touched her wrong." Later, investigators came to interview the girl, and she disappeared from the pod.

In quiet moments in her cell, Aida reflected on how Rosie had helped her just by listening. And so Aida began to listen, deliberately and with new empathy, to anyone who wanted to talk. Her sense that an American upbringing made her different from, and maybe better than, "migrants" and "*sureños*" melted. All the women in Eloy shared stories of trauma and separation. They were survivors, like Aida. She could learn from them, and she could help them. And just as Rosie had said, helping others helped her heal.

Tomasita became her closest friend, part mother figure and part accomplice. Together, they consoled and advised and, at the end of the day, sat together in Aida's cell. Tomasita would recline on Aida's bed with her feet up, while the younger woman brewed a packet of instant coffee in their one precious mug purchased from the commissary. Aida would scoot the plastic chair up next to the bed, and they'd sip from the same cup until lights-out. Other times, Aida would bring Tomasita her coffee in the common room, and the two would sit with everyone watching *Flor salvaje* or *Rosa diamante*.

IN THE DAYS before her next hearing, Aida made another discovery in the library—a several-page description of an immigration remedy called cancellation of removal. Against her better judgment, the text rekindled hope for her own case. Looking up from the pamphlet, she saw one of the nicest guards in Eloy staffing the library post. He was a large, gangly guy who brought a camera on Saturdays so detainees could take pictures for their families. He always seemed to enjoy organizing the photo shoots—posing the women, waving wildly, and bellowing for everyone to look at the lens. He called Aida "Cheesy" because she wanted to appear in every photograph.

"Hey, Cheesy, come here," he'd greet her. "We're taking pictures. Come join us."

Aida slipped into a kittenish pose and held out the legal manual.

"Excuse me, sir." Her voice could be low and gravelly when she wanted, a Southwest-tinted Mae West. "I know it's not allowed, but could you make a copy of this for me?"

"You know I can't."

She arched an eyebrow and said, "Sir, please."

"I could get fired for that." The guard shook his head, but Aida knew that he would make the copy. She left the pamphlet open on the table when she returned to the pod. A day later, she found it waiting in the same place, with three stapled sheets of paper slipped underneath.

Once again, Luz proposed hiring a lawyer, and Aida agreed. The papers, hidden under her tunic, gave her a reason. Jack had some savings left. It was enough to make a down payment for a really good lawyer, Luz promised. "God will provide the rest, somehow, *mija*." In other words, Luz would scrimp and save and find a way to make it work.

Aida polled the guards assigned to her pod: "Who is the best lawyer here?"

"Jesse Evans-Schroeder," each replied in turn. In the yard, she asked the detainees in khaki scrubs. Women in brown had minor criminal convictions that supposedly made them more dangerous than women in green, like Aida. Khaki detainees could spend years in Eloy waiting for their cases to grind toward likely loss and almost inevitable deportation. No one knew more about the attorneys who served Eloy.

"There's only one who wins," they said, showing Aida a dog-eared business card. "Jesse Evans."

"Jesse Evans," Aida repeated.

An assistant met with Aida to assess her case. To Aida, it felt like an audition. Two weeks later, a day before Aida's next hearing, Jesse Evans-Schroeder arranged to meet her. Aida recognized her immediately. Every time she'd met with Charles Vernon or Elizabeth Juarez, she'd seen this attorney sweeping through the sticky fluorescent visitation room, all high heels and long blond hair, slinging files and attitude. She looked, Aida thought, like a model crossed with a cop. Guards deferred to her, Aida noticed. Even hardened *cholas*, swaggering in the dark blue scrubs indicating serious criminal records, visibly shrank in her presence. All their cocky belligerence melted into pure attention when Jesse Evans-Schroeder flipped to their paperwork and began to talk. Why, Aida kicked herself, didn't I hire her in the first place?

When they were sitting, facing each other across a plastic table, Aida extracted the slightly sweaty Xeroxes from her shirt.

"Can we try this?" Aida asked, laying the papers in front of Jesse.

"Where on earth did you get those?" A smile showed on the lawyer's face. There was something different about this client.

Jesse moved to reschedule Aida's next hearing to allow time to prepare a defense. She had come to the law via work at women's shelters and liked to take on difficult cases. She combined empathy, charisma, and intelligence into a single package and won more cases than a lot of other attorneys serving Eloy. But Aida's case wasn't just hard; it seemed impossible.

Aida and Jesse agreed to proceed on multiple legal fronts at once. They filed two types of "withholding of removal" petitions and a claim to protection under the international Convention Against Torture. Her stronger case stemmed—as Aida's law book suggested—from her experience of domestic violence at the hands of a U.S. citizen. That winter, the once reliably bipartisan Violence Against Women Act was under attack by Republican legislators. But it still extended legal residence to victims of extreme cruelty committed by U.S. citizen spouses or domestic partners.

Aida's experience with David easily met those criteria, but petitions for VAWA protection were highly subjective. Getting the judge to acknowledge Aida's experience of violence and cruelty was the easy part. The judge would also have to accept Aida as a woman of good moral character. Deepseated presumptions about what made women deserving or undeserving weighed heavily on hearings like this.

People close to Aida saw value in her life and dignity in her survival, but to outside observers the facts of her story wouldn't fit images of the model immigrant. Aida's teen pregnancy and struggles with poverty, her shoplifting offense, and her humanitarian visa overstay would burden the case. Her false citizenship claim at the border would probably sink it. Letters of support from community members in Douglas might help, but the ultimate outcome rested almost entirely on Aida's self-presentation. Aida and Jesse began to work together on her testimony.

Back in the pod, women, having seen the way Aida had helped Tomasita, began to approach her with questions: a Salvadoran shopkeeper driven out of business by gangs, a woman from central Mexico who fled after getting caught between police and cartels. Aida started with bond petitions and moved on to explaining notices, translating statements, and writing letters for detainees who couldn't even write in Spanish. Sometimes her efforts paid off. Her "clients" received bonds, ICE attorneys assigned to cases responded quicker, and unrepresented women understood a little better what happened in their hearings. Often, though, her efforts fell short. Aida was not an attorney, and the system remained entirely rigged against people defending themselves in one of the most complicated arenas of U.S. law. But people figured that they were better off with her help than without it.

Statements like "We can't let them walk all over us" and "We're going to figure this out" punctuated her speech. She didn't charge precious commissary credit for her help, but she accepted prayers, hugs, and cookies. Often

Aida's connection with detainees would end after she helped them. Other times, it would blossom into friendship.

ASIDE FROM TOMASITA, no one was closer to Aida in those months than Katy Manzanedo. This, even though their friendship began with a deception. Like Aida, Katy had kept to herself during her first weeks at Eloy. At meals, Aida had tried to include the new girl. "Don't sit there all alone. Come sit with us," she urged. Aida was twenty-four, and Katy, just twenty, seemed so young.

During yard time one day, Aida took her by the hand. "Let's walk," she said.

The two young women did laps around the gravel plaza. At first, Aida gushed about Gabriel. He'd inherited his father's handsome face but none of his malice. Then she told Katy harder truths. Her separation from Gabriel was torture beyond anything she could imagine. Gabriel's teacher reported that the boy had stopped paying attention and couldn't focus on school since her arrest. He'd once been a strong student but had begun to struggle. She recounted phone calls with her son: the boy's pleading for her to come home soon. Slowly, Katy began to talk, but not about herself. The conversation shifted, and they lightened the day with chatter about movies, music, and books.

Through all this, Katy kept quiet about what had brought her to Eloy. When Aida pressed for details, she lowered her eyes. Eventually, Aida drew a story out of her new friend, but it was a thin sketch of the most generic migrant's journey. Not much more than "I came through the desert in search of a better life." Something about it seemed off.

"But why are you *here*?" Aida asked, suspicious. Most women in the pod either had lived in the United States for many years and were fighting to stay or had fled violence and persecution and were fighting for asylum. Women caught in the desert "in search of a better life" usually didn't end up in Pod 200.

Katy paused, trying to decide how much of her real story to share. Since coming to Eloy, she'd kept the reasons for her flight from Mexico secret. She didn't know whom she could trust. She didn't even know who was looking for her or how far their reach extended. Arizona and Sonora seemed like a small town sometimes, despite their vast geographies. Katy worried that news of her whereabouts would make its way to the wrong person in Mexico on the lips of a deported detainee. She had begun to trust Aida, though, so she settled on a version of her story built of half-truths and omissions rather than outright lies.

When she finished, Aida squinted at her new friend, weighing what she'd heard. Katy's account still didn't sound right.

"You need to talk to a lawyer," Aida said after a long pause. "You have a difficult case. I've never heard of anything like this."

Katy laughed and said, "I can't pay for a lawyer."

Aida nodded like a therapist. She had devised a strategy that worked for other women. "Find a lawyer who offers free intake interviews," she instructed Katy. "Go to the consultation and learn everything you can. Ask a lot of questions. Then find another and another. Little by little you can figure out what you need to do for your case."

Aida handed her one of Jesse's well-worn business cards. "Start with her," she said.

Matthew Green, the head of Jesse's law firm, showed up for Katy's intake interview. He listened as she recounted the full story of what had brought her to Eloy. When she finished, Matthew Green exhaled and said, "You shouldn't be here."

His firm would represent her at no cost. "Pro bono."

Katy had never heard the phrase before, but its big round sounds were like a glowing sun. She practically danced back to the pod and rushed to find Aida.

"I want you to know the truth about why I'm here," Katy began after sharing her good news. "I didn't really come through the desert." Until a year earlier, Katy had lived a comfortable lower-middle-class life in Hermosillo. Like Aida in Agua Prieta, she grew up in a government-subsidized house. Aida could easily picture the matchbook-sized, two-story cement home. It would have been identical to the one she'd grown up in.

One evening, Katy's family was eating dinner when a metallic banging on the patio outside caught their attention. Her mother crossed the miniature living room to check the front door. An older man who lived across the way and fashioned himself a one-person neighborhood watch hailed her through his front window. He'd seen a man with a gun snooping around their house. Don't worry, he said, I called the police.

Through their own barred window, a few minutes later, they saw officers talking with a stranger and watched as he sauntered away. Crime had been on the rise in Hermosillo for years. Drug addicts burgled houses. Small-time crooks shook down businesses.

Katy's family returned to the dinner table, shaken but grateful. They were talking about the fact that their neighborhood had been spared the worst of cartel violence when a hand smashed through the front window. They barely had time to stagger up, sending chairs flying, when they heard the shots, impossibly loud in the concrete room.

Katy was a university student at the time, but for several years she had worked part-time, following her mother's footsteps. They were both Red Cross paramedics, assigned to ambulance duty, but all their training could not save Katy's father that night. He bled out on the living room floor as his wife and daughter worked on him and his young children watched.

Theories and rumors spread rapidly. With no discernible motive for the shooting, people's fantasies filled in the blanks. A city newspaper published a story saying that Katy's father had been a *narco*, but it published a retraction after her mother protested. Was it a case of mistaken identity? An act of random drug-addled violence? Some secret business Katy's father had never revealed? Even in a country where most crimes went unpunished, the speed with which police dropped this investigation raised suspicions.

Katy's remaining family moved to a different house, and she stopped attending the university. Months of grief and confusion passed before they slid back into old routines. Eventually, Katy and her mother concluded that what had happened to Katy's father was a senseless, indiscriminate act. No deeper meaning could be found. There was nothing else to do but continue living.

On the day Katy returned to the university to reenroll in classes, she received a call from the oldest of her little sisters. Katy could barely understand her hysterical message. Their mother was dead. She had piled the kids into the car for a trip to the supermarket. As she pulled away from the curb, a man stepped casually in front of the vehicle. Katy's sister said that her mom braked, assuming the man was a friend who wanted to say hello. Instead, he opened fire through the windshield.

And then Katy was alone—the sole adult left in her demolished family. This time, the rumors about the attack against her family were worse. It didn't seem possible that the police could do less to investigate this shooting than they did the first, but they managed. That, in itself, stirred suspicion. A popular theory settled on Katy's mom, who had enjoyed reading tarot cards. It was a hobby really, but sometimes she accepted paying clients. Angry neighbors had, more than once, accused her of being a witch. Maybe, people speculated, she had consulted her deck for a *narco* who got angry because he didn't like his fortune? It had happened before. Cartels were superstitious organizations. More likely, another theory went, whoever had murdered Katy's father killed her mother to clean up loose ends and possible witnesses to the original shooting. And now her mother's murder had left more loose ends: a carful of kids had seen the gunman.

Over the next few weeks, neighbors reported vehicles with dark-tinted windows circulating more frequently. People appeared to be watching the house, and a group of kids—not from the neighborhood—tried to befriend Katy's little brother. They plied him with questions about the family's schedule.

Maybe it was all a coincidence. Maybe it wasn't. Had her father been involved in something she didn't know about? Had her mother run afoul of a cartel? What if they'd just had the bad luck of stumbling into the path of a well-connected killer? Katy had no way to answer these questions and no way to know how much danger her family still faced.

As the "maybe"s and "if"s piled up, a close family friend Katy called *tía*—auntie—took her aside and told her something she already knew: "You need to take the children and get out of there." So, with her siblings in tow, Katy presented herself at the border crossing in Nogales and claimed asylum.

"My brother and sisters were sent to Texas." This was the hardest part for Katy to talk about. As minors, the three recent orphans had been taken from her and placed in a family detention center. "Don't worry, they'll be well cared for there," an official had told her. Katy fought the decision. At age twenty, she was the children's sole guardian. Their parents had just died. She was responsible for their safety. When it became clear that her siblings would be taken away no matter how much she protested, Katy had tried to console herself with officials' assurances about the care they'd receive in Texas. "As for you," her case manager had continued, "you'll be placed in

Eloy, Arizona, while a judge decides your case. It's a small town on the way to Phoenix."

Katy told Aida that she had believed that the official meant she would be living with a host family in Eloy or, at worst, in a kind of group home.

Aida rolled her eyes.

"Right?" Katy's freckled face went the color of her red hair. The memory still made her furious. When the bus had rolled up to Eloy just before dawn, it felt as if the official had shoved her off a cliff. Eloy was not a small town; it was a medium-security prison.

"I have a legal right to protection in the United States," Katy said. "There are laws and treaties." She didn't expect to be treated like a common criminal, stripped, probed, numbered, and bullied by guards. If this was her "small town," what was the supposedly comfortable and supportive place her little siblings had been sent to really like? She had no way of knowing. Her money had disappeared along the way to Eloy, so she had no commissary credit and, thus, no phone card. No one in the world knew where she was. Katy's *tía* was the closest thing she had to family at this point. And to that woman, it must have seemed as if Katy had vanished off the face of the earth. Two weeks of total isolation passed before another detainee had taken pity on Katy and shared a few minutes off a phone card, Eloy's most coveted commodity.

"The worst part of it all," Katy told Aida, "is not knowing why it all happened to us, and whether it's over."

AIDA CRIED AND KISSED her new friend. Katy's hair glowed red in the sun, and her freckles shone with a glaze of intermingled tears.

"*Pequitas*, my little freckle face, you are the strongest person I know."

Revelation encouraged revelation. Drinking coffee from a shared mug, Aida told Katy about the darkness that had been pulled over her outside Pachanga's. While the slash marks on her stomach prompted endless questions at shower time, Aida had not shared the whole story with more than a few women in the pod. In fact, most of the women with whom Aida shared every intimate function across every invariable day and every tedious hour had no idea what lay under her lighthearted exterior. They saw only the impish humor and impromptu displays of silly break-dance moves. They saw her deliver coffee to Tomasita and cheer-you-up cards to women pining for home. They saw her eagerness to help. But few people in Eloy knew about her plunge into darkness and mental instability after the attack.

That night, Aida poured out her entire blood-soaked past. Her story and Katy's story pooled and intermingled on the floor of Aida's cell. That night, they became blood sisters, ready for whatever came next.

"I know that we are both going to win our cases and get out of here," Aida assured her, "and we are going to be good friends on the outside, too."

And then the lights snapped off, and each person returned to her own darkness, alone.

27

AIDA AND EMA

KATY LEANED ON THE BLUE RAILING of the second-floor balcony, observing the scene in the common area below. The new *Ecuatoriana*, Ema Ponce, stood beside her. She had materialized in the pod's entrance a week or two earlier, remarkably unscathed by her long journey. She had wasted no time inserting herself into the community. As razor-wired purgatories went, this one wasn't so bad. Ema could do a lot worse than to be locked in limbo with forty or fifty women. She missed her mother and country, but aspects of life at Eloy that grated on other detainees—hierarchies of power, arbitrary rules, the lack of men—didn't bother her that much. Eloy roughed a person up, but it wasn't a dysentery-ridden stash house controlled by smugglers.

"Damn, she is beautiful," Ema said, gazing down at the common area.

"Who—Aida?" Katy replied, laughing at her new friend.

"My ideal woman: curly black hair, *morenita*, light as a dancer."

Below, Aida and Tomasita were sitting next to each other watching television. Ema had been watching Aida interact with other detainees since her arrival in Eloy. The young Mexican's combination of friendliness and ferocity attracted her. At that moment, something in the television program caught Aida's attention, and she cocked her head to whisper into Tomasita's ear. The older woman laughed heartily.

"Do you see that?" Ema asked. "If I had a wife, I'd want her to treat me like that."

"I thought you said that you never wanted to get married."

"I'd get married if *she* asked me."

"Well, she's not like that." Katy put a stop to the delusion. "She has a son. We talk about men."

Soon everyone in the pod could see how besotted Ema was—everyone, that is, except Aida. Pod mates answered her unending questions about Aida with bemused patience. When they caught her in mid-googly-eyed stare or operatic pining, they teased her. But Aida danced through her days, oblivious. If she thought of the new *Ecuatoriana* at all, it was only to wonder why her face always seemed frozen in an idiotic gape. More annoyed than intrigued, Aida could not stretch her generous spirit to cover the embarrassingly silly new woman.

Bumbling for a way to impress Aida, Ema only made things worse. Aida gave off the vibe of someone who went for rebels and rockers, Ema deduced, correctly. When gazing in a manner she thought, incorrectly, was sly and undetectable, Ema saw tiny flecks on Aida's face where old piercings had healed. A brilliant idea stirred in her head. Using craft supplies in direct contravention of prison rules, Ema impaled her nose. For a full day she strutted around the pod, risking write-up or a stretch in solitary. The paper-clip ring she'd fashioned dangled from her nose like a piece of tinsel deposited by a bird building a nest.

My God, Aida thought when the furtive piercing grew infected and Ema's swollen nose turned bright maroon. She is like a child.

MEANWHILE, AIDA FOCUSED on the statement for her hearing. Piece by piece, she wrote her life story. Her words were blunt and unadorned. Their form: neat backward-slanting handwriting that appeared to lean away from the events it described. As she wrote, the pace accelerated, each episode running into the next:

> One night, we were eating dinner and out of nowhere [David] started going crazy . . . he broke a wooden chair, threw the plate with all the food everywhere, then he went to Gabriel's room. He told me he was his baby. He wanted to get Gabriel out of the crib and take him. I tried to stop him but he started pushing me, throwing me down to the floor or against the wall. . . . The look in his eyes was weird. I had never seen it before.
>
> I was afraid of him hurting [Gabriel's] neck from the way he pulled him. I didn't want him to take Gabriel. He was always drunk and very aggressive. I didn't want him to take Gabriel in the car with him . . . but I went to the other side of the car and got Gabriel, took him inside the house. I locked the door. He started banging on the door telling me to open the fucking door or he was going to knock it down. I was afraid of the neighbors calling the cops. I knew it would [have] been me to get deported. He would just go to jail for a night. So I opened the door.
>
> He started spending the rent money, bills money, and food money. Giving me 20 dollars for food for a week. One time he invited two of his male friends. I cooked for them trying to be a good wife, but I noticed how he would look at me all mad. One of his friends helped me clean the table, and I noticed how he got mad. I saw it on his face, so I asked his friend to let me do it. I knew that would cause problems. As soon as they walked out of the door, [David] told me he knew I wanted to fuck him. I said please don't start David. He said, "I know you want to fuck them. You're a lil slut just like every single bitch here in Douglas." . . . He got super mad and said, "This is my fucking house! Get the fuck out!!" He picked me up by the hair and started pushing me towards the door. I didn't want to go because Gabriel was in the room sleeping and I didn't want him to do something stupid with him. He kept pushing but I was holding on to the door. He threw me down

3 steps. I landed on my hands and knees, then he kicked me again on my back. I fell and scratched my arm. When I looked up I saw my sisters and his friends standing there. They tried to go after him, but I stopped them. Begged them to leave.

At times he would race with Gabriel and me in the car while intoxicated. I would beg him not to do it because we had Gabriel in the car and I was afraid of an accident. . . . He would get super angry and tell me how annoying I was and boring that I wasn't fun like I use to be. He would push my head against the seat or pull me by the hair down to his legs to shut me up.

After writing, Aida would sleep for hours.

SOMETIMES AIDA REREAD the letters written by family and friends to support her bond request and establish good moral character. They were not nearly as well written as her own account, but they engulfed her in love.

"I Jazmin," her little sister wrote, "want to say this about Aida Hernandez. She is a really hard working person. Aida is one of the person I look up to. Also she is a loving, caring person. Aida has been through many thing like husband hitting her and she got stabbed in Mexico. But she still been strong."

I Jennifer Hernandez would like to take this time to plead to the court to release my sister. She is a good friend, sister, mother, and daughter and over all a great person. . . . She volunteers with the yearly cancer walk, with her son Gabriel at school activities, she also helps an elderly lady with no pay because the woman is bed [ridden.] She tends to her grandfather and step father who both are on O2.

Jack wrote as well: "She has cooked most of the meals and cleaned the house. We have really depended on her."

A friend of Aida's mother wrote, "Aida has volunteered to help with my son who at the time was 2 years old. . . . She is a very reasonable, loving and giving person. She also helps me at home with no pay because also I use O2 at all times that limit my daily chores. Aida would always lend a helping hand when needing. . . . I feel like she needs to be home to care of her son Gabriel and her family."

SHE READ BRIEF swirly notes from her mother, aunt, and friends. A half page in Spanish from her father was curt but brimming with secret emotion. Each letter made her feel less alone and more desperate to escape confinement. One drove her crazy. It was a spare memo from an attorney in Utah, fewer than fifty words long: "Our records indicate that your obligation to our client, Walmart Stores Inc. . . . has been paid in full." Luz had paid Walmart back for the stolen Lego kit. Such a small thing to have caused so much upheaval in her life. She wasn't sure yet whether her time in Eloy would prove to be a positive or a negative experience. She still could not quite imagine it as a "blessing in disguise," as the agent in Tucson suggested.

With Rosie's help, Aida had learned to look back at what she'd survived with pride. A new country and language. The way Saul blotted out the sun. David. The border. Her deportation, La Roca, Pachanga's, and the attack. She was one of the skinny trees that "send ferocious roots beneath the ground," that "grab the earth between their hairy toes and bite the sky with violent teeth and never quit their anger."

The Tucson Border Patrol agent's words, well-intentioned as they might have been, felt almost comically removed from her daily reality of metal bars, tedium, cardboard food, and wrenching separation from her son. And yet, without the arrest at Walmart, she would never have become *la abogada*, "the attorney," who helped the women of Pod 200 fill out their forms and fight their cases. She would not have had a chance to win legal residency in the United States.

As if all of this weren't confusing enough, she soon had other, even more perplexing feelings to worry about.

FROM TIME TO TIME, the guard who had nicknamed Aida "Cheesy" brought a digital camera to the pod. Detainees who purchased tickets from the commissary could have photographs taken. Some wanted pictures to send home to remind the world of their existence. Detainees cut off from family and social media, some of them thousands of miles from home, cast the images out like messages in bottles: Please don't forget what Mommy looks like.

Other detainees just liked the way photo days broke the stultifying sameness of prison life. The women took full advantage of the break, vamping and clowning for the camera. Guards could almost maintain Eloy's strict prohibition against physical contact between detainees on those jubilant afternoons—but not quite. Starved for touch, women risked hugs under the pretense of composing a shot. Green jumpsuits brushed against one another, fingers touched out of view. This was how Aida met Ema: they got pushed together in a group portrait of rowdy Central Americans and Ecuadorians.

Aida knelt in front and for some reason glanced up to see Ema behind her in the ranks of jumpsuits. Ema had planted herself there on purpose, focusing all of her attention on Aida, hoping the young Mexican would turn around. When she did, both women felt a lurch. Ema looked nothing like the ditzy child Aida imagined her to be. Thick, wide lips, high flushed cheeks, and a long spade nose framed imperious eyes. Ema's look commanded attention, unforgiving in its intensity, like an Incan empress.

"Hey, Cheesy," the guard yelled. "The camera's this way. Eyes front."

Eleven women, some with hands on hips, some striking fashion poses, some looking startled, others calm, and two with distinctly quizzical smiles. Then the flash, and it was over.

"HEY, *COLOCHITA*, how do you say *chévere?*"

"You know already, Ema."

"Owwsoom? Awesome?"

"Stop asking me," Aida said, laughing.

When Ema couldn't think of anything else to say, she'd interrupt Aida with questions about English. The two of them started playing board games and jogging in the yard together. Ema tried to teach Aida soccer, but the dancer floundered comically over the ball. They scrounged commissary ingredients to improvise birthday cakes for friends. Preposterous concoctions of Oreos, pudding, and gummy bears made them keel over in tandem laughter but raised spirits around the pod.

"Ay, look at *las enamoradas,*" Tomasita teased. Aida ignored her.

One day, Ema spoke to her mother by telephone. She'd saved money sent by a relative in New York until she had enough to make the expensive call to Ecuador. Placing the phone into its cradle after her allotted minutes,

Ema fell into a vortex of desolation. She'd maintained a forced optimism with her mother until shouting goodbye over the insentient robot operator. At that moment, she felt the layers of toughness and defensive humor that had sustained her for months peel off. She needed to find her friend from the desert. She needed Aida's volcanic black hair and smile like cactus flowers.

They sat side by side in Aida's cell. Ema unburdened herself, but not about her feelings for Aida. She spoke of older things. Huddled on the bed, she took Aida to Mitad del Mundo, nine years earlier. Spring exam season of Ema's final year in high school had come to the Colegio Velasco Ibarra. She'd passed her hardest exams on her way to her math and physics diploma. Only the final for mechanical drawing remained.

After Ema left Ecuador in January 2012, nothing hurt more than the separation from her mother. Since that night at the Causana Foundation, they had become so close. You cannot imagine, she told Aida, how much my mother has done for me, what it meant to be accepted by her. You cannot imagine how much I owe her, how hard it is to have half a world between us. Aida, for a moment in Ema's company, thought that yes, she could imagine all that.

"HEY, CURLY, what does 'Nothing Else Matters' mean in Spanish?" Ema asked Aida one day.

"You mean the Metallica song?"

Ema nodded, smiling as if the song held special meaning.

"Ema, you already know the answer." But Aida translated anyway. She remembered most of the lyrics.

> I never opened myself this way
> . . . All these words I don't just say
> And nothing else matters
> Trust I seek and I find in you
> . . . Open mind for a different view

HEARINGS CONTINUED IN quick succession. Aida had more than most women in the pod, partly because of frequent rescheduling, partly due to the complexity of her case. Guards had told her that before becoming an immigration judge four years earlier, Richard Phelps had been a senior attorney for ICE and, before that, a military judge. They said he had the most terrifying stare of any judge in Eloy, and maybe in Arizona. But mostly the hearings seemed to consist of registering paperwork. The thunk of Judge Phelps's "received" stamp made more noise on any given day than adversarial argument. He looked more harried than mean.

After President Obama took office in 2009, the Department of Homeland Security set a goal of executing 400,000 deportations a year. It achieved it, and more. The government also stepped up criminal prosecutions related to immigration, although Aida did not face one of these. By 2012, immigration-related violations accounted for 40 percent of all federal criminal prosecutions—more than drug and white-collar crime combined. As a result, the government criminalized and deported more immigrants during Obama's terms than under any other president in history.

The year before Aida arrived in Eloy, swamped immigration judges across the country completed an average of fourteen hundred "matters," including deportation hearings, bond determinations, and motions to reconsider past cases. This made immigration judges, as a group, some of the most overloaded magistrates in the country. The four judges at Eloy handled even more—an average of three thousand matters each in 2011. And even at that rate, they were falling behind: in 2011, more new matters piled onto their desks than they managed to clear.

Judges knew that a negative verdict, made under intense time pressure, might return a person to a war-torn country, to a cartel-controlled neighborhood, or into the arms of an abusive partner. On the flip side, they feared opening the gates of the United States too wide and experiencing blowback if they released someone who later committed a violent crime. In 2009, the head of the National Association of Immigration Judges declared that their work was "the equivalent of death penalty cases . . . conduct[ed] . . . in a traffic court setting." Immigration judges burned out quickly, especially at Eloy.

Jesse Evans-Schroeder worked on a stumbling block in Aida's case. In order to claim protection under the Violence Against Women Act, they needed to prove that Aida's abuser was a U.S. citizen, but David refused to help Aida in any way. He had not responded to requests for copies of his birth certificate, driver's license, or Social Security number. By this time, Jesse had accumulated court records of David's arrest and convictions in

New Mexico. News clippings suggested that the crime involved the attempted kidnapping of an underage girl. His family—Gabriel's grandmother, aunts, and uncles—was hesitant to cooperate. The government attorney offered to look for information about David but reminded Jesse that ICE didn't keep track of U.S. citizens. This was entirely up to her.

The next hearing, early on the morning of June 25, brought no resolution to the question of David's citizenship. To Aida's ears, the hearing hadn't appeared any different from any of the other preliminary sessions: Besides Jesse, it consisted mostly of the white-haired judge and a rotating crew of government attorneys fumbling to organize paperwork. The thump of Phelps's stamp, muttered questions about misplaced forms, and long periods of silent reading were all that Aida noticed. Yet the hearing did offer a crucial piece of good news. Amid the collating of papers and flipping through exhibits, Phelps observed that the government had filed a statement of non-opposition. It meant nothing to Aida, but Jesse probably smiled.

Statutes governing both VAWA and asylum contained long lists of conditions that disqualified applicants. With no criminal record other than the minor shoplifting incident, Aida probably didn't have to worry. But the list of disqualifying factors was expansive. Something might still trip up her case.

Congress created the special category of "aggravated felony" in 1988, wanting to ensure the exclusion of documented and undocumented immigrants who committed crimes such as murder. Over two decades, as demonstrating toughness on illegal immigration emerged as a hallmark of political campaigns, it augmented the list at every chance it got. By 2012, the list of "aggravated felonies" in immigration law included offenses that counted as misdemeanors when committed by a citizen. And there was no statute of limitation. In Arizona, offenses like serious shoplifting, criminal trespassing, and copying music CDs, committed many years earlier, could carry long enough sentences to qualify as aggravated felonies in immigration hearings.

Immigration statutes also barred immigrants guilty of "a crime involving moral turpitude." Like many aspects of immigration law, this category combined incendiary rhetoric, confusing specifics, and large doses of subjectivity. Crimes of moral turpitude involved "depraved or immoral acts," "reprehensible acts," and offenses characterized by "lewdness, recklessness, or malice"—as determined by an individual immigration judge or government attorney. The same offense, carried out under the same circumstances, might qualify as a crime involving moral turpitude in one courtroom but not in the one across the hall.

What worried Jesse Evans-Schroeder most was Aida's false claim of U.S. citizenship at the Douglas port of entry four years earlier. That panicked act hung over the whole proceedings. In fact, VAWA and asylum statutes specifically mentioned false citizenship claims as a disqualifying factor.

Aida remembered her stupid, desperate attempt to reach Gabriel on that awful morning: the ragged run from Raúl's house to the border, the melting feeling the second she opened her mouth at the inspection desk, the sick vertigo in the interrogation room as her expedited removal rushed forward without a lawyer or phone call. That one slow-motion disaster jeopardized everything she and Jesse had fought for.

"Exhibit thirteen," Judge Phelps announced, "is the government's non-opposition." Thud.

For once, the subjectivity of immigration law worked in Aida's favor. "Exhibit thirteen" indicated that the government had decided not to deem Aida ineligible for legal status in the United States because of her false citizenship claim. Reading the transcript of her interrogation at the border, it seemed clear that she'd recanted her lie immediately, without pressure from the interviewing officer. According to Bureau of Immigration Appeals rulings and the U.S. Citizenship and Immigration Services manual, this timely retraction meant that government attorneys could choose to disregard the offense. And they did.

This did not mean that the government wouldn't fight her petition. It didn't even mean that the government wouldn't hold the false citizenship claim against her at the hearing. But at least her case was eligible to proceed. And that was something.

That same morning, Judge Phelps set a date for Aida's final hearing. They'd have one more preliminary meeting in September and then reconvene at 1:00 p.m. on November 17. By 2:00 that same afternoon, Aida would know whether she could remain legally in the United States or face immediate removal to Mexico. As he consulted the calendar, Phelps asked Jesse, "Are you confident that you are ready to go?"

"Yes, Your Honor," she answered. But she did not feel all that confident. The government's non-opposition constituted a major victory, but many more factors still weighed against her. So far, the judge and government attorneys had evinced a modicum of impatient sympathy for Aida's application. But the young woman's written and oral testimony would carry enormous weight in the final hearing.

If Jesse could prove to the court that David was a U.S. citizen, the case would hinge on Aida's ability to convince the judge and government attorneys of three things: that she was a person of good moral character, that she had suffered cruelty and abuse, and that deportation would create extreme hardship for her and her son. Because Aida never reported David to the police, all they had to offer were letters from family members and Aida's own voice. In cases like this, outcomes often came down to highly subjective judgments about whether a particular woman looked and sounded credible.

If the VAWA application failed, Jesse and Aida would talk about the stabbing. That incident, at least, was well documented. But given the largely untested nature of gender-based asylum claims for Mexican women, and immigration officials' extreme reluctance to grant asylum to Mexicans in general, Jesse hoped that it didn't come to that. Neither woman knew it, but a study conducted in 2014 would reveal that between 2009 and 2013 Judge Phelps had the twelfth-highest asylum denial rate of any of the almost three hundred federal judges who handled more than one hundred immigration cases a year.

INSIDE THE COURTROOM, Aida felt meek and intimidated. Over the course of seven preliminary hearings, she had not said much more than "Yes, Your Honor" and "Thank you, Your Honor."

Outside, though, Aida had come into her own. She still helped her pod mates with translations for free, and a number of them had begun to trust her judgment. Ema, of course, loved the way the curly-haired *mexicana* sucked in her cheeks and stuck out her jaw in response to another outrage from the Corrections Corporation of America. And when prison officials cut the women's meager shampoo and toilet paper ration in half, Aida truly became a leader.

"This is not okay," she told Katy. "We can't let them get away with this."

Katy hesitated, reluctant to get involved, but Aida was right: ICE and CCA wanted prisoners to purchase high-priced toiletries from the commissary. Many women in the pod simply couldn't spend several dollars' worth of commissary credit for hotel-sized shampoo. Some had no credit at all.

"Think about her," Aida said, pointing to a young indigenous woman from Guatemala with no outside support.

Even those prisoners with access to commissary credit pinched pennies: family members worked hard on the outside, and Western Union claimed steep fees on transfers to prisoners' accounts. Like Aida, most women in the pod saved commissary credit for phone calls, tampons, and edible food. Ramen noodles, peanut butter, and cookies provided crucial supplements to the cafeteria's pasty rounds of *"pan, pasta, y papas."*

In the end, Katy looked on while Aida wrote a letter of protest and circulated through the pod collecting signatures. About a dozen women refused to sign, fearing retaliation from prison officials, but Aida persuaded most of the pod to join her struggle. The letter provoked quick action: a two-man team of ICE officers responded to the complaint, slapping Aida's letter on one of the pod's steel tables.

"What's going on here?"

Outraged women erupted in Spanish opprobrium all at once, and the agents visibly tensed.

Then Aida's voice cut through the noise, explaining, in English, the hardships the reduction created.

"But we implemented this in the male section with no problems," one of the officers countered. "Why is it that the male section uses so much less toilet paper than you women?" he demanded.

The retort slipped out before Aida could think. "Because you shake and we wipe."

One official couldn't stifle a laugh at this, but his partner plowed forward.

"What about the shampoo? Why do you use so much more than the men?"

Aida said nothing this time. Instead, not breaking eye contact, she removed a hair tie and shook out her long curls. The other women followed suit, waving their thick manes like protest flags.

AIDA WAS RIGHT to demand that their needs be recognized. The women in Pod 200 were not being held because they'd committed a crime, and by law immigration detention was not punishment. Yet CCA and ICE administered Eloy using a criminal incarceration model. They confinined women behind razor wire in a remote location and subjected them to shackles, locked quarters, solitary confinement, and strict, seemingly arbitrary rules. Indeed, in some ways immigration detention was worse than criminal prison. ICE based the standards of care for immigration detention on short-term, pre-trial criminal confinement. As a result, rules mandating services such as access to medical care were less stringent than those found in prison. One of the reasons immigration detention was so profitable for CCA was because it was so easy. The arbitrary cut in basic necessities smacked of unabashed profiteering.

To the women's surprise, Aida's words moved gears somewhere in the prison administration. That afternoon, guards delivered boxes of shampoo and toilet paper to Aida's pod.

Strange, she reflected, how it took getting sent to one of the worst immigration detention centers in the country to make her feel powerful.

AIDA AND EMA became inseparable. The Ecuadorian woman's company— and her worldly outlook—made Aida braver. But also confused. One evening, Aida, Ema, Tomasita, Katy, and a few other women crowded around a table playing cards. In this particular game, the winner of each hand got to ask another player a question that she had to answer truthfully. As soon as Ema won a round, she looked across the table at Aida.

"Do you think you could ever be with a woman?" Ema tried to make the question sound casual, half joking, half teasing. Everyone at the table knew how serious it was. The noisy common area contracted around the card table. Aida's cheeks burned and a sheen of sweat appeared instantly on her eyelids and upper lip.

"I don't—" She tried to play her answer cool, with an arched eyebrow to demonstrate good humor, but it came out flustered. "I don't know," she concluded.

Aida admired Ema's unflappable calm and scientific approach to life— perfect foils for her own impulsiveness. She even conceded that Ema looked beautiful playing soccer. When she chose to be honest with herself, Aida admitted that she had found women attractive since she was a teen, but that didn't make it right. She was not gay.

Homosexuality did not fit into Luz's Catholic worldview or Raúl's

1960s Marxism. They instilled Aida with a strong sense that homosexuality was, depending on which parent spoke, "sinful" or "unscientific." *Joto, maricón, marimacha*, and *tortillera* had flowed freely as general-purpose put-downs in their household. And so, as a teen, she'd found nonthreatening explanations for the way women caught her eye. I appreciate beauty of all kinds, and women are one of God's beautiful things, she had told herself for years. It doesn't mean anything.

Aida repeated that mantra through the early summer of 2012. At night, when images of Ema settled her into sleep, Aida reminded herself that she was not gay, and she repeated the words in the morning when she woke up happy, her first thoughts of the day dedicated to the beautiful Ema.

IN THE END, it was irrelevant. Since meeting Aida, Ema had secretly discouraged her New York family's efforts to raise money for her release on bond. But after three months in Eloy, her sister put up the money for Ema's release. When a guard appeared in the pod, yelling, "Roll it up, Ponce!" Ema howled, "Noo! That's not right." It was likely the first time this had ever occurred in the history of CCA Eloy. Other women looked on, some mystified, some angry that one of their ranks would treat a coveted shot at freedom so flippantly. A few probably chuckled to themselves or exchanged arch looks with other women in the know.

It took the guard a moment to recover from the shock. Usually people cried with joy, not anger. And even more perplexing, Ema had begun to argue with him, questioning the paperwork. Finally, he came to his senses and ordered the strange woman to pack her things.

Aida sat, glued to a television in the common area, unable to watch as Ema gave away her commissary items to friends on the second floor. Practically the whole pod squeezed into Ema's cell to say goodbye and wish her luck on the outside. Aida stared straight ahead at the screen. Ema's impromptu going-away celebration spilled out onto the catwalk, and Aida sat stiffly, earbuds inserted, her back to the tumult. When she heard Ema descending the stairs, Aida couldn't stand it any longer. She stood up, almost flipping the plastic chair, and clattered across the polished concrete floor. They stood facing each other at the bottom of the stairs for something close to a lifetime. Then they hugged.

The guard saw it coming: "No touching, ladies."

Aida could get a write-up for embracing another detainee, or even a stint in solitary, depending on the guard. But she pressed harder, folding Ema's prison-soft curves into her acute angles. It wasn't clear whose tears were whose anymore.

"No touch, no touch," the guard repeated. "Come on, break it down," he said, waiting. "Come on, ladies, you're going to get me in trouble."

They unclasped, and Ema disappeared through the blue metal door into the hundred-degree July sunshine. Aida returned to her cell and wept openly for days.

28

GOING AWAY TO
COME BACK

AIDA LIFTED A SWOLLEN EYE. Tomasita tugged at her body, sprawled over the bed.

"Okay, up you go—come on."

Aida burrowed deeper into her half sleep, and Tomasita stopped trying to rouse her. The older woman, Aida's Eloy "mother," scrunched her face and gave a knowing snort.

"*¿Ya te enamoraste, verdad, cabrona?*"

"Yes," Aida said, rolling over to face her friend. "I fell in love."

"*Ayy*, girl, what will your mother say?"

"I don't care."

"At least get out of bed."

Aida managed to drag herself out of bed that day, and all the ones that followed, but she was not the same person. Tomasita looked after her, and freckle-faced Katy could still make her laugh. Without Ema, though, the agony of detention with no fixed end and little hope of success flattened her. Unlike a criminal sentence with its clear terminus, civil confinement in Eloy was indefinite, chained to the slow march of an overtaxed immigration system. Rationing her telephone minutes for calls to Gabriel and cut off from the internet, Aida lost track of Ema. All she knew was that her friend had melted into the hundreds of thousands of Ecuadorians living in and around New York City. Without Ema, Aida's separation from the world felt infinite.

As women before her had learned, there were only two ways to terminate immigration detention early: you took your own life, or you petitioned for voluntary departure. Rumors of suicide haunted CCA Eloy. More detainees had taken their lives at Eloy than in any of the United States' 250 other immigration prisons. But Aida had survived too much already to contemplate suicide. In July, medical staff from an international human rights clinic had examined her for the asylum claim. The report enumerated ten stab wounds—left arm, hand, stomach, and back—as well as indications of PTSD and battered woman syndrome. Aida took fierce pride in her ability to survive.

The seductive closure that came from electing voluntary departure, on the other hand, engulfed her. Judge Phelps had offered to grant voluntary departure at Aida's first hearing, and the option tormented her.

Anyone who hadn't been convicted of an aggravated felony could petition for this kind of release. If it was granted, Aida would walk out of Eloy and return to Mexico on her own. In exchange, she'd give up all of her current claims to legal permanent residence and waive her right to an appeal. A ten-year bar on entering the United States for any reason would prevent her from acquiring a tourist visa or a border-crossing card. Returning to Douglas before that bar expired could earn Aida years in federal prison. But living in Agua Prieta, she'd be closer to Gabriel. She would be able to see home through gaps in the wall.

Days became an endless three-way tug-of-war between Aida's fear of returning to Mexico, her yearning to win a place in the United States, and the overwhelming heaviness of detention. Voluntary departure meant forfeiting almost any hope of ever living in the United States legally, but women disappeared from the pod that way almost every week. Aida's cellmate Blanca was inching inevitably toward that decision herself.

Blanca had arrived in April. Before that, she told Aida, she'd spent seventeen months in Sheriff Arpaio's infamous Estrella women's prison on the southwest side of Phoenix. A routine traffic stop had swept Blanca into the sheriff's dirty war on immigrants. For years, Arpaio had flouted federal investigations, court rulings, and lawsuits to run dragnets against brown-skinned Phoenix residents. He coordinated mass raids on Latino neighborhoods, searching and detaining people without lawful reasons. He organized checkpoints and championed policies that made Latinos four to nine times more likely than non-Latinos to be stopped by police in Maricopa County. Disregarding court rulings and federal investigations, he effectively enforced his own immigration law, in violation of the Constitution.

When undocumented residents like Blanca fell into his grasp, they often faced serious criminal charges for document fraud or the bizarre crime of conspiracy to smuggle themselves. Using a fake ID landed Blanca her seventeen-month criminal sentence.

Arpaio bragged about targeting Latinos, but he took particular pride in the brutal conditions in his jails. Inmates at Estrella toiled on chain gangs, and pregnant women went into labor with their arms and legs shackled. Guards brutalized the "Mexican bitches," and prisoners received two meals a day. In 2012, according to news sources, each meal consisted of a roll, an orange, and a carton of milk. Salt, condiments, coffee, and mirrors were forbidden. Televisions were tuned to only two sadistic stations: the Weather Channel, to remind women of the blast-furnace temperatures in which they worked, and the Food Channel, to taunt the starving prisoners. Twice, a federal judge ruled that medical care under Arpaio's rule was so bad that it violated the Constitution. Arpaio boasted that the draconian conditions saved taxpayer money. In fact, Arpaio's tactics cost taxpayers a lot: during the twenty-four years he served as sheriff, his department would spend $140 million litigating and settling lawsuits over civil rights violations.

When Blanca's criminal sentence ended, Maricopa County officials turned her over to ICE custody. After seventeen months in Estrella, Blanca came to Eloy raw, her spirit already lacerated. She doubted she could last much longer. That summer, she and Aida read a guide to applying for voluntary departure produced by Charles Vernon's organization.

SEPTEMBER IN THE Sonoran Desert brought a whisper of relief. After four or five months of blistering heat, temperatures inched downward. At higher elevations, frost appeared in the night. Hillsides erupted in golden blossoms, and, lower down, cactus fruits ripened, red, yellow, and plum. For Aida, though, September 2012 was a pitiless season.

The first week of the month, she dreamed that Fulgencio was sitting on a lawn chair in a field of wildflowers. She saw herself carrying two cups of ranch-style coffee, one for him and one for her. He was young and handsome again and wearing the tailored gray *charro* suit he always wore to weddings and *quinceañeras*. Aida handed her grandfather one of the coffees, and a second chair appeared. She sat down and leaned back to sip her own coffee. Then she turned to say something to her grandfather. He was gone. She was all alone in the field of flowers.

Aida startled awake and called out to Blanca on the bunk above, "Are you up?"

"What do you want?"

"I think my *tata* died."

"Go back to sleep, Aida. It was just a dream."

During early September, Aida's nightly news programs clogged with blurry images of Benghazi and loud, vainglorious shots of the Democratic National Convention. For detainees in Eloy, they seemed like events taking place in the distant future of a different Earth-like planet. The Arizona news, meanwhile, spat out nothing but relevant, dispiriting stories: On September 7, the Department of Homeland Security trumpeted historic numbers of formal deportations, despite continued decline in the number of people crossing the border without permission. In 2011, immigration officials had deported 391,953 people—more than in any other year in U.S. history except 2009. What the Department of Homeland Security touted as a banner accomplishment was, to Aida, 391,953 people who had fought their cases, just like the women of Pod 200.

That's us, Aida thought to herself when she heard the statistic.

Two days earlier, a federal judge had denied a request by civil rights organizations seeking to block the most controversial provision of the notorious

Arizona law S.B. 1070. The judge's decision paved the way for implementing the requirement that police verify the immigration status of anyone they believed might be in the country without papers. Fears of increased racial profiling of people who "looked illegal" ignited again. There was one glimmer of good news, though. The judge blocked a provision of the law making it a crime to transport an undocumented person in Arizona. At least now, police couldn't arrest Jack for driving Luz to work.

As the deportation machine ground away at people inside Eloy, life got more dangerous for their family members outside. Arizona law now made it increasingly clear that local police could be extensions of the Border Patrol. Douglas's police chief worked hard to win the trust of undocumented residents, but state lawmakers undermined his efforts.

Aida worried about her trapped family. Luz's green card application had been denied. Her children had no cases on their own. Border Patrol checkpoints sliced Douglas from the rest of the state. Aida knew that there were now more ways than ever before for Luz, Jennifer, Cynthia, Jazmin, and Emiliano to end up like her.

Gabriel's birthday fell in the second week of September. Aida had resisted calling home for weeks, saving all the minutes on a phone card for his big day. She had also mailed a new set of her drawings for him to open on his birthday. Along with the usual superheroes, she slaved over a self-portrait. When he opened the envelope, it would feel almost as if she were there in person. It wasn't much, she knew, but at least he would have something to open and a visual reminder of her love.

The day arrived and Gabriel picked up the phone, brimming with excitement.

"Guess what, Mom."

Aida could feel his happiness bursting through the line, and it lifted her spirits.

"I have a real cake! And Emiliano is going to take me to GameStop to buy a video game!"

"Oh, Gabriel, that's wonderful. I—"

The call ended a minute later. Gabriel couldn't wait to go to GameStop. Aida could hear him bouncing with excitement, and she rushed her "happy birthday"s and "I love you"s to fit them in before he bolted away. Gabriel half listened, impatient to leave for the store.

Aida replaced the receiver in its cradle and stared at the phone. Her painstakingly hoarded phone card still had most of its minutes. Gabriel was having the perfect birthday, without her. Her son's pleasure made her both dizzy with happiness and utterly crushed. That was the first time she cried outside her cell, in the middle of the pod common area.

That September, Gabriel was starting first grade for the second time. Severe attention problems are a common symptom of secondary trauma in children. When Gabriel had faced the same struggle in kindergarten, Aida had been there for him, volunteering in the classroom almost every day. With his mother at his side, Gabriel relaxed and focused. By the end of the year, the teacher confirmed, "Gabriel has matured this year academically." First grade had started on the same upward trajectory, but after Aida's detention he slid backward. A school counselor met with him shortly after Aida's arrest and reported, "He appeared to be friendly and . . . after about three meetings, Gabriel began speaking freely regarding his home life. However, he did remain guarded with regards to his mother. . . . Usually he would tell me that she was 'coming home in two weeks.'" After six months of counseling, "Gabriel remained avoidant regarding his academics and his mother." In June 2012, Gabriel's teachers decided to hold him back to repeat first grade.

All Aida could think of for the rest of Gabriel's birthday was the promise she had made to him after she'd returned from the hospital four years earlier, the promise that hadn't really been hers to make: "I will never leave you again."

THE NEXT WEEK, when she called home, Aida spoke to her mother. Something about Luz's voice sounded wrong.

"*Mama*, how is *Tata*?" The dream about her grandfather still ached, like an old bruise.

"*Bien*. Fine." Luz brushed away the question.

"Can I talk to him?"

"He's sleeping, *mija*."

Luz didn't need to say anything else. Her too-cheerful tone told Aida everything she needed to know: Fulgencio was dead.

Detention stretched longer that day, and the lure of voluntary departure pulled harder than ever. The gut pain from missing family and home was excruciating without end—each breath, each thought. Aida and Blanca talked about ending their incarceration. They wanted to rejoin the world so badly that they were almost willing to suffer the decades of exile it would entail. Aida wrote out her longhand request for voluntary departure and addressed it to the Honorable Judge Phelps. Then she tore it up and vowed to persevere.

Around that time, Matthew Green and Jesse Evans-Schroeder managed to get Katy released on her own recognizance while the remainder of her case played out. As unaccompanied minors, her younger siblings had soared through the system in Texas. Their asylum petition already granted, they had returned to Arizona to live with a distant relative. Katy's attorneys didn't have a hard time convincing the judge that the young orphans needed their older sister. The news still came as a surprise. Aida, Katy, and Tomasita were watching television together when a guard said the most important phrase in Eloy, "Roll it up, Katy Manzanedo."

In a flash Katy was gone—out the blue door, into the sunlight.

Aida celebrated her friend's escape for the rest of the evening. Almost dancing, she exchanged "can you believe it"s and "she's so lucky"s with the women left behind. They were all jealous, of course, but agreed that the three orphaned children needed their older sister. If only the judges would show the same concern for the rest of the women's small children, many of them U.S. citizens, abandoned on the outside like Gabriel.

AIDA FELT HER WORLD diminish. With Ema and Katy gone, only Tomasita remained of the tight sisterhood they'd crafted in the middle of misery.

On September 17, Aida appeared before Judge Phelps at another preliminary hearing. David still refused to help, and the notarized statement his mother sent attesting that she gave birth to him in Safford, Arizona, didn't count. Jesse's voice crackled with irritation.

"David Rojas has been completely unwilling to submit any verification of his citizenship status. . . . I recognize that the evidence we have right now is circumstantial."

Phelps understood the difficulty and acknowledged that Congress had recognized the potential for precisely this kind of problem when they passed VAWA. But he still needed to see proof. Without evidence of David's U.S. citizenship, the judge could not even consider Aida's case for protection under VAWA's immigration provisions, or "special rule cancellation of removal," as it was known in legalese.

"I don't think that we're fooling anyone here," the government attorney added, "by mentioning that the special rule cancellation is by far [Aida's] stronger case, and I have to agree with the court that we do want to get the eligibility clear on the record."

Gabriel's birth certificate emerged as a possible way forward. Phelps thought that Arizona birth certificates required proof of parents' place of birth. If David's name appeared on the certificate, it would reveal his citizenship status. Jesse agreed to look for the document and scheduled the next hearing for three weeks later.

By this time, Aida had accustomed herself to the court's unsettling rhythm of bureaucratic tedium punctuated by jolts of terror. As Judge Phelps prepared to adjourn that day, Jesse dropped a casual question.

"Are there currently visa numbers available for cancellation of removal?"

It hadn't occurred to Aida that the number of VAWA visas might be capped and that all this work could have been for nothing.

"I have not been notified of any constraints on my ability to grant under 240(a)(b)," Phelps answered.

The cryptic response, like most of what went on in court, left Aida more confused. But Jesse smiled at her and gave a discreet thumbs-up.

FINALLY, SEPTEMBER ENDED. Through the latter part of the month, Jesse and Aida had worked together on written testimony and rehearsed for oral questioning. The outline of Aida's story took shape on yellow legal paper with scribbled questions and arrows crowding the drafts. "No convictions" circled in black. Notes filled the margins. "PTSD." "Legs around neck," "Stabbed a door w/knife by her head," "Broke wooden chair." "Step-dad, cancer, oxygen." Aida's life looked as chaotic on paper as it sounded coming out of her mouth.

During the first week of October, Aida celebrated her twenty-fifth birthday. It fell near Columbus Day that year. For most holidays, the prison administration did something special: slightly better food at lunchtime, extra rec time outside. For this Columbus Day, the cafeteria served double cheeseburgers, a breathtaking respite from the endless bread, pasta, and potatoes. Everyone at Aida's table gave the birthday girl one of their patties and half a bun, allowing her to make an exuberant, towering burger.

Prison officials wrote up anyone caught taking cafeteria leftovers to their pod. Saving a bit of food for the long stretches between meals cut into commissary profits and was considered a serious infraction. One of the more sympathetic guards hovered over Aida as she grappled with her culinary creation.

"I am going to stand here until you finish, Hernandez," she said, "because you are going to want to take that back to your pod."

Aida and the butch guard had passed whole afternoons talking about music—particularly their shared passion for 1980s hard rock—but Aida knew that the guard would still cite her if she didn't cooperate. It didn't matter in the end. Aida had no trouble finishing the best lunch she'd eaten in months.

Back in the pod, the women called her to join them while Blanca carried in a plate. When she set it down, half the women shrieked. The rest hooted. Blanca had assembled something like a cake out of commissary items: Little Debbie honey buns glazed with melted chocolate bars. It was not a great work of art, culinary or representational, but the shape was unmistakable: a penis cake, big enough for all of them. Happy birthday, Aida.

That night, women from Mexico, South America, Central America, China, and India sang "Happy Birthday" in Spanish and English. Some prayed over her. Others broke the rules to give her a much-needed hug. Someone produced decks of Uno cards, and they played en masse, with Aida explaining the game to newbies, until lights-out.

The women of Pod 200 had spent a fortune—the real equivalent of many minutes on the phone with family—to celebrate Aida's birthday.

"Even though I've been through so much," she said to the gathering, "amazing people are coming into my life and I am so grateful."

Going to sleep that night, she realized that the Border Patrol agent in Tucson had been prophetic. This *was* a blessing in disguise. His arrogance had pissed her off so many months ago, but even jerks could be right sometimes. Quietly, she recommitted to winning her case. All thoughts of voluntary departure vanished. Losing her case could mean a ten-year bar on entering the United States, so she would have to win it.

THE MORNING AFTER Aida's birthday celebration, Judge Phelps and the government trial attorney accepted Gabriel's birth certificate as proof of David's U.S. citizenship. This last obstacle cleared, Jesse confirmed the final hearing date set for mid-November. Every technicality that could formally preclude

Aida from receiving VAWA protection had been addressed—at least every one Jesse could think of.

All Aida's life, she'd listened to people talk about "the law" with awe and respect. She could imagine immigration statutes filling thick, impersonal tomes in Jesse's Tucson office. Words like "criminal alien," "illegal immigrant," "citizen," and "inadmissible" sounded concrete and indisputable on the news. But Jesse reminded her that immigration law only looked dispassionate from the outside. Inside, subjective calls and moral judgments reigned. But Aida and Jesse had built the best legal case they could. Barring technical surprises, success or failure now depended entirely on Aida's testimony. Or rather, the case hinged on how two men, Judge Richard Phelps and the government attorney Alec Niziolek, viewed Aida's character and credibility.

So far, the white-haired former air force JAG officer's demeanor in this case had conformed to his reputation: impatient and stern, but sympathetic. Still, there was no getting around the blunt reality of his 95 percent denial rate. A deportation order wrapped in kind words was still a deportation order.

With the appointment of Alec Niziolek as trial attorney for Aida's final hearing, on the other hand, Jesse felt a bit reassured. The young attorney came across as tightly wound. Even in the most brutal summer months, he wore a three-piece suit. But compared with many other government trial attorneys, he was willing to take individual detainees' life circumstances seriously. Or so Jesse thought.

As November ticked closer, Jesse told Aida that as long as she handled her spoken testimony well, she had a fifty-fifty chance of winning. It was the equivalent of a coin flip, but better odds than what most women in Pod 200 could expect if and when their cases made it to a final hearing.

Painstakingly, Aida and Jesse gathered hours of discussion into bullet points and numbered lines. Aida noticed that telling her story had gotten a little easier. Speaking about her life didn't revive old fears or trigger flashbacks as much as it used to. For the first time, narrating the events of her childhood and young adulthood in a clear, loud voice filled Aida with a sense of her own inner worth. She told her story to reclaim her life.

BLANCA DID NOT make it. Days before Aida's final hearing, Blanca petitioned for voluntary departure. Extreme violence had driven the woman out of her home in northern Mexico, but the criminal conviction she received after one of Sheriff Arpaio's dubious roundups clouded her case for asylum. After twenty-four months in jail and detention, the future looking bleak, she decided that she couldn't bear another hour away from her husband and children. Now she'd have to choose between relocating her U.S. family to the place she'd fled from, hiding alone in Mexico, or risking years in jail to return home to Phoenix.

In twenty-four hours, Aida would either win permission to live with her family or face the same cruel options her roommate now confronted.

WITH BLANCA GONE, the night before Aida's hearing would be the first night in over ten months she'd spent in a room alone. Pacing in the dark after lights-out, she tried to review her testimony. Her brain refused to concentrate at first, tallying the reasons for optimism and fear over and over in an anxious loop. Carefully prepared questions darted in and out of focus. Were you ever abused by your mom's boyfriend? You talk in your declaration about struggling with alcohol and marijuana—when did you start drinking and smoking? Why did you drop out of school when you became pregnant? When did you begin to experience abuse by David? Do you remember any specific instance of physical violence by David? How would Gabriel react?

She knew that Jesse wouldn't talk about the attack in Mexico unless Phelps rejected the VAWA petition. Even leaving the attack aside, Aida could hardly believe what she'd overcome. She thought of her father. "You survived death. You can do anything."

Blanca had left a transistor radio, and Aida plugged in earbuds. The song that came on the radio first would reveal her fate, she decided. A staticky Phoenix station played the slow groove of "Down on Me" by Jeremih and 50 Cent. The song held no particular meaning for her, but she'd always liked it. It was a good omen, she thought. Standing in the center of the empty cell, Aida swayed to the beat, her body loosening. She murmured the simple chorus, smooth rhythm waving through her hips and arms. While she was lost in the music, something settled in her. She imagined freedom, and then she slept.

EVERY BIT OF confidence vanished in the freezing courtroom air. Passing into the chamber, not much bigger than an office, Aida sensed Luz sitting in the narrow gallery a few feet behind her. She'd braved Border Patrol stops and Eloy ID checks to be there for her daughter. Aida wanted to see her. No, she wanted to hurl herself over the barrier and fly into her mother's embrace. It had been more than ten months since she'd held a member of her family. But she had heard a rumor from other prisoners: if she reached out to her mother, the hearing would be canceled. So she locked her gaze on the Justice Department seal. Her body shivered with fear in Eloy's over-refrigerated artificial air.

The room rose for Judge Phelps, and Jesse gave Aida a reassuring look. As always, paperwork was shuffled, forms were exchanged, and technical questions were clarified. This time, though, there was nothing new for Phelps to stamp.

Instead, he lifted two thick files in the air and addressed Aida. "I'm showing you your two applications. The one in my right hand is your application for cancellation of removal. The one in my left hand is your application for asylum and withholding," he said. "Are you familiar with the contents of both applications?"

Aida shuddered a nod.

"The answers to *all* the questions?"

Aida hesitated, then said, "Yes, Your Honor."

For a long time, Phelps and the two attorneys addressed one another, and Aida strained to follow the conversation. She could think of nothing but her testimony and the feeling of her mother's anxious breath a few feet behind her. Finally, everyone went silent, and no sounds disturbed the room except for the scratch of Phelps's pen as he signed the two applications, ready to commence.

"Miss Hernandez, I would invite you, ma'am, to come up to the witness stand." The bailiff indicated an office chair next to the judge and adjusted the height as she stepped forward.

"Watch your step going up that rise, ma'am." The judge spoke in his gentle drawl. "Now, ma'am, Miss Evans-Schroeder is going to ask you some questions. Mr. Niziolek is probably going to ask you some questions. I might even ask you some questions. If any of us asks you a question that you don't understand, please don't hesitate to tell us that you don't understand the question. That happens *all* the time. And if it happens to you, it is no reflection on you and your inability to understand us. It means that we haven't done a very good job of framing our question."

Guards had told Aida that Judge Phelps wanted his witnesses close enough to detect truth and fiction as it radiated off their bodies. In the cramped room, this meant Aida's knees were squeezed against Phelps's dais as she prepared to speak.

The questions began, slow and formal. "Good afternoon," Jesse said.

"Good afternoon," Aida replied.

At first Jesse's questions were almost longer than Aida's nervous answers.

"When did you first come to the United States?"

"When I was six years old."

Aida confused dates and ages through the start of her testimony; she was just under nine when her mother moved her to Douglas. It was not dissimulation. Ever since the attack, chronologies taxed her. She had a natural storyteller's ability to summon astounding levels of detail about her life, but PTSD altered her sense of time.

She fought onward, and a feeling of confidence returned. Her story grew steady and precise as it spooled out. Her voice had the round, melodic timbre of southwestern border English, but the words were savage. She began with Saul. She spoke in intimate detail about his brutality, each humiliation, gut kick, and attack on her mother. Next, she talked of her traumatized flight into drinking and rebellion, and her ferocious battles with Luz.

A few yards away, Aida's mother struggled to understand the English, but the fragments she grasped upended her. While Aida forged ahead, her petition for mercy sounding more and more like an indictment of the whole world, Luz began to weep. Heavy makeup streaked on her face.

Aida's witness seat looked out at the gallery, but she kept her eyes leveled on the judge's gaze and proceeded.

"Everything we've heard is on the record already," Phelps interrupted, asking Jesse and Aida to focus on essential matters. "The record is very comprehensive," he added. It wasn't clear whether he was trying to spare Aida and her mother or just wanted to move along.

Jesse paused and refocused. "Your mom is here today, and I imagine that it's hard to talk about those things when she's present. How is your relationship with your mom now?"

"It's totally different now. We help each other out. We're there for each other."

After the judge's interruption, Aida focused almost entirely on David's abuses. She told of knives plunged into walls beside her head, Gabriel shaken over his crib, rug burns, and bruises. At times, Jesse sounded as if she would rather have been anywhere on earth other than in front of Aida, asking the questions she needed to ask. But Aida's voice grew clearer and more courageous as she went along. She explained what it was like to survive on the twenty dollars a week David allotted for food and diapers. Her words dissected David's behavior almost clinically but humanized him as well. His plummet from gifted boy to trapped outcast, shattered by the impossibility of life in Douglas. It tempered her reproof. Jesse asked her why she never called the police.

"One part was because I was illegal," Aida replied with the practiced answer, and then added, "Another was because I loved David and didn't want to hurt him."

"What kind of child is Gabriel?" Jesse asked.

"He's an amazing kid. He's smart, kind, loving; he's funny." She smiled something like her old smile. Her voice lightened and expanded, sparkling for the first time all afternoon. She brimmed with pride describing her son, and then she suddenly crashed. It would be the only time she broke down during the hearing.

"He's in his second time in first grade. . . . Since I was here, detained, I couldn't go anymore [to volunteer in Gabriel's classroom]. I couldn't help him. They said, me being in here, the depression . . . I remember talking to him, and he said, 'Mom, I can't concentrate. I'm always thinking about you.'" Sobbing now, she mimicked her son's small voice: "'I try, I try, and I can't.' And they flunked him."

When Jesse asked her last question, Alec Niziolek looked up from his notes and asked eight rapid-fire questions.

"Does Gabriel have [Medicaid] benefits?"

"Yes."

"Do you have a job lined up if you were to return to Douglas?"

"Other than employment, what plans do you have?"

The questions continued and Aida handled each one deftly, strange and unexpected as they were.

"Do you know where [GED] courses are offered in Douglas?"

"Yes."

And then he stopped abruptly. "Thank you. I have no further questions."

Aida returned to her seat. She sat down, face flushed and mind blank, staggered by the conclusion of her testimony. It had happened so fast. They'd entered the unknown territory of the hearing's final stage.

"Mr. Niziolek," Phelps asked, "does the government have a position on the application for special rule cancellation?"

"No opposition, Your Honor," the trial attorney blurted out, almost jolly.

"Ma'am, I'm going to grant your application for special rule cancellation," the judge said. "Does the government reserve its right to appeal?"

"No, Your Honor."

"This is a final order. Miss Hernandez, I wish you and your son well. Court adjourned."

Aida sat bolt upright as the attorneys slid papers into their briefcases. She thought that she'd won, but couldn't be sure. The judge paused his preparation for the next case.

"Miss Hernandez, do you have any questions?"

"Am I going home tonight to see my son? To hold my son tonight?"

"Yes, Miss Hernandez."

Jesse signaled that she should celebrate. It was over. She'd won.

Aida could barely move. She thanked the judge and the trial attorney. She stood for a moment, dazed. As Jesse and the bailiff walked her back to the holding cell, her mind raced to catch up with the abrupt end of a legal process that had taken almost a year, or maybe a lifetime. She'd been relegated to the margins and shadows of her world since she was eight and a half years old; for sixteen and a half years, she'd been fully a part of the United States and yet excluded from it. Now she would have a green card and a path to citizenship. It would take a long time for "legal permanent resident" to sink in.

The courtroom door clanked shut behind her. She couldn't grasp what Phelps's decision meant for her in the long run, but she knew one thing: she was going home to Gabriel. Emotion poured in all at once. She leaped into the air and whooped. She howled and cheered, a joyous eruption audible in the courtroom behind the metal door.

BACK IN THE POD, Aida distributed her brush, her earbuds, and other commissary items. She held her hard-won tampons and shampoo for a moment and then passed them out. Women crowded around her. Some, like Toma-sita, had become close friends over the past ten months. Others just wanted to stand close to success. As she left the courtroom, Jesse had handed her a pile of business cards. "You'll need these," the attorney had said, grin-ning. After handing out the cards, Aida improvised a speech.

"Ten months I was here. They said there was no way I could do it, but I didn't give up. Look at me. Don't give up." Then she said goodbye and walked through the blue door and into the evening light.

AIDA HAD SPENT 316 days in immigration detention. She had committed no crime worse than shoplifting, posed no threat to public safety, and, with her long ties to one hometown, was unlikely to have fled Douglas. Never-theless, U.S. taxpayers paid approximately $52,000 to keep her locked down in medium-security prison conditions. That year, Corrections Corporation of America, the company operating Eloy, logged almost $160 million in profits. And the money trail didn't end there. The private contractor that ran the commissary where Aida bought food, stamps needed to send pictures to Gabriel, earbuds for the television, a single mug for coffee with Tomasita, and phone cards to call home made a fortune off captive consumers. As did the telecom contractor that connected detainees' calls home. And before either of those companies could charge their inflated prices, Aida had to receive money transfers into her prison account at a dear cost via Western Union. If Aida's almost year in Eloy accomplished anything for the United States, it was to make a lot of money for corporate shareholders.

As the last chain-link gate clanked shut behind her, Aida knew that she had done something extraordinary. Not only had she won a place for herself in the country she still, improbably, loved with all her heart, but she had changed herself. Walking away on the heels of victory, she knew that despite the horrendous conditions, the desperate loneliness, and the daily humiliations, she had done more than just survive.

IT WAS DARK when Luz and Aida reached a cousin's house in Tucson. Aida walked into the empty living room, and dismay rolled over her. The high from her hearing and release had worn off in the car. Only the hope of see-ing Gabriel that night had propelled her forward through exhaustion. The thought of having to wait to see her boy until she made it to Douglas the next day bled the last bit of adrenaline from her body. She slumped onto a couch in a wreck of disappointment.

The lights flicked on. And the air filled with cheers and laughter. Sisters and cousins flooded out from their hiding spots. Gabriel ran ahead of them, his arms and eyes opened joyfully wide. It was all Aida had ever wanted. They hugged for what seemed like hours, and it could not be enough.

That night, Aida ate a dozen of her mother's ground-beef tacos, savoring food that wasn't prison carbs, *pan, pasta, y papas*. She paused only to stroke Gabriel's cheek and thick hair. He was eight years old. In her time away, he had grown a lot. He looked like a little man in his *quinceañera* vest and button-down shirt. Everyone at the party asked her what she would do now that she was a legal permanent resident of the United States.

It was a good question. But for as long as that night lasted, the answer didn't matter. For the moment, she would just hold her boy in her arms. Tomorrow she would set herself to the task of figuring out what came next.

29.

TO BATTERY PARK

ROSIE MENDOZA COULDN'T FIGURE who would be bringing her flowers for Valentine's Day. She didn't have time to stop working either, but she told the receptionist to let the person in anyway. On top of her regular client meetings at the clinic, Rosie now spoke at conferences on domestic violence and sexual assault around the country. On top of that, she stepped in to help with local child abuse campaigns, cancer runs, and community health fairs.

Some early mornings, she joined teams of health *promotores* taking the Chiricahua Community Health Centers' mobile clinic out to the rich agricultural district north of Douglas. The men and women who cared for the state's pecan, pistachio, apple, peach, cotton, grape, and chili crops worked such long hours that they couldn't take care of their own health. Many couldn't have made it into town for medical treatment, even if their work schedules permitted it: the short drive to Douglas meant passing a Border Patrol checkpoint where agents kept watch for people who looked like farmworkers. So the clinic went to them, bringing cholesterol, diabetes, and blood pressure screening into the fields. Rosie helped with the basic health workups, but her real reason for making the trip was to watch for a particular flat look on workers' faces. A look that spoke of abuse.

Aida popped through the office door carrying a pot of peace lilies. "This is for you, Rosie. This is for everything that you've done for me." When Rosie set the flowers on a table, Aida engulfed her in a hug. Rosie leaned backward and then gave in. She had never been a hugging person. When members of Frontera de Cristo or her church leaped at her for their whole-body embraces, Rosie usually threw out her arm for a handshake. But Rosie had to admit Aida had made her more of a hugger.

In recent months, Rosie had seen Aida almost weekly thanks to the young woman's new job. Aida tended bar at the Warehouse, Rosie's favorite place to relax. Rosie stopped in every Thursday to drink strong, fruity cocktails with friends. The place was a microcosm of Douglas: ranchers in starched shirts, vests, and Stetsons drank Crown and Coke alongside *cholos* drinking shots. The mayor could often be found there after work. At shift's end, Border Patrol agents sometimes joined the mix. On one set of vinyl stools, women with rough hands, white hair, and western shirts might talk grazing allotments, while their neighbors, businessmen from across the line in Agua Prieta, debated the relative merits of the Mexican writers Carlos Monsiváis and Octavio Paz.

Bartending suited Aida well, Rosie realized: Mixing drinks, serving rounds, stocking coolers, and wiping counters gave her a place to channel her hyperkinetic energy. Her open charm enchanted customers. Regulars soon learned to expect Aida's trademark greeting: she leaned over the bar on tiptoes offering a shout of joy and welcoming hug.

Though bartending was a good fit, it wasn't a cure. Rosie knew that Aida's all-consuming panic attacks had not completely disappeared since her return from Eloy.

"It's not like the flu, *mija*," Rosie reminded her. "PTSD doesn't go away after a week. You'll probably always have it, but you can learn not to let it rule your life."

By spring 2014, the results of a landmark Centers for Disease Control study on adverse childhood experiences (ACEs) were well-known in the domestic violence and sexual assault counseling community. The multiyear investigation quantified a disturbing truth long intuited by practitioners like Rosie: people who experienced ACEs—such as suffering physical or sexual abuse; witnessing domestic violence against a parent; losing a parent to death, divorce, or abandonment; or lacking basic necessities like food, clothing, and housing before age eighteen—were far more likely than people with stable, supportive upbringings to have serious problems as adults. Their odds of developing depression and a wide range of chronic illnesses and cancers soared astronomically higher than the general population's. They were also more likely to commit suicide, perform poorly in school, and suffer financial troubles as adults. The study helped launch trauma-informed counseling, school curricula, and police protocols, but its bleak findings could seem like a death sentence to people with high ACE scores. And Aida's life experiences gave her a nine out of ten.

"That doesn't mean you can't live a good life," Rosie assured Aida. "I also scored a nine, and look at me."

AIDA WAS, IN FACT, on her way to constructing a better life. She'd begun cleaning the Warehouse in the early mornings, her first job as a legal permanent resident of the United States.

"Don't you recognize me?" the bar owner had asked her on her first day.

Aida hesitated. He looked familiar.

"Mr. 06664?" he prompted her.

She almost jumped into the air when she remembered. "Eddie Alvarez, account number 06664. *Mr. 06664!*" He had been one of her favorite customers at Movies 'n' More. It seemed like lifetimes ago.

Eddie offered Aida a chance to move from cleaning to tending bar. Nervous, she dropped bottles, spilled drinks, and cringed when asked to mix a "Wet Pussy" or "Panty Dropper." Customers didn't seem to notice. Once she gained confidence making drinks on her own, even the other bartenders warmed to her.

Aida had never earned so much money in her life, and the constant movement eased her nerves. More important, though, working the night shift allowed her to spend large chunks of every day with Gabriel. The two of them walked everywhere together, or, more accurately, they skipped and danced down the street together. They made a strangely joyous sight in a town of pickup trucks, wide streets, and empty sidewalks. Even total strangers commented how happy they looked. At Christmastime, she took Gabriel to the downtown hayrides and the small outdoor ice rink the city installed during the winter holidays. Gabriel got chosen to play Frosty in his school pageant. He sang and danced onstage in a puffy white costume and Aida cheered. She tried to maintain her hard-rocking image with nose and lip piercings, but there was a new softness about her. Her favorite T-shirt was torn and black but emblazoned with a sparkly silver "Moms Rock." When she cooked Gabriel's favorite meal, hamburger and fries, she squirted love notes in ketchup on the plate.

In the year after Aida returned from Eloy, both Jennifer and Cynthia were deported. Both cases began with police calls during heated arguments with boyfriends. Neither of the sisters wanted to risk the high stakes of an illegal reentry, so they tried to make their lives in Agua Prieta. Cynthia resigned herself to this fate. With her high school diploma and knowledge of English, she worked her way up to supervisor at a maquiladora. She earned about two dollars an hour, but she hoped to save up enough to attend college in Mexico. Jennifer was not so resigned. She resisted adapting to her new home and still considered Agua Prieta a place of exile.

With her legal immigration status, Aida could visit her sisters, but both she and her son balked at the idea of crossing the border. Only once or twice did they work up the courage to enter Mexico. Aida still had Jazmin, though. They grew ever closer, and when Jazmin graduated from high school that spring, it was one of the proudest days in Aida's life. Sometimes Jazmin would join her sister and nephew, the three of them tangoing down the street to Gabriel's school, to the store, or to pick up *pan dulce* at La Unica.

Aida had come a long way since a quarrel outside that bakery almost destroyed her life. But something was missing.

WHEN AIDA LOGGED BACK IN to Facebook after leaving Eloy, she expected to find a friend request from Ema. The queue held several new requests, including one displaying Katy Manzanedo's beaming face. Dozens of unseen birthday messages, six-month-old Mother's Day greetings, and perplexed queries from acquaintances who wondered where she'd gone crowded her feed. But nothing from Ema. As word of her release spread around Douglas, "welcome home" messages poured in, but nothing from Ema.

It took weeks before Aida realized that Ema had disguised her account on Facebook. There had been a friend request waiting for Aida under a different name.

Ema's immigration case still hung in limbo, but she had found decent work in New York City as a night clerk in a company that wired remittances to Latin America. Aida and Ema sent Facebook messages back and forth and then began passing hours every day talking on the phone. On one side of the country, Aida reclined in a string hammock on her porch or walked and talked in the desert twilight. Ema carried her side of the conversation while walking home from work under the elevated tracks on Roosevelt Avenue in Queens. Neither woman wanted to hang up, and the calls often extended long after midnight.

Aida stopped telling herself that she wasn't bisexual.

That summer, Aida and Ema pooled their earnings to pay for a flight to New York. Aida had wanted to visit the city since her days on the playground in Agua Prieta, and she needed to know if she was really in love.

The arrival at JFK was cinematic: Aida and Ema ran toward each other through the crowd in baggage claim, falling into each other's arms at long last. What followed was less so: Aida started vomiting.

While Aida shook and sweat cold torrents back at Ema's shared apartment, Ema fretted and asked, "Am I doing something wrong?"

"No, *mi amor*," Aida said, clutching the toilet.

The next morning, Aida admitted herself to Elmhurst Hospital in Queens. Doctors spent days probing for the source of jagged pains slicing through the places where she'd been stabbed years ago. They could find nothing physically wrong. Test after test revealed scar tissue and haywire blood chemistry, but no clear cause for the pain. It was another expression of long-term trauma, something else that she'd have to accept and manage. In coming years, she'd learn to expect her body to collapse into a convulsing tangle of unexplainable symptoms every few months. Her body had become so conditioned to trauma that high-stress life events—job loss, the threat of eviction, or even reuniting with a lover—could catapult it into total crisis.

During the hospitalization, Ema hovered beside Aida, trying to make her comfortable. Ema pestered the nurses for boxes of apple juice, the one thing Aida could hold down. And when they left, hand in hand, a few days later, one thing was clear. They *were* a couple.

"PLEASE LET ME be the one to take you to see the ocean for the first time," Ema said once they'd begun to venture out for slow walks around Corona. Just after the Fourth of July, they took the subway to Coney Island, Aida in her new "I ❤ NY" T-shirt. The nervous collapse had left her too frail to swim, but she sprawled on the sand, in love, feeling the universe open up.

When Aida returned to Douglas, their long-distance relationship settled into a comfortable pattern. At opposite ends of the country, they watched the first season of *Orange Is the New Black* together. The show got every detail wrong, they thought, but they loved it. While dissecting each episode over the phone, they almost felt as if a continent hadn't come between them. At night they signed off over Facebook.

"*Me dejas sin palabras, mi amor.*" The high school dropout's messages were neat and grammatical.

"*Te aaaaammmooooo FLAKITA.*" The university-trained engineer's, not so much.

IN THE SPRING of 2014, Aida's panics and flashbacks intensified as they often did when the anniversaries of her deportation and attack crept closer. The seasonal storm flooded receptors in her brain and overwhelmed her defenses. Aida scrubbed the bar top harder and delivered drinks faster. She sloshed Bud Light on the parquet with a brittle smile. Constant movement kept her a step ahead of disaster, but she crashed in screaming, shaking, sobbing torrents after work. She pulled herself together and skipped cheerfully to school with Gabriel in the mornings. But even as she executed a funny walk to make him laugh, Aida counted down the minutes left until she would be alone and afraid. After days of this, her skin stopped twitching. She disengaged from everything except Gabriel, crawling inside her lonely carapace.

During this period, Aida sent Ema's calls to voice mail and deleted her panicked texts. After work, she arranged bottles of Indio beer in a neat line on the bar top and drank with angry precision. There was no way she could let Ema any closer to the inner edge of her terror. Afraid that even a glimpse of her panics and paranoia would drive Ema away, Aida did everything she could to drive Ema away.

Instead, Ema phoned from LaGuardia with a message: She'd collected her savings and borrowed money from a friend. She'd be in Tucson by nightfall.

DURING THE SURPRISE VISIT, Aida decided to come out to her family, formally.

She told them one by one, saving Jazmin for last. Her opinion mattered, and Aida worried that the devout Pentecostal would reject her when she learned the truth. Raúl's response had been hard enough.

"It's not correct," he had insisted. "Not natural. Unscientific." He vowed to wait for his daughter to come to her senses with the same sure patience he applied to the rest of life.

Luz also protested at first, but came around. The strangest thing about Ema, from Luz's perspective, was the fact that she hated spicy food. Ema could not even pretend to tolerate the spicy pozole Luz served during the visit. This was as incomprehensible to Luz as her daughter's sexuality. Finally, Aida approached Jazmin in the kitchen.

"I need to tell you something," she said.

"What," Jazmin sassed back, "you're a lesbian?"

Aida turned to stone. "How did you know?" she managed to sputter.

And then it was Jazmin's turn to freeze, suddenly grasping that her wisecrack had unintentionally hit the mark.

"Please don't hate me," Aida said, prepared to kneel down in front of her sister to beg.

"Of course not—you're my sister. I'll always love you."

And with that, Ema was family. Aida and Gabriel moved to New York City the next month.

Jazmin accompanied them. Of all the siblings, Jazmin seemed the least affected by trauma. Despite her undocumented status, she had completed high school without drama. For a few months, she had even adventured around the country taking odd jobs in Nevada, Pennsylvania, and Rhode Island with a friend—a poor person's working vacation. Perhaps she escaped the worst impacts of a Hernandez childhood because she was Saul's biological daughter, or maybe because she found community in her church.

At some level, though, she knew that she partly owed her life to Aida. When the house shuddered with blows, it was Aida who had shielded her, emotionally and physically. When Luz worked endless hours to support the family, it was Aida who'd brushed Jazmin's hair, made her lunch, and sent her off to school. For this reason, Jazmin—eighteen and sparrow small—agreed to serve as Aida's worldly escort to New York City.

The four of them, Aida, Ema, Gabriel, and Jazmin, rented a small room in an apartment shared with two Mexican men and a Dominican family. Ema found two used beds and a television. Aida decorated with posters of cartoon characters Gabriel adored and a lucky bamboo shoot she found in Flushing.

Ema felt at home in Queens: walking under the Roosevelt Avenue elevated tracks past Ecuadorian, Colombian, and Venezuelan restaurants was almost like returning to the Andes. Aida took longer to adjust. The subway map swarmed in front of her eyes. She despaired at venturing into the city without Ema. At red lights, New Yorkers seethed around her as she stood paralyzed, completely unable to jaywalk. But she learned. The first time she told off a harasser on the 7 train, she knew that she'd truly found her home. There was no big entirely white apartment in her future, or even money to feed an opinionated white cat—yet. But it didn't matter.

EVEN IN THE close quarters of their rented room, Aida and Ema tried to hide the nature of their relationship from Gabriel. Aida, Jazmin, and Gabriel crowded into one bed, while Ema slept in the other. Aida wondered when she should approach her son with the truth. He had turned nine in New York and would soon start third grade at a public school with a program designed for kids who had experienced early childhood trauma. Tests would soon confirm what Aida already knew: Gabriel was highly intelligent but had lost the ability to read.

He would make excellent progress in the trauma-informed curriculum and, in a few years, read at grade level. He held himself tall and sported a *mango chupado* haircut like all the professional soccer players. There was an economy to his movement and an openhearted patience in his slightly bucktoothed smile. During those first months in New York, he shrugged off disappointments like someone used to shrugging off disappointments. He kept anxious watch on his mother.

"I know, Mom," Gabriel said when Aida confessed. "Ema is your girl-friend. Everyone knows that."

ON JULY 28, 2014, Aida, Ema, Jazmin, and Gabriel made a long trip on the 7 and 4 trains to the Office of the City Clerk in lower Manhattan. The temperature was well over eighty, and they paused to buy water bottles outside the entrance. The Bangladeshi woman who sold them had dispensed water and soda for nervous throats on the same corner for ten years. She laughed when she tried to think how many couples she had seen tie the knot.

Aida and Ema had not planned to marry so soon, but Jazmin would return to Douglas in a week. Aida wanted at least one member of her family present at the ceremony.

Before they went inside, Jazmin, feeling sentimental, bought a bouquet of roses from a vendor on Worth Street. When the wedding party emerged from the court building, she ran ahead, plucking the petals and sprinkling fistfuls onto the steps. Her sister and new sister-in-law descended into a new life on a carpet of flowers.

After the wedding ceremony, they took cell phone photographs and then walked south, past the hard-hat men and police officers, past lawyers in slouchy suits and interns in white blouses. They skirted tourists with back-packs and cameras starting out over the Brooklyn Bridge. All the while, Aida and Ema hollered "Just married!" to anyone who could hear.

They crossed Broadway arm in arm. The space narrowed and the crowd thickened, flowing toward Ground Zero. They wandered through tour groups in matching T-shirts. The map guys, the helicopter-tour guys, the commemorative-picture-book guys pattered in Spanish and English at them. Aida and Ema weren't listening; they were staring up.

The site was unfinished, like all of New York. Like their new lives.

A bay breeze cooled them in Battery Park. They rested for a while under shade trees and then posed for more pictures in front of a sailing ship. This time, no guards stopped them when they touched. Then Aida and Ema leaned out over the water. Aida went suddenly quiet taking in the scene. When she looked up, the Statue of Liberty was silhouetted in the distance. The statue looked out over the world with an expression that did not smile, did not warn, did not beckon or divide. All were equal within her impassive, expansive gaze. For a brief moment, Aida was full of hope.

EPILOGUE:
THE LIFE OF AIDA HERNANDEZ

HOW TO WRITE THE END of the beginning? Don't. That is my first instinct. It would be easier to stop at the tip of Manhattan, full of hope. But this is not an American fairy tale. It is not a reassuring allegory where the good are rewarded and hard work always pays off. It might not end well. "Empowering narratives do not necessarily give us happy endings," the ethnic studies scholar Lisa Marie Cacho writes. "Nor do they always leave us inspired."

For people in Aida's position, "empowerment is not contingent on taking power or securing small victories. Empowerment comes from deciding that the outcome of struggle doesn't matter as much as the decision to struggle." That is the lesson at the end of the beginning. Here is the story.

.   .   .

"SORRY," AIDA SAID to the toothbrush, apologizing for disturbing it. Her hands flew across the counter, arranging each toiletry in a precise row. Their owner would feel cared for when he returned later. She bowed to empty the trash, and her hair fell out of its bun. She shoved it back, twisted, and stooped to wipe down the Euro-modern shower. Each time she moved, her oversized glasses tumbled off. She replaced them again and again. The glasses gave her the same bug-eyed look as the hipster women trickling into Long Island City, but not intentionally. They were just cheaper than a pair that fit.

Aida worked at breakneck pace. Two completed rooms yielded an hour's pay, no matter how long they took. If the occupant was neat, she advanced. If she opened the door on strewn laundry, mangled sheets, spilled food, or vomit, she knew that she'd fall irrecoverably behind. If a guest was present and declined housekeeping, she lost pay for that room. If occupancy was low that day, she got fewer rooms. And always, the subcontractor took a cut of everything she earned, except tips.

A night at the hotel cost almost a week of her pay, but guests rarely left more than five dollars. Once she stopped to talk with a businessman from Dubai for ten minutes, and he left her a twenty. She would have chatted with him anyway. She loved to learn about guests who flew in from around the world and left their things for her to straighten. Usually, though, she didn't have time for enjoyment.

Sweat glistened on Aida's forehead. No matter how she streaked through the rooms in a blur of wet rags and wild hair, she always finished last. The other women took shortcuts that she refused to imitate. Guests would not want to see what her coworkers did to cut corners. Aida also paused frequently to help newcomers learn the job. After a year at the hotel, she was the unofficial, unremunerated trainer. In return, women brought her plates of homemade *arepas*, cheesy corn pancakes from South America that Aida had come to love. Her coworkers gossiped about how much weight she'd lost, and tried to ply her with food. Aida was grateful for their offerings. Without Styrofoam plates and tinfoil packages passed to her by coworkers, she would subsist mostly on coffee and pastry. She saved grocery money for her preteen boy.

Aida was rail thin but rippled with muscle. Heaving those mattresses was like going to the gym eight hours a day. Strangers stopped her on the street to ask if she was a "lady boxer." "No, I'm a housekeeper," she bragged. She loved this job and had an "Employee of the Month" photograph hanging in the break room to prove it.

But Aida also knew that her churning pace was not efficient. Her psychologist had added a diagnosis of OCD on top of her dissociative PTSD. Hotel housekeeping was both a good and a bad job for someone with OCD. Sometimes she hoisted the thick mattress cover into the air twelve times before the crisp of her duvet fold satisfied her. If she kept moving at a break-neck pace, though, she could keep a step ahead of panic. Cleaning rooms alone left so much time for intrusive thoughts, and her life in New York provided ample fodder. She spent the first day at her job curled in a supply closet, shaking with fear and drowning in the smell of cleaning fluids.

The Dominican maintenance man who lifted her out of the closet spoke a kind of Spanish that she couldn't follow, but she understood his kindness. Her coworkers learned to love her but also to walk delicately around her. Their faces were caring and wary, wanting to help, but afraid something they'd say would send Aida spinning into convulsions.

AIDA RODE THE Q66 along Northern Boulevard, reading *The Four Agreements: A Practical Guide to Personal Freedom.* She hoped that terror might spare her that afternoon. Mostly Aida was able to sidestep full-blown attacks long enough to complete her rooms at the hotel, but often panic returned as soon as she boarded the bus for home. On her way back to Corona, Queens, she practiced observing the electric scratch dispassionately as it rose in her neck and hands. If she named the anxiety and accepted it, it might float by rather than claw in. Sometimes she succeeded.

She named the voice of her PTSD *chona*—slang for a gossipy old woman who loves to criticize. This took some of its power away, but the warning sirens in her brain still felt so real. On bad days, every fellow passenger, every lurch of the bus, became a potential threat. Her senses detected danger in every expression and gesture.

She'd been staring out the Q66 bus window for months and knew Northern Boulevard well. This great Queens thoroughfare was almost as wide as an ordinary street in big, empty Arizona. It just lacked the enormous sky and endless mountain views. Instead, the bus passed *iglesias*: Iglesia de Dios, Iglesia de Cristo, Iglesia de Gracia, Iglesia de Avivamiento. She thought often of returning to Arizona, especially as she contemplated storefront law offices advertising help with the seven plagues of poverty: Accidents, Immigration, Workers' Comp, Wages & Overtime, Divorce, Bankruptcy, and DUI.

During her first months in Queens, Aida lost all of her savings from the Warehouse to a job-placement con that preyed on immigrants. When an attorney filed a class action suit against the fake agency, Aida testified in court, reveling in her newfound voice. They won, but it would take ages to get her money back, and what she did receive just disappeared to pay overdue bills.

After the scam, it took several months for Aida to find a job that she could hold. She loved interacting with people behind the counter at a Grand Central Terminal coffee shop, but in those early months riding the subway to work unhinged her. Night-shift jobs nearby were easier to secure, but she needed to be home for Gabriel in the mornings before school. When she finally found the hotel housekeeping job, it paid only $150–$300 a week, depending on how steadily she was able to work.

So Ema's wages supported the family, and they were not enough. Life became a continual falling behind. The smallest unexpected expense—a new medicine for Aida, bigger shoes for Gabriel's growing feet—threw them further off balance. Ema used a mechanical pencil and ruler to chart the money she had borrowed from friends when they came up short on rent or installment payments on Aida's old hospital bills.

None of Ema and Aida's new friends believed that a person could survive as an island or must be forced to pull herself up by her bootstraps. The poorest among them lent money to one another in times of need. Even Aida parted with a hundred dollars from her tax return when a coworker fell short on rent. But Ema's debts had risen to a point where repayment became a fantasy.

ON A TYPICAL afternoon, Aida would collect Gabriel from a friend's house where he went after school. They'd walk past the vinyl-sided row houses and ornamental fences of residential Queens to their building. Ema would be at work already. They'd scale three flights of stairs to their apartment and retreat immediately into their eight-by-twelve-foot room. The young Mexican men and Dominican family took up the rest of the apartment. The young men worked long hours and kept to themselves, but the family played loud music and fought late into the night. Aida, Ema, and Gabriel mostly stayed in their room. They only ventured into the apartment's kitchen when the family was gone. But even in the cramped quarters, Ema and Aida rarely saw each other. When they did, it was on the edge of exhausted sleep.

Ema woke up long after Aida took Gabriel to school, and left for work before they came home. Aida had begun staying up until 2:00 or 3:00 every night so she and Ema could have some time together, but this meant she rarely got more than four or five hours of sleep a night herself. She tried to convince herself that she was young and strong and didn't need more sleep, but it was hard to will her way out of sleep deprivation. Over time, exhaustion unscrewed her mental state further.

When Ema and Aida did find time to talk, it was mostly about money and their inability to make more of it despite the long hours of work. The insecurity and relentless grind had torn the fascia of their new marriage beyond repair. They could not find a way to fix it.

When their days off overlapped, Ema slept late into the afternoon, while Aida sat on the bed, her mind spinning. These were long, almost catatonic vigils, during which Aida contemplated returning to Arizona. She had come close to leaving several times after fights with Ema.

Good news reached her from Arizona from time to time. Aida's U.S. citizen cousin Camila had almost achieved her dream. She wasn't an elementary school teacher yet, but she worked at a preschool and loved it. In 2015, Rosie received the Arizona Coalition to End Sexual and Domestic Violence's Guara Award for outstanding service. Alvaro was still drug-free. He'd moved to Tucson, married, gone back to school, and now worked as a licensed massage therapist. Fall 2015 marked the fiftieth anniversary of the GPG's attack on the Madera barracks. Events, books, and commemorative issues of magazines across Mexico celebrated Raúl's contribution to the country. And Jazmin had a beautiful newborn boy that Aida longed to hold.

The news from Arizona was not all good. Some of it reminded her of why she'd left. Blanca, Aida's cellmate at Eloy, had risked many years in federal prison to reunite with her husband and child in Phoenix. She lived deep underground and in constant fear. Katy lived in Tucson under an assumed name, always wondering whether an unknown killer, or killers, still searched for her and her siblings. Meanwhile, Cynthia and Jennifer struggled with exile in Agua Prieta.

On good days, Aida's sisters resigned themselves to not returning home. They talked about opening a beauty salon in Agua Prieta together. Mostly they laughed about the idea of styling *las buchonas*, the glitzy new-rich girlfriends of *narcos*. Neither of the sisters knew how to cut hair, but they could learn. On bad days, Cynthia longed to be able to continue her studies in Arizona and maybe earn an associate's degree at Cochise College. Jennifer just ached to see her U.S. citizen children whenever she wanted. And Aida's mother? Luz continued to work endless hours, take care of grandchildren, and hold together a household. Rosie Mendoza and Jesse Evans-Schroeder encouraged her to apply for legal permanent residency again, this time through VAWA. Luz had a strong case, but she lacked time and money for the long application process. And more than that, decades of accumulated fear and trauma had left her too frayed to try.

The number of undocumented migrants crossing the border through Douglas continued to fall. Spending on border security did not. Since Silvestre Reyes debuted the new border security paradigm in 1993, the number of Border Patrol agents posted on the southwest border had ballooned fivefold, from 3,444 to 17,026. The terrain covered by substantial border barriers stretched from effectively around a dozen miles to nearly seven hundred. The Border Patrol budget had increased almost tenfold. In 2012, funding for Customs and Border Protection and Immigration and Customs Enforcement surpassed the budgets of the FBI, DEA, Secret Service, ATF, and U.S. Marshals Service combined, with enough left over to run all of the country's national parks for a year. By 2016, that figure had grown to just under twenty billion dollars a year, and that did not include the cost of strains on the federal court system or National Guard troops stationed at the border.

Aida did not want to reenter that world. She would find a way to survive in New York, just as she always found a way to survive. She was stubborn and smart, and she saw that New York was good for Gabriel.

When Gabriel enrolled in his new school at age ten, he had no reading level. Two years later, he read at a fourth-grade level. Teachers in his special-ed classroom cared in a way that Aida didn't remember from Douglas. They enjoyed resources Douglas lacked and had been trained in classroom techniques sensitive to the needs of traumatized students. In January 2016,

Aida and Gabriel worked together on a science fair project. Their experiment demonstrating "the power of fruit" took first place.

Whatever her faults, Aida loved Gabriel madly. The two of them were inseparable opposites. She was frenetic and anxious, her curly hair and leopard eyes twitching—a featherweight boxer body in perpetual motion. Gabriel took in the world from a place of stillness, smiling his chubby-cheeked smile, arms quiet at his side. At age eleven, he exuded a confidence underlaid with worry—the attitude of a boy who, from a young age, has had to take care of his mother as much as she has cared for him.

"We were not born in New York," they'd tell each other, "but we *are* New Yorkers."

ONE NIGHT, Aida's nightmares came on stronger than usual. Tangled in the sheets, she punched and kicked with the same desperate fury that had saved her life in the railroad yard almost a decade earlier. She half awoke, soaked with sweat in a freezing November. Ema crumpled to the floor, having taken all the blows, blood streaming down her face. Aida knelt up in bed and saw what she'd done. She gave a stuttering moan. Her wild black curls stuck to her face and caught in her piercings.

Ema's voice seeped through the panic: "*Soy yo.* Aida, it's me. *Soy yo.*"

In return, Aida howled, "*Lo siento. Lo siento.* I'm sorry. *Mi amor.* Not again. Please. Not again."

Then, still not entirely awake, Aida picked up a phone and called the police on herself.

Rosie always told Aida that legal permanent residency was permanent probation. "Everyone else makes mistakes, but immigrants can never make mistakes," Rosie said, and she was right. If not for a sympathetic prosecutor who listened to Ema and Aida's pleas and reduced the charges from domestic violence to disorderly conduct, Aida might have been deported. As it was, the nonprofit counseling center that treated her PTSD dropped her as a patient. They told her that the agency's grants did not allow them to work with perpetrators.

Ema lived in limbo, not in immediate danger of deportation, but not safe from it either. She might have qualified for a work permit, but her TV-advertising attorney failed to file for it. So Ema worried constantly about losing her job. And as her own anxiety grew, her response to Aida's attacks deteriorated. Before, she had hummed steady reassurance when Aida shouted and writhed on the floor. But now she shook Aida, angry and desperate to make the attacks stop. They were wretched together. At night they no longer spoke. Instead, Ema stayed up playing *Plants vs. Zombies* on her phone until dawn, spitting anger at the screen.

In the summer of 2016, Aida and Gabriel took refuge with the family of the Dominican man who'd helped when she collapsed on her first day at the hotel. For a time, her old dreams poked through the thick carpet of despair. She researched GED programs and once again imagined becoming a therapist to help women with PTSD. But she couldn't afford her share of the new rent, and financial stress amplified her attacks. When she ran out of money to pay for medications, the attacks got worse. The Dominican family asked her to leave.

Aida learned to navigate New York's social service system, but it had little to offer. She felt that she faced a choice between taking Gabriel to a homeless shelter or returning to Ema. So she returned to Ema. The Ecuadorian insisted that they could begin again. Aida was not so sure; she had been shaken too many times. But they made an effort: Ema joined an indoor soccer team that played in a gym in Flushing, they started wearing makeup again, and for a fluttering moment Aida recalled the joy of watching her Ema dance on the field.

It didn't last, though, and by the spring of 2017 it was over.

The police came again, and this time they took Ema away. Poverty, instability, and untreated depression all contributed to the dissolution of Ema's composure. Her fortitude crumbled, and she spiraled into abuse. She began to drink heavily and steal her wife's medications. When Aida went numb and blank or convulsed in panic on the floor, Ema kicked and shook her. "*Snap out of it! Stop!*" When the police took Ema away after the couple's last night together, bruises covered Aida's arms and face.

ON HER OWN, Aida redoubled the pace of her work. Most weeks, she could earn $300, which was enough to cover rent and food, unless an unexpected expense appeared. She needed to find a place to live that cost less than her $750-a-month room, but moving required saving enough to pay the first and last months' rent. Aida tried to minimize expenses even further. Once again, she went weeks surviving on coffee and sweet bread. One weekend, she set up a blanket on the sidewalk and sold her possessions: shoes that Gabriel had outgrown, used paperback copies of *Playful Parenting* and *Boy Erased*, T-shirts, tights, and an old handbag. Everything she could spare, except Gabriel's Legos. This helped, but every time she got close to having the money, something intruded: The final bill from a hospital visit she'd made a year earlier wiped out one month's rent, and she began saving again. A school uniform, supplies, and an unexpected class field trip destroyed another start at savings. She might have qualified for Social Security Disability Insurance coverage, but she was determined to make it on her own.

On the brighter side, Aida's most severe attacks receded a bit after Ema left, and she allowed herself to think about going back to school once she found a cheaper room. When panic eased its grip, she would remember how smart she was. Navigating social service agencies, she became *la abogada* again. With help, she started the paperwork to petition David for child support, something she'd never received in the past. But then panic would return. The plans would fall apart.

One day, the electricity went out in her apartment. Aida's first thought was that a man was coming to kill her under the cover of darkness. She fought back that image and left the apartment to investigate the outage. She came to believe that the landlord was trying to drive her out so he could remodel the apartment and charge more rent. He'd threatened to do that before. Then she discovered a cache of unpaid utility bills Ema had secreted away for months. Her apartment mates argued that the electricity was Aida's responsibility now and refused to help pay. They disappeared, finding places to stay with friends. Aida and Gabriel were all alone, and the bills totaled hundreds of dollars.

Aida and Gabriel spent four nights in candlelight. She tried to make it into a fun adventure, but she could tell that the darkness unsettled him. This was clearly not a normal way to live, no matter how much they enjoyed playing *Lotería* together in the warm glow of votive candles.

As Gabriel's own panic attacks intensified, Aida spent hours on the phone with Con Edison and legal aid. In a moment of desperation, she applied for a second job at a strip club. Memories of La Roca and Pachanga's reared up, but she drove them away, took a deep breath, and went in for an interview. The club called her back, but she couldn't bear to accept the job. The homeless shelter now loomed more likely than ever.

At home, Gabriel was anxious in the dark. Aida persevered on the phone with the power company. Finally, they reached agreement on an almost-feasible payment plan. The first installment wiped out all progress toward saving for a cheaper apartment, but the look on Gabriel's face when the power came on was worth it.

They were sitting at the kitchen table playing Mexican bingo by candlelight again when it happened. As a joke—to raise Gabriel's spirits—Aida had put on an old football helmet they'd found on the street. Gabriel was close to winning; Aida's card had barely begun to fill. The lights blinked on.

"Mom!" Gabriel triumphed. "You did it!"

She sat frozen still for a moment waiting for the lights to flicker off again. They didn't. Aida laughed in agreement. "Yes, I did."

ABOUT THIS BOOK

"There is a woman—a client who became a friend," Rosie Mendoza said over breakfast at the Gadsden Hotel in January 2014. It was a year and two months after Aida's release from Eloy and six months before her move to New York. "I can't tell you anything about her," Rosie said, "but I will tell *her* about you."

Gold-leafed columns and a grand marble staircase in the Gadsden lobby evoked a more prosperous era. A Tiffany window turned the lobby leafy green. Rosie fancied the Gadsden's coffee and pancakes. The hotel was also a block from her office at the Chiricahua Community Health Centers.

"If she wants to call you, she will. If she does call," Rosie told me, "you should talk with her."

I went to Douglas that winter hoping to understand how people lived their lives amid America's ever-hardening social, political, and economic borders. I was an academic looking to write a book, but also a person committed to immigrant rights work in my own rural eastern Washington community. The distant border spoke to me as a place where challenges faced in communities across the country could be seen in stark relief: economic restructuring, changing demographics, anti-immigrant fervor, and militarized policing of communities of color. It also exerted a personal force on me. Twenty years earlier, during a formative time, I had worked for four years as an educator and activist in communities on both sides of the Arizona-Sonora border, including Douglas and Agua Prieta. In the decades that followed, I found ways to return often to the powerful, stark landscape of divisions and connections.

That winter, Rosie became one of my primary guides to Douglas, but her friend did not call. For weeks, I immersed myself in listening to people talk about how they navigated the economic abandonment and intensified policing that defined the area's recent history. I interviewed teachers, community organizers, journalists, the mayor, two former mayors, assorted city officials, and several unofficial town historians. I sat with former smelter workers and their children, church pastors, a former police chief, and people I met hanging out at cafés. One day, I talked with an Iraq War veteran visiting the Douglas Historical Society. He told me that when he returned to Douglas after his tours of duty, he found that what the border had become in his absence triggered flashbacks to the Green Zone.

I came and went between Douglas and my home in Washington State. Rosie's friend still did not call. On the border, I spoke with immigrant rights attorneys, community college students, a regional economist, and the unemployed guys hanging out in the Tenth Street Park. I attended community meetings on both sides of the line and visited with Wendy Glenn, an incisive rancher raising cattle in one of the area's heaviest smuggling corridors. Some mornings, I walked along the border with Jack and Linda Knox. They were Mennonites who retired to Douglas to work for peace. Before beginning their full days volunteering with organizations that sought to heal divides between Douglas and Agua Prieta, they paused to pray at the base of the modern double wall and its medieval moat.

One night in March, I met the mayor for drinks at the Warehouse bar.

The owner of the radio station where Rosie worked many years earlier joined us. Another businessman appeared later. I'd seen ads for his family-owned furniture showroom: it was going out of business, another casualty of big-box stores and economic decline. Somewhere along the way, a Mexican poet, an architect from Agua Prieta who was married to a Douglas judge, and a quiet cowboy drinking Jack and Seven popped into the conversation. No matter how divided Douglas sometimes felt, from November through March the Warehouse brought people together under the red-and-blue banner of University of Arizona basketball. That night, the Wildcats squeaked out a crucial tournament win, and the celebration went loud and late.

I didn't know it, but Rosie's friend was tending bar at the Warehouse. In a town as small as Douglas, she guessed who I was, and she watched me closely as I mingled with the crowd. The next day she called.

AIDA HERNANDEZ AND I met at the Tenth Street Park. As Aida walked toward me across wintry brown grass, her gait articulated contradictory planes. She moved with the confident limber of a street dancer and the inward folding of a hurt bird. I was completely unprepared for what I was about to hear.

Aida and I exchanged awkward greetings and sat on a bench near a fountain spraying clumsily on a cold spring afternoon. The park looked as it always did. I noticed customers queuing at Lico's Sonoran hot-dog truck. Teenage laughter from the park's concrete plaza and mothers' voices calling after toddlers faded into the background. Aida and I talked at length about my time in Douglas. We laughed about her undying love for David Bowie's cult film *Labyrinth*. Then she began to tell her story. Not all of it that first time, but a lot of it.

Before that afternoon, I had not considered writing about trauma and violence against women. Aida's account made it instantly clear that the large forces at work in Douglas couldn't be understood apart from those subjects. I also realized something about the nature of immigration debates roiling the United States.

By framing support for undocumented immigrants in the language of virtue and achievement—"hardworking," "family values," "not criminals," and "success stories"—I, and some parts of the immigrant rights movement, had tacitly condemned people like Aida who could not fit their lives into our narrow windows of approval. Emphasis on "model immigrants" and the "deserving poor" can help win important improvements for select groups, but it falls short for the vast majority of people—people with tougher, more complicated stories.

For them, winning rights—or even basic recognition as humans—requires distancing themselves from the slightest taint of criminality, mistakes, and unworthiness. In many cases, this requisite disavowal is a trap, impossible to achieve for people caught between economic abandonment, racial discrimination, and intensified police scrutiny. If successful, it often means getting cast in the role of supplicant victim, worthy of pity but lacking agency.

When Aida told me her story that day in Douglas, she refused the trap of disavowing her life. Her words did not solicit my pity. They conveyed immeasurable suffering, yes, but also brimmed with wit, humor, and a certain brio that comes from navigating adversity by the seat of one's pants. They demanded a greater reckoning with my—and all of our—complicity in creating laws and policies that made her life almost unlivable. And they also blazed with evident pride. What Aida shared that day asserted the act of sheer survival in a world like hers as a form of dignity and worth, as hard-earned and valuable as any affluent person's achievements.

I SPENT WHAT felt like much of the next year trying to talk myself and Aida out of working on a book together. The many borders of race, gender, class, education, and age dividing us felt insurmountable and strewn with ethical dangers. The risk that the project would retraumatize Aida was real. At the same time, we knew that remembering and recounting trauma can aid healing. Each time I mentioned the dangers of telling her story in public, Aida took a moment to think and then restated her commitment to the project. Her words took different forms at different times, but they had a common theme: I have already lived through death. Maybe working on this book can help turn all that badness into something good, something that can help other people. At the very least, the book could bear faithful witness to a kind of story that most people in the United States don't hear.

Once we decided to proceed, the difficult work began. Aida's memories formed the heart of this book. They emerged over some forty-five hours of formal interviews; thousands of texts, Facebook messages, and voice mails;

and time spent just hanging out together. After she moved to New York in the summer of 2014, I visited as often as I could. We walked through Queens, shared meals, rode the F train, and picked Gabriel up from school. I hovered awkwardly, chatting with her coworkers, while she cleaned hotel rooms. Eventually, we formed an unlikely friendship.

The first shift in our relationship came when I shared my own history of debilitating anxiety. It poured out unexpectedly after what would prove to be the first of many of Aida's crises I witnessed. After that, there was no room for cold academic remove in our alliance, if there ever had been. Aida looked out for me, expressing concern and sympathy when needed. I did small things to help her navigate social services, health-care bureaucracy, and the law. When I learned that she'd been surviving on coffee and sweet bread in order to feed Gabriel after paying an unexpected medical bill, I bought groceries. Once, after hearing that Aida, on the edge of homelessness, had applied for the job at a strip club, I gave her money to pay a month's rent. Mostly I listened and encouraged while she struggled to afford New York, hold down jobs, keep the lights on, raise Gabriel, figure out her relationship with Ema, and grapple with panic—nearly all on her own.

When frightened texts arrived at all hours—"Something is wrong"; "I'm in danger"; "Help me"—I tried to respond in the ways she said helped. During tough moments in my life, Aida responded in kind with her own encouraging messages.

Every time we met in person, I repeated some form of the three caveats that I offered Aida when we first decided to proceed.

First, she could end the project if she, or her therapists, felt that participation was unhealthy. On two occasions that I know of, Aida talked to her therapists about the project. She reported that those conversations bolstered her belief that the book would help her heal and find meaning in her experiences.

Second, she could read and comment on drafts of the book. If there were things she regretted telling me, or parts of the story she felt could not appear in print, I would consider taking them out. She did read drafts and offered invaluable feedback. In the end, there weren't pieces that she wanted removed, although we agreed to use pseudonyms for many people who appear in the book.

Finally, I said that I would do my best to portray her as a real person, not a saint or a demon. If we proceeded, it was important to tell a complex human story independent of the larger political and economic issues swirling around it. Aida's story would matter on its own, not just as a representative type of "immigrant experience."

Aida's account of her life evolved considerably as trust grew between us over four years. By 2018, the somewhat idealized tale she spun at the Tenth Street Park had evolved into the frank, nuanced, sometimes horrifying narratives that made this book possible. Two years into the project, after completing the bulk of our collaboration, I broached the question of money with Aida. After considering several options, we agreed to divide book proceeds evenly among Aida, the Chiricahua Community Health Centers to support services for people dealing with domestic violence or sexual assault, and myself to offset the costs of writing the book.

MEMORY IS A capricious beast, particularly for people suffering from PTSD. For this reason, I put as much time into cross-checking and verifying Aida's recollections as I did talking with her directly. Aida gave me access to hundreds of pages of medical, immigration, police, family, court, and school records, as well as three CDs of court recordings from Eloy. These primary sources proved invaluable for confirming facts, clarifying blurry sections in Aida's recollections, and reconstructing chronologies. In general, I discovered that Aida commanded an excellent recall of the tone and texture of distant events, but a poor grasp on time and duration. Later, I read that confusion about timelines is common in people with PTSD.

Dozens of interviews with family members, friends, coworkers, fellow Eloy detainees, and other people whose lives intersected with Aida's filled in blank spots, corrected some details, and corroborated her accounts. Aida's parents and siblings were extraordinarily generous with their time and emotions. I reached out to Saul and David, hoping that they would share their sides of the story. David declined to participate, and Saul did not reply to messages that I left for him.

Abundant material published by journalists and historians facilitated the chapters about Aida's father, as did his two memoirs, *El asalto al cuartel de Ciudad Madera* and *Del cuartel a Lecumberri*. The remarkable Arturo Ripstein documentary *El palacio negro* illuminated life in the political prisoner wing of Lecumberri prison. Most important, Raúl spent many hours talking with me about his youth.

Rosie's story is drawn entirely from her memories. As with the stories of people who make brief appearances in the book, it should be read as a kind of oral history. News coverage of controversies surrounding lesbian soccer in Ecuador, along with interviews of people affiliated with the team, fleshed out aspects of Ema's story. Research and reporting on migration through Central America and Mexico and my own experience in Chiapas and Altar filled in other aspects. Nevertheless, the account of Ema's life and her flight from Quito to Eloy should also be read as her memories and self-representation (interpreted by me). My account of Ema's life is grounded in many hours of interviews, but Ema and Aida's unpleasant separation disrupted the process of cross-checking details of her story.

When various accounts of Aida's past conflicted with one another, I tried to untangle the contradictions. When I couldn't, I either left those parts out of the story or went with Aida's memories of her own life. Sorting out details required constant collaboration. Often Aida and I messaged back and forth while I wrote, conferring on pieces of the story. We scoured Google Street Views of Douglas, talked about family photographs, and, one time, looked at *chola* makeup tutorials together to get details right.

Some dialogue in the book was recorded by me, transcribed in Border Patrol reports, or captured directly in Aida's immigration file. Mostly I reconstructed dialogue from participants' (sometimes contradictory) recollections.

I made a rule to avoid attributing thoughts or internal dialogue to people unless they specifically told me what they had thought about in that particular moment. I also avoided creating composite scenes, although, when one compresses whole lifetimes into discrete memories, details inevitably blur—particularly when reaching back to childhood. Fleshing out scenes from Aida's life required authorial imagination, of course, but I grounded this process firmly in interview material, primary documents, secondary sources, and my own observations.

For example, Aida, Raúl, her mother, and her sisters all shared strong but incomplete memories of the family's breakup and taxi ride from Agua Prieta to Douglas on March 8, 1996. These memories included rich descriptions of dialogue and people's actions, but I filled in details. To do this, I retraced the route the taxi would have taken and recalled my own trips to Agua Prieta in the mid-1990s. I checked documents to confirm dates and read historical weather reports. I also considered how, in that moment, the girls would have voiced the intense feelings they recalled many years later. Finally, Aida read drafts of the chapter to offer corrections and suggestions.

THIS BOOK FALLS somewhere between journalistic nonfiction and ethnography, two traditions with directly opposed views on the use of subjects' real names. While journalism insists on subjects' true names under most circumstances, the social sciences and ethnography default to pseudonyms and identity protection. Because of the continued vulnerability of the book's central characters, as well as the many sensitive topics addressed in the book, I opted for the latter approach, using pseudonyms for the immediate circle of Aida's family and friends. Aida, Alex, Alvaro, Cynthia, David, Ema, Emiliano, Fulgencio, Gabriel, Irma, Jazmin, Jennifer, Katy, Luisa, Luz, and Saul's names are pseudonyms. The names of the eight detainees at Aida's first hearing are also pseudonyms. All other names are real.

With the exceptions of Fulgencio (who passed away in 2012), David and Saul (discussed above), Luisa, Alex, Irma, and the eight detainees from Aida's first hearing, I interviewed all pseudonymous characters, often multiple times. While Aida is the book's main source, I corroborated her narrative through cross-checking interviews and official documents as well as I could, particularly when it touched on the stories of people I was not able to interview.

In addition to people directly connected to Aida's life, I interviewed immigration attorneys, physicians, and other professionals who helped me verify the plausibility of different aspects of Aida's story. These perspectives proved particularly important because Aida, as any of us would, often struggled to understand the many proceedings to which she was subjected. About one hundred interviews with Douglas community leaders, public officials, law enforcement officers, journalists, teachers, ranchers, religious leaders, community organizers, amateur historians, and ordinary citizens also provided crucial background and local details. These interviews lasted from thirty minutes to nine hours each and contained enough unused material to write a second book. One of my greatest regrets is that because of the nature of Aida's story, I did not have as many chances as I would have liked to highlight all the incredible work those people have done to lift up Douglas and Agua Prieta and heal divides severing DouglaPrieta.

Along with Aida, several people who appear in the book read and commented on drafts. This list includes Raúl, Rosie, Cynthia, Jazmin, Alvaro, Luz, Xavier Zaragoza, Jesse Evans-Schroeder, Mark Adams, Charles Vernon, and Ginny Jordan. They offered many valuable observations and perspectives, for which I am grateful.

Toward the end of the writing process, I hired a professional fact-checker to review the manuscript. She scrutinized details and empirical claims in the book derived from primary and secondary documents, photographs, field notes, and supporting interviews.

Finally, to get a better sensory understanding of the memories conveyed to me in interviews, I visited nearly every important location described in the book, from the railroad yard in Agua Prieta, to the Guatemala-Mexico border region, to the CCA detention center in Eloy. In the spirit of full disclosure, my visits to the Lecumberri prison in Mexico City; Huehuetenango, Guatemala; Quito, Ecuador; Altar, Sonora; and the mountains of Chihuahua took place before this project came into existence. I also spent time in Douglas and Agua Prieta during the years of Aida's childhood and adolescence, long before we knew each other. Those real-time memories of the story's settings proved invaluable.

In sum, I strove to ground even the book's smallest details in rigorous research. Still, as the cultural critic Walter Benjamin wrote long ago, storytelling "does not aim to convey the pure essence of a thing, like information or a report. It sinks the thing into the life of the storyteller, in order to bring it out of him [or her] again. Thus traces of the storyteller cling to the story the way the handprints of the potter cling to the clay vessel."

THIS PROJECT OCCUPIES a space between journalism and ethnography, with a dash of oral history and biography. One thing it is not is first-person testimony. Instead, the book emerged out of a long process of intensive collaboration. Differences, two-way learning, and expressions of mutual respect animated that work. In the end, though, I was the author. This meant confronting the way my very different social position and personal experiences shaped the story and my relationship with Aida. A caution voiced by the anthropologist Philippe Bourgois (paraphrasing Laura Nader) hung over me—literally. I had printed it out and posted it above my desk at the start of the project: "Don't study the poor or powerless because everything you say will be used against them." Even well-meaning scholarship on poor people in America has sometimes helped reinforce the objectifying assumptions through which comfortable people blame struggling people for their own suffering. That sad observation applies acutely to accounts of women, people of color, and survivors of sexual violence. Throughout the life of this project, I listened to and tried to learn from scholars and activists who are women and people of color as one way to check that danger.

Equally important, I strove to ensure that—surface appearances aside—*The Death and Life of Aida Hernandez* wasn't only a book about Aida Hernandez. Nor is Aida's story intended to represent or symbolize a general type of immigrant experience. Her life does not—cannot—stand for millions of other lives, as varied, as rich, as hopeful, and as traumatic as hers. No one's life could bear the objectifying weight of that. Instead, I hoped this book would stand as a critical account of the world the rest of us have made for Aida Hernandez, as well as a tribute to the tenacity with which she and others around her navigate and remake that world.

For U.S. readers—particularly those who observe border and immigration debates from a comfortable remove—this book should be a look in the mirror as much as it is a portrait of Aida. After all, the forms of institutional violence against immigrants and border communities described here are carried out *in our name*—purportedly to keep us "secure."

In this sense, *The Death and Life of Aida Hernandez* is not really about Aida Hernandez. It is a story told in collaboration with Aida about the brutal consequences of policies she was, in Audre Lorde's poetic language, "never meant to survive." Her hard-won expert knowledge of systems and policies that few Americans understand, and her willingness to share that knowledge, made this book possible.

THE STORY OF Aida's life is individual and specific, not representative, but it still tells us things about the world we've created. What does it suggest?

First, contrary to popular perceptions, current border and immigration policies are not broken. They are working just fine for many people, and *that* is the problem. Enforcement-only policies designed to deter undocumented immigration have only minimally affected the number of unauthorized crossings. Instead, they have funneled migrants from place to place along the border. They have pushed the business of migration into the hands of dangerous cartels. In the absence of efforts to address the root causes of migration, they have increased the vulnerability and exploitability of immigrants. And they have fueled a vast, lucrative, and often corrupt immigration industrial complex. All this has cost thousands of lives and hundreds of billions of taxpayer dollars.

On the surface, it sounds like a fantastic failure. And yet we should think twice before following politicians and the media in declaring the border and immigration system "broken." Many people, corporations, and agencies benefit directly from the current arrangement: polarizing politicians, nativist social movements, private prison companies, ordinary people in search of decent jobs, local governments struggling to increase revenue, employers seeking exploitable undocumented workers, massive federal law enforcement bureaucracies, and countless private security contractors. All these actors have a stake in maintaining perpetual crisis on the border.

Women have paid a disproportionate price for this "successful failure"— sometimes with their lives, often with their bodies, and certainly with their futures. Shocking levels of rape, abuse, and intimidation perpetrated against undocumented immigrants and border residents are not accidental side effects of border enforcement. Nor are they only the result of a supposedly macho culture. Rather, they are integral to the operation of immigration policy. As currently conceived, border "security" makes many women's lives less secure. It's not just that corruption, abuse, and "bad apples" permeate the United States' official immigration enforcement agencies. The current enforcement-only, deterrence-based paradigm was *designed* to push migrants into dangerous spaces and the hands of criminal organizations. This, in turn, has created ripe conditions for violence to proliferate in more general ways. We "outsource" some of the worst violence of deterrence, this exacts terrible costs, and then we pretend that it has nothing to do with our actions.

Not all violence against women on either side of the border can be attributed to economics, immigration policy, or the militarized forms of masculinity that accompany those policies, of course. Violence against women arises from many different socioeconomic contexts and for many different reasons. Placing violence against women in relation to socioeconomic policy, as this book has, does not flatten its complexity or exonerate individual abusers of their responsibility. What it does do is focus our attention on the fact that gender violence on the border is not an aberration or an accident. Much of it is the result of policies that people have chosen.

Second, much has been written about deindustrialization, de-unionization, and the decline of the white working class since the 1980s. The deindustrialization of communities of color has received far less attention. As a country, we do not generally see brown skin when we picture the struggling industrial working class. For this reason, it is possible to look at a place like Douglas and believe that it has always been the way it appears today: full of vacant lots, desperate for new opportunities, dependent on government services, and bristling with law enforcement. It has not.

To be blunt: White working-class decline elicits sympathy. Black and brown working-class decline yields "tough on crime" policies targeting communities of color for intensified surveillance, prosecution, and incarceration. As much as Aida's was a southwest border story, her fate was also bound up in a larger American story of race, economics, and policing. In that context, the kinds of small mistakes, poor choices, and miscalculations central to any coming-of-age story carried outsize consequences for Aida.

Finally, Aida's trials and triumphs should make us skeptical about the way that many immigrant stories, pro and con, stick to black-and-white binaries: the rule breaker and the hard worker, the criminal alien and the model immigrant. In our political moment, the "good" immigrant, worthy of sympathy and rights, does not exist without its foil: the alien who has made mistakes and therefore deserves the punishment she gets. But Aida's life—and the lives of most immigrants—are messier than those binaries allow.

Our increasingly punitive immigration system makes this worthiness contest worse by labeling an ever-growing list of minor offenses committed by immigrants as dangerous-sounding "aggravated felonies." In lockstep with this trend, Congress has steadily reduced room for forgiveness, second chances, and taking life circumstances into account in immigration proceedings. Immigrants are less likely to commit crimes than their citizen counterparts. But they are more likely to be judged fundamentally undeserving when they do make mistakes. As Rosie Mendoza has often said, "Humans make mistakes. Immigrants cannot."

WHILE NATION-STATES EXIST in their current form, they will almost certainly have borders and make decisions about membership. They will define who belongs to the nation and who doesn't. These arrangements will inevitably include some people and exclude others. This does not mean that the paradigm of borders and belonging described in these pages is natural, inevitable, or worthy of the United States. As I wrote most of this book, Donald Trump, in his campaign and then first eighteen months of office, began to champion a vision of American belonging skewed far toward the extremes of exclusion and fear. Advised by radical nativist leaders, he has demonized undocumented and legal immigrants alike, painting vast swaths of ordinary people as depraved criminals.

These efforts have not gone unopposed. A powerful upwelling of voices—led in great part by immigrant youth—has arisen. This movement claims space for a braver, more generous vision of membership and belonging. This movement speaks a powerful truth about the meaning of citizenship: People like Aida and those around her—people who have led messy, human lives, struggling against difficult odds—have forged legitimate places for themselves in their communities and country. They should be given a chance to establish this belonging under the law, and not just by defining themselves as supplicant victims. They are active makers of their communities and nation.

At the same time, voices from the border have emerged to challenge the idea that "securing the border" requires militarizing communities along the international divide. They point to rich histories of culture, commerce, and coexistence that thrive despite, not because of, walls.

Meanwhile, the Trump administration has doubled down on the enforcement-only paradigm. It has done this despite—or perhaps because of—that approach's record of failure and crisis generation. Little in Trump's first eighteen months of immigration and border policy is new. Border walls, shortcutting of due process in immigration enforcement, the creeping criminalization of civil immigration law, and mandatory mass detention of immigrants who pose no threat to their communities all have roots in earlier administrations. The same is true for the president's efforts to expand "due process lite" expedited-removal proceedings, limit the legal right to seek asylum, and deploy brutal family separation practices in the name of deterrence. The current administration has simply taken these policies to crueler extremes.

In the minds of many proponents, policies like these are not anti-immigrant or betrayals of the country's rich immigration history. They simply reflect an overriding respect for the rule of law. The statement "But they're *criminals*!" accompanies and seeks to justify the massive economic, social, and moral costs of war against "illegals."

This argument presents current policies as disinterested law enforcement, rather than racially motivated nativism. It is a facade that ignores the extensive histories of racial bias and discrimination that produced U.S. immigration laws in the first place. Trump and his immigration team have made it all too clear that attacks on immigrants have little to do with public safety or respect for the rule of law.

A few examples suffice. During his first week in office, the president revoked late Obama-era guidelines that concentrated enforcement efforts on immigrants with serious criminal records. As a result, arrests of immigrants with no criminal record, or whose only crimes are minor immigration-related offenses such as misdemeanor illegal entry, have soared. This stands in direct contradiction to the president's rhetorical focus on protecting the public from dangerous criminals.

The administration's "zero-tolerance" approach to minor criminal offenses related to immigration drains resources from efforts to address serious crime. It has also escalated ongoing practices of family separation and incarceration to crisis proportions. If this were simply about race-blind law enforcement, the administration would have to explain why minor immigration offenses merit such a massive, expensive, and extreme response.

Despite preaching respect for law, the administration has worked to make it harder for people to exercise their legal right to seek asylum through lawful channels. Of particular relevance to this book, former attorney general Jeff Sessions tried to chip away at the legal foundations for seeking immigration protection in cases of gender violence. The administration has also worked tirelessly to limit *legal* immigration by challenging family-based immigration, targeting legal residents for deportation, and stripping naturalized immigrants of their citizenship. And finally, largely unnoticed by the general public, the administration has implemented numerous procedural changes designed to make it harder and riskier for people to apply for legal immigration statuses.

All this will likely seem quite troubling to anyone moved by Aida Hernandez's story, but there are reasons for hope. While the president's anti-immigrant vitriol rallies a fierce activist base terrified by demographic change, it flies in the face of increasingly positive national attitudes toward immigrants and immigration. Paradigms can and do change.

Smelter jobs are not coming back to Douglas, but that does not mean we need to accept a future of deepening divides between haves and have-nots, buttressed by militarized policing and blamed on immigrants. Gender violence on the border is complex and deeply rooted but also confrontable. Nation-state-based immigration systems will always include some people and exclude others, but they do not need to take their current, increasingly punitive and enforcement-bloated form. The good news is that these socio-economic systems are the products of human choices, not inevitable natural phenomena. Changes—both systemic overhauls and small tweaks that would make big differences—are achievable. Readers seeking concrete ideas about how to transform border security and the U.S. immigration system may consult a supplementary essay that will be posted on my website.

While the rest of us seek the courage to join with people—Aida included—who are taking risks to bring about needed changes, Aida will find the courage to survive another day. She will fend off the next economic setback and win another small victory against PTSD. Or sometimes she won't. Then it may take months for her to regain lost ground. Her dreams of finishing high school and college, becoming a therapist, and ensuring that Gabriel's future is better than her past will recede a bit. The world we have made will seem a little less survivable those days. Then she will pick herself up and try again.

NOTES

1. GIRL IN A LABYRINTH

16 *their family friend Saul's house*: While my attempts to interview Saul were unsuccessful, I was able to cross-check and confirm the violent nature of his relationship with Luz and her family. Aida is the main source for these stories, but Luz, Jennifer, Cynthia, Jazmin, and Raúl confirmed their general tenor and some of the precise details. At least two people outside Aida's immediate family provided additional corroboration.

17 *Pirtleville, a dusty neighborhood*: This section is based on interviews with Ginny Jordan, Lupe Jordan, David Velasco, and Hector Salinas, as well as Josiah Heyman, "The Oral History of the Mexican American Community of Douglas, Arizona, 1901–1942," *Journal of the Southwest* 35, no. 2 (1993): 186–206.

17 *Douglas had been a relatively prosperous place*: I am grateful to numerous residents for helping me understand Douglas's history in general and the overbearing importance of Phelps Dodge in particular. Interviews with Mark Adams, Ray Borane, Michael Gomez, Cindy Hayostek, Elizabeth Henson, Ginny Jordan, Lupe Jordan,

Hector Salinas, Keoki Skinner, and Xavier Zaragoza contributed greatly to my account. Cindy Hayostek generously helped me access archival material at the Douglas Historical Society. Additional sources are cited below.

17 *whose population never exceeded twenty thousand*: *Census of Population and Housing*, U.S. Census Bureau, 1910, 1920, 1930, 1940, 1950, 1960, 1970, 1980, 1990, 2000, and 2010.

17 *James Douglas journeyed*: "Biographical Note," MS 1031, Dr. James Douglas Collection, 1863–1935, Arizona Historical Society; James Douglas, *Notes on the Development of Phelps, Dodge & Co.'s Copper and Railroad Interests* (1906; Bisbee: Frontera House, 1995); Robert S. Jeffrey, "The History of Douglas, Arizona" (master's thesis, University of Arizona, 1951); John Mason Hart, *Empire and Revolution: The Americans in Mexico Since the Civil War* (Berkeley: University of California Press, 2006), 141; "Oral History Interview with Walter Douglas, Grandson of James Douglas, Conducted in His Home on May 16, 1985," typescript, Arizona Historical Society Library.

17 *He chose a spot*: Edward Buck, *Douglas: Its Resources and Development* (Douglas, Ariz.: Nacozari Railroad, 1904), 3; "Douglas History as Recalled Back in 1936 by Dr. Lynne J. Tuttle, Mayor of Douglas," reprint of a Feb. 1936 mayoral address, *Douglas Dispatch*, Feb. 3, 1960; Jeffrey, "History of Douglas," 2. In addition to the water and border location, Douglas appreciated the valley's gentle slope toward mines in Sonora and Arizona. Hoppers full of ore could roll down to the smelter on their own power. George B. Lee, "Reduction Works at Douglas, Arizona," *Transactions of the Institution of Mining and Metallurgy*, 22nd Session (1913), 566.

17 *establishing the border*: Joint Mexican and U.S. military efforts to brutally extirpate the Apaches were crucial to the consolidation of the border in this region. On the conquest and consolidation of the U.S.-Mexico border, see Katherine Benton-Cohen, *Borderline Americans: Racial Division and Labor War in the Arizona Borderlands* (Cambridge, Mass.: Harvard University Press, 2009); Brian DeLay, *War of a Thousand Deserts: Indian Raids and the U.S.-Mexican War* (New Haven, Conn.: Yale University Press, 2008); Rachel St. John, *Line in the Sand: A History of the Western U.S.-Mexico Border* (Princeton, N.J.: Princeton University Press, 2011); Samuel Truett, *Fugitive Landscapes: The Forgotten History of the U.S.-Mexico Borderlands* (New Haven, Conn.: Yale University Press, 2006). In a romanticized—but still revealing—turn of phrase, an early twentieth-century tourist brochure referred to the border between Douglas and Agua Prieta as "an imaginary line." One image drives this home: for many decades, the Douglas airport was truly international. With runways that crossed the border, planes could taxi between countries. Douglas Borderland Climate Club, *On the Romantic Mexican Border, Douglas, Arizona* (Douglas, Ariz.: Borderland Climate Club, ca. 1920), L9791.D73 Pam. 8, University of Arizona Library Special Collections; *Land Anytime in Douglas, Arizona, by Plane, Train, or Auto* (Douglas: Arizona Chamber of Commerce and Mines, ca. 1929), L9791.D73 Pam. 2, University of Arizona Library Special Collections.

18 *burgeoning new town*: Buck, *Douglas*, 2–5; *Draft Downtown Douglas Revitalization Plan* (Douglas, Ariz.: City of Douglas, 2011); *Facts You Should Know About Douglas, Arizona: Copper, Cattle, Climate* (Douglas, Ariz.: Chamber of Commerce

and Mines, 1939); Jeffrey, "History of Douglas," 14. Agua Prieta, across the border, grew in the shadow of its industrial neighbor, but slowly. In 1939, it was less than half the size of Douglas, populated largely by farmers and ranchers. *Sonora, Secretaría de la Economía Nacional, Dirección General de Estadística, Censo de Población* (1940). For a classic anthropological account of Agua Prieta's development, see Josiah Heyman, *Life and Labor on the Border: Working People of Northeastern Sonora, Mexico, 1886–1986* (Tucson: University of Arizona Press, 1991).

18 *twin smelters rose from the desert*: The Calumet & Arizona smelter fired its furnaces in 1901, and the Phelps Dodge Copper Queen came on line in 1904. In the wake of the Great Depression, Phelps Dodge took over the Calumet & Arizona smelter to create a single consolidated complex. Jeffrey, "History of Douglas," 21, and "Smelter Hits Million Mark in Copper Run," *Los Angeles Times*, June 21, 1937. Long based on John Street in lower Manhattan, Phelps Dodge established its western headquarters in Douglas. The offices brought executives, scientists, and engineers to the town. "Phelps Dodge & Co.," *Los Angeles Times*, Oct. 17, 1901, A3; Gene Varn, "Douglas' Love for Smelter Drifts Away," *Arizona Republic*, Jan. 20, 1985.

18 *the town had nearly ten thousand people*: *Census of Population and Housing*, U.S. Census Bureau (1920), https://www.census.gov/prod/www/decennial.html.

18 *its smelters could pour almost a million pounds*: "Smelter Hits Million Mark in Copper Run," A16.

18 *Douglasites called the company*: This section draws heavily from the interviews cited above.

18 *Copper attracted virtuoso violinists*: Cindy Hayostek, "Simply Grand: Douglas' Premier Theater and Irma D. Bond," *Borderland Chronicles* 7 (2009).

18 *During market gluts and strikes*: Interviews with Xavier Zaragoza and Lupe Jordan. For examples of this pattern, see Jeffrey, "History of Douglas," 113–18, and "Accord Reached in Copper Strike," *New York Times*, Aug. 2, 1955, 12; "Copper Workers Strike Over Pay," *New York Times*, July 16, 1967, 50; "Mine-Mill Union Widens Walkouts," *New York Times*, Aug. 21, 1959, 46; "No. 2 Producer of Copper Calls Operations Halt," *Los Angeles Times*, April 8, 1982, F1; "The Slump in Copper," *Los Angeles Times*, Sept. 15, 1907; "Smelter to Shut Down for Three Months Also Because of Big Surplus of Copper," *New York Times*, May 12, 1933, 28.

18 *a reputation for violent union busting*: This section draws heavily on Jonathan D. Rosenblum's masterful history, *Copper Crucible: How the Arizona Miners' Strike of 1983 Recast Labor-Management Relations in America* (Ithaca, N.Y.: ILR Press, 1995). Also Heyman, "Oral History," and interviews with Elizabeth Henson.

18 *two-tier wage system*: Heyman, "Oral History," 189.

19 *mutual aid societies*: Ibid., 198. Groups like the Sociedad Mutualista de Obreros Mexicanos pooled dues from the town's Mexican American residents to provide medical and burial insurance for community members. They also provided a free space where people could criticize PD. Many interviewees credited participation in the Sociedad Mutualista de Obreros Mexicanos with forming their and their parents' political consciousnesses.

19 *The "Phelps Dodge rule"*: Rosenblum, *Copper Crucible*, 30–33.

19 *Wages rose steadily from the 1950s to the 1970s*: Calculated from: "Accord

Reached," 12; "Mine-Mill Union," 46; "Classic Confrontation: Clean Air vs. Jobs," *Los Angeles Times*, May 2, 1976; Rosenblum, *Copper Crucible*, 45.

19 *despite discrimination*: Many residents reported long-standing patterns of discrimination and informal segregation during the smelter years. Lupe Jordan, for example, recalled seeing buses that wouldn't stop for brown residents and getting turned away with her fiancé from an Anglo dance. Numerous interviewees remembered policies that barred Mexican American residents from the YMCA swimming pool. In his autobiography, Raúl Castro—Arizona's first and, to date, only Mexican American governor—also cites incidents of discrimination encountered while living in Douglas. Raúl H. Castro, *Adversity Is My Angel: The Life and Career of Raúl H. Castro*, with Jack L. August (Fort Worth, Tex.: TCU Press, 2009). For a scholarly account of extralegal segregation in Douglas, see Jeanne M. Powers, "On Separate Paths: The Mexican American and African American Legal Campaigns Against School Segregation," *American Journal of Education* 121 (Nov. 2014): 29–55.

19 *PD closed the smelter*: See chapter 2 for a more detailed discussion of the closure.

19 *ranked as one of the poorest*: By per capita income, Pirtleville was the 367th poorest out of over 25,000 census-designated places, putting it in the poorest 2 percent. "Per Capita Income in 1999, All Places," U.S. Census Bureau, Census 2000, Summary File 3, generated using American FactFinder, http://factfinder2.census .gov.

2. ENGLISH WITHOUT BARRIERS

25 *dust heavy with arsenic, cadmium, and lead*: Petitioned Public Health Assessment: Phelps Dodge Corp Douglas Reduction Works, Douglas, Cochise County, Arizona, U.S. Department of Health and Human Services, Public Health Service, Agency for Toxic Substances and Disease Registry, Division of Health Assessment and Consultation (1995), AZDOO8397143, and "Town Hall Meeting, January 17, 1985," University of Arizona Special Collections, "Groups Against Smelter Pollution (GASP) Records," MS 402 (hereafter cited as GASP), box 2, Communications Files, Newsletter, 1984–86 Folder; "Comments on AZ DHS Public Meeting on 1985 Operating Permit Application by PD Reduction Works by Michael Gregory, SW Regional Conservation Committee Sierra Club," April 3, 1985, in GASP, box 9, and an interview with a Douglas City official speaking on the condition of anonymity.

25 *In 1980, the U.S. economy dipped*: Richard C. Auxier, "Reagan's Recession," Pew Research Center, Dec. 14, 2010, http://www.pewresearch.org/2010/12/14 /reagans-recession/.

25 *At first, the recession*: "Copper Mine Outlook Dim," *New York Times*, May 6, 1982; "No. 2 Producer of Copper," F1; Jonathan D. Rosenblum, *Copper Crucible: How the Arizona Miners' Strike of 1983 Recast Labor-Management Relations in America* (Ithaca, N.Y.: ILR Press, 1995), 52.

26 *Taking over as chair*: This is obviously a brief and simplified account of a complex moment. A nice introduction to the crisis can be found in this debate between Paul Krugman and Robert Samuelson: Paul Krugman, "Presidents and the Economy," *New York Times*, Jan. 4, 2015; Robert J. Samuelson, "Volcker, Reagan, and History," *Washington Post*, Jan. 11, 2015; Robert J. Samuelson, "Setting the

Record Straight on Reagan, Volcker, and Inflation: Part 2," *Washington Post*, Jan. 21, 2015.

26 *the policy shift rocked Latin America*: This pivotal moment generated an enormous scholarly literature. Key sources consulted include All Party Parliamentary Group on Overseas Development, *Managing Third World Debt: Report of the Second Working Party Established by the All Party Parliamentary Group on Overseas Development* (London: Overseas Development Institute, 1987); Sebastian Edwards, *The Latin American Debt Crisis: The Evolving Role of the World Bank* (Washington, D.C.: World Bank, 1994); Patrice Franko, *The Puzzle of Latin American Economic Development* (Lanham, Md.: Rowman & Littlefield, 2003), chap. 4; Jeffrey Sachs, "Managing the LDC Debt Crisis," *Brookings Papers on Economic Activity* 2 (1986); and a special issue of the journal *Latin American Perspectives* on Latin American debt and world economic crisis, *Latin American Perspectives* 16, no. 1 (Jan. 1989).

26 *windfall profits*: *The Impact of the Latin American Debt Crisis on the U.S. Economy*, Joint Economic Committee of Congress, May 10, 1986, 18–36; Sachs, *Managing the LDC Debt Crisis*, 402–11. Thanks to structural adjustment programs imposed on Latin American countries, U.S. banks enjoyed snowballing debt repayments in the wake of the crisis. As the Joint Economic Committee report noted, "Bank profits have grown steadily since the onset of the debt crisis" (36).

26 *For poorer mineral-producing nations*: Rosenblum, *Copper Crucible*, 50; also James Ferguson, *Expectations of Modernity: Myth and Meanings of Urban Life in the Zambian Copper Belt* (Berkeley: University of California Press, 1999).

27 *In the face of competition*: This section draws on Rosenblum, *Copper Crucible*, 47–55, 154–64.

27 *no postwar precedents for a private company*: Ibid., 9.

27 *Morenci and Clifton, Arizona*: Ibid., chaps. 3–8; Barbara Kingsolver, *Holding the Line: Women in the Great Arizona Mine Strike* (Ithaca, N.Y.: ILR Press, 1996).

27 *Union supporters shut down Park Avenue*: Rosenblum, *Copper Crucible*, 178.

28 *PD was again earning healthy profits*: Ibid., 10; Nicholas Kristof, "Profit Follows Cost Cutting," *New York Times*, March 19, 1986.

28 *the largest single manufacturing source of sulfur dioxide pollution*: Iver Peterson, "Acid Rain Starting to Affect Environment and Politics in the West," *New York Times*, May 30, 1985. Mexican smelters about to come on line just south of the border added to the urgent need for pollution control. Environmentalists warned that three smelters operating in the Arizona-Sonora borderlands would blanket the entire Mountain West in a vast, poisonous cloud. Scott McCartney, "Country Town's Air Goes Up in Smoke of Copper Smelters," *Los Angeles Times*, July 27, 1986; Marjorie Miller, "'Triangle of Gray' Looms over Border," *Los Angeles Times*, Aug. 24, 1984.

28 *Regulators and a burgeoning local environmental movement*: Interviews with Elizabeth Henson, Rosie Mendoza, Ginny Jordan, Keoki Skinner, and other people who preferred not to be named, as well as numerous documents found in GASP. News sources consulted include "Suit Adds to Copper Firms' Woes," *Los Angeles Times*, Jan. 1, 1985; "Classic Confrontation: Clean Air vs. Jobs," *Los Angeles Times*, May 2, 1976; "Clean Air Costly for Arizona Town," *Los Angeles Times*, Jan. 5, 1987; McCartney, "Country Town's Air Goes Up in Smoke of Copper Smelters"; Miller, "'Triangle of Gray'"; Peterson, "Acid Rain."

28 *On Monday, January 12, 1987*: "Bouncing Back in Smelter City," *New York Times*, May 3, 1987; "Copper Smelter Closes," *Journal of Commerce*, Jan. 15, 1987; "Last Copper Is Poured at Polluting Smelter," *New York Times*, Jan. 15, 1987. My descriptions of copper-smelting practices in Douglas, here and elsewhere, are based on David King Ingman, "Copper Smelting as Practiced at Douglas, Arizona" (master's thesis, Colorado Agricultural College, 1931); *Inorganic Arsenic Emissions from Low-Arsenic Primary Copper Smelters—Background Information for Proposed Standards*, U.S. Environmental Protection Agency, Emissions Standards and Engineering Division (April 1983), EPA-450/3-83-010a.

29 *Douglas's mayor estimated it cost*: "Copper Smelter Closes," 16B.

29 *40 percent of the population*: "Poverty Status in 1999 by Age, Douglas City, AZ, and United States," U.S. Census Bureau, 2000 Census, Summary File 3, generated using American FactFinder, http://factfinder2.census.gov.

29 *had already left*: Interviews with Del Cabarga, Ginny Jordan, Hector Salinas, and Xavier Zaragoza.

3. A SUDDEN STORM

35 *It had been a week of storms*: Along with news sources cited below, many people helped me understand the tone, texture, and emotional resonance of the events described in this chapter. Interviews with Charlie Austin, Rosie Mendoza, and Xavier Zaragoza were crucial. Other people whose insights shaped my thinking about this chapter include Mark Adams, Ray Borane, Del Cabarga, Jazmin Hernandez (no relation to the book character), Danny Ortega, and Ray Ybarra.

35 *more than three inches*: Pamela Hartman, "Drowning Toll May Rise to 7," *Tucson Citizen*, Aug. 7, 1997.

35 *Four inches of standing water*: Christine Ermey, "Mayor Wants Feds to Be Responsible for Border," *Douglas Dispatch*, Aug. 8, 1997; Pamela Hartman, "Child, Second Woman Feared Dead in Ditch," *Tucson Citizen*, Aug. 8, 1997.

37 *removed sections of ramshackle chain link*: Hartman, "Drowning Toll."

37 *segments of which dated to the 1950s*: Eric Schmitt, "A Small Border War Turns, but Is Not Yet Won," *New York Times*, Feb. 24, 2001.

37 *an eighteen-foot-high barrier*: Christine Ermey, "New Fence Rising," *Douglas Dispatch*, July 25, 1997; Pamela Hartman, "Arrests Surging on Ariz. Border," *Tucson Citizen*, Sept. 6, 1997; Ralph Vartabedian, "In a State of Emergency, City's Relaxed," *Los Angeles Times*, Aug. 26, 2005.

37 *most substantial barrier ever installed*: Minimal border fences (for example, barbed-wire strand) date to the late 1930s in this area ("25 Miles of Modern Fence Called For in Bids to Be Opened Sept. 20 for Boundary Line West of Douglas," *Douglas Dispatch*, Aug. 23, 1938; "Engineer Reports Border Fencing Project Finished," *Douglas Dispatch*, Jan. 5, 1939). Chain-link fences followed at some point after that. Construction of substantial barriers (for example, more than a simple chain-link fence) on the U.S.-Mexico border began in 1993, but this work did not spread beyond San Diego until the late 1990s. Blas Nuñez-Neto and Michael John Garcia, *Border Security: The San Diego Fence*, U.S. Library of Congress, Congressional Research Service (2007), RS22026.

37 *had gathered to chat*: "Border Barrier Begins Taking Shape," *Douglas Dispatch*, Aug. 22, 1997.

37 *hazmat suits*: Hartman, "Drowning Toll."

38 *He had come out purple*: Lee Morgan II, *Reaper's Line: Life and Death on the Mexican Border* (Tucson, Ariz.: Rio Nuevo, 2006), 305.

38 *had been rare*: While pre-1997 numbers are hard to come by, the *Douglas Dispatch* reported that there were only sixty-nine deaths on the entire Arizona border between 1993 and 1996 (Christine Ermey, "Douglas Police Interview Two Flood Survivors," *Douglas Dispatch*, Aug. 11, 1997). A 2006 GAO report demonstrated that border deaths declined fairly steadily between the late 1980s and the mid-1990s. *Border-Crossing Deaths Have Doubled Since 1995; Border Patrol's Efforts to Prevent Deaths Have Not Been Fully Evaluated*, Government Accountability Office (2006), GAO-06-770.

38 *The number of bodies recovered*: The Tucson Border Patrol sector saw eight deaths in 1995 according to a landmark study on the topic: *A Continued Humanitarian Crisis at the Border: Undocumented Border Crosser Deaths Recorded by the Pima County Office of the Medical Examiner, 1990–2012* (University of Arizona, Binational Migration Institute, 2013), 12.

38 *among the first of thousands*: The most conservative estimate of border deaths—that compiled by the U.S. Border Patrol itself—records almost 3,000 deaths in the Tucson Sector between 1998 and 2017 (*Southwest Border Sectors: Southwest Border Deaths by Fiscal Year* [U.S. Customs and Border Protection, U.S. Border Patrol, 2017], https://www.cbp.gov/newsroom/media-resources/stats). The Tucson Sector includes Douglas. An exhaustive study by the Binational Migration Institute at the University of Arizona concluded that the number of migrant deaths was significantly higher than Border Patrol estimates. Raquel Rubio-Goldsmith et al., *The "Funnel Effect" & Recovered Bodies of Unauthorized Migrants Processed by the Pima County Office of the Medical Examiner, 1990–2005* (University of Arizona, Binational Migration Institute, 2006).

39 *Late on August 5*: My re-creation of this night is based on interviews with Charlie Austin and Xavier Zaragoza and the following news sources. Reporting in the *Douglas Dispatch* by Christine Ermey: "Seven Undocumented Immigrants"; "Dogs Assist Search for Remaining Victims," Aug. 7, 1997; "Mayor Wants Feds to Be Responsible for Border"; "Survivor's Sister's Phone Call Prompts Search for Additional Drowning Victims," Aug. 9–10, 1997; "Douglas Police Interview Two Flood Survivors"; "Two More Bodies Found in Border Ditch," Aug. 19, 1997. Reporting in the *Tucson Citizen* by Pamela Hartman: "Drowning Toll May Rise to 7"; "Child, Second Woman Feared Dead in Ditch"; "Arrest Total Along Border Here Declines," Oct. 9, 1997; and Ignacio Ibarra, "Three Survivors of Flood Are Sent Back into Mexico," *Arizona Daily Star*, Aug. 12, 1997; Morgan, *Reaper's Line*; "Six Bodies Found in Ditch at Arizona Border Town," *New York Times*, Aug. 7, 1997.

40 *On August 17, a second summer monsoon*: Pamela Hartman, "Storm Uncovers 2 More Flood Victims," *Tucson Citizen*, Aug. 19, 1997.

41 *praised the country's pro-market policies*: Stephany Griffith-Jones, *Global Capital Flows: Should They Be Regulated?* (New York: St. Martin's, 1998), 114; Nora Lustig, "Life Is Not Easy: Mexico's Quest for Stability and Growth," *Journal of Economic Perspectives* 15, no. 1 (2001): 85.

41 *a growing cadre of Mexican billionaires*: John Summa, "Mexico's New Super Billionaires," *Multinational Monitor* (Nov. 1994).

41 *left many Mexicans far behind*: This has been the subject of a vast literature and much debate. A selection of sources include Emmanuel Alvarado, "Poverty and Inequality in Mexico After NAFTA: Challenges, Setbacks, and Implications," *Estudios Fronterizos* 9, no. 17 (Jan.–June 2008); Enrique Dussel Peters, *Polarizing Mexico: The Impact of Liberalization Strategy* (Boulder, Colo.: Lynne Rienner, 2000); Agustín Escobar Latapí and Mercedes González de la Rocha, "Crisis, Restructuring, and Urban Poverty in Mexico," *Environment and Urbanization* 7, no. 1 (April 1995): 57–76; Kevin J. Middlebrook and Eduardo Zepeda, eds., *Confronting Development: Assessing Mexico's Economic and Social Policy Challenges* (Stanford, Calif.: Stanford University Press, 2003); Gerardo Otero, ed., *Neoliberalism Revisited: Economic Restructuring and Mexico's Political Future* (Boulder, Colo.: Westview, 1996); Pablo Ruiz Nápoles, "Neoliberal Reforms and NAFTA in Mexico," *Economía UNAM* 14, no. 41 (May–Aug. 2017): 75–89.

41 *And in 1994 and 1995, a financial collapse*: A number of internal factors in Mexico, including the 1994 Zapatista uprising and conflicts within the ruling PRI party, contributed to the crisis. In broad strokes, political instability in Mexico helped pop a speculative bubble driven by wildly enthusiastic investors. While Mexico ultimately bore the economic and social costs of the crisis, actors in the United States bear a good deal of blame for its onset. Aldo Musacchio, "Mexico's Financial Crisis of 1994–1995," Harvard Business School Working Paper No. 12-101, May 2012; Joseph A. Whitt Jr., "The Mexican Peso Crisis," *Economic Review of the Federal Reserve Bank of Atlanta* (Jan.–Feb. 1996), https://www.frbatlanta.org/-/media/documents/filelegacydocs/Jwhi811.pdf.

41 *By August 1997, the meltdown*: Frank D. Bean and Robert G. Cushing, "The Relationship Between the Mexican Economic Crisis and Illegal Migration to the United States," *Trade Insights* 5, no. 1–4 (Aug. 1995); Daniel Chiquiar and Alejandrina Salcedo, "Mexican Migration to the United States: Underlying Economic Factors and Possible Scenarios for Future Flows," Migration Policy Institute, April 2013, https://www.migrationpolicy.org/research/mexican-migration-united-states-underlying-economic-factors-and-possible-scenarios-future. Both studies note that the peso crisis alone cannot explain increased migration. Strong labor market conditions in the United States also played a role during this period.

41 *Agricultural provisions of NAFTA*: It should be noted that the longer-term trends in the liberalization of Mexican agriculture played as much of a role in migration as NAFTA itself. Literature on this topic includes Patricia Fernández-Kelly and Douglas Massey, "Borders for Whom? The Role of NAFTA in Mexico-U.S. Migration," *Annals of the American Academy of Political and Social Science* 610 (March 2007): 98–118; Gisele Henriques and Raj Patel, "Agricultural Trade Liberalization and Mexico," Food First! Institute for Food and Development Policy, Policy Brief 7 (Aug. 2003), https://foodfirst.org/publication/agricultural-trade-liberalization-and-mexico/; Luis Hernandez Navarro, "Migration and Coffee in Mexico and Central America," *Counterpunch*, Dec. 15, 2004; Demetrios G. Papademetriou, "The Shifting Expectations of Free Trade and Migration," in *NAFTA's Promise and Reality*, ed. John J. Audley et al. (Washington, D.C.: Carnegie Endowment for International Peace, 2004); Marie-Christine Renard, "The Mexican Coffee Crisis," *Latin American Perspectives* 37, no. 2 (2010): 21–33.

42 *no policies had limited migration*: Joseph Nevins, *Operation Gatekeeper and Beyond* (New York: Routledge, 2010), chap. 2; Rachel St. John, *Line in the Sand: A History of the Western U.S.-Mexico Border* (Princeton, N.J.: Princeton University Press, 2011).

42 *racist immigration quota system*: This section draws on Mae M. Ngai, *Impossible Subjects: Illegal Aliens and the Making of Modern America* (Princeton, N.J.: Princeton University Press, 2004), chap. 1.

42 *excluded Mexicans and other Western Hemisphere residents*: Another key factor helps explain the differential treatment of Mexican immigrants: Since the 1790s, U.S. law had declared foreign-born "nonwhites" ineligible for citizenship. The new immigration system extended that proposition to restrict *immigration* by people ineligible for citizenship (i.e., deemed nonwhite). During this period, however, the law categorized most Mexicans and Mexican Americans as white, and therefore eligible for citizenship. The 1920s saw an increase in legal attacks on that classification by eugenicists and nativists. Natalia Molina, "'In a Race All of Their Own': The Quest to Make Mexicans Ineligible for Citizenship," *Pacific Historical Journal* 79, no. 2 (2010): 161–201.

42 *bias still affected the treatment*: St. John, *Line in the Sand*, chap. 5; Nevins, *Operation Gatekeeper*, 66; Jeffrey St. Clair and Alexander Cockburn, "A Short History of Zyklon-B on the U.S.-Mexico Border," *Counterpunch*, March 18, 2016.

42 *officials staged mass expulsions*: Francisco E. Balderrama and Raymond Rodriguez, *Decade of Betrayal: Mexican Repatriation in the 1930s* (Albuquerque: University of New Mexico Press, 2006); Neil Betten and Raymond A. Mohl, "From Discrimination to Repatriation: Mexican Life in Gary, Indiana, During the Great Depression," *Pacific Historical Review* 42, no. 3 (Aug. 1973): 370–88; Kelly Lytle Hernandez, *Migra! A History of the U.S. Border Patrol* (Berkeley: University of California Press, 2010), chaps. 7–8; National Commission on Law Observance and Enforcement, *Report on Enforcement of the Deportation Laws of the United States* (Washington, D.C.: U.S. Government Printing Office, 1931); Ngai, *Impossible Subjects*, chap. 2 and 155–56.

42 *the border was essentially open*: This was not the case, however, for migrants from Asia (and, to a lesser extent, southern Europe and the Middle East) who tried to cross the Mexican border. Racial exclusion laws applied to them, and the border was anything but open. The first migrant-smuggling operations on the border came into existence to guide those immigrants into the United States. Patrick Ettinger, *Imaginary Lines: Border Enforcement and the Origins of Undocumented Immigration, 1882–1930* (Austin: University of Texas Press, 2009), chap. 4.

43 *Cattle thieves had plied their trade*: Most regional histories discuss cross-border banditry at some point. Two books with accounts placing banditry in social and political context are Samuel Truett, *Fugitive Landscapes: The Forgotten History of the U.S.-Mexico Borderlands* (New Haven, Conn.: Yale University Press, 2006), and St. John, *Line in the Sand*. The early twentieth-century journalist George Marvin wrote a fascinating contemporaneous account: "Bandits in the Borderlands," *World's Work* 32 (1916): 656–63.

43 *merchants trafficked guns and ammunition*: Linda Biesele Hall and Don M. Coerver, *Revolution on the Border: The United States and Mexico, 1910–1920* (Albuquerque: University of New Mexico Press, 1988), 146–52; Truett, *Fugitive*

Landscapes, 158; St. John, *Line in the Sand*, 123; Tim Steller, "Smuggled Guns Are History of Border," *Arizona Daily Star*, April 7, 2013.

43 *During the U.S. Prohibition era*: During Prohibition, the Border Patrol focused its resources on intercepting smuggled liquor. Nevins, *Operation Gatekeeper*, 37. Gabriela Recio argues that present-day drug-smuggling routes on the border have their roots in Prohibition-era liquor trafficking ("Drugs and Alcohol: US Prohibition and the Origins of the Drug Trade in Mexico, 1910–1930," *Journal of Latin American Studies* 34 [Feb. 2002]: 21–42). The proximity of legal drinking in Mexico also turned Douglas into a lively tourist destination. Robert S. Jeffrey, "The History of Douglas, Arizona" (master's thesis, University of Arizona, 1951), 107.

43 *first narco-tunnel*: Interview with Keoki Skinner; Douglas Jehl, "$1-Million Drug Tunnel Found at Mexico Border," *Los Angeles Times*, May 19, 1990.

43 *a set of liberal reforms*: This section draws heavily on Ngai, *Impossible Subjects*, chap. 7, and Douglas S. Massey and Karen A. Pren, "Unintended Consequences of US Immigration Policy: Explaining the Post-1965 Surge from Latin America," *Population and Development Review* 38, no. 1 (2012): 1–29.

44 *The Bracero Program*: Ngai, *Impossible Subjects*, chap. 4; Deborah Cohen, *Braceros: Migrant Citizens and Transnational Subjects in the Postwar United States and Mexico* (Durham: University of North Carolina Press, 2011).

44 *as many as half a million Mexican migrants*: Douglas S. Massey, "America's Immigration Policy Fiasco: Learning from Past Mistakes," *Daedalus* 14, no. 2 (2013): 7; Massey and Pren, "Unintended Consequences," 12.

44 *The sudden and dramatic change*: Massey and Pren, "Unintended Consequences."

45 *the number of visas available*: Ngai, *Impossible Subjects*, chap. 7; Massey and Pren, "Unintended Consequences," 3. As Massey and Pren wrote, "In sum, illegal migration rose after 1965 not because there was a sudden surge in Mexican migration, but because the temporary labor program had been terminated and the number of permanent resident visas had been capped, leaving no legal way to accommodate the long-established flows" (3).

45 *Border Patrol agents arrested*: Massey and Pren, "Unintended Consequences," 3.

45 *"flood" of Mexicans without papers*: For a classic account of media and popular culture in this moment, see Leo R. Chavez, *The Latino Threat: Constructing Immigrants, Citizens, and the Nation* (Stanford, Calif.: Stanford University Press, 2013). Other factors contributing to mounting concerns about immigration at this moment included white anxieties fueled by Chicano civil rights organizing, as well as the rise of the broader "war on crime." Nevins, *Operation Gatekeeper*, 81–83.

45 *The "illegal immigrant" was thus invented*: I owe the idea of the "invention" of the "illegal immigrant" to Mae Ngai's *Impossible Subjects* and Cecilia Menjívar and Daniel Kanstroom's excellent edited volume, *Constructing Immigrant "Illegality": Critiques, Experiences, and Responses* (Cambridge, U.K.: Cambridge University Press, 2013).

46 *citizens without citizenship*: This turn of phrase plays on the double meaning of "citizenship." The word refers to both a formal legal status of belonging, as recognized by a nation-state, and the active practice of forging belonging by participating in and contributing to one's community (as in the phrase "be a good citizen"). For an extended reflection on this conundrum, in the context of U.S.

immigration, see Linda Bosniak, *The Citizen and the Alien: Dilemmas of Contemporary Membership* (Princeton, N.J.: Princeton University Press, 2006).

46 *Immigration Reform and Control Act*: Muzaffar Chishti, Dorris Meissner, and Claire Bergeron, "At Its 25th Anniversary, IRCA's Legacy Lives On," Migration Policy Institute, Policy Beat, Nov. 16, 2011, http://www.migrationpolicy.org /article/its-25th-anniversary-ircas-legacy-lives.

46 *"amnesty for illegals"*: For example, this piece from the anti-immigration think tank Center for Immigration Studies: David North, "Before Considering Another Amnesty, Look at IRCA's Lessons," Center for Immigration Studies, Jan. 11, 2013, https://cis.org/Considering-Another-Amnesty-Look-IRCAs-Lessons.

46 *Rising inequality in the United States*: Pierrette Hondagneu-Sotelo makes this point in her book *Doméstica: Immigrant Workers Cleaning and Caring in the Shadows of Affluence* (Berkeley: University of California Press, 2001).

47 *had virtually no possibility*: At this point, the number of visas available to Mexicans without specific family or employment ties to the United States was so small and backlogged as to be essentially irrelevant to Aida. The only real way for an undocumented Mexican immigrant to "get in line" was to have an eligible U.S. citizen child, parent, or spouse sponsor the person. Even this did not guarantee a green card. Many factors could disqualify an applicant. Legal permanent residents could sponsor spouses and unmarried children, with the same caveats. Perhaps the only pathway for Aida was her mother's sister: U.S. citizens can sponsor siblings, although the wait for Mexicans going this route stretches into decades. Had she pursued this, about fifteen to twenty years after her sister began the process, Luz might have received a green card. By that point, however, Aida would likely have aged out of eligibility for sponsorship by her mother or married (which also would have disqualified her). As a preteen, Aida was unlikely to receive an employment-based visa.

47 *a new enforcement paradigm*: Nevins, *Operation Gatekeeper*; Wayne A. Cornelius, "Controlling 'Unwanted' Immigration: Lessons from the United States, 1993–2004," *Journal of Ethnic and Migration Studies* 31, no. 4 (2005): 775–94; *Border Control: Revised Strategy Is Showing Some Positive Results*, U.S. Government Accountability Office (1994), GGD-95-30; Jason De León, *The Land of Open Graves: Living and Dying on the Migrant Trail* (Berkeley: University of California Press, 2015); *Illegal Immigration: Southwest Border Strategy Results Inconclusive*, U.S. Government Accountability Office (1997), GGD-98-21; Massey, "Immigration Fiasco"; Rubio-Goldsmith et al., *"Funnel Effect"*; Fernanda Santos and Rebekah Zemansky, "Arizona Desert Swallows Migrants on Riskier Paths," *New York Times*, May 20, 2013.

47 *apprehensions of undocumented border crossers fell*: Wayne A. Cornelius, "Efficacy and Unintended Consequences of U.S. Immigration Control Policies," *Population and Development Review* 27, no. 4 (2001): 662. Given the difficulty of counting clandestine border crossings, most observers use the number of apprehensions as a rough proxy for trends in unauthorized migration. It is an imperfect proxy, but is widely used by scholars and policy makers. I follow that practice in this book.

48 *In the mid-1990s, Rahm Emanuel*: "Memo on Domestic Policy," Rahm Emanuel to President William Jefferson Clinton, Nov. 12, 1996, Clinton Presidential

Library, publicly posted at https://www.scribd.com/doc/230512565/Nov-1996
-Emanuel-Memo-to-Clinton.

48 *Mushrooming budgets and an energetic new sense*: For a quick overview of the growth
in immigration enforcement budgets, see *The Cost of Immigration Enforcement and
Border Security*, American Immigration Council, Jan. 25, 2017, https://www
.americanimmigrationcouncil.org/research/the-cost-of-immigration-enforce
ment-and-border-security. Also see Dorris Meissner et al., *Immigration Enforcement in the United States: The Rise of a Formidable Machinery*, Migration Policy Institute, Jan. 2013, http://www.migrationpolicy.org/research/immigration-enforcement
-united-states-rise-formidable-machinery.

48 *quickly becoming the largest*: In 2006, *The New York Times* reported that Border Patrol might soon overtake the FBI as the country's biggest federal law enforcement
agency. It did. And by 2009, Customs and Border Protection (which includes Border Patrol) was not just the country's largest federal law enforcement agency. It
was the country's largest law enforcement agency, period. That is still the case, as
of this writing. See Randal Archibold, "Border Patrol Draws Scrutiny as Its Role
Grows," *New York Times*, June 4, 2006; Steve Vogel, "Border Agency to Hire More
Army Reservists," *Washington Post*, April 21, 2009; "Two out of Three Border Patrol Job Applicants Fail Polygraph Test, Making Hiring Difficult," *Los Angeles
Times*, Jan. 13, 2017.

48 *smugglers charged*: Cornelius, "Death at the Border," 688.

48 *Deaths from exposure*: Rubio-Goldsmith et al., *"Funnel Effect."*

49 *Zaragoza snapped a photograph*: A thank-you to Xavier Zaragoza for passing this
image on to me. The photograph also hung in the Douglas Fire Department station, where I interviewed Frank Hone.

4. MILES OF WALL AND NO TIME TO SLEEP

52 *In 1999, Border Patrol detained*: The figure for 1999 is calculated from Tanis J.
Salant et al., *Illegal Immigrants in U.S.-Mexico Border Counties: Costs of Law Enforcement, Criminal Justice, and Emergency Medical Service* (U.S.-Mexico Border
Counties Coalition, University of Arizona Institute for Local Government, 2001),
27. The figure for 2000 comes from Xavier Zaragoza, "Record Number of Immigrants, 31,243, Caught in January," *Douglas Dispatch*, Feb. 1, 2000; Cheryl Devall,
"New Focus of Border Action Arizona Ranchers Angered by Crush of Illegal Immigrants Making Dangerous Crossing," *San Jose Mercury News*, July 29, 2000. For a
concise overview of the ups and downs of border apprehensions, see Ana Gonzalez-
Barrera, "Apprehensions of Mexican Migrants at U.S. Borders Reach Near-Historic
Low," Pew Research Center, April 14, 2016, http://www.pewresearch.org/fact
-tank/2016/04/14/mexico-us-border-apprehensions/. Other sources consulted on
the intense period discussed in this chapter include Scott Baldauf, "After Being
Overrun, Douglas Takes Back Its Community," *Christian Science Monitor*, Feb. 17,
2000; Hilary MacKenzie, "State of Anger: Arizona Dams Migrant Flood," *Calgary
Herald*, Oct. 9, 2000; Cindy Hayostek, "County at Top of List for Uncompensated
Healthcare," *Douglas Dispatch*, Oct. 16, 2002; Michael Coronado, "Wary Groups in
Border Watch; Border Patrol Not Thrilled by Arrival of Minuteman Volunteers
Seeking to Discourage Illegal Immigrants," *Orange County Register*, April 5, 2005;

Michael Coronado, "Minutemen Monitor, Get Monitored; Only One Has Crossed a Line, and Issue of Illegal Immigration Is Front and Center," *Orange County Register*, April 10, 2005; Sam Dillon, "Boom Turns Border to Speed Bump," *New York Times*, Jan. 18, 2000; Barbara Ferry, "Aid Groups Shift Sights to N.M. Border," *Santa Fe New Mexican*, Nov. 2, 2002; Michael Janofsky, "Immigrants Flood Border in Arizona, Angering Ranchers," *New York Times*, June 18, 2000; Jan McGirk, "Blood and Bullets Along the Border as Arizona's Private Posses Hunt Mexican Immigrants for Sport," *Independent*, May 6, 2000; Eric Schmitt, "A Small Border War Turns, but Is Not Yet Won," *New York Times*, Feb. 24, 2001; Elliot Blair Smith, "Armed Rancher Acts as One-Man Border Patrol," *USA Today*, April 28, 2000; Morris Thompson, "Border Tightens, Risk Heightens for Mexicans Entering Despite Debate on Wrongs and Rights, Reality Shows Many Are Willing to Die to Get to U.S.," *Philadelphia Inquirer*, July 28, 2000; reporting in the *Douglas Dispatch* by Xavier Zaragoza: "Border Patrol: Targeting Smugglers May Help Agua Prieta's Migrant Problem," April 19, 2000, and "Despite National Attention, Is Anyone Listening?," July 24, 1999.

52 *Migrants caught and returned*: That migrants who were caught and returned to Mexico or Central America during this period simply tried again is well-known. It is recognized by different sides of immigration debates. More controversial is the question why. And what does this tell us about whether deterrence through intensified border enforcement works on its own terms? A recent comprehensive study by Edward Alden noted diminishing returns of border enforcement build-ups. Deterrence, it concluded, does not work well on migrants fleeing violence or trying to reunite with family members (Edward Alden, "Is Border Enforcement Effective? What We Know and What It Means," *Journal on Migration and Human Security* 5, no. 2 [2017]: 481–90). Another landmark study surveyed recently deported migrants on their reasons for trying again (or not). It found that increasing the punitive nature or cruelty of what Border Patrol euphemistically calls "Consequence Delivery Systems" had little effect on migrant decision making (Jeremy Slack et al., "In Harm's Way: Family Separation, Immigration Enforcement Programs, and Security on the US-Mexico Border," *Journal on Migration and Human Security* 3, no. 2 [2015]: 109–28). One of the central reasons many migrants try again (and why deterrence fails) is debt incurred in order to pay smugglers. In other words, intensified enforcement ironically *decreases* the effectiveness of deterrence by raising the cost of smuggling (Richard L. Johnson and Murphy Woodhouse, "Securing the Return: How Enhanced US Border Enforcement Fuels Cycles of Debt Migration," *Antipode*, published online Feb. 2018, https://onlinelibrary.wiley.com/doi/pdf/10.1111/anti.12386). The conclusion one can draw from all this is nicely presented by Douglas S. Massey in an article for the libertarian CATO Institute: "Backfire at the Border: Why Enforcement Without Legalization Cannot Stop Illegal Immigration," Center for Trade Policy Studies, CATO Institute, June 13, 2005, https://object.cato.org/sites/cato.org/files/pubs/pdf/tpa-029.pdf.

52 *increased cruelty would deter*: The hypothetical scenario in which a thirteen-year-old girl was separated from her family and returned to Mexico alone is something I personally witnessed in Nogales, Sonora, in the mid-2000s. For comprehensive documentation of Border Patrol practices described in this paragraph, see *Culture*

of Cruelty: Abuse and Impunity in Short-Term Border Patrol Custody, No More Deaths/No Más Muertes (2011), http://forms.nomoredeaths.org/wp-content /uploads/2014/10/CultureOfCruelty-full.compressed.pdf. Also see Slack et al., "In Harm's Way."

52 *Backed by President Bill Clinton*: Like prevention through deterrence on the border, these two bills signaled a decisive shift toward the emerging enforcement-only approach to immigration policy. Ironically, the catalyst for this sea change had little to do with immigration or the border. Instead, AEDPA and IIRIRA arose in response to the 1995 Oklahoma City bombing, as well as the Democratic president's desire to steal a page from Republicans' "tough on crime" playbook. "Analysis of Immigration Detention Politics," ALCU.org, n.d., accessed Aug. 5, 2018, https://www.aclu.org/other/analysis-immigration-detention-policies; Susan Bibler Coutin, "Exiled by Law: Deportation and the Inviability of Life," in *Governing Immigration Through Crime: A Reader*, ed. Julie A. Dowling and Jonathan Xavier Inda (Stanford, Calif.: Stanford University Press, 2013); Dana Greene, "Exploring the Relationship Between Contemporary Immigration and Crime Control Policies," in *U.S. Criminal Justice Policy: A Contemporary Reader*, ed. Karim Ismaili (Sudbury: Jones & Bartlett, 2011), 252; Dawn Marie Johnson, "AEDPA and the IIRIRA: Treating Misdemeanors as Felonies for Immigration Purposes: The Legislative Reform," *Journal of Legislation* 27, no. 2 (2001); Dara Lind, "The Disastrous, Forgotten 1996 Law That Created Today's Immigration Problem," Vox.com, April 28, 2016, https://www.vox.com/2016/4/28/11515132 /iirira-clinton-immigration; Nancy Morawetz, "Understanding the Impact of the 1996 Deportation Law and the Limited Scope of Proposed Reforms," *In Defense of the Alien* 23 (2000): 1–30; Ana María Tejada, "The Anti-terrorism and Effective Death Penalty Act (AEDPA) and the Illegal Immigration Reform and Immigrant Responsibility Act (IIRIRA): The Retroactive Effects on Lawful Permanent Residents Convicted of Aggravated Felonies and Drug Offenses," *Rutgers Race and the Law Review* (1999): 381–427. I borrow the concept of an enforcement-only approach from the former INS commissioner Dorris Meissner; for example, see Dorris Meissner, "DHS and Immigration: Taking Stock, Correcting Course," Migration Policy Institute (April 2009), https://www.migrationpolicy.org/pubs /DHS_Feb09.pdf.

53 *IIRIRA also established "expedited removal"*: *A Primer on Expedited Removal*, American Immigration Council, Feb. 3, 2017, https://www.americanimmigration council.org/research/primer-expedited-removal; Alison Siskin and Ruth Ellen Wasem, *Immigration Policy on Expedited Removal of Aliens*, U.S. Library of Congress, Congressional Research Service (2005), RL 33109; David G. Savage, "Trump's Fast-Track Deportations Face a Legal Hurdle: Do Unauthorized Immigrants Have a Right to a Hearing Before a Judge?," *Los Angeles Times*, July 12, 2017; Catherine E. Shoichet, "Can Immigrants Be Deported Without a Court Hearing?," CNN.com, March 3, 2017, https://www.cnn.com/2017/03/03/politics /deportations-without-court-hearings/index.html.

53 *Agua Prieta's population to increase*: Interviews with Mark Adams, Del Cabarga, Amando Padilla, Keoki Skinner, and Xavier Zaragoza; "Agua Prieta, cruce privilegiada para migrantes," Organización Editorial Mexicana, April 14, 2008; Thompson, "Border Tightens, Risk Heightens."

53 *Hundreds of overcrowded "guesthouses"*: Interviews with Keoki Skinner, Xavier Zaragoza, Amando Padilla, and Del Cabarga; Janofsky, "Immigrants Flood Border"; Alan Zarembo, "Coyote Inc.," *Newsweek*, Aug. 29, 1999.

53 *the deterrent effects of punitive enforcement played a modest role*: Edward Alden, "Is Border Enforcement Effective?"; Slack et al., "In Harm's Way." The conclusion one can draw from all this is nicely presented by Douglas S. Massey in "Backfire at the Border."

53 *Many migrants had taken out debts*: Johnson and Woodhouse, "Securing the Return."

54 *Douglas simply didn't have the infrastructure*: Interviews with Ray Borane, Michael Gomez, and Danny Ortega. Perhaps more than any other institution, Douglas's already struggling rural hospital reeled. Day and night, Border Patrol agents dropped migrants at the Southeast Arizona Medical Center suffering contusions, exposure, dehydration, and broken bones incurred fleeing across a rough landscape. Over seven years, the small hospital wrote off more than fifty million dollars in unreimbursed emergency medical care for undocumented migrants. Hayostek, "County at Top of List."

55 *hit its boiling point*: A number of interviewees named a 1999 town hall meeting in Bisbee as the moment when the crisis hit its boiling point. The meeting is described in Xavier Zaragoza, "About Immigrants: Do Something. Do It Right, Residents Say," *Douglas Dispatch*, April 27, 1999.

55 *Wendy Glenn was one of those*: Material in this section from author's interviews.

55 *familiar cyclical migration came to a crashing halt*: Douglas S. Massey and Karen A. Pren, "Unintended Consequences of US Immigration Policy: Explaining the Post-1965 Surge from Latin America," *Population and Development Review* 38, no. 1 (2012): 1–29.

57 *"A big wall isn't the answer"*: Quoted in Xavier Zaragoza, "Napolitano in Douglas, Listens to Law Enforcement on Illegal Immigration," *Douglas Dispatch*, Nov. 3, 2005.

57 *Larry Vance, a rancher living a mile north of the border*: Baldauf, "After Being Overrun"; MacKenzie, "State of Anger."

57 *Roger Barnett, one of Douglas's most*: Janofsky, "Immigrants Flood"; MacKenzie, "State of Anger."

57 *Mayor Ray Borane*: Interview with Ray Borane; Ray Borane, "Do You Hire Illegal Immigrants?," *New York Times*, Aug. 30, 1999; Dillon, "Boom Turns Border to Speed Bump."

57 *"enforcement only" approach*: I borrow the concept of an enforcement-only approach from the former INS commissioner Dorris Meissner; for example, see Meissner, "DHS and Immigration."

57 *built to house forty agents*: Thompson, "Border Tightens, Risk Heightens"; Xavier Zaragoza, "Border Patrol Broke Ground Friday for New Douglas Station," *Douglas Dispatch*, Nov. 18, 2000.

57 *"biggest Border Patrol station"*: Zaragoza, "Broke Ground"; Tim Vanderpool, "Eye of the Storm," *Tucson Weekly*, May 14, 2009.

57 *billion-dollar high-tech virtual fence*: Julia Preston, "Homeland Security Cancels 'Virtual Fence' After $1 Billion Is Spent," *New York Times*, Jan. 14, 2011.

58 *"ground zero" for people smuggling*: See, for example, Dillon, "Boom Turns Border to Speed Bump"; MacKenzie, "Border War." Along with "ground zero," we see "hot

spot," "smuggling capital," "new immigration battleground," and other labels applied to Douglas in the 2000s. For example: Jerry Seper, "Thin Green Line Takes a New Strategy," *Washington Times*, Sept. 23, 2002; Dave Montgomery, "Debate over Illegal Immigration a Hot Topic for Border-State Voters," Knight Ridder News Service, Feb. 1, 2004; Carol Morello, "Living in Fear on the Border: Little Desert Town Is New Immigration Battleground," *USA Today*, July 21, 1999; Joyce Howard Price, "Bush's Immigration Plan Seen as Hispanic-Vote Ploy," *Washington Times*, Jan. 9, 2004; Paul Rubin, "For Those Living in Ground Zero for Drug Trafficking Along the U.S.-Mexico Border, the Illegal Immigration Crisis Is Personal," *Dallas Observer*, June 3, 2010.

58 *"new immigration battleground"*: Morello, "Living in Fear."

58 *number of migrant apprehensions in town fell*: "Fewer Illegal Entrants Being Caught Along Entire SW Border," *Douglas Dispatch*, Jan. 26, 2001; "Reasons for Decline in Migrants' Arrests Is Anyone's Guess," *Douglas Dispatch*, Jan. 27, 2001; Schmitt, "Small Border War."

58 *"Douglas has become a garrison"*: Quoted in Dillon, "Boom Turns Border to Speed Bump."

59 *Christopher Levy*: Christopher Levy, "Border Security: A Journey Without a Destination" (master's thesis, Naval Postgraduate School, 2013).

59 *Charlie Austin tried to downplay*: Vartabedian, "In a State of Emergency."

59 *Douglas's crime rate*: Interviews with Charlie Austin and Michael Gomez. See also Jack Gillum, "Arizona Border Cities Tout Lowest Crime Rates in State," *USA Today*, July 18, 2011.

59 *privately, he had to admit*: Author's interview.

60 *truly believed they were at war*: On the Border Patrol's increasingly militarized sense of purpose, see Todd Miller, *Border Patrol Nation: Dispatches from the Front Lines of Homeland Security* (San Francisco: City Lights, 2014), and comments by Internal Affairs officers quoted in Mark Binelli, "10 Shots Across the Border," *New York Times Magazine*, March 3, 2016. An amicus curiae brief before the U.S. Supreme Court by former officials of the Border Patrol is quite revealing as well, noting the "increasing militarization" of the law enforcement agency: Amicus Curiae, *Jesus C. Hernandez et al. v. Jesus Mesa Jr.*, 15 U.S. 118 (2016), http://www.scotusblog.com/wp-content/uploads/2016/12/15-118-amicus-petitioner-former-us-customers-and-border-protection-officials.pdf.

60 *They spent hundreds of thousands*: A 2002 investigation into travel reimbursement problems offers revealing insight into the economic impact of short-term Border Patrol assignments: *An Investigation of Travel Reimbursements in Connection with the INS's Operation Safeguard*, U.S. Department of Justice, Office of the Inspector General (2002).

60 *"Where are you from, Iowa?"*: Interview with Ray Ybarra.

60 *experiment in the psychology of fear*: A number of interviewees recounted versions of this parable. I have not tracked down the actual neighbors, but the tale offers valuable insight into the emotional tenor of Douglas during this period.

5. THE NEW MILLENNIUM, HER OWN QUIET WAR

69 *"I have begun my own quiet war"*: Sandra Cisneros, *The House on Mango Street* (New York: Vintage, 2013), 89.

6. BETTER LIVING THROUGH BORDER SECURITY

71 *Cinco de Mayo horse races*: Thanks to Cindy Hayostek for sharing photographs of this event. Also see "15,000 Attend Cinco de Mayo Horse Race," *Douglas Dispatch*, May 8, 2001; Brady McCombs, "Life Along the Border: Then Horse Race Celebrated Sister-City Camaraderie," *Arizona Daily Star*, Dec. 13, 2011.

72 *"They say enemies build walls"*: Quoted in McCombs, "Life Along the Border."

73 *One of them, Glenn Spencer*: "Glenn Spencer," Southern Poverty Law Center, n.d., accessed Aug. 5, 2018, https://www.splcenter.org/fighting-hate/extremist-files/individual/glenn-spencer; Roxanne Doty, *The Law into Their Own Hands: Immigration and the Politics of Exceptionalism* (Tucson: University of Arizona Press, 2016), 29; Leo R. Chavez, "Spectacle in the Desert: The Minuteman Project on the U.S.-Mexico Border," in *Governing Immigration Through Crime: A Reader*, ed. Julie A. Dowling and Jonathan Xavier Inda (Stanford, Calif.: Stanford University Press, 2013), 115–25.

73 *the Texan Jack Foote*: Doty, *Law into Their Own Hands*, 30; Thomas Korosec, "Soldiers of Misfortune," *Dallas Observer*, Sept. 11, 2003.

74 *no other law enforcement agency*: The New York Police Department may come close. Estimated from "Police Department Race and Ethnicity Data," *Governing*, n.d., accessed Oct. 2, 2018, http://www.governing.com/gov-data/safety-justice/police-department-officer-demographics-minority-representation.html; James Pinkerton, "Hispanics Hold 52 Percent of Border Patrol Jobs," *Houston Chronicle*, Dec. 29, 2008.

74 *"It's kind of like the Irish"*: Interview with David Velasco. As Josiah Heyman noted presciently, border militarization has created a situation in which "more and more people work for the watchers or are watched by the state." "Why Interdiction? Immigration Law Enforcement at the United States–Mexico Border," *Regional Studies* 33 (1999), 628.

75 *one in thirteen employed adults*: Calculated from "S2401 Occupation by Sex and Median Income, Douglas City, Arizona," U.S. Census Bureau, American Community Survey, 2007–2011 and 2010–2014, generated using American FactFinder, https://factfinder.census.gov.

75 *By comparison, only about one*: The numbers for New York, Tucson, and Phoenix were calculated from "S2401 Occupation by Sex and Median Income, New York City, Tucson & Phoenix," U.S. Census Bureau, American Community Survey, 2007–2011, generated using American FactFinder, https://factfinder.census.gov.

75 *Law enforcement jobs carried wages*: Interviews with Danny Ortega and Carlos de la Torre; "S2401 Occupation by Sex and Median Income, Douglas City, Arizona," U.S. Census Bureau, American Community Survey, 2007–2011, generated using American FactFinder, https://factfinder.census.gov.

76 *"didn't get the materials"*: Interview with Robert Carreira.

76 *"It's like the military"*: Interview with city official speaking on the condition of anonymity.

76 *El Chef was one of the town's most popular*: Interviews with Fernando Betancourt, Mark Adams, and Xavier Zaragoza.

77 *abraded the lives of women*: Sylvanna M. Falcón makes these connections powerfully in "Rape as a Weapon of War: Advancing Human Rights for Women at the U.S.-

Mexico Border," *Social Justice* 28, no. 2 (2001), 31–50. Also see Kathleen A. Staudt, Tony Payan, and Z. Anthony Kruszewski, eds., *Human Rights Along the U.S.-Mexico Border: Gendered Violence and Insecurity* (Tucson: University of Arizona Press, 2009).

77 *the U.S. government's overarching border security strategy*: Joseph Nevins, *Operation Gatekeeper and Beyond* (New York: Routledge, 2010); Wayne A. Cornelius, "Controlling 'Unwanted' Immigration: Lessons from the United States, 1993–2004," *Journal of Ethnic and Migration Studies* 31, no. 4 (2005): 775–94; *Border Control: Revised Strategy Is Showing Some Positive Results*, U.S. Government Accountability Office (1994), GGD-95-30; Jason De León, *The Land of Open Graves: Living and Dying on the Migrant Trail* (Berkeley: University of California Press, 2015); *Illegal Immigration: Southwest Border Strategy Results Inconclusive*, U.S. Government Accountability Office (1997), GGD-98-21; Douglas S. Massey, "America's Immigration Policy Fiasco: Learning from Past Mistakes," *Daedalus* 14, no. 2 (2013); Raquel Rubio-Goldsmith et al., *The "Funnel Effect" & Recovered Bodies of Unauthorized Migrants Processed by the Pima County Office of the Medical Examiner, 1990–2005* (University of Arizona, Binational Migration Institute, 2006); Fernanda Santos and Rebekah Zemansky, "Arizona Desert Swallows Migrants on Riskier Paths," *New York Times*, May 20, 2013.

77 *was* designed *to make unauthorized border crossing more dangerous*: De León, *The Land of Open Graves*, 32–34.

79 *had outsourced the ugliest work of "deterrence"*: Research by Gilberto Rosas helped spark this idea. Gilberto Rosas, *Barrio Libre: Criminalizing States and Delinquent Refusals of the New Frontier* (Durham, N.C.: Duke University Press, 2012).

7. DANCE STEPS

82 *David Rojas*: While David declined my requests to interview him, I was able to cross-check and confirm the violent nature of his relationship with Aida. Aida is the main source for these stories, but Luz, Jennifer, Cynthia, Jazmin, and Raúl confirmed their general tenor and some of the precise details. Aida's written and oral testimony in immigration court supported the interview material.

84 *profound impacts of 9/11 on Douglas*: "Border on High Alert," *Douglas Dispatch*, Sept. 11, 2001; Xavier Zaragoza, "Tightened Security Hurting Business," *Douglas Dispatch*, Sept. 19, 2001.

84 *militarized sense of purpose*: Todd Miller, *Border Patrol Nation: Dispatches from the Front Lines of Homeland Security* (San Francisco: City Lights, 2014), and comments by Internal Affairs officers quoted in Mark Binelli, "10 Shots Across the Border," *New York Times Magazine*, March 3, 2016. An amicus curiae brief before the U.S. Supreme Court by former officials of the border is quite revealing as well, noting the "increasing militarization" of the law enforcement agency: Amicus Curiae, *Jesus C. Hernandez et al. v. Jesus Mesa Jr.*, 15 U.S. 118 (2016), http://www.scotusblog.com/wp-content/uploads/2016/12/15-118-amicus-petitioner-former-us-customers-and-border-protection-officials.pdf.

86 *Violence Against Women Act*: This section draws on Margaret E. Adams and Jacquelyn Campbell, "Being Undocumented and Intimate Partner Violence (IPV): Multiple Vulnerability Through the Lens of Feminist Intersectionality," *Women's Health and Urban Life* 11, no. 1 (2012): 15–34; Maria Theresa Mayorga and Katie Gillespie, "Experiences of Immigrant Women Who Self-Petition Under the Vi-

olence Against Women Act," *Violence Against Women* 16, no. 8 (2010): 859–60; Edna Erez, Madelaine Adelman, and Carol Gregory, "Intersections of Immigration and Domestic Violence: Voices of Battered Immigrant Women," *Feminist Criminology* 4, no. 1 (2009): 32–56; Cecilia Menjívar and Olivia Salcido, "Immigrant Women and Domestic Violence: Common Experiences in Different Countries," *Gender and Society* 16, no. 6 (2002): 898–920; Elizabeth Newman, "Reflections on VAWA's Strange Bedfellows: The Partnership Between the Battered Immigrant Women's Movement and Law Enforcement," *University of Baltimore Law Review* 42, no. 2 (2013): 229–76; Mariela Olivares, "Battered by Law: The Political Subordination of Immigrant Women," *American University Law Review* 64, no. 2 (2014): 231–83; Nancy Whittier, "Carceral and Intersectional Feminism in Congress: The Violence Against Women Act, Discourse, and Policy," *Gender and Society* 30, no. 5 (2016): 791–818.

87 *few people understood the law*: Interview with Rosie Mendoza. On obstacles to petitioning for VAWA immigration relief, see Mayorga and Gillespie, "Experiences of Immigrant Women."

87 *fuzzy third category*: Mariela Olivares makes a similar point in Olivares, "Battered by Law," 280.

87 *The Development, Relief, and Education for Alien Minors (DREAM) Act*: For an overview, see "The Dream Act, DACA, and Other Policies Designed to Protect Dreamers," American Immigration Council, Sept. 6, 2017, https://www .americanimmigrationcouncil.org/research/dream-act-daca-and-other-policies -designed-protect-dreamers. On Durbin and Hatch's role, see Kathryn Rodgers, "Domestic Abuse Law Deserves Praise," *New York Times*, July 25, 1995.

87 *"Particularly moving are the stories"*: Quoted in Testimony of the Hon. Orrin Hatch, U.S. Congress, Senate, Committee on the Judiciary, June 20, 2002, https:// www.judiciary.senate.gov/imo/media/doc/hatch_statement_06_20_02.pdf.

88 *five continuous years of residence*: "Durbin, Reid, Menendez, 30 Others Introduce the DREAM Act," press release, May 11, 2011, https://www.durbin.senate.gov /newsroom/press-releases/durbin-reid-menendez-30-others-introduce-the -dream-act.

89 *only one in ten Douglas residents*: Including associate degrees and bachelor's degrees. "Educational Attainment by Sex, 2000," U.S. Census Bureau, 2010 Census, Summary File 2, generated using American FactFinder, http://fact finder2.census.gov.

8. AMERICAN DREAMING

93 *autumn Friday nights*: I am grateful to Cindy Hayostek for sharing her memories of this remarkable image.

96 *twelve miles of eighteen-foot steel wall*: Ralph Vartabedian, "In a State of Emergency, City's Relaxed," *Los Angeles Times*, Aug. 26, 2005.

96 *record number of migrant deaths in Arizona*: Raquel Rubio-Goldsmith et al., *The "Funnel Effect" & Recovered Bodies of Unauthorized Migrants Processed by the Pima County Office of the Medical Examiner, 1990–2005* (University of Arizona, Binational Migration Institute, 2006); *Southwest Border Sectors: Southwest Border Deaths by Fiscal Year*, U.S. Customs and Border Protection, U.S. Border Patrol (2017), https://www.cbp.gov/newsroom/media-resources/stats.

97 *Wendy complained to Governor Janet Napolitano*: Quoted in Xavier Zaragoza, "Napolitano in Douglas, Listens to Law Enforcement on Illegal Immigration," *Douglas Dispatch*, Nov. 3, 2005.

97 *haul away tons of material*: Final Report: *Developing a Collaborative to Manage and Mitigate Undocumented Migrant (UDM) Waste in Arizona's Borderlands*, Arizona Department of Environmental Quality (2011), TAA08-064.

97 *In April 2005, a thousand volunteers*: Interviews with Ray Borane, Del Cabarga, Angela Nuñez, Ray Ybarra, and Xavier Zaragoza; "About Jim Gilchrist," Minuteman Project, n.d., accessed Aug. 10, 2018, http://baesic.net/minutemanproject /jim-gilchrist/; Leo R. Chavez, "Spectacle in the Desert: The Minuteman Project on the U.S.-Mexico Border," in *Governing Immigration Through Crime: A Reader*, ed. Julie A. Dowling and Jonathan Xavier Inda (Stanford, Calif.: Stanford University Press, 2013), 122; Meredith Hoffman, "Whatever Happened to Arizona's Minutemen?," Vice.com, March 22, 2016, https://www.vice.com/en_us/article /xd7jmn/what-happened-to-arizonas-minutemen; Xavier Zaragoza, "Minuteman Launches Protest," *Douglas Dispatch*, April 2, 2005; Xavier Zaragoza, "Legal Observers to Provide Update on Minuteman Activities to Public at Free Dinner," *Douglas Dispatch*, April 15, 2005.

97 *"It's racism. . . . We don't want them here"*: Quoted in Michael Coronado, "Wary Groups in Border Watch; Border Patrol Not Thrilled by Arrival of Minuteman Volunteers Seeking to Discourage Illegal Immigrants," *Orange County Register*, April 5, 2005.

97 *boycott of Douglas businesses*: Xavier Zaragoza, "A Day Without a Mexican," *Douglas Dispatch*, April 21, 2005.

97 *FBI agents had arrested a key figure*: This section draws on "Arizona Jury Finds Vigilante Rancher Liable for Attack on Immigrants," MALDEF, Feb. 18, 2009, http://www.maldef.org/news/releases/vicente_barnett_2_18_09/index.html; David Holthouse, "Nativist Leader Arrested for Double Murder," Southern Poverty Law Center, June 15, 2009, https://www.splcenter.org/hatewatch/2009/06/15 /nativist-leader-arrested-double-murder; "Minuteman Founder Must Pay Former Close Ally He Smeared," Southern Poverty Law Center, Oct. 9, 2012, https://www.splcenter.org/hatewatch/2012/10/09/minuteman-founder-must -pay-former-close-ally-he-smeared; Leah Nelson, "Reality Show Celebrates Hate Group Leader as American Patriot," Southern Poverty Law Center, Feb. 23, 2012, https://www.splcenter.org/hatewatch/2012/02/23/reality-show-celebrates -hate-group-leader-american-patriot; Dean Schabner, "Border Vigilante Shawna Forde Sentenced to Death for Home Invasion," ABCnews.com, Feb. 22, 2011, https://abcnews.go.com/US/minutemen-vigilante-shawna-forde-sentenced-death -deadly-arizona/story?id=12976687; Tim Stellar, "Blog: How Border-Militia Members Got a Bad Name," *Arizona Daily Star*, June 21, 2012, splcenter.org /hatewatch/2016/06/13/ex-minuteman-chris-simcox-meets-rul.

98 *Governor Napolitano declared a state of emergency*: Ralph Blumenthal, "Citing Violence, 2 Border States Declare a Crisis," *New York Times*, Aug. 17, 2005.

98 *Mayor Borane bristled*: Vartabedian, "In a State of Emergency."

98 *lower crime rates*: "Crime Reported by Douglas Police Department, Arizona," and "Estimated Crime in Arizona," Federal Bureau of Investigations, Uniform Crime Reporting Statistics, table generated using https://www.ucrdatatool.gov/;

Jack Gillum, "Arizona Border Cities Tout Lowest Crime Rates," *USA Today*, July 18, 2011.

99 *"Women in town say"*: Vartabedian, "In a State of Emergency."

9. NO COUNTRY FOR YOUNG WOMEN

104 *$100 million for further border security*: Howard Fischer, "State Tired of Waiting, Taking Action Along the Mexico Border," *Douglas Dispatch*, Feb. 7, 2006; Mike Sunnucks, "Governor Extends State of Emergency at Mexican Border," *Phoenix Business Journal*, Feb. 16, 2006; Xavier Zaragoza, "Napolitano Announces $100 Million for Border Security," *Douglas Dispatch*, Jan. 27, 2006.

104 *a salvo of bills*: "2006 State Legislation Related to Immigration: Enacted and Vetoed," National Council of State Legislatures, Oct. 31, 2006, http://www.ncsl .org/research/immigration/immigrant-policy-2006-state-legislation-related -t.aspx#Education; "Overview of State Legislation Related to Immigration and Immigrants in 2007," National Council of State Legislatures, April 11, 2007, http://www.ncsl.org/research/immigration/2007-state-legislation-immigration .aspx; "2009 State Laws Related to Immigrants and Immigration, Jan. 1–Dec. 31, 2009," National Council of State Legislatures, n.d., accessed Aug. 10, 2018, http://www.ncsl.org/research/immigration/2009-state-immigration-laws.aspx; Alia Beard Rau, "Limit on Illegal-Immigrant Lawsuits Faces Test of Constitutionality," *Arizona Republic*, May 30, 2011.

104 *Flows of migrants through the area dwindled*: Jonathan Clark, "Federal Government Extends Border Fencing to Huachuca," *Douglas Dispatch*, Aug. 22, 2006.

105 *sliced into the number*: Ana Gonzalez-Barrera, "More Mexicans Leaving Than Coming to the U.S.," Pew Research Center, Nov. 19, 2015, http://assets .pewresearch.org/wp-content/uploads/sites/7/2015/11/2015-11-19_mexican -immigration__FINAL.pdf; *Southwest Border Sectors Total Illegal Alien Apprehensions by Fiscal Year (Oct. 1st through Sept. 30th)*, U.S. Customs and Border Protection, U.S. Border Patrol (2017), https://www.cbp.gov/sites/default/files/assets /documents/2017-Dec/BP%20Southwest%20Border%20Sector%20Apps%20 FY1960%20-%20FY2017.pdf.

105 *By 2008, that number had fallen*: Calculated from *Border Patrol Agent Staffing by Fiscal Year* and *Southwest Border Sectors Total Illegal Alien Apprehensions by Fiscal Year*, U.S. Customs and Border Protection, U.S. Border Patrol (2017), both found at https://www.cbp.gov/newsroom/media-resources/stats.

105 *declines in border apprehensions*: Examples of this claim can be found in "Druglords Taking Over Business of Smuggling Migrants, Using as Decoys," *Douglas Dispatch*, May 2, 2007; Jay Mayfield, "Finishing the Job," *Frontline: U.S. Customs and Border Protection* 4, no. 2 (2011); *Performance and Accountability Report, FY 2011*, U.S. Customs and Border Protection (March 2013); "What Would It Take to Secure the U.S.-Mexico Border?," *Week*, March 13, 2013.

105 *In August 2006*: Jonathan Clark, "Committee Talks Border Security," *Douglas Dispatch*, Aug. 18, 2006.

105 *horrific spike in violence*: Kimberly Heinle, Cory Molzahn, and David A. Shirk, *Drug Violence in Mexico: Data and Analysis Through 2014* (San Diego: Justice in Mexico Project, 2015); "Mexico's Kingpin Strategy Against Cartels," *New York Times*, Feb. 16, 2016.

105 *In 2006, Felipe Calderón*: "Mexico Votes 2006, an Interactive Primer," *Washington Post*, n.d., accessed Aug. 10, 2018, http://www.washingtonpost.com/wp-srv/world /interactives/mexico06/.

106 *Calderón's declaration of all-out war*: Sources consulted for this section include June S. Beittel, *Mexico's Drug-Related Violence*, U.S. Library of Congress, Congressional Research Service (2009), R40582; Patrick Corcoran, "Mexico's Success in Taking Out Kingpins Has Done Little to Change What's Driving the Drug War," *Business Insider* and *InSight Crime*, June 6, 2017; "Mexico's Kingpin Strategy Against Cartels"; Reggie Thompson, "A Decade into Mexico's War on Drugs," *Stratfor Worldview*, Dec. 11, 2016. Dawn Marie Paley's *Drug War Capitalism* (Oakland: AK Press, 2014) provides both an excellent introduction to this topic and a critical perspective on mainstream reporting about the so-called war on drugs.

106 *Most regions of Mexico remained far safer*: See, for example, "How Safe Is Mexico? A Traveler's Guide to Safety over Sensationalism," n.d., accessed Aug. 10, 2018, http://howsafeismexico.com/mexico_states_safety.html.

106 *far from a "failed state"*: Use of this (wildly exaggerated) label spiked in U.S. media reports around 2008–2009 thanks to a notorious Pentagon report that warned of the potential for a "failed state" across the United States' southern border. For example, see Joel Kurtzman, "Mexico's Instability Is a Real Problem: Don't Discount the Possibility of a Failed State Next Door," *Wall Street Journal*, Jan. 16, 2009.

106 *Sinaloa Cartel, Mexico's most powerful*: "Druglords Taking Over Business of Smuggling Migrants, Using as Decoys"; Juan Carlos Ruiz Olvera, "La ola de violencia se recrudece en Sonora," *Dossier Político*, Aug. 1, 2008, http://www .dossierpolitico.com/vernoticiasanteriores.php?artid=40352&relacion=dossier politico.

106 *Little* pueblos *south of Agua Prieta*: The copper-mining town of Cananea was particularly affected. Ruiz Olvera, "La ola de violencia"; "Cartels Target Mexican Police," *Douglas Dispatch*, May 20, 2008.

107 No Country for Old Men: Joel and Ethan Coen (Los Angeles: Miramax Films and Paramount Vantage, 2007).

112 *"Voluntary Return" box pre-checked*: A class action lawsuit filed in 2013 brought this and other coercive practices to public attention. The ACLU, which filed the lawsuit, noted that "as a matter of standard practice, ICE and Border Patrol have misinformed immigrants about the consequences of 'voluntary return.' . . . And in many cases, immigration officers used pressure and threats to force people to sign 'voluntary return' orders" (Mitra Ebadolahi and Gabriela Rivera, "Victory! Immigration Authorities Must Stop Coercing Immigrants into Signing Away Their Rights," ACLU, Blog of Rights, Aug. 27, 2014, https://www.aclu.org/blog/victory -immigration-authorities-must-stop-coercing-immigrants-signing-away-their -rights). Representatives of the American Immigration Lawyers Association also reported similar patterns of coercion in a 2010 meeting with government officials. ("Questions and Answers: Albuquerque ICE/DRO Liaison Meeting with AILA/New Mexico Member," June 15, 2010, http://www.ailatexas.org/wp -content/uploads/2013/03/QA-ICEDRO-061510.pdf). The U.S. government agreed to a settlement in 2014 that would establish safeguards against coercion in the

voluntary return process ("Settlement Agreement and Release," *Lopez-Venegas v. Johnson*, Aug. 8, 2014, https://www.aclu.org/sites/default/files/field_document /settlementagreement90-4.pdf).

113 *thwarted migrants accumulated there*: Author's interviews and observations during the period in question, as well as Damien Cave, "Crossing Over, and Over," *New York Times*, Oct. 2, 2011.

113 *Was it 60,000 residents or 200,000?*: The Southeast Arizona Economic Development Group noted, "Population estimates for Agua Prieta vary widely, ranging from about 60,000 to 150,000, although some estimates have placed the city's population close to 200,000." See "Agua Prieta," in Southeast Arizona Economic Development Group, *2016 Douglas Economic Outlook*, accessed Aug. 14, 2018, http://www.saedg.org/douglas.html#agua_prieta. Also see "Agua Prieta, cruce privilegiada para migrantes," Organización Editorial Mexicana, April 14, 2008.

10. HUNGER IS WORSE

117 *An angel was speaking*: This chapter draws primarily on the author's interviews with Raúl Florencio Lugo, as well as Raúl Florencio Lugo, *El asalto al cuartel de Ciudad Madera* (Chapingo: Universidad Autónoma de Chapingo, 2006); Raúl Florencio Lugo and Francisco Ornelas, "Testimonios," *La Jornada del Campo* 96 (Sept. 19, 2015); and Raúl Florencio Lugo, "Mi participación en la lucha campesina," typed manuscript provided by the author (n.d.). Other key sources include Armando Bartra, "Encuentros en la Sierra," *La Jornada del Campo* 96 (Sept. 19, 2015); Elizabeth Henson, "Madera 1965: Primeros Vientos," in *Challenging Authoritarianism in Mexico*, ed. Fernando Herrera Calderón and Adela Cedillo (New York: Routledge, 2012); Miguel Méndez García, "50 Aniversario de asalto al cuartel militar de Madera," *El Diario de Nuevo Casas Grandes*, Sept. 23, 2015; Jesus Vargas, "Madera Rebelde," *La Jornada del Campo* 96 (Sept. 19, 2015).

118 *some of North America's most important*: On the nineteenth-century dispossession of peasant communities in Chihuahua and subsequent agrarian struggles, see John Mason Hart, *Empire and Revolution: The Americans in Mexico Since the Civil War* (Berkeley: University of California Press, 2002); Henson, "Madera 1965"; Friedrich Katz, *The Secret War in Mexico: Europe, the United States, and the Mexican Revolution* (Chicago: University of Chicago Press, 1981); Daniel Nugent and Ana María Alonso, "Multiple Selective Traditions in Agrarian Reform and Agrarian Struggle: Popular Culture and State Formation in the *Ejido* of Namiquipa, Chihuahua," in *Everyday Forms of State Formation: Revolution and the Negotiation of Rule in Mexico*, ed. Gilbert M. Joseph and Daniel Nugent (Durham, N.C.: Duke University Press, 1994); Mark Wassserman, "The Social Origins of the 1910 Revolution in Chihuahua," *Latin American Research Review* 15, no. 1 (1980): 15–38.

118 *After the revolution, Article 27*: Jorge Luis Ibarra Mendívil, *Propiedad agraria y sistema político en Mexico* (Mexico D.F.: Porrúa, 1989); Laura Randall, ed., *Reforming Mexico's Agrarian Reform* (London: Routledge, 1996).

118 *agrarian reform had begun to carve*: On agrarian reform processes and the *ejido* system, see Wayne A. Cornelius and David Myhre, eds., *The Transformation of Rural Mexico: Reforming the Ejido Sector* (San Diego: Center for US-Mexican Studies, 1998); Arnulfo Embriz and Laura Ruiz, *Archivo General Agrario: Guía*

General, Vols. 1–2 (Mexico D.F.: RAN and CIESAS, 1998); Ibarra, *Propiedad agraria*; Randall, *Reforming Mexico's Agrarian Reform*.

118 *Three hundred wealthy individuals*: Bartra, "Encuentros en la Sierra."

119 *Arturo Gámiz, a charismatic young teacher*: "39 años del asalto al cuartel de ciudad Madera," El Comité Primeros Vientos, Sept. 24, 2004, Madera1965.com.mx; Elizabeth Henson, personal communication.

120 *General Union of Mexican Peasants and Workers*: Bartra, "Encuentros en la Sierra"; Henson, "Madera 1965."

120 *most hallowed practices of nonviolent agrarian mobilization*: Henson, "Madera 1965"; Lugo, "Mi participación."

121 *Seven UGOCM activists died*: Bartra, "Encuentros en la Sierra."

122 *To all appearances, Mexico was a democracy*: On the Mexican political system and PRI rule during this period, see Hector Aguilar Camín and Lorenzo Meyer, *In the Shadow of the Mexican Revolution: Contemporary Mexican History, 1910–1989* (Austin: University of Texas Press, 1993); Paul Gillingham and Benjamin T. Smith, eds., *Dictablanda: Politics, Work, and Culture in Mexico, 1938–1968* (Durham, N.C.: Duke University Press, 2014); Fernando Herrera Calderón and Adela Cedillo, eds., *Challenging Authoritarianism in Mexico* (New York: Routledge, 2012); Gilbert Joseph and Jürgen Buchenau, *Mexico's Once and Future Revolution* (Durham, N.C.: Duke University Press, 2013); Tanalís Padilla, *Rural Resistance in the Land of Zapata: The Jaramillista Movement and the Myth of the Pax Priista* (Durham, N.C.: Duke University Press, 2008).

122 *"the Mexican miracle"*: On the so-called economic miracle and its rural discontents, see Aguilar Camín and Meyer, *In the Shadow of the Mexican Revolution*; Joseph and Buchenau, *Mexico's Once and Future Revolution*; Enrique C. Ochoa, *Feeding Mexico: The Political Uses of Food Since 1910* (Lanham, Md.: Rowman & Littlefield, 2001).

123 *the number of peasant land reform petitioners killed*: Bartra, "Encuentros en la Sierra"; Padilla, *Rural Resistance*.

123 *the army retaliated against land reform petitioners*: Bartra, "Encuentros en la Sierra."

11. MADERA

127 *Madera*: This chapter draws primarily on the author's interviews with Raúl Florencio Lugo, as well as Raúl Florencio Lugo, *El asalto al cuartel de Ciudad Madera* (Chapingo: Universidad Autónoma de Chapingo, 2006); Florencio Lugo and Francisco Ornelas, "Testimonios," *La Jornada del Campo* 96 (Sept. 19, 2015); and Raúl Florencio Lugo, "Así terminó aquella batalla," typed manuscript provided by the author (n.d.). Other key sources include Francisco Perez Arce Ibarra, "Querían tierra," *La Jornada del Campo* 96 (Sept. 19, 2015); Elizabeth Henson, "Madera 1965: Primeros Vientos," in *Challenging Authoritarianism in Mexico*, ed. Fernando Herrera Calderón and Adela Cedillo (New York: Routledge, 2012); Miguel Méndez García, "50 Aniversario de asalto al cuartel militar de Madera," *El Diario de Nuevo Casas Grandes*, Sept. 23, 2015; Jesus Vargas, "Madera Rebelde," *La Jornada del Campo* 96 (Sept. 19, 2015); Rubén Villalpando, "Falleció el guerrillero Salvador Gaytán," *La Jornada*, April 24, 2011. Elizabeth Henson generously provided additional background and crucial feedback.

128 *heard rumors that most of the soldiers in the barracks would leave*: Vargas, "Madera rebelde."

128 *With seven thousand inhabitants*: *VIII Censo General de Población, Estado de Chiapas, 1960* (Mexico DF: Secretaría de Industría y Comercio, 1963), 88. The remainder of this section is drawn from Vargas, "Madera rebelde," and Henson, "Madera 1965."

130 *Black clouds of smoke*: An iconic image of the attack can be found at Colloqui.org: http://www.colloqui.org/colloqui/2015/9/22/50-aniversario-del-asalto-al-cuartel-madera.

132 *"They were fighting for soil"*: Quoted in Perez Arce, "Querían tierra."

132 *Díaz Ordaz immediately decreed*: On post-Madera land redistribution, see Henson, "Madera 1965," 19.

132 *it did inspire groups across the country*: Fernando Herrera Calderón and Adela Cedillo, "The Unknown Mexican Dirty War," in Calderón and Cedillo, *Challenging Authoritarianism in Mexico*; Rosa Albina Garavito Elías, "El poder simbólico del asalto al cuartel madera," *La Jornada del Campo* 96 (Sept. 19, 2015); Jesús Zamora García, "Revisión histórica de la guerrilla en Guadalajara: Las fuerzas revolucionarias armadas del pueblo (1972–1982)" (Ph.D. diss, CIESAS, 2014).

132 *a group of urban guerrillas*: Zamora, "Revisión histórica," 244.

12. EXILE AND BELONGING

139 *"One Thousand and One Nights style"*: Author's interview with Keoki Skinner; Zoyada Gallegos, "Amado Carillo edificó su casa de las mil y una noches," *El Universal*, Sept. 12, 2011; "Narquitectura: Los palacios fortificados de los capos del narcotráfico en México," Marcianosmx.com, n.d., accessed June 22, 2018, https://marcianosmx.com/narquitectura-los-palacios-fortificados-de-los-capos-del-narcotrafico-en-mexico/.

140 *Luis Pericles Drabos*: Interview with residents speaking on the condition of anonymity.

13. LA ROCA

146 *subject to expedited removal*: *A Primer on Expedited Removal*, American Immigration Council, Feb. 3, 2017, https://www.americanimmigrationcouncil.org/research/primer-expedited-removal; David G. Savage, "Trump's Fast-Track Deportations Face a Legal Hurdle: Do Unauthorized Immigrants Have a Right to a Hearing Before a Judge?," *Los Angeles Times*, July 12, 2017; Catherine E. Shoichet, "Can Immigrants Be Deported Without a Court Hearing?," CNN.com, March 3, 2017, https://www.cnn.com/2017/03/03/politics/deportations-without-court-hearings/index.html.

146 *severe criminal penalties*: *A Primer on Expedited Removal*; *What to Do if You Are in Expedited Removal or Reinstatement of Removal*, Florence Immigrant and Refugee Rights Project (2002), http://firrp.org/media/ExpeditedReinstatement-en.pdf.

146 *act of fraud*: "False Claim to U.S. Citizenship," in U.S. Citizenship and Immigration Services, *USCIS Policy Manual*, vol. 8, part K (Washington, D.C.: USCIS, 2018).

15. THE BLACK PALACE

159 *The Black Palace*: This chapter draws primarily on the author's interviews with Raúl Florencio Lugo, as well as Raúl Florencio Lugo, *Del cuartel a Lecumberri* (Salaices: Asociación de Egresados de la Escuela Normal Rural de Salaices and El Colegio de Egresados de Aguilera A.C., 2005).

160 *Lecumberri prison, the Black Palace*: See Edmundo Arturo Figueroa Viruega and Minerva Rodríguez Licea, "La penitenciaría de Lecumberri en la Ciudad de México," *Revista de Historia de las Prisiones* 5 (July–Dec. 2017): 98–119; Alberto Ulloa Bornemann, *Surviving Mexico's Dirty War: A Political Prisoner's Memoir* (Philadelphia: Temple University Press, 2007). Arturo Ripstein's 1977 documentary, *Lecumberri: El palacio negro*, offers a tremendous inside view of the prison, including O-West, around the time of Raúl's confinement.

163 *"Fully convinced that I had to keep struggling"*: Raúl Florencio Lugo, *El asalto al cuartel de Ciudad Madera* (Chapingo: Universidad Autónoma de Chapingo, 2006), 101.

164 *"In this study," he began*: Raúl Florencio Lugo, *Salud y belleza a través del yoga* (Mexico D.F.: Siglos, 1976), 15.

16. TRAUMA RED

169 *Earlier that summer, cartel hit men*: "Authorities in Mexico Probe Recent Deaths," *Douglas Dispatch*, Aug. 9, 2008; Jonathan Clark, "20 Dead Following Shootout in Sonora: Four Police Officers Killed Wednesday," *Douglas Dispatch*, May 18, 2007; "Drug-Cartel Bloodshed Puts Sonoran Residents on Edge," *Tucson Citizen*, Sept. 8, 2008; Michel Marizco, "La fuga de Agua Prieta," Borderreporter .com, July 14, 2008, http://borderreporter.com/2008/07/la-fuga-de-agua-prieta/; Juan Carlos Ruiz Olvera, "Ejecutan a policía municipal en Agua Prieta," *Dossier Político*, June 26, 2008, http://www.dossierpolitico.com/vernoticiasanteriores.php ?artid=38803&relacion=dossierpolit; Xavier Zaragoza, "Agua Prieta Police Chief Killed, Shot Three Times," *Douglas Dispatch*, Feb. 27, 2007; Xavier Zaragoza, "Former Naco Police Chief, Brother of Slain AP Chief, Arrested for Smuggling Pot," *Douglas Dispatch*, March 3, 2007.

169 *they probably wouldn't have taken Aida's case seriously*: On police ignoring reports of violence against women in Mexico, see Liliana Alcántara, "CNDH ve impunidad en 99% de delitos," *El Universal*, Dec. 15, 2008; Observatorio Ciudadano Nacional del Feminicidio, *Informe cualitativo y cuantitativo: Avances y retrocesos en la protección de las mujeres, víctimas de violencia familiar* (Mexico D.F.: Católicas por el Derecho de Decidir AC, 2015); Adrian Ortiz Ortega, "Women's Sexualities, Sexual Rights, and Violence in Mexico," in *The Essential Handbook of Women's Sexuality*, ed. Donna Marie Castañeda (Santa Barbara, Calif.: Praeger, 2013).

169 *Attitudes toward violence against women*: Mexico has one of the highest rates of violence against women in the world. One of the most important studies on the topic found that three out of five women had experienced violence in the previous year. (Florinda Riquer Fernandez and Roberto Castro, *Estudio nacional sobre las fuentes, orígenes, y factores que producen y reproducen la violencia contra las mujeres* (Mexico D.F.: Comisión Nacional para Prevenir y Erradicar la Violencia Contra las Mujeres, 2012), 5. Other studies confirm the magnitude of the prob-

lem, including "Estadísticas a propósito del Día Internacional de la Eliminación de la Violencia contra la Mujer," Instituto Nacional de Estadísticas y Geografía (INEGI), Nov. 23, 2015; "Women's Struggle for Justice and Safety: Violence in the Family in Mexico," Amnesty International, Aug. 1, 2008, 16, https://www.amnesty.org/en/documents/AMR41/021/2008/en/. For short English-language discussions of this topic, see Rosa-Linda Fregoso, "Coming to Grips with Feminicide," Truthout.org, Jan. 13, 2012, https://truthout.org/articles/coming-to-grips-with-feminicide/#6; *The World's Women 2010: Trends and Statistics* (New York: United Nations, 2010), 131–32, https://unstats.un.org/unsd/demographic-social/products/worldswomen/ww2010pub.cshtml; "Conflict Profile: Mexico," Women's Media Center, n.d., accessed June 21, 2018, https://www.womensmediacenter.com/women-under-siege/conflicts/mexico. This violence is not a timeless feature of Mexican culture. In fact, levels of violence against women had been declining in the 1980s. Scholars and activists have pointed to globalization and the so-called war on drugs as key factors in skyrocketing rates of violence after that. Riquer and Castro, *Estudio nacional*, 34; Renee Lewis, "Violence Against Women Soars in Mexico," *Al Jazeera America*, Nov. 25, 2014; Girish Gupta, "Mexico's Disappeared Women," *New Statesman*, Feb. 17, 2011; Alicia R. Schmidt Camacho, "Ciudadana X: Gender Violence and the Denationalization of Women's Rights in Ciudad Juárez, Mexico," *CR: The New Centennial Review* 5, no. 1 (2005), 255–92; Kathleen Staudt and Zulma Y. Méndez, *Courage, Resistance, and Women in Ciudad Juárez: Challenges to Militarization* (Austin: University of Texas Press, 2015); Melissa W. Wright, "Necropolitics, Narcopolitics, and Femicide: Gendered Violence on the Mexico-US Border," *Signs* 36, no. 3 (2011): 707–31; Katrina Pantaleo, "Gendered Violence: An Analysis of the Maquiladora Murders," *International Criminal Justice Review* 20, no. 4 (2010): 349–64; Melissa Wright, "Public Women, Profit, and Femicide in Northern Mexico," *South Atlantic Quarterly* 104, no. 5 (2006): 681–98.

169 *"Public women"—the kinds of women*: Wright, "Necropolitics" and "Public Women."

169 *Mexico's federal legislature*: Observatorio Ciudadano Nacional del Feminicidio, *Órdenes de protección en México* (Mexico D.F.: Católicas por el Derecho de Decidir AC, 2013), 21, 80, 147. Based on a review of 58,000 cases.

17. LUCKY EMA

179 *Lucky Ema*: This chapter is primarily based on interviews with Ema Ponce, along with cross-check interviews with Ane Barragán and Leticia Rojas, leaders of the Causana Foundation during the period covered here. Other sources are indicated below. See "About This Book" for more information on research methods and Ema's story.

183 *decriminalized same-sex relationships*: Patricio Benalcázar Alarcón, "Noviembre, 20 años de despenalización de la homosexualidad en el Ecuador," *El Telégrafo*, Nov. 14, 2017; Judith Salgado, "Análisis de la interpretación de inconstitucionalidad de la penalización de la homosexualidad en el Ecuador," *Aportes Andinos: Revista de Derechos Humanos* 11 (Oct. 2004), http://hdl.handle.net/10644/679. It is worth noting that even the Ecuadorian Constitutional Tribunal's decriminalization of same-sex relationships was rife with homophobia.

187 *inaugurated an informal soccer program*: For academic studies of the team, see Karla Sofía Ayora Jara, "Reportaje multimedia acerca del análisis de las percepciones sociales del fútbol femenino a partir del estudio de caso: Club deportivo femenino Guipuzcoa" (bachelor's thesis, Universidad de las Américas, 2013); Leticia Alexandra Rojas Miranda, "Grupos de fútbol parroquiales y la politicazación de lo lésbico en Quito" (master's thesis, FLASCO, 2010).

187 *League officials harassed them*: Rojas Miranda, "Grupos de fútbol parroquiales y la politicazación de lo lésbico en Quito"; "Equipo de futbol lésbico expulsado por beso gana acción judicial en Ecuador," *El Universo*, Sept. 16, 2010.

187 *the tribunal concluded*: Quoted in Salgado, "Análisis," 6.

18. ALL THE MONSTERS AT ONCE

189 *All the Monsters at Once*: The sources on PTSD and CPTSD consulted for this chapter include Christine A. Coatis and Julian D. Ford, eds., *Treating Complex Traumatic Stress Disorders: An Evidence-Based Guide* (New York: Guilford, 2009); "Conversations with History: Judith L. Herman," University of California Television, Feb. 7, 2008, https://www.youtube.com/watch?reload=9&v=USTK mffoQms; *Diagnostic and Statistical Manual of Mental Disorders: DSM-III, DSM-III-R, and DSM-IV* (Arlington, Va.: American Psychiatric Association, 1980, 1987, 1994); George S. Everly and Jeffrey M. Lating, *A Clinical Guide to the Treatment of the Human Stress Response* (London: Springer, 2013), chap. 21; Matthew J. Friedman, "PTSD History and Overview," U.S. Department of Veterans Affairs, National Center for PTSD, accessed June 20, 2018, https://www .ptsd.va.gov/professional/ptsd-overview/ptsd-overview.asp; Judith L. Herman, *Trauma and Recovery: The Aftermath of Violence—from Domestic Abuse to Political Terror* (New York: Basic Books, 2015); Austin Sarat, Nadav Davidovitch, and Michal Alberstein, eds., *Trauma and Memory: Reading, Healing, and Making Law* (Stanford, Calif.: Stanford University Press, 2007); "Complex PTSD," U.S. Department of Veterans Affairs, National Center for PTSD, n.d., accessed June 20, 2018, https://www.ptsd.va.gov/professional/PTSD-overview/complex -ptsd.asp; Sarah Willen, "'Illegality,' Mass Deportation, and the Threat of Violent Arrest: Structural Violence and Social Suffering in the Lives of Undocumented Migrant Workers in Israel," in Sarat, Davidovitch, and Alberstein, *Trauma and Memory*; Mary Beth Williams and John F. Sommer Jr., eds., *Simple and Complex Post-traumatic Stress Disorder: Strategies for Comprehensive Treatment in Clinical Practice* (New York: Haworth Press, 2002).

198 *Two hundred and two migrants had died*: *Southwest Border Sectors: Southwest Border Deaths by Fiscal Year*, U.S. Customs and Border Protection, U.S. Border Patrol (2017), https://www.cbp.gov/newsroom/media-resources/stats.

19. THE HEALER

204 *"leaving your husband without a court order"*: The Mexican law that, under some circumstances, punishes women who flee the home is *abandono de hogar*. U.S. domestic violence survivor advocates report that it is not uncommon for Mexican immigrant women to fear that this law exists in the United States. Gaudalupe T. Vidales, "Arrested Justice: The Multifaceted Plight of Immigrant Latinas Who Faced Domestic Violence," *Journal of Family Violence* 25, no. 6 (2010): 539.

20. LEAVING THE WORLD AND FIGHTING TO REJOIN IT

210 *In 1980, the American Psychiatric Association*: Dr. Judith Herman proposed complex PTSD (CPTSD) as a diagnosis in 1992. The *DSM*'s editors have, thus far, declined to create a separate category for it. This has not stopped caregivers and patients from taking up the banner of CPTSD as a way to make sense of their experiences. CPTSD may involve conditions such as fugue states, unexplainable chronic pain, obsessive-compulsive behavior, reckless impulsivity, phobias, detachment from one's identity, and severe mood swings. The sources on PTSD and CPTSD consulted for this chapter include Christine A. Coatis and Julian D. Ford, eds., *Treating Complex Traumatic Stress Disorders: An Evidence-Based Guide* (New York: Guilford, 2009); "Conversations with History: Judith L. Herman," University of California Television, Feb. 7, 2008, https://www.youtube.com /watch?reload=9&v=USTKmffoQms; *Diagnostic and Statistical Manual of Mental Disorders: DSM-III, DSM-III-R, and DSM-IV* (Arlington, Va.: American Psychiatric Association, 1980, 1987, 1994); George S. Everly and Jeffrey M. Lating, *A Clinical Guide to the Treatment of the Human Stress Response* (London: Springer, 2013), chap. 21; Matthew J. Friedman, "PTSD History and Overview," U.S. Department of Veterans Affairs, National Center for PTSD, accessed June 20, 2018, https://www.ptsd.va.gov/professional/ptsd-overview/ptsd-overview.asp; Judith L. Herman, *Trauma and Recovery: The Aftermath of Violence—from Domestic Abuse to Political Terror* (New York: Basic Books, 2015); Austin Sarat, Nadav Davidovitch, and Michal Alberstein, eds., *Trauma and Memory: Reading, Healing, and Making Law* (Stanford, Calif.: Stanford University Press, 2007); "Complex PTSD," U.S. Department of Veterans Affairs, National Center for PTSD, n.d., accessed June 20, 2018, https://www.ptsd.va.gov/professional/PTSD -overview/complex-ptsd.asp; Sarah Willen, "'Illegality,' Mass Deportation, and the Threat of Violent Arrest: Structural Violence and Social Suffering in the Lives of Undocumented Migrant Workers in Israel," in Sarat, Davidovitch, and Alberstein, *Trauma and Memory*; Mary Beth Williams and John F. Sommer Jr., eds., *Simple and Complex Post-traumatic Stress Disorder: Strategies for Comprehensive Treatment in Clinical Practice* (New York: Haworth Press, 2002).

213 *noted sociologist Kai Erikson*: Kai Erikson, *A New Species of Trouble: The Human Experience of Modern Disasters* (New York: W. W. Norton, 1994), 233–37.

214 *"new immigration battleground"*: Carol Morello, "Living in Fear on the Border: Little Desert Town Is New Immigration Battleground," *USA Today*, July 21, 1999.

214 *redevelopment of downtown*: Author's interviews and *Draft Downtown Douglas Revitalization Plan* (Douglas: City of Douglas, 2011), https://douglasaz.org/pdf /Administration/2014/FINAL%20AECOM%20PLAN%20(2).pdf.

214 *unemployment rates hovered over 10 percent*: *City Unemployment Report, 2009–2015*, Arizona Unemployment Statistics Program, n.d., accessed June 20, 2018, https:// laborstats.az.gov/sites/default/files/documents/files/pr-laus-04cit-09to14-nsa .pdf.

214 *Real household median income*: Calculated from 1980 U.S. Census data tables accessed through IPUMS NHGIS, University of Minnesota, https://www.nhgis .org, and "Median Income in the Past 12 Months," U.S. Census Bureau, American Community Survey, 2006–2010, generated using American FactFinder,

http://factfinder2.census.gov. Inflation adjustments made using https://data.bls
.gov/cgi-bin/cpicalc.pl.

214 *A third of Douglas households earned*: Calculated from "Poverty Status in the Past 12
Months of Families by Household Type by Numbers of Workers in Family," U.S.
Census Bureau, American Community Survey, 2006–2010, generated using
American FactFinder, http://factfinder2.census.gov.

215 *paid a median wage of around fourteen thousand dollars*: Calculated from "Occupa-
tion by Sex and Median Earnings in the Past 12 Months," U.S. Census Bureau,
American Community Survey, 2006–2010, generated using American Fact-
Finder, http://factfinder2.census.gov, and "2009 HHS Poverty Guidelines," U.S.
Department of Health and Human Services (2009), https://aspe.hhs.gov/2009
-hhs-poverty-guidelines.

215 *federal public benefits*: Tanya Border, Avideh Moussavian, and Jonathan Blazer,
"Overview of Immigrant Eligibility for Federal Programs," National Immigration Law Center, Dec. 2015, https://www.nilc.org/issues/economic-support
/overview-immeligfedprograms/.

215 *Rumors of his whereabouts*: Court records and news reports confirm these
rumors.

215 *On aggregate, the children of poor parents*: For a discussion of research on this topic,
see Matt O'Brien, "Poor Kids Who Do Everything Right Don't Do Better Than
Rich Kids Who Do Everything Wrong," *Wonkblog* (blog), *Washington Post*,
Oct. 18, 2014, https://www.washingtonpost.com/news/wonk/wp/2014/10/18
/poor-kids-who-do-everything-right-dont-do-better-than-rich-kids-who-do
-everything-wrong/?utm_term=.d4212cdccfd8.

21. THE "SHOW ME YOUR PAPERS" STATE

220 *Robert Krentz lay sprawled*: This section draws on two extended interviews with
Wendy Glenn; Randal Archibold, "Ranchers Alarmed by Killing near Border,"
New York Times, April 4, 2010; "Robert N. Krentz, Jr., June 3, 1951–March 27,
2010," *Douglas Dispatch*, March 30, 2010; Natalie Lakosil, "Releasee of Reports
Provides Detail, but Little New Information on Krentz Death," *Douglas Dispatch*,
June 17, 2010; Shar Porier, "Krentz Described as a Humanitarian," *Douglas Dis-
patch*, March 31, 2010; Bruce Whetten, "Sheriff's Office Continues Search for
Killer of Area Rancher," *Douglas Dispatch*, March 29, 2010; Bruce Whetten,
"Rancher Shot," *Douglas Dispatch*, March 31, 2010.

221 *a Border Patrol agent shot*: Brady McCombs, "AZ Border Agent Cleared in Fatal
Shooting," *Arizona Daily Star*, March 9, 2010.

221 *Brewer looked to balance the budget*: David R. Berman and Kristin Borns, "Bud-
geting in Arizona: Hard Decisions for Hard Times," Western Political Science
Annual Meeting (2010), http://gardner.utah.edu/_documents/westernstatesbudgets
/wpsa-10/arizona-2010.pdf; Howard Fischer, "Brewer's Cuts Impact Schools,
AHCCCS, and More," *Douglas Dispatch*, Jan. 20, 2010; Tim Gaynor, "Transplant
Patients a Target of Arizona Budget Cuts," Reuters News Service, March 5,
2010; Alia Beard Rau, "Needy Arizona Children to Lose Health Care, Medicine
Coverage," *Arizona Republic*, March 20, 2010.

221 *Douglas's city council began the year*: "Agenda with Actions Taken, Regular Meeting," Mayor and Council, City of Douglas, Jan. 13, 2010.

221 *harshest state-level statutes*: Randal C. Archibold, "Arizona Enacts Stringent Law on Immigration," *New York Times*, April 23, 2010.

221 *Maricopa County, home to Phoenix*: Jill Williams and Geoffrey Alan Boyce, "Fear and Loathing and the Everyday Geopolitics of Encounter in the Arizona Borderlands," *Geopolitics* 18, no. 4 (2013): 895–916.

221 *hate crimes had increased*: Ibid., 910.

221 *S.B. 1070 promised to make it*: Randal C. Archibold, "Judge Blocks Arizona's Immigration Law," *New York Times*, July 28, 2010; James Orlando, "Summary of Arizona Immigration Legislation and Legislation in Other States," Connecticut General Assembly, Office of Legislative Research Report, May 14, 2010, https://www.cga.ct.gov/2010/rpt/2010-R-0213.htm; "Text of SB 1070—Arizona Illegal Immigration Law," *Tucson Sentinel*, April 29, 2010, http://www.tucsonsentinel.com/local/report/042910_1070_text/text-sb-1070-arizona-illegal-immigration-law/.

221 *"Show Me Your Papers Law"*: For example, see Raf Sanchez, "Arizona Judge Clears Path for 'Show Me Your Papers' Immigration Law," *Telegraph*, Sept. 6, 2012.

221 *Arizona police chiefs*: Spencer Hsu, "U.S. Police Chiefs Say Arizona Immigration Law Will Increase Crime," *Washington Post*, May 27, 2010; "Interview with Clarence Dupnik," KGUN-TV 9, April 7, 2010, https://www.youtube.com/watch?v=dH1E5uCmIT4.

222 *"drives a wedge between us"*: Alan Greenblatt, "Arizona Immigration Law Is a Challenge for Police," NPR.org, July 28, 2010, https://www.npr.org/templates/story/story.php?storyId=128820774.

222 *Mass protests spread across*: Nicholas Riccardi, "Thousands in Phoenix Protest Arizona's Immigration Law," *Los Angeles Times*, May 29, 2010.

222 *Governor Brewer used the occasion to lambast*: "Governor Jan Brewer Calls on Feds to Immediately Approve Troop Increase on Arizona Border," press release, March 29, 2010, archived at https://votesmart.org/public-statement/495957/governor-jan-brewer-calls-on-feds-to-immediately-approve-troop-increase-on-arizona-border; Muzaffar Chishti and Claire Bergeron, "Political Considerations Surround Decision to Deploy National Guard to Southwest Border," Migration Policy Institute, Policy Beat, June 15, 2010, https://www.migrationpolicy.org/article/political-considerations-surround-decision-deploy-national-guard-southwest-border.

222 *The "migrant hunter" Roger Barnett*: William LaJeunesse, "Illegal Immigrant Suspected in Death of Rancher," FoxNews.com, March 30, 2010, http://www.foxnews.com/us/2010/03/30/illegal-immigrant-suspected-murder-arizona-rancher.html.

222 *On March 31, Congresswoman Gabrielle Giffords*: Photographs and descriptions of the event: "Border Security Fact or Fiction? More Boots on the Border Now Than Ever Before! Some Call for Militia, Marshall [sic] Law to Stop the Invasion!," *Southwest Photo Journal*, Oct. 11, 2012, https://southwestphotojournal.com/2012/10/11/; Leo W. Banks, "Our Lawless Mexican Border," *Wall Street Journal*, April 9, 2010.

222 *one-quarter of a murder a year*: In the Douglas Police Department jurisdiction. "Crime Reported by Douglas Police Dept, Arizona, 1985–2014," Federal Bureau of Investigations, Uniform Crime Reporting Statistics, table generated using www.ucrdatatool.gov/.

222 *one of seven reported*: Cochise County Criminal Justice Data Profile, Arizona Criminal Justice Commission (2014), http://www.azcjc.gov/sites/default/files /pubs/Cochise_County_Profile.pdf, 12.

222 *violent crime rates in Arizona border towns*: Jack Gillum, "Arizona Border Cities Tout Lowest Crime Rates in State," *USA Today*, July 18, 2011.

222 *undocumented immigrants committed fewer crimes*: Reviews of research on this issue include Chris Nichols, "Mostly True: Undocumented Immigrants Less Likely to Commit Crimes Than U.S. Citizens," Politifact: Fact-Checking U.S. Politics, Aug. 3, 2017, http://www.politifact.com/california/statements/2017/aug/03/antonio -villaraigosa/mostly-true-undocumented-immigrants-less-likely-co/; Alex Now-rasteh, "Immigration and Crime: What the Research Says," CATO Institute, July 14, 2014, https://www.cato.org/blog/immigration-crime-what-research-says; Jane C. Timm, "Fact Check: No Evidence Undocumented Immigrants Commit More Crimes," NBCNews.com, June 28, 2017, https://www.nbcnews.com/politics /white-house/fact-check-no-evidence-undocumented-immigrants-commit-more -crimes-n777856. See also Graham C. Ousey and Charis E. Kubrin, "Immigration and Crime: Assessing a Contentious Issue," *Annual Review of Criminology* 1, no. 1 (June 2017): 63–84; Walter A. Ewing, Daniel E Martínez, and Rubén G. Rumbaut, "The Criminalization of Immigration in the United States," American Immigration Council, July 2015, https://www.americanimmigrationcouncil.org/research /criminalization-immigration-united-states.

223 *Giffords called for the deployment*: Shar Porier, "Time to 'Listen to Us': Giffords Meets with Ranchers About Safety Following Death of Robert Krentz," *Douglas Dispatch*, April 7, 2010.

223 *The Krentz family issued*: "Statement from the Krentz Family," *Douglas Dispatch*, April 7, 2010.

223 *promoting a security plan*: "Ranchers Take Message to Legislators," *Douglas Dispatch*, April 14, 2010.

223 *Pearce had tried and failed*: Williams and Boyce, "Fear and Loathing."

223 *Janet Napolitano, Arizona's former*: Shar Porier, "Napolitano Cites Actions Since Death of Robert Krentz," *Douglas Dispatch*, April 21, 2010.

223 *National Guard soldiers reached*: Chishti and Bergeron, "Political Considerations."

223 *Ranchers like John Ladd*: Author's interview with John Ladd and Wendy Glenn.

224 *Public outcry over the rancher's murder*: Williams and Boyce, "Fear and Loathing."

224 *received a bump in popularity*: Sean Alfano, "Arizona Immigration Law SB 1070 May Have Been Weakened, but Governor Jan Brewer Strong as Ever," *New York Daily News*, July 29, 2010; Terry Greene Sterling, "Jan Brewer, Arizona Gov., Meets with Obama," *Daily Beast*, June 3, 2010, https://www.thedailybeast.com /jan-brewer-arizona-gov-meets-with-obama.

224 *Russell Pearce, the Arizona state senator*: Luige del Puerto, "Immigration Hawk Pearce Elected President of Arizona Senate," *Arizona Capitol Times*, Nov. 3, 2010.

224 *Kobach would go on to play*: Suzy Khimm, "Kris Kobach, Nativist Son," *Mother Jones*, March/April 2012.

224 *preliminary injunction blocking the most*: Archibold, "Judge Blocks Arizona's Im-migration Law."

224 *Only 15 percent of Latinos in Arizona*: Eileen Diaz McConnell, "Latinos in Ari-zona: Demographic Context in the SB 1070 Era," in *Latino Politics and Arizona's*

Immigration Law SB 1070, ed. Lisa Magaña and Erik Lee (New York: Springer, 2013), 13.

224 *May 12 Douglas City Council meeting*: Author's interviews; "Special Meeting Agenda with Actions Taken," Mayor and Council, City of Douglas, May 12, 2010; Larry Blasky, "City Blasted for Not Opposing SB 1070," *Douglas Dispatch*, May 19, 2010.

224 *two hundred people marched*: Author's interviews; Jonathan Shacat, "Two-Hour Event Features Speakers," *Douglas Dispatch*, May 19, 2010.

225 *Douglas's city attorney released*: Blasky, "City Blasted."

225 *S.B. 1070* forced *local jurisdictions*: Orlando, "Summary of Arizona Immigration Legislation."

225 *Under the new law*: "Text of SB 1070-Arizona Illegal Immigration Law."

226 *Mayor Michael Gomez, by his account*: Author's interview with Michael Gomez, Ginny Jordan, and Del Cabarga.

226 *the council voted 5–1*: "Agenda with Actions Taken," Mayor and Council, City of Douglas, May 19, 2010.

226 *At the next scheduled city council meeting*: Author's interviews; "Agenda with Actions Taken," Mayor and Council, City of Douglas, June 9, 2010.

227 *a petition supporting their cause*: Author's interviews with Ginny Jordan.

227 *They arrived early and sat*: Author's interviews; "July 6 Special Meeting Minutes," Mayor and Council, City of Douglas, July 6, 2010; Natalie D. Lakosil, "City Votes Against Safe Border Resolution, Again," *Douglas Dispatch*, July 14, 2010.

227 *campaign to recall the mayor*: "Michael Gomez Recall, Douglas, Arizona," Ballotpedia.org, n.d., accessed June 20, 2018, https://ballotpedia.org/Michael _Gomez_recall,_Douglas,_Arizona_(2011); Larry Blaskey, "Recall May Be Called Off Due to Invalid Petitions," *Douglas Dispatch*, Jan. 5, 2011; "Douglas Mayor Not Seeking Re-election," Tucson News NOW-KOLD, Jan. 17, 2012, http:// www.tucsonnewsnow.com/story/16541673/douglas-mayor-not-s.

227 *Danny Ortega, the city's next mayor*: Author's interviews.

228 *Alberto Melis had already begun*: Author's interviews with Mark Adams and Rosie Mendoza.

228 *less likely to report crimes*: Nik Theodore, *Insecure Communities: Latino Perceptions of Police Involvement in Immigration Enforcement*, University of Illinois at Chicago, Lake Research Partners, PolicyLink, May 2013, http://www.policylink .org/sites/default/files/INSECURE_COMMUNITIES_REPORT_FINAL .PDF; *Police Chiefs Guide to Immigration Issues*, International Association of Chiefs of Police (2007), http://www.theiacp.org/Portals/0/pdfs/Publications /PoliceChiefsGuidetoImmigration.pdf.

23. SLIPKNOT

237 *The previous day's* Douglas Dispatch: Bruce Whetten, "Douglas Brings in Quiet New Year," *Douglas Dispatch*, Jan. 4, 2012; "Douglas Population Drops as Does Cochise County," *Douglas Dispatch*, Jan. 4, 2012; Jason DeParle, "Harder for Americans to Rise from Lower Rungs," *New York Times*, Jan. 4, 2012.

239 *"Dead Memories" by Slipknot*: Released on the album *All Hope Is Gone* (Roadrunner, 2008).

239 *The U.S. legal system*: Regardless of its devastating life consequences, even when it amounts to exile for life from one's home—even when it delivers deportees into unsafe conditions in another country—deportation is not considered punishment under the law. As such, people in deportation proceedings do not receive many of the legal protections granted to criminal defendants. For reviews of this mismatch between legal procedures and real-world consequences, see Peter L. Markowitz, "Deportation Is Different," *University of Pennsylvania Journal of Constitutional Law* 13 (2011): 1299–361. This extends to the legal framing of immigration detention as well: César Cuauhtémoc García Hernández, "Immigration Detention as Punishment," *UCLA Law Review* 61 (2014): 1346–414.

240 *U.S. law required the supervisor*: "Credible Fear FAQ," U.S. Citizenship and Immigration Services, n.d., accessed June 5, 2018, https://www.uscis.gov/faq-page /credible-fear-faq.

241 *agents often failed to follow the law*: Joshua Partlow, "Rights Groups Sue U.S. Government, Alleging It Is Turning Away Asylum Applicants at Mexico Border," *Washington Post*, July 12, 2017; "You Don't Have Rights Here: U.S. Border Screening and Returns of Central Americans to Risk of Serious Harm," Human Rights Watch, Oct. 16, 2014, https://www.hrw.org/report/2014/10/16/you-dont-have -rights-here/us-border-screening-and-returns-central-americans-risk.

24. EMA'S JOURNEY

246 *Guipuzcoa sued and won a partial victory*: Ema's memories accord with published accounts of the team's history. See Pamela Juliana Aguirre Castro, Dayana Avila Benavidez, and Vladimir Bazante Pita, eds., *Rendición de cuentas del proceso de selección, 2008–2013: Corte Constitucional del Ecuador* (Quito: Corte Constitucional del Ecuador), 258–60; Karla Sofía Ayora Jara, "Reportaje multimedia acerca del análisis de las percepciones sociales del fútbol femenino a partir del estudio de caso: Club deportivo femenino Guipuzcoa" (bachelor's thesis, Universidad de las Américas, 2013); "Defensoría del Pueblo presenta acciones de protección en defensa al derecho a la no discriminación," Defensoría del Pueblo de Ecuador, press release no. 34, Feb. 9, 2012, http://repositorio.dpe.gob.ec/bitstream/39000 /286/1/Boletín%20034%20%28No%20discriminación%29.pdf; "Equipo de futbol lesbio expulsado por beso gana acción judicial en Ecuador," *El Universo*, Sept. 16, 2010; "El Juez dio la razón al equipo lésbico," *El Comercio*, Sept. 16, 2010; Ramiro Rivadeneira Silva, "Sentencia-acción de protección 572–2010," Defensoría del Pueblo de Ecuador, n.d., accessed June 2, 2018, http://repositorio.dpe.gob.ec /bitstream/39000/747/1/SS-001-DPE-2011.pdf; Leticia Alexandra Rojas Miranda, "Grupos de fútbol parroquiales y la politicazación de lo lésbico en Quito" (master's thesis, FLASCO, 2010), chap. 3.

247 *The country's new constitution*: *Constitución de la República del Ecuador 2008*, https:// www.oas.org/juridico/pdfs/mesicic4_ecu_const.pdf.

247 *Around 550,000 Ecuadorians lived*: The 2010 U.S. Census counted 553,919 people of Ecuadorian descent in the United States, including 309,800 living in the New York metro region. "Allocation of Hispanic or Latino Origin, Population: Ecuadorian, New York–Northern New Jersey–Long Island Metro Area," U.S. Census Bureau, 2010 Census, Summary File 2, generated using American FactFinder, http://factfinder2.census.gov.

247 *about a third of them undocumented*: A rough estimate based on "Ecuadorians in the United States, 1980–2008," Graduate Center, City University of New York, Center for Latin American, Caribbean & Latino Studies, Latino Data Project, April 2011, Report 40, 8.

247 *Ema and Juana boarded an airline flight*: On the difficulties of Ecuadorian migration through Central America and Mexico around this time period, see Nancy Ann Hiemstra, "The View from Ecuador: Security, Insecurity, and Chaotic Geographies of U.S. Migrant Detention and Deportation" (Ph.D. diss., Syracuse University, 2011).

247 *massacre of seventy-two South and Central American*: For an English-language discussion of this incident, see Gary Moore, "Unravelling Mysteries of Mexico's San Fernando Massacre," *InSight Crime*, Sept. 19, 2011, https://www.insightcrime.org/investigations/unravelling-mysteries-of-mexicos-san-fernando-massacre/.

247 *Accounts of more mundane extortion*: *Human Rights of Migrants and Other Persons in the Context of Human Mobility in Mexico*, Inter-American Commission on Human Rights (2013), http://www.oas.org/en/iachr/migrants/docs/pdf/report-migrants-mexico-2013.pdf; *Invisible Victims: Migrants on the Move in Mexico*, Amnesty International (2010), https://www.amnestyusa.org/reports/invisible-victims-migrants-on-the-move-in-mexico/; Adam Isacson, Maureen Meyer, and Gabriela Morales, *Mexico's Other Border: Security, Migration, and the Humanitarian Crisis at the Line with Central America* (Washington, D.C.: Washington Office on Latin America, 2014), https://www.wola.org/sites/default/files/Mexico%27s%20Other%20Border%20PDF.pdf.

252 *On average, two hundred Guatemalan migrants*: *Perfil migratorio de Guatemala, 2012*, Organización Internacional para las Migraciones (2012), http://publications.iom.int/system/files/pdf/mpguatemala_11july2013.pdf, 21.

252 *Debt burdens crushed both groups*: For two excellent studies of this phenomenon, see Richard L. Johnson and Murphy Woodhouse, "Securing the Return: How Enhanced US Border Enforcement Fuels Cycles of Debt Migration," *Antipode*, published online Feb. 2018, https://onlinelibrary.wiley.com/doi/pdf/10.1111/anti.12386; and Diane L. Rus and Jan Rus, "Trapped Behind the Lines: The Impact of Undocumented Migration, Debt, and Recession on a Tsotsil Community of Chiapas, Mexico, 2002–2012," *Latin American Perspectives* 41, no. 3 (April 2014): 154–77.

253 *Mexico had militarized* its *southern border*: Isacson, Meyer, and Morales, *Mexico's Other Border*.

253 *into a "vertical border"*: Sources used for reference while writing this section include Xiomara Chávez-Suárez, "Immigration Policy Responses to Transmigrants in Mexico," *Cornell Policy Review* 3, no. 2 (2013): 39–58; Rebecca B. Galemba, "'He Used to Be a Pollero': The Securitisation of Migration and the Smuggler/Migrant Nexus at the Mexico-Guatemala Border," *Journal of Ethnic and Migration Studies* 44, no. 5 (2018): 870–86; Isacson, Meyer, and Morales, *Mexico's Other Border*; Leigh Anne Schmidt and Stephanie Buechler, "'I Risk Everything Because I Have Already Lost Everything': Central American Female Migrants Speak Out on the Migrant Trail in Oaxaca, Mexico," *Journal of Latin American Geography* 16, no. 1 (April 2017): 139–64; Amarela Varela Huerta, "La 'securitización' de la gubernamentalidad migratoria mediante la 'externalización' de las

fronteras estadounidenses a Mesoamérica," *Contemporánea* 4 (2015), http://con
-temporanea.inah.gob.mx/del_oficio/amarela_varela_num4.

253 *twenty thousand migrants went missing*: "Secuestran a 10,000 migrantes en seis
meses: CNDH," *El Economista*, Jan. 6, 2011.

255 *Altar, Sonora, 60 miles south*: Based on multiple visits by author in the mid-1990s
and the 2000s. See also stories in the series "Altar, Sonora: The Business of Smuggling," by David Rochkind, Pulitzer Center, https://pulitzercenter.org/projects
/north-america/altar-sonora-business-smuggling.

257 *Sexual assault was endemic*: *Invisible Victims: Migrants on the Move in Mexico*, 5.

25. THE UNDERWORLD

262 las hieleras, *the iceboxes*: Aida's account of her time in the Tucson Border Patrol
station was consistent with the picture painted by media reports and judicial inquiries of these supposedly short-term holding facilities. See Guillermo Cantor,
"Detained Beyond the Limit: Prolonged Confinement by U.S. Customs and
Border Protection Along the Southwest Border," American Immigration Council, Special Report, Aug. 2016, https://www.americanimmigrationcouncil.org
/sites/default/files/research/detained_beyond_the_limit.pdf; Camila Domono-
ske, "Surveillance Stills from Border Patrol Facilities Show Crowded, Trash-Filled
Cells," NPR.org, Aug. 19, 2016, https://www.npr.org/sections/thetwo-way/2016
/08/19/490624225/surveillance-stills-from-border-patrol-facilities-show
-crowded-trash-filled-cell; Melvin J. Félix and Rachel Glickhouse, "Arizona
Court Releases Photos from Inside 'Freezers' at Immigrant Processing Centers,"
Univision.com, Aug. 18, 2016, https://www.univision.com/univision-news
/immigration/arizona-court-releases-photos-from-inside-freezers-at-immigrant
-processing-centers; Paul Ingram, "Judge Orders Halt to Controversial BP Detention Practices," *Tucson Sentinel*, Nov. 18, 2016, http://www.tucsonsentinel.com
/local/report/111816_bp_order/judge-orders-halt-controversial-bp-detention
-practices/; Rob O'Dell, "The Republic Intervenes in Lawsuit over Conditions at
Border Patrol Detention Facilities," *Arizona Republic*, Jan. 1, 2016; Ed Pilkington,
"Freezing Cells and Sleep Deprivation: The Brutal Conditions Migrants Still
Face After Capture," *Guardian*, Dec. 12, 2014.

265 *Corrections Corporation of America*: Changed its name to CoreCivic in 2016.

269 *Though FIRRP could directly represent only a hundred people*: "Snapshot of Florence
Project 2012 Services," *La Línea* (Spring 2013), 2.

271 *initial master hearing*: Respondent names are pseudonyms.

272 *Immigration courts were notoriously skeptical*: J. Anna Cabot, "Problems Faced by
Mexican Asylum Seekers in the United States," *Journal on Migration and Human
Security* 2, no. 4 (2014): 361–77. Analysis of data from FY 2012–2017 revealed
that asylum claims by Mexicans had the highest denial rate in the U.S. immigra-
tion system, with almost nine of ten petitions rejected. "Asylum Representation
Rates Have Fallen amid Rising Denial Rates," Syracuse University, Transactional
Records Access Clearinghouse, Nov. 28, 2017, http://trac.syr.edu/immigration
/reports/491/.

272 *issue a withholding of removal*: "Withholding of Removal and CAT," Immigration
Equality Legal Resources, n.d., accessed June 2, 2018, https://www.immigra
tionequality.org/get-legal-help/our-legal-resources/asylum/withholding-of

-removal-and-cat/#.WxLLUS2n_K0; *How to Apply for Asylum, Withholding of Removal, and/or Protection Under Article 3 of the Convention Against Torture,* Florence Immigrant and Refugee Rights Project, Oct. 2011, http://www.unhcr.org /589258db4.pdf.

272 *women's experience of gender violence*: Author interview with Jesse Evans-Schroeder.

273 *Aida's humanitarian parole*: "Humanitarian or Significant Public Benefit Parole for Individuals Outside the United States," U.S. Citizenship and Immigration Services, n.d., accessed June 2, 2018, https://www.uscis.gov/humanitarian/humanitarian-or -significant-public-benefit-parole-individuals-outside-united-states; author interviews with Jesse Evans-Schroeder, Danielle Alvarado, and Wendy Hernandez.

26. AIDA'S VOICE

275 *"Four skinny trees with skinny necks"*: Sandra Cisneros, *The House on Mango Street* (New York: Vintage, 1991), 74, 110.

279 *No one knew more about the attorneys who served Eloy*: According to Aida, detainees in blue scrubs had more serious criminal histories but were segregated from the women in green and khaki.

280 *Violence Against Women Act was under attack*: Jonathan Weisman, "Women Figure Anew in Senate's Latest Battle," *New York Times,* March 14, 2012.

280 *easily met those criteria*: "Immigration Relief for Vulnerable Populations," U.S. Citizenship and Immigration Services, July 2011, https://www.uscis.gov/sites /default/files/USCIS/Humanitarian/T-U-VAWA-relief.pdf.

280 *petitions for VAWA protection*: Author interviews with Jesse Evans-Schroeder.

27. AIDA AND EMA

293 *"I never opened myself"*: Metallica, "Nothing Else Matters" (Lars Hatfield and Kirk Hammett, composers), on *Metallica* (Elektra, 1991).

294 *400,000 deportations a year*: Spencer S. Hsu and Andrew Becker, "ICE Officials Set Quotas to Deport More Illegal Immigrants," *Washington Post,* March 27, 2010; Ginger Thompson and Sarah Cohen, "More Deportations Follow Minor Crimes, Records Show," *New York Times,* April 6, 2014.

294 *criminal prosecutions related to immigration*: *United States Attorneys' Annual Statistical Report,* 2012, U.S. Department of Justice (2013), https://www.justice.gov/sites /default/files/usao/legacy/2013/10/28/12statrpt.pdf, 10.

294 *judges at Eloy handled*: Number of matters calculated from *FY 2012 Statistical Yearbook,* U.S. Department of Justice, Executive Office for Immigration Review (2013), https://www.justice.gov/eoir/statistical-year-book, B3–B5. Number of judges estimated from "Judge-by-Judge Asylum Decisions in Immigration Courts, FY 2011–2016," Syracuse University, Transactional Records Access Clearinghouse, http://trac.syr.edu/immigration/reports/447/include/denialrates.html.

294 *"the equivalent of death penalty cases"*: Quoted in Jennifer Ludden, "Immigration Crackdown Overwhelms Judges," *All Things Considered,* National Public Radio, Feb. 9, 2009, https://www.npr.org/templates/story/story.php?storyId=100420476.

295 *conditions that disqualified applicants*: Immigration and Nationality Act §§ 240A(b)(2)(A)(i)-(v). See also Rebecca Story, Cecilia Olavarria, and Moira Fisher Preda, "VAWA Cancellation of Removal," National Immigrant Women's

Advocacy Project, n.d., accessed Aug. 15, 2018, http://library.niwap.org/wp-content/uploads/IMM-Man-Ch9-VAWACancellationofRemoval.pdf.

295 *special category of "aggravated felony"*: "Aggravated Felonies: An Overview," American Immigration Council, Dec. 2016, https://www.americanimmigrationcouncil.org/research/aggravated-felonies-overview; Dawn Marie Johnson, "AEDPA and the IIRIRA: Treating Misdemeanors as Felonies for Immigration Purposes," *Journal of Legislation* 27, no. 2 (May 2001): 477–91.

295 *In Arizona, offenses like*: Katherine Brady et al., *Quick Reference Chart and Annotations for Determining Immigration Consequences of Selected Arizona Offenses*, Immigrant Legal Resource Center, Florence Immigrant and Refugee Rights Project, and Maricopa County Office of the Public Defender (2016), https://firrp.org/media/Arizona_Chart_2016-Update-FINAL.pdf.

295 *"a crime involving moral turpitude"*: "§ N.7 Crimes Involving Moral Turpitude," Immigrant Legal Resource Center (Jan. 2013), https://www.ilrc.org/sites/default/files/resources/n.7-crimes_involving_moral_turpitude.pdf; and author interviews.

296 *this timely retraction meant*: Interview with Jesse Evans-Schroeder and "Adjudicating Inadmissibility," in U.S. Citizenship and Immigration Services, *USCIS Policy Manual*, vol. 8, section J, chapter 3 (Washington, D.C.: USCIS, 2018).

297 *reluctance to grant asylum to Mexicans*: See J. Anna Cabot, "Problems Faced by Mexican Asylum Seekers in the United States," *Journal on Migration and Human Security* 2, no. 4 (2014): 361–77. Analysis of data from FY 2012–2017 revealed that asylum claims by Mexicans had the highest denial rate in the U.S. immigration system, with almost nine of ten petitions rejected. "Asylum Representation Rates Have Fallen amid Rising Denial Rates," Syracuse University, Transactional Records Access Clearinghouse, Nov. 28, 2017, http://trac.syr.edu/immigration/reports/491/.

297 *Phelps had the twelfth-highest*: "Immigration Judge Reports: Richard A. Phelps," Syracuse University, Transactional Records Access Clearinghouse (2014), http://trac.syr.edu/immigration/reports/judge2014/00327ELO/index.html.

298 *immigration detention was not punishment*: The law professor César Cuauhtémoc García Hernández provides an overview of this issue in his Crimmigration blog: "Lifting the Legal Fiction That Immigration Detention Isn't Punishment," March 10, 2017, http://crimmigration.com/2017/03/10/lifting-the-legal-fiction-that-immigration-detention-isnt-punishment/. Also see César Cuauhtémoc García Hernández, "Immigration Detention as Punishment," *UCLA Law Review* 61 (2014): 1346–414; David Brotherton and Sarah Tosh, "The Sociology of Vindictiveness and the Deportable Alien," in *Immigration Policy in the Age of Punishment: Detention, Deportation, and Border Control*, ed. David Brotherton and Philip Kretsedemas (New York: Columbia University Press, 2017); Mark Dow, "Designed to Punish: Immigrant Detention and Deportation," *Social Research* 74, no. 2 (Summer 2007): 533–46; Mark Noferi, "Making Civil Immigration Detention 'Civil,' and Examining the Emerging U.S. Civil Detention Paradigm," *Journal of Civil Rights and Economic Development* 27, no. 3 (2014): 533–85.

299 *using a criminal incarceration model*: García Hernández, "Immigration Detention as Punishment"; Dora Schiro, *Immigration Detention Overview and Recommendations*, Department of Homeland Security, Immigration and Customs Enforce-

ment, October 6, 2009. On conditions and treatment in immigration detention, see "Unseen Prisoners: A Report on Women in Immigration Detention Facilities in Arizona," University of Arizona, James E. Rogers College of Law, Southwest Institute for Research on Women, Jan. 2009, http://law2.arizona.edu/depts /bacon_program/pdf/Unseen_Prisoners.pdf; "Warehoused and Forgotten: Immigrants Trapped in Our Shadow Private Prison System," American Civil Liberties Union of Texas and American Civil Liberties Union, June 2014, https://www.aclu.org/other/warehoused-and-forgotten-immigrants-trapped-our -shadow-private-prison-system.

299 *standards of care for immigration detention*: Dora Schiro, *Immigration Detention Overview*; American Bar Association, *ABA Civil Immigration Detention Standards* (Washington, D.C.: American Bar Association, 2012).

299 *so profitable for CCA*: Meredith Kolodner, "Immigration Enforcement Benefits Prison Firms," *New York Times*, July 19, 2006.

28. GOING AWAY TO COME BACK

304 *civil confinement in Eloy was indefinite*: César Cuauhtémoc García Hernández, "Immigration Detention as Punishment," *UCLA Law Review* 61 (2014): 1346–414; Domenico Montanaro, Nina Totenberg, and Richard Gonzalez, "Supreme Court Ruling Means Immigrants Could Continue to Be Detained Indefinitely," NPR.org, Feb. 27, 2018, https://www.npr.org/2018/02/27/589096901/supreme -court-ruling-means-immigrants-can-continue-to-be-detained-indefinitely; Nathaniel Gier, "(In)Definite Detention: *Jennings* and the Backwards Detention System for Non-citizens Seeking Relief," *Minnesota Law Review* 102, no. 3 (2018).

304 *overtaxed immigration system*: In June 2012, the number of pending immigration court cases hit an all-time high at over 300,000. The average completion time for immigration cases was 526 days, although detained cases typically proceeded more quickly than non-detained cases. The size of the immigration court backlog has continued to rise since 2012, hitting 692,000 in 2018. "Immigration Backlog, Wait Times, Keep Rising," Syracuse University, Transactional Records Access Clearinghouse, July 19, 2012, http://trac.syr.edu/immigration/reports/286/; "Backlog of Pending Cases in Immigration Courts as of March 2018," Syracuse University, Transactional Records Access Clearinghouse, March 2018, http://trac .syr.edu/phptools/immigration/court_backlog/apprep_backlog.php.

304 *Ecuadorians living in and around New York City*: The 2010 U.S. Census counted 553,919 people of Ecuadorian descent in the United States, including 309,800 living in the New York metro region. "Allocation of Hispanic or Latino Origin, Population: Ecuadorian, New York–Northern New Jersey–Long Island Metro Area," U.S. Census Bureau, 2010 Census, Summary File 2, generated using American FactFinder, http://factfinder2.census.gov.

304 *petitioned for voluntary departure*: "Voluntary Departure," U.S. Citizenship and Immigration Services, Federal Register Publications (CIS, ICE, CBP) [70 FR 4743] [DHS 6-05], Voluntary Departure (2005), https://www.uscis.gov/ilink/docView /FR/HTML/FR/0-0-0-1/0-0-0-102229/0-0-0-106136/0-0-0-106514/0-0-0 -106604.html.

304 *More detainees had taken their lives*: Megan Jula and Daniel González, "Eloy Detention Center: Why So Many Suicides?" and "Eloy Migrant Detention Center

Has the Worst Suicide Rate in U.S., Raising Questions About Care," *Arizona Republic*, July 28 and 29, 2015.

304 *meant forfeiting*: *How to Apply for Voluntary Departure*, Florence Immigrant and Refugee Rights Project, Oct. 2011, https://www.justice.gov/sites/default/files /eoir/legacy/2013/01/22/Voluntary%20Departure%20-%20English%20 %2813%29.pdf, 8, 12–13.

305 *conspiracy to smuggle themselves*: "Court: Immigrants Subject to Smuggling Law," Associated Press, July 17, 2008; Michael Kiefer, "County Ends Prosecution for Conspiracy to Smuggle Humans," *Arizona Republic*, July 30, 2014.

305 *Inmates at Estrella toiled*: Matt Clarke, "Conditions in Maricopa County, Arizona, Jails Still Unconstitutional," *Prison Legal News*, May 2009, 28; John Dickerson, "Inhumanity Has a Price," *Phoenix New Times*, Dec. 20, 2007; "Undercover Reporter Details Stay Inside Maricopa County Jail," KPHO Broadcasting, Aug. 14, 2014, http://www.azfamily.com/story/26295248/undercover-reporter -details-stay-inside-maricopa-county-jail.

305 *chain gangs, and pregnant women*: Nigel Farndale, "The World's Only Female Chain Gang," *Telegraph*, Nov. 27, 2012; "Sheriff Runs Female Chain Gang," CNN.com, Oct. 29, 2003, http://www.cnn.com/2003/US/Southwest/10/29/chain .gang.reut/; Jacques Billeaud, "Maricopa County to Pay $200,000 to Settle Lawsuit over Restraining Pregnant Inmate," Associated Press, Nov. 21, 2016; Ray Stern, "Pregnant Inmate Who Was Shackled in County Jail Loses Lawsuit Against Sheriff Arpaio," *Phoenix New Times*, Jan. 24, 2014; "Practice of Shackling Pregnant Women Called into Question," BBHO Broadcasting, Feb. 17, 2012, http://www.azfamily.com/story/16963408/jail-birth-called-into-question.

305 *"Mexican bitches"*: Thomas E. Perez, Roy L. Austin Jr., and Jonathan M. Smith, "Complaint Filed in the United States District Court for the District of Arizona," *United States v. Maricopa County et al.* (May 10, 2012), https://www.justice .gov/iso/opa/resources/512012510134311376158.pdf, 2.

305 *according to news sources*: The sources consulted on Arpaio's policies and practices in this section include Jacques Billeaud, "Joe Arpaio Convicted of Crime for Ignoring Judge's Order," *Arizona Capitol Times*, July 31, 2017; Joe Hagen, "The Long, Lawless Ride of Sheriff Joe Arpaio," *Rolling Stone*, Aug. 2, 2012; Marc Lacey, "U.S. Finds Pervasive Bias Against Latinos by Arizona Sheriff," *New York Times*, Dec. 15, 2011; Nathan J. Robinson, "Wait, Do People Actually Know Just How Evil This Man Is?," *Current Affairs*, Aug. 26, 2017; "Ortega Melendres et al. v. Arpaio et al.," American Civil Liberties Association, Sept. 13, 2017, https://www .aclu.org/cases/ortega-melendres-et-al-v-arpaio-et-al; "United States' Investigation of the Maricopa County Sheriff," Letter from Assistant Attorney General Thomas E. Perez to Maricopa County Attorney Bill Montgomery, Dec. 15, 2011, https://www.justice.gov/sites/default/files/crt/legacy/2011/12/15/mcso _findletter_12-15-11.pdf; Thomas E. Perez, Roy L. Austin Jr., and Jonathan M. Smith, "Complaint Filed in the United States District Court for the District of Arizona," *United States v. Maricopa County et al.* (May 10, 2012), https://www .justice.gov/iso/opa/resources/512012510134311376158.pdf; Ray Stern, "Arpaio Boasts of Arresting 4,000 Illegal Immigrants in Under Four Months," *Phoenix New Times*, July 8, 2009. See also the Pulitzer Prize–winning series of articles

on Joe Arpaio by Ryan Gabrielson and Paul Giblin of the *East Valley Tribune* collected here: http://www.pulitzer.org/winners/ryan-gabrielson-and-paul-giblin.

305 *$140 million litigating and settling lawsuits*: Laurie Roberts, "Joe Arpaio Just Cost You Another $4.5 Million," *Arizona Republic*, Sept. 21, 2016.

306 *guide to applying for voluntary departure*: How to Apply for Voluntary Departure.

306 *officials had deported 391,953 people*: This figure did not include another 324,000 people removed from the country without a formal hearing or removal order. John Simanski and Lesley M. Sapp, "Immigration Enforcement Actions: 2011," Department of Homeland Security, Office of Immigration Statistics (Sept. 2012), https://www.dhs.gov/sites/default/files/publications/immigration-statistics/enforcement_ar_2011.pdf; Julia Preston, "Record Number of Foreigners Were Deported in 2011, Officials Say," *New York Times*, Sept. 7, 2012.

306 *a federal judge had denied*: Fernanda Santos, "Arizona Immigration Law Survives Ruling," *New York Times*, Sept. 6, 2012. The U.S. Supreme Court would later rule against most of the law's provisions, but leave intact the requirement that police verify immigration statuses of people they suspect of being in the country without permission. "Arizona v. United States," Scotusblog.com, http://www.scotusblog.com/case-files/cases/arizona-v-united-states/?wpmp_switcher=desktop; and Adam Liptak, "Blocking Parts of Arizona Law, Justices Allow Its Centerpiece," *New York Times*, June 25, 2012. For an update on the law, see Nigel Duara, "Arizona's Once-Feared Immigration Law, SB 1070, Loses Most of Its Power in Settlement," *Los Angeles Times*, Sept. 15, 2016.

309 *"special rule cancellation of removal"*: Immigration and Nationality Act §§ 240A(b)(2)(A)(i)-(v). See also Rebecca Story, Cecilia Olavarria, and Moira Fisher Preda, *VAWA Cancellation of Removal*, National Immigrant Women's Advocacy Project, n.d., accessed Aug. 15, 2018, http://library.niwap.org/wp-content/uploads/IMM-Man-Ch9-VAWACancellationofRemoval.pdf.

318 *committed no crime*: As noted earlier, undocumented presence in the United States is a civil, not a criminal, offense. Aida had shoplifted, but this was not the legal reason for her detention.

318 *U.S. taxpayers paid approximately $52,000*: Based on the average daily cost calculated by the National Immigration Forum. In FY2012, this was $164 per daily bed. "The Math of Immigration Detention," National Immigration Forum, Aug. 22, 2013, https://immigrationforum.org/article/math-immigration-detention/.

318 *almost $160 million in profits*: Corrections Corporation of America, "FY 2012 Form 10-K," U.S. Securities and Exchange Commission website, https://www.sec.gov/Archives/edgar/data/1070985/000119312513080296/d452767d10k.htm#fin452767_2.

318 *money trail didn't end there*: For a global study of this phenomenon, see Deirdre Conlon and Nancy Hiemstra, eds., *Intimate Economies of Immigration Detention: Critical Perspectives* (New York: Routledge, 2017).

29. TO BATTERY PARK

323 *adverse childhood experiences*: Vincent J. Felitti et al., "Relationship of Childhood Abuse and Household Dysfunction to Many of the Leading Causes of Death in Adults: The Adverse Childhood Experiences (ACE) Study," *American*

Journal of Preventative Medicine 14, no. 4 (May 1998): 245–58; "Adverse Child-hood Experiences (ACEs)," Centers for Disease Control and Prevention, n.d., accessed Aug. 15, 2018, https://www.cdc.gov/violenceprevention/acestudy/index .html.

EPILOGUE: THE LIFE OF AIDA HERNANDEZ

331 *"Empowering narratives do not"*: Lisa Marie Cacho, *Social Death: Racialized Rightlessness and the Criminalization of the Unprotected* (New York: New York University Press, 2012), 32.

336 *The number of undocumented migrants*: *Southwest Border Sectors Total Illegal Alien Apprehensions by Fiscal Year (Oct. 1st Through Sept. 30th)*, U.S. Customs and Bor-der Protection, U.S. Border Patrol (2016), https://www.cbp.gov/newsroom /media-resources/stats.

336 *the number of Border Patrol agents*: *Border Patrol Agent Nationwide Staffing by Fis-cal Year (FY 1992–2017)*, U.S. Customs and Border Protection, U.S. Border Pa-trol (2017), https://www.cbp.gov/newsroom/media-resources/stats.

336 *The terrain covered by substantial border barriers*: Chain-link fences date to the early twentieth century, but 1993 is generally considered the beginning of substantial border barriers, with the exception of a fourteen-mile San Diego wall built in 1990. Blas Nuñez-Neto and Michael John Garcia, *Border Security: The San Diego Fence*, U.S. Library of Congress, Congressional Research Service (2007), RS22026; Ted Robbins, "Bush Signs Border Fence Act; Funds Not Found," NPR.org, Oct. 26, 2006, https://www.npr.org/templates/story/story.php?storyId=6388548; *Southwest Border Security: Additional Actions Needed to Better Assess Fencing's Contributions to Operations and Provide Guidance for Identifying Capability Gaps*, U.S. Government Accountability Office (2017), GAO-17–331.

336 *The Border Patrol budget*: *U.S. Border Patrol Fiscal Year Budget Statistics (FY 1990– FY 2015)*, U.S. Customs and Border Protection, Jan. 12, 2016, https://www.cbp .gov/newsroom/media-resources/stats.

336 *In 2012, funding for Customs*: Dorris Meissner et al., *Immigration Enforcement in the United States: The Rise of a Formidable Machinery*, Migration Policy Institute, Jan. 2013, 9, http://www.migrationpolicy.org/research/immigration-enforcement -united-states-rise-formidable-machinery.

336 *enough left over to run*: Calculated from ibid. and 2012 net cost of National Park Service. *Agency Financial Report FY 2012*, U.S. Department of the Interior, Of-fice of Financial Management (2013), 9, https://www.doi.gov/pfm/afr.

336 *By 2016, that figure had grown*: Budget-in-Brief (FY 2016), U.S. Department of Homeland Security, (2016), https://www.dhs.gov/dhs-budget. For an overview of immigration enforcement spending, see *The Cost of Immigration Enforcement and Border Security*, American Immigration Council, Jan. 25, 2017, https:// www.americanimmigrationcouncil.org/research/the-cost-of-immigration -enforcement-and-border-security.

ABOUT THIS BOOK

343 *the language of virtue and achievement*: A growing number of immigrant groups, such as United We Dream, Immigrant Youth Coalition, UndocuBlack Net-work, Immigrant Youth Justice League, and National Day Laborer Organizing

Network, are leading the way in challenging the limits and exclusions of dominant immigrant deservingness narratives. See, for example, Tania A. Unzueta Carrasco and Seif Hinda, "Disrupting the Dream: Undocumented Youth Reframe Citizenship and Deportability Through Anti-Deportation Activism," *Latino Studies* 12, no. 2 (June 2014): 279–99. For discussions of the challenges of immigrant deservingness narratives, see Lisa Marie Cacho, *Social Death: Racialized Rightlessness and the Criminalization of the Unprotected* (New York: New York University Press, 2012); Christina Gerken, *Model Immigrants and Undesirable Aliens: The Cost of Immigration Reform in the 1990s* (Minneapolis: University of Minnesota Press, 2013); Alfonso Gonzales, *Reform Without Justice: Latino Migrant Politics and the Homeland Security State* (Oxford: Oxford University Press, 2013); Fanny Lauby, "Leaving the 'Perfect DREAMer' Behind? Narratives and Mobilization in Immigration Reform," *Social Movement Studies* 15, no. 4 (Feb. 2016): 374–87; Grace Yukich, "Constructing the Model Immigrant: Movement Strategy and Immigrant Deservingness in the New Sanctuary Movement," *Social Problems* 60, no. 3 (Aug. 2013): 302–20.

344 *but also brimmed with wit, humor, and a certain brio*: Encountering Héctor Tobar's essay, "Avoiding the Trap of Immigration Porn" (*New York Times*, Aug. 7, 2017), late in the process of writing this book crystallized the importance of highlighting this wit and brio. Instead of "immigration porn," which reduces immigrant lives to iconic scenes of suffering, Tobar suggests depicting "the ineffable qualities of the immigrant present: weariness and hopefulness, uncertainty and pride. [The immigrant's] dignity and his burdens would be plain to see, but perhaps also a certain raffish quality—the lively brown eyes of a man who has found his way through adversity with wit and wiles." Hopefully, this book conveyed the "beauty and complexity," wit, and brio of Aida's and others' lives.

346 *confusion about timelines is common*: For a review of research and debates around this topic, see Maria Crespo and Violeta Fernández-Lansac, "Memory and Narrative of Traumatic Events: A Literature Review," *Psychological Trauma: Theory, Research, Practice, and Policy* 8, no. 2 (March 2016): 149–56.

349 *"does not aim to convey"*: Walter Benjamin, *Illuminations* (New York: Schocken Books, 1968), 91.

350 *"Don't study the poor or powerless"*: Philippe Bourgois, *Selling Crack in El Barrio* (Cambridge, U.K.: Cambridge University Press, 1995), 18, paraphrasing Laura Nader, "Up the Anthropologist: Perspectives Gained from Studying Up," in *Reinventing Anthropology*, ed. Dell Homes (New York: Random House, 1972).

350 *"never meant to survive"*: Audre Lorde, "Litany for Survival," in *The Black Unicorn* (New York: W. W. Norton, 1995).

350 *Enforcement-only policies*: Sources for the claims summarized in this section are cited in chapters 3, 4, and 6.

351 *And they have fueled a vast, lucrative*: On the growth of a "border security industrial complex," see Renaud Bellais and Vincent Boulanin, "Border Security: A New Market for the Military Industrial Complex?" (paper presented at the EAEPE 25th Annual Conference, Nov. 2013); Tanya Golash-Boza, "The Immigration Industrial Complex: Why We Enforce Immigration Policies Destined to Fail," *Sociology Compass* 3 (2009): 295–309; Josiah Heyman, "Capitalism and US Policy at the Mexican Border," *Dialectical Anthropology* 36, nos. 3–4 (2012): 263–77;

Kyle Longley, "Industry of Border Security Creates Extra Layer of Regional Problems," *Austin Statesman*, Jan. 21, 2012; Todd Miller, *Border Patrol Nation: Dispatches from the Front Lines of Homeland Security* (San Francisco: City Lights, 2014); Kathleen Staudt, Tony Payan, and Timothy J. Dunn, "Bordering Human Rights, Social Democratic Feminism, and Broad-Based Security," in Kathleen A. Staudt, Tony Payan, and Z. Anthony Kruszewski, eds., *Human Rights Along the U.S.-Mexico Border: Gendered Violence and Insecurity* (Tucson: University of Arizona Press, 2009).

351 *hundreds of billions of taxpayer dollars*: For a quick overview of the growth in immigration enforcement, see *The Cost of Immigration Enforcement and Border Security*, American Immigration Council, Jan. 25, 2017, https://www.americanimmigration council.org/research/the-cost-of-immigration-enforcement-and-border-security. Also see Dorris Meissner et al., *Immigration Enforcement in the United States: The Rise of a Formidable Machinery*, Migration Policy Institute, Jan. 2013, http://www .migrationpolicy.org/research/immigration-enforcement-united-states-rise -formidable-machinery.

351 *a stake in maintaining perpetual crisis*: I owe this realization to Jenna Loyd, "Race, Capitalist Crisis, and Abolitionist Organizing: An Interview with Ruth Wilson Gilmore," in *Beyond Walls and Cages: Prisons, Borders, and Global Crisis*, ed. Jenna Loyd, Matt Mitchelson, and Andrew Burridge (Athens: University of Georgia Press, 2012).

351 *Women have paid a disproportionate price*: See Sylvanna M. Falcón, "Rape as a Weapon of War: Advancing Human Rights for Women at the U.S.-Mexico Border," *Social Justice* 28, no. 2 (2001): 31–50. Also see Staudt, Payan, and Kruszewski, *Human Rights*.

351 *"successful failure"*: Gilberto Rosas's *Barrio Libre: Criminalizing States and Delinquent Refusals of the New Frontier* (Durham, N.C.: Duke University Press, 2012) and Loyd's "Race, Capitalist Crisis, and Abolitionist Organizing" helped inspire my thinking about the "productive" power of failed immigration enforcement.

351 *corruption, abuse, and "bad apples"*: See, for example, Bill Chappell, "Former ICE Chief Counsel Gets 4 Years in Prison for Stealing Immigrants' Identities," NPR .org, June 28, 2018, https://www.npr.org/2018/06/28/624207450/former-ice-chief -counsel-facing-prison-time-for-stealing-immigrants-identities; "Cracks in the Wall: When Border Watchdogs Turn Criminal," *Texas Tribune* and *Reveal*, July 7, 2016, https://apps.texastribune.org/bordering-on-insecurity/when-border -watchdogs-turn-criminal/; "Crossing the Line: Corruption at the Border," Center for Investigative Reporting, n.d., accessed Aug. 15, 2018, http://border corruption.apps.cironline.org; *Final Report of the CBP Integrity Advisory Panel*, Homeland Security Advisory Council, March 16, 2016, https://www.dhs.gov /sites/default/files/publications/HSAC%20CBP%20IAP_Final%20Report _FINAL%20(accessible)_0.pdf; "ICE Attorney Sentenced to Nearly 18 Years on Corruption Charges Stemming from Multi-Agency Probe Involving ICE OPR," U.S. Immigration and Customs Enforcement, news release, March 21, 2011, https://www.ice.gov/news/releases/ice-attorney-sentenced-nearly-18-years -corruption-charges-stemming-multi-agency-probe; Garrett M. Graff, "The Green Monster: How the Border Patrol Became America's Most Out-of-Control Law Enforcement Agency," *Politico Magazine*, Nov./Dec. 2014, https://www

.politico.com/magazine/story/2014/10/border-patrol-the-green-monster
-112220; Mike Heuer, "Corrupt ICE Agent Wreaked Havoc, Business Owners
Say," Courthouse News Service, Jan. 20, 2017, https://www.courthousenews.com
/corrupt-ice-agent-wreaked-havoc-business-owners-say/; Jeremy Raff, "The Border Patrol's Corruption Problem," *Atlantic*, May 5, 2017; Bryan Schatz, "New
Report Details Dozens of Corrupt Border Patrol Agents—Just as Trump Wants
to Hire More," *Mother Jones*, April 24, 2018.

352 *deindustrialization of communities of color*: Several notable exceptions to this trend
include Thomas J. Sugrue, *The Origins of the Urban Crisis: Race and Inequality in
Postwar Detroit*, rev. ed. (Princeton, N.J.: Princeton University Press, 2014);
Gregory D. Squires, *Capital and Communities in Black and White: The Intersec-
tions of Race, Class, and Uneven Development* (Albany: State University of New York
Press, 1994); Ruth Wilson Gilmore, *Golden Gulag: Prisons, Surplus, Crisis, and
Opposition in Globalizing California* (Berkeley: University of California Press, 2007).
See also Jenna M. Loyd and Anne Bonds, "Where Do Black Lives Matter? Race,
Stigma, and Place in Milwaukee, Wisconsin," *Sociological Review Monographs* 66,
no. 4 (2018): 898–918.

352 *dangerous-sounding "aggravated felonies"*: Sources for the claims summarized in this
section are cited in chapters 4 and 27.

352 *Immigrants are less likely to commit crimes*: Reviews of research on this issue include
Chris Nichols, "Mostly True: Undocumented Immigrants Less Likely to Commit Crimes Than U.S. Citizens," Politifact: Fact-Checking U.S. Politics, Aug. 3,
2017, http://www.politifact.com/california/statements/2017/aug/03/antonio
-villaraigosa/mostly-true-undocumented-immigrants-less-likely-co/; Alex Now-
rasteh, "Immigration and Crime: What the Research Says," CATO Institute,
July 14, 2014, https://www.cato.org/blog/immigration-crime-what-research-says;
Jane C. Timm, "Fact Check: No Evidence Undocumented Immigrants Commit More Crimes," NBCNews.com, June 28, 2017, https://www.nbcnews.com
/politics/white-house/fact-check-no-evidence-undocumented-immigrants
-commit-more-crimes-n777856. See also Graham C. Ousey and Charis E. Kubrin, "Immigration and Crime: Assessing a Contentious Issue," *Annual Review
of Criminology* 1, no. 1 (June 2017): 63–84; Walter A. Ewing, Daniel E Martínez, and Rubén G. Rumbaut, "The Criminalization of Immigration in the
United States," American Immigration Council, July 2015, https://www
.americanimmigrationcouncil.org/research/criminalization-immigration-united
-states.

353 *They will define who belongs*: Linda Bosniak, *The Citizen and the Alien: Dilemmas of
Contemporary Membership* (Princeton, N.J.: Princeton University Press, 2006).

353 *A powerful upwelling of voices*: For example: United We Dream, Immigrant Youth
Coalition, UndocuBlack Network, Immigrant Youth Justice League, and National
Day Laborer Organizing Network. Tania A. Unzueta Carrasco and Seif Hinda,
"Disrupting the Dream: Undocumented Youth Reframe Citizenship and Deport-
ability Through Anti-Deportation Activism," *Latino Studies* 12, no. 2 (June 2014):
279–99.

353 *voices from the border*: Frontera de Cristo, featured prominently in this book, is
one example. Others include the Southern Border Communities Coalition, the
Border Action Network, and la Coalición de Derechos Humanos.

353 *the Trump administration*: Anti-immigration nativists have filled key positions in the Trump administration. For example: Julie Kirchner, Trump campaign adviser and former executive director of the Federation for American Immigration Reform (FAIR). Kirchner was appointed by the Trump administration to serve as citizenship and immigration services ombudsman at the Department of Homeland Security. According to the Southern Poverty Law Center, FAIR is an "anti-immigrant hate group" whose leaders have ties to white supremacist groups and a strong commitment to limiting the number of nonwhites entering the United States (Stephen Piggott, "Julie Kirchner, Former FAIR ED, Named New Citizenship and Immigration Ombudsman," Southern Poverty Law Center, May 1, 2017, https://www.splcenter.org/hatewatch/2017/05/01/julie-kirchner-former -fair-ed-named-new-citizenship-and-immigration-services-ombudsman; "FAIR," Southern Poverty Law Center, n.d., accessed Aug. 15, 2018, https:// www.splcenter.org/fighting-hate/extremist-files/group/federation-american -immigration-reform). Before his appointment as attorney general, Jeff Sessions was one of the fiercest opponents of both illegal and legal immigration in the U.S. Senate (Adam Serwer, "Jeff Sessions's Fear of Muslim Immigrants," *Atlantic*, Feb. 8, 2017, and a collection of sources compiled by Zachary Mueller, "A Session in Hate," *America's Voice*, July 19, 2018, https://americasvoice.org /sessionsinhate/). As attorney general, Sessions oversaw ICE attorneys, immigration judges, and other important components of the immigration system. The anti-immigrant firebrand and former Sessions Senate staffer Stephen Miller is credited with helping define some of the most controversial components of Trump's immigration platform. According to the Southern Poverty Law Center, Miller has ties to nativist and white supremacist groups ("Stephen Miller: A Driving Force Behind the Muslim Ban and Family Separation," Southern Poverty Law Center, Hatewatch, June 21, 2018, https://www.splcenter.org /hatewatch/2018/06/21/stephen-miller-driving-force-behind-muslim-ban -and-family-separation-policy; Sophie Tatum, "How Stephen Miller, the Architect Behind Trump's Immigration Policies, Rose to Power," CNN.com, June 23, 2018, https://www.cnn.com/2018/06/23/politics/stephen-miller-immigration -family-separation/index.html). Kris Kobach, one of the authors of Arizona's S.B. 1070, has also played a significant role in the Trump White House. Suzy Khimm, "Kris Kobach, Nativist Son," *Mother Jones*, March/April 2012.

354 *respect for the rule of law*: It's worth noting the many times when immigration enforcers demonstrate a willingness to bend or break the law in order to facilitate deportations. Prominent examples include systemic use of unlawful detentions and violations of regulations governing immigration detention. See, for example, Paige St. John and Joel Rubin, "ICE Held an American Man in Custody for 1,273 Days. He's Not the Only One Who Had to Prove His Citizenship," *Los Angeles Times*, April 27, 2018; *Concerns About ICE Detainee Treatment and Care at Detention Facilities*, Department of Homeland Security, Office of the Inspector General, Dec. 11, 2017, OIG-18-32; Elizabeth M. Frankel, "Detention and Deportation Without Adequate Due Process," *Duke Forum for Law and Social Change* 3 (2011): 63; Michael Kagan, "Immigration Law's Looming Fourth Amendment Problem," *Georgetown Law Journal* 124 (2015): 125; *Immigration Detainers Legal Update*, Immigrant Legal Resource Center, July 2018, https://

www.ilrc.org/sites/default/files/resources/immig_detainer_legal_update
-20180724.pdf; *Legal Issues with Immigration Detainers*, Immigrant Legal
Resource Center, Nov. 2016, https://www.ilrc.org/sites/default/files/resources
/detainer_law_memo_november_2016_updated.pdf; Robin Urevich, "Investigation Finds ICE Detention Center Cut Corners and Skirted Federal Detention
Rules," *The World*, PRI, March 15, 2018, https://www.pri.org/stories/2018-03
-15/investigation-finds-ice-detention-center-cuts-corners-and-skirted-federal.
News reports and pending lawsuits alleging that Border Patrol agents illegally
turn away asylum seekers have received increased attention in recent years
("Challenging Customs and Border Protection's Unlawful Practice of Turning
Away Asylum Seekers," American Immigration Council, n.d., accessed Aug. 15,
2018, https://www.americanimmigrationcouncil.org/litigation/challenging-cus
toms-and-border-protections-unlawful-practice-turning-away-asylum-seekers;
Amrit Cheng, "'Turn the Plane Around': Government Wrongfully Deports Asylum Seekers," ACLU.org, Aug. 9, 2018, https://www.aclu.org/blog/immigrants
-rights/deportation-and-due-process/turn-plane-around-government-wrong
fully-deports; Mica Rosenberg, "Asylum Seekers Turned Away at U.S.-Mexico
Border Sue U.S. Government," Reuters News Service, July 12, 2017).

354 *extensive histories of racial bias and discrimination*: Mae M. Ngai, *Impossible Subjects:
Illegal Aliens and the Making of Modern America* (Princeton, N.J.: Princeton University Press, 2004).

354 *the president revoked*: Trump revoked earlier enforcement guidelines focusing enforcement efforts on immigrants with serious criminal records and laid out his
own priorities in the January 25, 2017, Executive Order, "Enhancing Public Safety
in the Interior of the United States." For overviews of enforcement priorities under
Trump and Obama, see "The End of Immigration Enforcement Priorities Under
the Trump Administration," American Immigration Council, March 7, 2018,
https://www.americanimmigrationcouncil.org/research/immigration-enforce
ment-priorities-under-trump-administration; "Understanding Trump's Executive
Order Affecting Deportations and 'Sanctuary Cities,'" National Immigration Law
Center, Feb. 24, 2017, https://www.nilc.org/issues/immigration-enforcement/exec
-order-deportations-sanctuary-cities/; Tal Kopan, "How Trump Changed the
Rules to Arrest More Non-criminal Immigrants," CNN.com, March 2, 2018,
https://www.cnn.com/2018/03/02/politics/ice-immigration-deportations/index
.html.

354 *arrests of immigrants with no criminal record*: Immigration detentions increased
by 41 percent during Trump's first year in office. Thanks to the change in enforcement priorities discussed in the previous endnote, arrests of immigrants without
criminal records accounted for most of this increase. The proportion of immigrants
detained with no criminal record increased 171 percent during Trump's first year
in office (Kopan, "How Trump Changed the Rules"). We should also take reported arrests of so-called criminal immigrants with a grain of salt. In 2017, ICE
included people charged with offenses *but not convicted* in its count of "criminals"
arrested. Finally, the vast majority of immigrants with actual criminal convictions
(or pending charges) arrested by ICE committed minor traffic offenses or nonviolent, immigration-related offenses such as misdemeanor illegal entry ("The End
of Enforcement Priorities"; Chantal da Silva, "Most Charges in ICE Criminal

Crackdown Related to Traffic Offenses," CNN.com, Feb. 14, 2018, https://www .newsweek.com/ice-arrested-more-immigrants-over-traffic-offenses-including -duis-any-other-806467). This was the case under Obama-era policies as well: Christie Thompson and Anna Flag, "Who Is ICE Deporting?," Marshall Project and *Fusion*, Sept. 26, 2016, https://www.themarshallproject.org/2016/09/26 /who-is-ice-deporting#.33a8mxjT5; Ginger Thompson and Sarah Cohen, "More Deportations Follow Minor Crimes, Record Shows," *New York Times*, April 6, 2014.

354 *"zero-tolerance" approach*: "Attorney General Announces Zero-Tolerance Policy for Criminal Illegal Entry," Department of Justice, Office of Public Affairs, press release, April 6, 2018, https://www.justice.gov/opa/pr/attorney-general-announces -zero-tolerance-policy-criminal-illegal-entry; Miriam Valverde, "What You Need to Know About the Trump Administration's Zero-Tolerance Immigration Policy," Politifact: Fact-Checking U.S. Politics, June 6, 2018, https://www.politifact .com/truth-o-meter/article/2018/jun/06/what-you-need-know-about-trump -administrations-zer/.

354 *Jeff Sessions tried to chip away*: Tal Kopan, "Trump Admin Drops Asylum Protections for Domestic Violence Victims," CNN.com, June 11, 2018, https://www .cnn.com/2018/06/11/politics/jeff-sessions-asylum-decision/index.html; Mark Joseph Stern, "Jeff Sessions Just Barred Most Domestic Violence Victims from Applying for Asylum," Slate.com, June 11, 2018, https://slate.com/news-and -politics/2018/06/jeff-sessions-bars-most-domestic-violence-victims-from -asylum.html.

354 *worked tirelessly to limit* legal *immigration*: Peter Baker, "Trump Supports Plan to Cut Legal Immigration by Half," *New York Times*, Aug. 2, 2017; Steve Chapman, "Column: Trump Leads Attack on Legal Immigration," *Chicago Tribune*, Feb. 14, 2018; Britnny Mejia, "Under Trump, the Rare Act of Denaturalizing U.S. Citizens Is on the Rise," *Los Angeles Times*, Aug. 12, 2018; Kanyakrit Vongkiatkajorn, "The Trump Administration Is Working to Deport More Legal Immigrants," *Mother Jones*, Jul. 17, 2017.

355 *make it harder and riskier*: Christina DiPasquale, "Trump Administration Plan to Initiate Removal Proceedings Against a Larger Number of Immigrants Will Cause More Panic and Fear," Immigrant Legal Resource Center, July 6, 2018, https://www.ilrc.org/new-memo-trump-administration-plan-initiate-removal -proceedings-against-larger-number-immigrants.

GLOSSARY

This list includes Spanish words and phrases that are not translated in the body of the text.

abogada: Lawyer (*fem.*).
águila: Eagle.
bailes folklóricos: Folkloric dances of Latin America.
banda: A type of music associated with northern Mexico.
barbacoa: Meat, often mutton, cooked slowly over a fire.
bien: Well.
birote: A type of Mexican bread roll.
bolita: A cheap plastic hair tie popular in the 1990s.

caldo: Stew.

campesino: Peasant.

carcelazo: Stir-craziness due to incarceration, as described by Raúl.

casita: In-law house or guesthouse behind a larger house.

¡Chale! . . . No mames . . . Pinche güey: Slang associated with Mexico City. Roughly: No way . . . Stop messing with me . . . Stupid idiot.

charro: Mexican rodeo festival.

chayotes: A type of edible gourd.

chévere: Awesome or cool.

chilango: Derogatory slang term for a person from Mexico City.

cholo/a: Tough street style, or a person associated with that style.

colegio: Roughly equivalent to middle and high school in Ecuador.

Colochita: Term of endearment referencing Aida's curls.

como mexicanas: Like Mexican women.

compañeras: Comrades (*fem.*).

corridos: Mexican ballads.

coyotes: Human smugglers.

Créanme, chiquitas: Believe me, little girls.

cumbia: A folkloric style of music.

Ecuatoriana: Ecuadorian (*fem.*).

enamoradas: Lovebirds.

ejidatarios: Members of an *ejido*.

ejido: A communal landholding, the basic unit of agrarian reform in Mexico.

en el barrio: In the neighborhood.

Flor salvaje *and* Rosa diamante: Literally, Savage Flower and Diamond Rose. Dramatic television series.

guapo: Handsome man.

güera: Blond (*fem.*).

¿Hablas español?: You speak Spanish?

hermana: Sister.

hierba del manso: A plant used in herbal medicine, usually *Anemopsis californica* (yerba mansa).

hija: Daughter.

hotel de mala muerte: Literally, hotel of bad death. A dive hotel.

iglesias: Churches.

Ingles sin barreras: English Without Barriers. A language-learning program.

jarabe tapatío: A type of dance from the Mexican state of Jalisco.

jarocho: A style of folkloric music from Veracruz, Mexico.

joto, maricón, marimacha, *and* tortillera: Derogatory slang terms for gay and lesbian men and women.

los Unites: Slang. The United States.

Lotería: Mexican game similar to bingo.

mango chupado: Literally, sucked mango. A hairstyle.

mangonadas: A sweet and spicy drink made with mango, lime, and chili powder.

Me dejas sin palabras, mi amor: You leave me without words, my love.

merengue: A musical style originally from the Dominican Republic.

mestizo: Used to indicate mixed indigenous and Spanish ancestry.

mi amor: My love.

migra: Slang. The Border Patrol or Immigration and Customs Enforcement.

mijo/a: My son/daughter. Affectionate term.

milagros: Religious charms.

Mira la negra fea: Look at the ugly dark-haired girl.

mojaditas: Little wetbacks. A derogatory term. In this case, used affectionately by Luz.

morenita: Term of endearment for a dark-haired woman.

narco: Drug trafficker.

ni modo: Difficult-to-translate expression of resignation.

norteño: A person from northern Mexico. Also, a type of music originating in northern Mexico.

oye: Hey.

pan dulce: Mexican sweet bread.

pan, pasta, y papas: Bread, pasta, and potatoes.

Pequitas: Term of endearment for a woman with freckles.

por Dios: For God's sake.

por supuesto: Of course.

por un pinche dólar: For one damn dollar.

pozoleada: A water torture described by Raúl. The word plays on *pozole*, a popular type of stew.

promotores: In this context, public health educators.

pueblos: Towns.

quinceañera: Often elaborate and ritualized traditional celebration of a girl's fifteenth birthday.

ranchera: A type of Mexican country music.

remate: A pattern of steps in folkloric dance.

risueña: Literally "giggly," but figuratively "having a sunny disposition."

rurales: Mexican federal police.

señoras: Married women.

Sí, por favor. Muchísimas gracias: Yes, please. Thank you very much.

sicarios: Hit men.

Soy yo . . . Lo siento: It's me . . . I'm sorry.

sureños: Southerners. In this context the label refers to people from southern Mexico and has a derogatory tenor.

tata: Grandfather.

Te aaaaammmmooooo FLAKITA: I looooooove you, SKINNY GIRL.

telenovela: A Latin American evening soap opera.

tragona *and* comelona: Greedy eater.

tienda: Store.

tierra caliente: Tropical lowlands.

tigre: Tiger.

triste recuerdo: Sad memory. "Triste recuerdo" is a classic Mexican ballad.

urgencias: Emergency room.

¿Ya te enamoraste, verdad, cabrona?: You really fell in love, didn't you, tough girl?

zapatillas: Dance shoes for Latin American folkloric dance.

EXPLANATION OF TERMINOLOGY

Deportation or Removal?

Since 1997, the process referred to in everyday speech as "deportation" has been labeled "removal" by U.S. immigration officials. While acknowledging that "removal" is the current legal term, this book employs the more familiar word "deportation."

Detention or Prison?

Legally, immigration detention is not punishment and immigration detention centers are not prisons. Yet the words "detainee" and "detention center" don't do justice to the system's harsh conditions and brutal treatment. Detention *feels* like imprisonment even when it's dressed up as "civil confinement." For that reason, the book sometimes employs the technically less accurate terms "prisoner" and "prison" when discussing immigration detention.

Hispanic, Latino, Mexican American, or Latinx?

Nearly all people of Latin American descent living in Douglas trace their roots to Mexico. For some (like Aida), this connection is recent. For others, it extends back four generations. This book uses the term "Mexican American" to refer collectively to this group. Elsewhere, this book uses the terms "Latino" (masculine) and "Latina" (feminine). Debates about how to refer collectively to people of Latin American descent living in the United States are long, fraught, and can't be weighed in this brief note. Instead, the book simply follows the lead of immigrant rights organizations around the country. For a variety of reasons, "Latino" and "Latina" tend to prevail over "Hispanic" in those organizations. In many ways, it would be better to use the neologism "Latinx." This term offers a gender-neutral and nonbinary way to avoid the exclusively masculine or feminine Spanish forms. Nevertheless, few if any of the Latinos and Latinas who populate these pages use—or would have recognized—this new term. To remain faithful to their speech and self-labeling, the book uses "Latino" and "Latina."

Illegal, Undocumented, or Unauthorized?

The book employs "undocumented," and in certain cases "unauthorized," to refer to people in the United States without valid immigration status. "Illegal"—used alone as a noun, or in the phrase "illegal immigrant"—is inaccurate and dehumanizing. While a person labeled that way may have committed a civil violation (and, in some cases, an immigration-related crime), offenses do not define people's identities. We do not speak of a person who drove while intoxicated as an "illegal" or "illegal driver." "Illegal" paints people with too broad a brush. "Undocumented" and "unauthorized," while not perfect labels, are more specific. Several exceptions apply: This book uses "illegal immigration" to refer to the way many politicians and the media have framed undocumented immigration as a problem. It also refers to "illegality"—the state of having one's very existence defined as "illegal" by the larger society. Finally, in a few places, the book uses "illegal" or "illegal immigrant" as self-descriptions. This does not validate the term. Rather, it reflects the way that even undocumented people can internalize the hateful rhetoric of anti-immigrant campaigns.

Immigrant or Migrant?

An immigrant is a person making a permanent life in a new country. A migrant moves across borders and may not choose to make a permanent life in the new country. In the United States, we typically ignore this distinction—probably because we assume that anyone who comes to the United States *must* want to make a permanent life here. That is not always the case, and key differences in people's experiences go missing as a result of the elision. The book tries to maintain a clear distinction between migration and immigration. Bowing to colloquial usage, however, the book defaults to "immigrant" and "immigration" in two cases: when it is not clear whether a person is a migrant or an immigrant, and when referring to the larger system governing the transnational movement of people (e.g., immigration law, immigration enforcement).

ACKNOWLEDGMENTS

This book owes its existence to the courage and generosity of Aida Hernandez and her family. Their participation in the project took grit, love, and a bold belief that a greater good could come from sharing Aida's story. It's hard to express even a small part of the admiration and gratitude I feel toward them.

Rosie Mendoza also played a pivotal role. She introduced Aida and me, agreed to have her life featured in the book, and was a constant source of encouragement and support in the years that followed. When Aida talks about Rosie, she says, "Rosie is my hero!" I feel the same way. Special thanks also go out to Alvaro, Camila, Ema, Katy, Aida's work colleagues, and all the other people close to her who shared their lives and memories.

This book would not have been possible without crucial assistance from Rev. Mark Adams, who introduced me to DouglaPrieta; Jesse Evans-Schroeder, who pulled so many threads of the story together; and Xavier Zaragoza, who offered friendship and a thoughtful sounding board. (Write that border noir novel, Xavier!) Jack and Linda Knox welcomed me and provided a place to stay in Douglas. Their radical hospitality and their thirst for justice are continuing sources of inspiration.

My deepest gratitude goes out to the many people around Douglas and Agua Prieta who shared their experiences and expertise, including Charlie Austin (1949–2016), Fernando Betancourt, Ray Borane, Aaron Cardona, Wendy Glenn (1940–2014), Michael Gomez, Howard Henderson, Jazmin Hernandez (no relation to any book character), Erik Hinajosa, Frank Hone, John Ladd, Liz Madrid, Angela Nuñez, Becky Orozco, Daniel Ortega, Hector Salinas, Mary Siqueiros, Carlos de la Torre, David Velasco, and many others who spoke on condition of anonymity. Del Cabarga, thank you for guiding me through "freakin' stressful, crazy interesting" cross-border life. Keoki Skinner, center of *el mitote*, thank you for your reporter's recall. Beth Henson, your scholarship and political insight were crucial to this book—thank you. Cindy Hayostek, thank you for everything you do at the Douglas Arizona Historical Society. Lupe and Ginny Jordan, thank you for sharing your passion for the people, history, and politics of Douglas.

Farther afield, special thanks are due to Ane Barragán, Geoff Boyce, Robert Carreira, Ramesh Karra, Eric Lee, Leticia Rojas, and Ray Ybarra. Tom Brightman and Patty Atkins offered a refuge in Tucson. Danielle Alvarado and Viviana Gordon provided moral support and whip-smart sounding boards in New York. Years ago I was privileged to have them as students; now the learning all goes in the other direction.

A wide range of primary and secondary sources informed the book and are cited in endnotes. Nevertheless, several scholarly texts shaped my overall thinking about the project to such a degree that I'd like to acknowledge them directly. They are: Lisa Marie Cacho, *Social Death: Racialized Rightlessness and the Criminalization of the Unprotected*; Judith L. Herman, *Trauma and Recovery: The Aftermath of Violence—from Domestic Abuse to Political Terror*; numerous pieces by the anthropologist Josiah Heyman; Cecilia Menjívar and Daniel Kanstroom, *Constructing Immigrant "Illegality": Critiques, Experiences, and Responses*; Joseph Nevins, *Operation Gatekeeper and Beyond:*

The War on "Illegals" and the Remaking of the U.S.-Mexico Boundary; Mae M. Ngai, *Impossible Subjects: Illegal Aliens and the Making of Modern America*; and Gilberto Rosas, *Barrio Libre: Criminalizing States and Delinquent Refusals of the New Frontier.*

I am grateful to the many people who appear in the book and also read and commented on drafts of the manuscript—a number of their names are listed in "About This Book." Legions of other people read and offered advice on all or part of the text, from the initial proposal stage to the final draft. Special thanks to Sharon Alker, Danielle Alvarado, Andrea Berg, Hana Bobrow-Strain, Kate Bobrow-Strain, Geoff Boyce, Rachel Hope Cleaves, Guillermo Corro, Susanne Freidberg, Daphne Gallegos, Beth Henson, Wendy Hernandez (no relation to any book character), Kazi Joshua, Jack and Linda Knox, Jennifer Lopez, Bruce Magnusson, Arden Mahlberg, Everett Maroon, Lydia McDermott, Cecilia Menjívar, Todd Miller, Lindsay Naylor, Joe Nevins, Dawn Paley, Jason Pribilsky, Nathan Sayre, Kisha Lewellyn Schlegel, Daniel Strain, and Megan Ybarra. I'm particularly grateful to Jennifer Boyden for brilliant editorial guidance early in the project. Thanks also to Hilary McClellen, the book's meticulous fact-checker. All remaining errors are, of course, my own.

Generous financial support from the Whitman College Politics Department and Provost and Dean of Faculty's Office made this book possible. Thank you to my colleagues in the Politics Department, generations of U.S.-Mexico Border Program students, and the inspiring student-activists of BAM. Cassandra Baker, Rachel Needham, and Andrea Berg provided crucial research assistance along the way.

To my agent, Matt McGowan, thank you for saying, "This is the one" (and for rejecting all those other book ideas). Working with everyone at Farrar, Straus and Giroux has been a fantastic experience. Thanks to Dominique Lear for keen insights on the manuscript and for keeping production on track. Most of all, my deepest gratitude to Alex Star for his faith, for his patience, and for his extraordinary capacity to understand what I was trying to do and then make it so much better.

Long before this book was even an idea, conversations with residents of the Arizona-Sonora borderlands shaped the way I understand that intense, beautiful landscape. I'm grateful to the staff and resource people of Border-Links, where I worked in the 1990s and where I returned year after year.

The profound insights of people like Lupe Castillo, Jim and Pat Corbett, John Fife, Raquel Rubio-Goldsmith, Teresa Leal, and Rick Ufford-Chase echoed in my head as I tried to write about the border. I don't expect that I've done their wisdom justice, but I am grateful nonetheless.

A big shout-out to the hardworking volunteers of the Walla Walla Immigrant Rights Coalition. Thank you for giving immigrant justice work such a strong voice in a small, rural corner of Washington State, and thank you for your friendship along the way.

Finally, I am so fortunate to have a loving, supportive family. My parents, Charles and Dianne, brother Daniel, and amazing sister-in-law Holly inspire me every day. As do Carol Blue and Ken Bobrow, who is in this book in spirit. Working on this book skinned me alive and turned me inside out. Thank you to my dearest ones—my wife, Kate, and children, Hana and Sam—for putting up with all that rawness and for making me laugh and remember to focus on what is really important.

A NOTE ABOUT THE AUTHOR

Aaron Bobrow-Strain is a professor of politics at Whitman College in Washington State, where he teaches courses dealing with food, immigration, and the U.S.-Mexico border. His writing has appeared in *The Believer*, *The Chronicle Review*, *Salon*, and *Gastronomica*. He is the author of *White Bread: A Social History of the Store-Bought Loaf* and *Intimate Enemies: Landowners, Power, and Violence in Chiapas*. In the 1990s, he worked on the U.S.-Mexico border as an activist and educator. He is a founding member of the Walla Walla Immigrant Rights Coalition in Washington State.